I dream of a new Tibet — a free land, a zone of peace — where my six million people can restore our spiritual way of life while becoming attuned to the best aspects of the modern world. I see it as a place where all people — not excluding our eastern neighbours — can visit and enjoy the fresh air and brilliant mountain light — can find inspiration in a peaceful, spiritual way of life, and perhaps can learn to understand their own worlds better by getting away for a little while to meditate at our high altitude. With your help we can return there.

—*Tenzin Gyatso*
Fourteenth Dalai Lama of Tibet

Quoted, with the permission of His Holiness the Dalai Lama, from his letter to students of Buddhism worldwide, 1994

tibetan transit

LOLO HOUBEIN

Kangaroo Press

Other books by Lolo Houbein
Walk a Barefoot Road
Wrong Face in the Mirror
Vreemdeling in de Spiegel (Dutch)
The Sixth Sense
Lily Makes A Living

First published in Australia in 1999 by Kangaroo Press
an imprint of Simon & Schuster (Australia) Pty Limited
20 Barcoo Street, East Roseville NSW 2069

A Viacom Company
Sydney New York London Toronto Tokyo Singapore

National Library of Australia
Cataloguing-in-Publication data

Houbein, Lolo. 1934–

  Tibetan transit.

  Includes index.
  ISBN 0 7318 0809 6
  1. Tibet (China) - Description and travel. 2. Tibet (China) -
  History - 1951- I. Title

915.1504

Cover design: Gyana Murphy

Set in Bembo 10.7
Printed by Kyodo Printing Co., Singapore

10 9 8 7 6 5 4 3 2 1

For Rimpoche

Exiled since 1959 from the world's last
self-contained civilisation and beloved teacher
of those who seek to know its wisdom.

NOTE: For the protection of all Tibetans met in Tibet during
these journeys, they remain nameless. Non-Tibetans have
been given fictitious names.

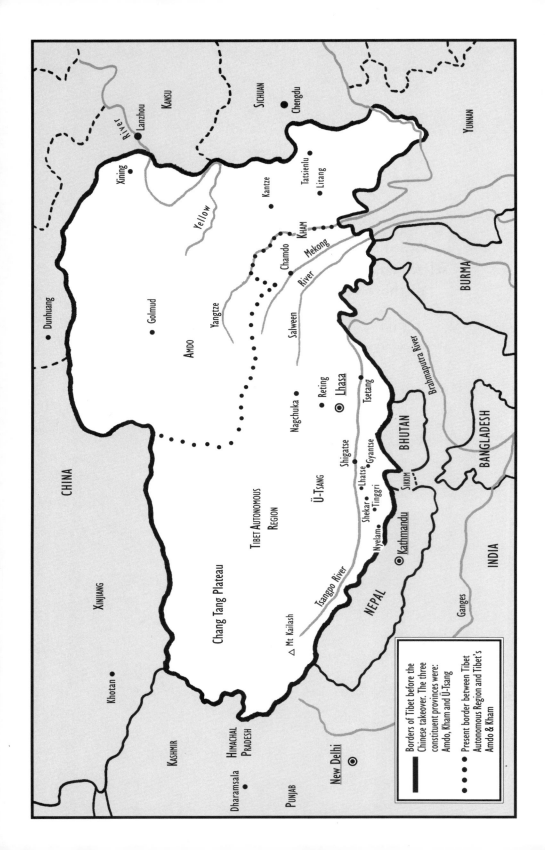

KANSU

SICHUAN

YUNNAN

Lanzhou

River

Chengdu

Xining

Tatsienlu

Kantze

Litang

Yellow

KHAM

Chamdo

Mekong

Dunhuang

BURMA

Golmud

Yangtze

River

Salween

AMDO

Brahmaputra River

CHINA

Reting

Lhasa

BANGLADESH

Nagchuka

Tsetang

Ü-TSANG

BHUTAN

Shigatse

Gyantse

TIBET AUTONOMOUS

REGION

Lhatse

Shekar

Tinggri

SIKKIM

Nyelam

Kathmandu

XINJIANG

Chang Tang Plateau

△ Mt Kailash

Tsangpo River

NEPAL

INDIA

Khotan

Ganges

KASHMIR

HIMACHAL
PRADESH

New Delhi

Dharamsala

PUNJAB

Borders of Tibet before the
Chinese takeover. The three
constituent provinces were:
Amdo, Kham and Ü-Tsang

Present border between Tibet
Autonomous Region and Tibet's
Amdo & Kham

Contents

Prologue

When His Holiness the Dalai Lama made a tour of Australia in 1992, tens of thousands of people flocked to hear him. At one venue I was honoured to recite a poem about one of his great concerns, humanity's effect on the global environment. Tibet's environment is extremely fragile and has been subjected to relentless exploitation for half a century by its Chinese occupiers, through straightforward exploitation and the transferral of millions of Chinese peasants. The message the Dalai Lama delivered during his tour was: 'Go to Tibet and see for yourself, then tell the world what you have seen'.

Until then Tibet had been a drawcard of unusual magnitude to me. How deeply I felt about Tibet is not something I could talk about then, nor now that I have been there. I had read about its history, culture and religion, seen films, even written background articles to news events leaking out from the closed shop Tibet had become since the Chinese communists occupied the country in 1950, such as the imprisonment of the Panchen Lama.

The First Panchen Lama was the Fifth Dalai Lama's teacher. In subsequent reincarnations the elder of the two became the teacher of the younger lama, but although the Dalai Lama's powers were secular as well as religious, the Panchen Lama remained a purely religious leader until the Tenth Panchen Lama stood up for the Tibetan people's human rights and was imprisoned by the Chinese for fourteen years, while the Western press dubbed him a Chinese puppet.

Always a 'forbidden' country to Westerners, Tibet nevertheless had a lively border trade with southern neighbours as well as China before 1950. Since then, Tibetan news issuing from Xinhua Newsagency has been cut and coloured to suit Beijing's view of Tibet as 'an inalienable part of the Motherland'.

China's contemporary history hardly ever reaches the outer world before two decades have passed. It takes that long for the regime to feel it can admit that 'mistakes have been made in the past'. Modern intrusive communications are speeding up the process. In the absence of popular criticism and investigative journalism, and with laws that interpret criticism as interfering with 'state secrets' or damaging 'state security', Chinese people and China's minority peoples put up and shut up, or lose their citizens' rights, possessions, liberty or even life.

Thus, the Cultural Revolution, the Great Famine and the South-West China civil war (1967–1968) took place in one decade while the world believed China was peacefully modernising agriculture and raising peasants from poverty. In the seventies there were signs that China wanted to foster trade with other countries, but the world was unaware that part of China's huge offering of consumer goods was the product of labour prisons run by the People's Liberation Army (PLA) disguised as state-run enterprises. In the eighties China opened up for the tourist dollar, but package tours to the Great Wall, emperors' graves, palaces and famed gardens showed but relics of a vanished world, historical islands in a new China of communes and hasty urban development. 'Friendship stores', where tourists bought copies of the art of vanished China, were the culture temples of the new China.

But in Tibet, the Land of Snows, travellers found a living tradition, a vibrant religion that would not make way for communist ideology, a people eager to meet strangers and tell their stories. So popular did Tibet become as a travel destination that it fed Tibetan hopes that three decades of confinement in the Chinese motherland's suffocating embrace were coming to an end. The mistakes of the Cultural Revolution had at last been admitted, some temples and monasteries were allowed to be restored, and the Panchen Lama — released from prison in 1979 after fourteen years of incarceration — though forced to live in Beijing, was allowed to visit. Tibetans began to sing songs of independence. Nuns and monks were in the forefront of demands for a free Tibet. In 1987, Chinese authorities clamped down. Tibetans were killed and imprisoned. Tibet's door began to gradually close once more against foreign witnesses. In 1989 came the sudden death of the Tenth Panchen Lama, tireless and courageous mediator for the welfare of the Tibetan people, followed by the Tiananmen Square massacre that changed world opinion and awakened many to what had happened routinely in Tibet for decades.

In the nineties, individual travellers were being discouraged, refused visas and finally told they were no longer welcome in Tibet. Many had kept the People's Armed Police busy through accessing 'state secrets' by photographing a bridge or overnighting in an unapproved village. They were made to write self-criticisms. Simultaneously, Tibetan guides replaced Chinese guides to ensure tourists felt they were given a genuine Tibetan experience. More temples reopened, more peasants were made to dance in Tibetan costume for foreign film cameras.

Groups have to present itineraries to get visas and are only permitted to stop, eat and sleep as planned in Chinese-managed hotels. Permits are required for stopovers. Hotels serve food only on meal tickets issued to group leaders. All groups have guides and Chinese drivers. Group travellers can be watched, traced, controlled, and their outgoing mail, phone calls and faxes are checked.

Travel in Tibet is somewhat like living in a movable tourist prison. Any possession can be confiscated if, in the eyes of Chinese authorities, it threatens state security. Travellers have had to relinquish passports, cameras, film, diaries, photos, letters, tapes, videos or anything arousing suspicion. Some travellers have foolishly attempted to personally liberate Tibet by publicly uttering democratic rhetoric. One traveller was lifted from his hotel bed, gaoled and expelled for what he innocently faxed to a homebound spouse about a loud noise in the night. Some travellers were injured when Chinese guns opened fire on Tibetan demonstrators. Travel in Tibet is not always a picnic.

In 1997, Tibetan guides who had returned to Tibet after being educated in India were dismissed. All tourist guides in Tibet are now Chinese-trained. Individual travel has virtually dried up due to official harassment. Group travel is strictly controlled. The population is scared to talk to foreigners because of repercussions. Only fearless Khambas and some monks and nuns approach foreigners. Temples and monasteries keep being restored and maintained by underfed monks and nuns. In them rests the essence of Tibet's beleaguered culture.

In the mid-nineties, the repression of Tibetan culture and religion became evident to the world through the fantastic contortions performed by China's leaders to groom their own Panchen Lama for the new communist Buddhism they reluctantly decided to create. Jiang Zhemin's calligraphy now graces Tibetan temples. Subsequently the Dalai Lama has announced he will not seek rebirth in a Tibet under Chinese control.

In 1993 I decided to follow the Dalai Lama's advice. Well-travelled but showing wear and tear, I needed that push to undertake what from all accounts was not an easy ride. Despite years of reading I found I knew less about Tibet than I had hoped. No book could fill in the millions of interstices between fabled places, buildings and customs. Not a thousand photos could prepare me for the reality of standing at the foot of the incredible Potala or some nameless mountain of sheer granite beauty.

Every traveller's transit of Tibet is unlike anything read in books, hence they continue to write new books about the Tibet they did not read about. In this way the vestiges of Tibetan culture can be recorded before they disappear. As long as Tibet remains a forbidden country — for vast areas are still out of bounds — travellers must write to fill out the picture of how Tibet was, how it is, how it changed. In matching observations by earlier travellers to locations now personally remembered, I not infrequently arrived at new insights. I made a second journey to consolidate these.

When I booked my first fare, I had no intention of writing a book on Tibet. The idea was born when later I tried to tell what I had seen. As I began to write to capture the overall picture of Tibet's predicament, I bent over backwards at first to be fair to China, but found I could only be fair to those Chinese people who are trying to improve their lives without consciously harming others. What the Chinese communist regime has done in Tibet can only arouse unending regret for what is lost forever, for what has been and is being suffered, until the Buddhist principle of impermanence is fully grasped.

I had to rewrite this book several times before I could admit that trying to be fair to China amounted to being foul to humanity. I began to realise that a Chinese army of three million soldiers, plus nuclear arms and everything threatening in between, is what encourages the world to 'be fair to China'. But China proves daily that it will not be influenced by quiet diplomacy, favourable trading contracts and shutting up about human rights. It only uses these to get its own way on its own terms. China's regime will in the long term only be contained by analyses of its recent history at home and in its colonies.

Tibet has become the litmus test for truthfulness in China and in the global conscience. One of the world's unique civilisations, centred in a highly developed philosophy and motivated by spiritual rather than material notions, Tibet is fast being wiped out as the world carries on with business as usual.

Lolo Houbein
1999

PART I

THE FIRST JOURNEY – 1993

Sleepless in Hong Kong

All packed but for my toothbrush. Three agonising days to departure. Rereading old favourites: Abbé Huc on his adventures with Abbé Gabet in Lhasa in the 1840s; the intrepid Alexandra David Neel, in search of spiritual magic, traversing Tibet on foot and horseback for many years until 1925, disguised as an old Tibetan woman. For contrast, *A Winter in Tibet*, written in the mid-1980s by English teachers Charles and Jill Hadfield. In a dark corner of the bookcase sits J. McDonald Oxley's *Lhasa at Last*, dating from the first decade of this century. A fictional take-off from Abbé Huc's real journey, peppered with opinions rooted in raj and empire and riding on the back of the British invasion of Tibet in 1904, it reveals how Tibet was then regarded as an international football for powerful nations to play with in the notorious Great Game of influence and espionage in Central Asia.

My mind pictures the whitewashed domes of Samyé, the oldest monastery in Tibet, through a hole in the clouds as seen by the Hadfields when they flew in, but I am incapable of seeing myself walk through Samyé's fields and temples next Tuesday, a mere week from now. As I count hours instead of days to departure, my life is being reined in like a galloping horse approaching an abyss: there seems no foothold in an unimaginable future. Having lived all my life towards this journey, what will life be like after Tibet?

Departure day. I rise eagerly at 3 am. At the airport, TV monitors show people singing and dancing in the dark night, balloons bobbing. Sydney's bid has beaten China's to host the Olympic Games in 2000. Clutching my Australian passport with its valid visa for China, I have mixed feelings. It states my occupation as teacher. That is half-true. The writer half is not welcome in China at any time.

The Chinese representative at Monaco, where the Olympic decision was made, Mr Wu Zhongyuan, had spoken feelingly about his country in preceding days. China felt deeply about human rights, he said, and he exhorted the world not to forget that China lost 30 million people to gain its independence. Subsequently, Tibet lost over one million people when it lost its independence to China, a fact not mentioned by Mr Wu. And in all China's territories an uncountable number of millions lost their lives after China's 1949 independence. Mao Zedong's economic policies, combined with droughts and floods, saw harvest after harvest fail until, between 1959 and 1961, grim, unreported famines killed another 30 million people. Tibet, having never experienced famine, met its first severe food shortage nine months after occupation because its sparse arable land could not support the People's Liberation Army as well as the Tibetans. Tibet suffered famines in 1961-64 and 1968-73, when Tibetan crops were transported to China to relieve famines there. When Mao ordered wheat, instead of high-altitude barley, to be grown in Tibet for Chinese consumption, the food situation in Tibet grew from bad to worse.

Mr Wu, anticipating a lost bid, claimed that people criticising China had never been there. 'Come and see for yourself', he invites, echoing the Dalai Lama. 'Meet the people.' I would like to meet Gendun Rinchen, Lhasa tour guide and classed a Chinese citizen, although born a Tibetan. He was arrested in May 1993 on suspicion of passing on 'state secrets' to visiting European delegates. I heard he was a terrific guide, but I won't have the pleasure.

I can only think of going to Tibet, not of returning from there. I say my goodbyes and the journey begins. Floating across Australia I find myself apprehensive rather than excited. From the south coast it takes the remaining hours of daylight to get out of Australia. Dusk falls when the plane flies through a long gap between Hong Kong's skyscrapers on the spectacular approach to hemmed-in Kai Tek Airport.

After an introduction to high living at a hotel breakfast fit for a Moghul, the group meets in the lobby next morning. We are seven besides tour leader Jason. Most have just flown in from America and we stand jet-lagged together on purple-pink carpet. We utter truncated joking remarks, as people do when faced with having to live intimately with strangers. Jason has the kind of intellect that must have ascertained at an early age that knowledge is bliss. He speaks as many languages as there are spokes on the Buddhist Wheel of Life and his excitement is infectious. We go sightseeing in pouring rain.

In the late afternoon we gather to establish a travel philosophy. We must not endanger Tibetans by discussing politics, as fraternising with foreigners makes them suspect already. Gendun Rinchen's case is mentioned as an example. We are not to give to beggars. This is becoming a rule for international travellers, often requested by host countries' governments. Can we feed them? Debating this issue leads into realms of very unequal values. We stop debating it. The bottom line is that we can give a child a pen, but must not make her into a beggar.

We are also to remember that Chinese people are people and not confuse them with their government. We nod in unison, being educated people. Some of us like China, admire Chinese culture and people. But that millions of Chinese have migrated to Tibet, and still do, we may not like. We will join the migrant flight out of Chengdu. In Tibet we will have a Chinese driver all the time.

Finally we discuss Cyclone Dot, which sent all this rain. Already boats have capsized in the harbour and a man is feared drowned. We may not be able to take off at all tomorrow.

Gathering around a hotpot in a busy restaurant, we get to know each other's preferences. A nice bunch of people. The possibility of having to make life's most important journey marred by incompatibilities had niggled me more than I'd realised. Will tomorrow ever come?

Tibetan storytellers set up contexts and provide antecedents before telling a story. At night in bed I wonder how to begin this journey's story, should I want to tell it. How to sum up the context of contemporary Tibet.

Inevitably, on the outer perimeters are 'the Chinese', now living in the heart of Tibet. China's population, including fifty-five conquered minorities, is more than 1.2 billion, one-fifth of the world's population. It is likely that the 'Chinese' because of numbers, shared culture and language — whether native or imposed — will have an increasing influence on the other four billion global residents. But presently they — including Tibetans, Manchurians, Mongolians, Uighurs and fifty other national minorities — cannot readily leave China to learn first-hand about those other four billion. That is where the rub is. Small numbers of privileged Chinese can travel, but the only foreigners the Chinese masses are likely to meet are those allowed entry to trade, aid or sightsee. How can mutual understanding develop?

Historically the Han Chinese had good reasons to fear foreigners. Already in the sixteenth century Matteo Ricci, a Jesuit missionary who spent most of his life in China, said the Chinese viewed foreigners as enemies or evil spirits. United only periodically into one nation with rather fluid borders, Han Chinese were as often victims as aggressors. Continuing foreign encroachments since the sixteenth century, first by the Manchu then Britain and other Western powers, so undermined Chinese living conditions that the China ready for Mao Zedong's communist revolution was the product of those who would not stop interfering in China for their own gain.

The carving up of China into 'spheres of influence' for Russia, America and the European powers had been enough to cast a mortal fear of foreigners into the fortified heart of the Manchu empress dowager. There was a brief outreach for democracy and modern technology after Sun Yat-sen's 1911 revolution, followed by decades of civil war and the Japanese invasion. But in 1949, Mao's victory closed China as hermetically as the emperors tried to do before him.

Soon after, 'liberation from foreign devils' was the pretext for Mao's troops to invade Tibet, where a British agent and trading post had long been established. The Tibetan government had employed two British radio operators to relay

Chinese and world news broadcasts, but was otherwise notorious for not letting Westerners in at all. American radio reporter Lowell Thomas and his son had received permission to visit Lhasa in 1949, perhaps in an attempt to open up to a powerful nation. But they were only the seventh and eighth Americans to enter Tibet. That handful of aliens became Mao's excuse for invading Tibet.

Now, after thirty years of insulation and isolation and two decades of erratic 'opening up', Han Chinese leaders find they take certain things for granted that do not qualify as universal values in the global community. Chinese people's conception of the non-Chinese world is still being shaped by censored, government-selected information. The Chinese generation now approaching middle age grew up during the Cultural Revolution, has never voted, and chorused 'Death to Foreign Devils' in kindergarten.

The tag 'foreign devil' still gets transmuted into 'barbarian' when Han Chinese think unofficially of minority peoples, some of whom conquered China or Chinese territory in past centuries. These include notably the Mongols or Tartars and the Manchu, but also the Tibetans.

Memories are long and it may be sweet revenge to the Han to now be in military control of these erstwhile hordes who threatened or ruled the Han homeland, China proper along the Han River to the western shores of the Pacific Ocean. But it is hard to accept that Chinese leaders believe all those minority territories — Manchuria, Inner Mongolia, Xinjiang, East Turkestan, Tibet, Qinghai, Sichuan and Yunnan, making up five-sixths of the People's Republic, with Tibet being one-sixth of present day China — are really the Chinese motherland of old. Hence the regime — after widespread destruction of towns and monasteries, as in Tibet and Mongolia — adopts lusty population transfer programs, making conquered territories over in the Chinese mode.

Sleep will not come. I am no longer a China romancer, of whom there were many in the sixties and seventies when few knew what went on inside China. They were blissfully ignorant like the Soviet romancers of the twenties and thirties. If communism puts food in their mouths it must be good for the Chinese, I used to say. But nobody enters China or Tibet innocently in the nineties. Abroad, in conditions of freedom and lawful opportunity, the Chinese people I have known were pretty admirable, living easily with non-Chinese people, trading, partying, wooing, marrying them. Could one billion Chinese in China be so, given a change in policy?

The Chinese people, of course, do not choose their government. Sections of the Chinese population in China proper chose to support one of two warring factions until one, the communist army, won in 1949, giving rise to the regime that still rules China itself and reconquered or newly conquered minority territories, none of which had a say in these developments. The Chinese were a persecuted, oppressed and impoverished people desiring a better life as promised by Mao Zedong and his People's Liberation Army. Many a village chose between the frying pan and the fire for the sake of survival, hoping for better times. Choosing the 'wrong' side meant courting death. China has no democratic elections or opposition parties. Neither will Beijing let us forget what happened to the democracy movement on Tiananmen Square in 1989.

But in the decades following the communist victory, China watchers became excited by what seemed obvious progress in the living conditions of Chinese peasants. It appeared China was finally at peace, its numerous warlords subdued, its agriculture leaping ahead and famine a thing of the past. Knowledge of widespread famines raging through Chinese territories in the 1960s, killing 30 million people, was kept from the world. Mao's agricultural dictates and economic policies took no account of local conditions in the vast territories under his sway, causing harvests to fail. China's subsistence agriculture of forty centuries crashed while the government sent out its first overseas exhibitions, showing clay models of gigantic cabbages, unreal turnips and gourds, Chinese-made tractors and models of self-sufficient Chinese communes with fish and duck ponds, food gardens and cottonfields. But when visiting China in 1988 as an individual traveller, I was not allowed to see communes, villages or food gardens. No permit! declared my guide for the day.

Thoughts return at last to tomorrow's adventure of re-entering China. I must remember that the Tibetan society we will see has been forged by policies of Chinese regimes under Mao, Zhou and Deng with the assistance of Tibetan collaborators, the Chinese army, and seven million Chinese immigrants who obey their government or ignore its instructions at their peril, and have nothing to lose by leaving home. Never have I felt so intimidated on entering another country. I would wish to be innocent and ignorant, to meet Tibet unconditionally, but knowledge once gained cannot be returned.

I am going to Tibet to meet Tibetans and make a pilgrimage. The Chinese presence in Tibet, now nearly a lifetime — the average life expectancy of Tibetans is fifty years — may yet be of a temporary nature. I hope to find Tibetan culture still alive, despite reports that it is doomed and Tibetans are dying out through genocide and unaccustomed hardships.

Counting myself to sleep now. This journey will return me changed forever. My room-mate Nicola is fast asleep. Breathe in, breathe out, watch the breath, discard all thought, breathe in, out, watch, discard ...

Chengdu — Ancient City without History

Cyclone Dot is brewing up a storm, still pouring rain. At the airport people scrutinise Dot's progress on a wall chart. Delays are inevitable. Yet our plane takes off only seventy minutes late. As we gain height we sail out of Dot's foul aura into beautiful weather for the flight to Chengdu, capital of Sichuan province.

Chengdu, birthplace of Deng Xiaoping, is in festive mood. Street banners announce the 'Giant Panda Festival & Convention' and 'The Sichuan TV Conference for Producers'. Some banners proclaim recklessly: 'Let the world get to know Chengdu and let Chengdu open up to the world', and even more challenging: 'Peace and Harmony'. Another banner announces that giant pandas inspire peace within all humanity, nature's own sitting buddhas. Chengdu's population cycles under banner after banner, ignorant of opening up and peace and harmony with all humanity. What are English words to them?

But an English-speaking guide meets us. Near Renmin Boulevard looms the biggest statue I have ever seen. Mao, five storeys high, enigmatic smile pleating his lips, holds one hand up in greeting. Even the Buddha in the British Museum — probably stolen from China — is only three storeys high. Although Mao is history, Chengdu does not have the feel of a city aged 2500 years. Not like Rome, where ancient aqueducts, houses, statues, fountains, even gardens, thrilled me to bits. Here the Cultural Revolution was fiercely pursued and what we see of Chengdu looks as if it was erected since the 1960s in rather a hurry.

Chengdu is a claustrophobic experience. Two million people live in the inner city, another six million inhabit the suburbs, together equivalent to half the population of Australia. Therefore dimensions are small, spaces over-utilised, rooms tiny in rows of small apartment houses. Beyond a vast lobby, our hotel rooms are similar. The hotel proudly announces four-star rating, issued by the Chinese hotel association. This holds surprises for non-Chinese guests. The cashier runs out of money before half of us have exchanged travellers' cheques.

In Chengdu zoo we pay our respects to the greater pandas. Their vast shapeless bodies slump in corners of dank cages or lie stretched on concrete bunks, asleep with bamboo stalks still clutched in powerless paws. Even awake, they hardly move an eyeball. Barely breathing, they are exponents of imminent extinction, while a conference about their future is in progress. Being indigenous, the giant panda has become new China's emblem, but it is doomed.

I become uncomfortably aware that Chinese zoo visitors seem more amazed at confronting these huge, seemingly limbless creatures with their sad drooping eyes, than we are. Media-fed familiarity with the great panda's plight is for us merely confirmed by seeing them in the fur. But the Chinese treat the creatures as if they'd come from outer space. They laugh and mock them, entice them to no avail with bits of paper and plastic rubbish, throw pebbles. The weight of wildlife indoctrination we carry is of no use here.

On the edge of the zoo grounds rise the walls of an old temple or monastery, surrounded by wire fencing. A sense of quietude hovers among those overgrown ruins. My imagination turns back time, when the monastery stood here amidst fine-leaved trees, its garden laid out where carnival tents now cluster, its drums filling the air more harmoniously.

An old man on crutches, wearing a jacket with more colourless patches than it shows colourless cloth, picks over the rubbish in a bin. His goatee beard quivers in the breeze as his sinewy thin arm dips in again. Chinese bins contain little rubbish of value. What could this one hold to maintain the life of a poor man, fallen outside the system supposed to provide a living for everyone? Somehow he cuts a familiar figure that doesn't correspond to the bin. High forehead, flowing wispy beard, finely chiselled features, delicate movements. Considering the meditative way this man moves and handles objects, he might be pruning bonsai trees or dipping a calligraphy brush in an inkwell. Or tending the altar in the ruined temple, lighting incense long ago.

Then it dawns on me that in today's China the absolute outcast is likely to be a person of great refinement who made the most of his family's wealth by becoming an artist, intellectual, or learned monk with status — an abbot perhaps. I imagine the beggar in good robes, head raised, reciting poetry, teaching an assembly of young monks. He must have been in the prime of life when the Cultural Revolution attempted to rid China of intellectuals and those who had chosen the religious life.

The beggar, having found nothing edible, limps away on crutches. Were his legs broken, but not his spirit? It was I who called him beggar for his rags and bin sorting. Now I realise I have not seen him beg or look at anyone. He hobbles away without so much as casting a longing glance at our bags and pouches, which contain the means of many a good meal. He is no beggar. The second of five Buddhist precepts followed by lay people, always kept by monks, states: I shall refrain from taking what is not given. He probably keeps the other precepts as well.

Watching him go, slightly bent, awfully thin and no doubt hungry, my stomach contracts. Should I have given without his asking, remembering hunger so well? I want to rush after him to press money into his bony hand, but am inhibited by the group. Would I if I were on my own? Will I be inhibited by others who have voiced no objections whatsoever, when it comes to acting on my better instincts? We troop to the bus, watch streetlife through clean windows, incapable of interfering.

We dine at a restaurant hidden in a People's Park. Cyclone Dot behind us and the most forbidding mountain range ahead, we inhabit a time wedge where eating and sleeping become occupation, paying little tribute to this vast city, but effortlessly doing justice to its wonderful Sichuan food.

The upstairs dining room of this old-style building has very tall windows opening into the warm night, lending views into leafy crowns of mature trees. The air is humid. Local patrons keep up a steady buzz of conversation. They seem well-to-do. Communism has not wiped out inequalities. Beer flows copiously while the lame old man who is no beggar goes hungry. No system in the world seems able to control human greed enough to prevent some from having to search rubbish bins for life's essentials.

In days gone by this elegant room must have seen aristocrats and mandarins entertain their guests. Theoretically, mandarins could emerge from all classes, rising to high posts by hard study and passing exams. Now it is the people's dining room. Or are these jolly diners high cadres? The Mao jacket may equalise the Chinese in the eyes of ignorant tourists, but their living standards are not equal.

The ground floor functions as art and craft shop. We must walk through it to enter and leave, an old ploy. Spotting high on a wall old *thangkas,* Tibetan temple paintings framed in silk brocade, we crane necks and receive our first instruction in Tibetan iconography from Jason. My heart leaps at a Green Tara *thangka* from Kham, but the asking price exceeds my budget. Anyway, what is Green Tara doing here? Robbed from a Tibetan monastery, bought for a pittance? Once the communists destroyed Tibetan religious artefacts. Now they sell them at a price.

I buy a tiny Kuan Yin to wear on a chain. Kuan Yin and Tara are one, *bodhisattva* of compassion, protectress of life, granter of wisdom to her devotees. I love her for the stories that abound of the days she walked the earth. And if because of the passing of time Kuan Yin and Tara were once two women who merged into one deity, then it happened because they embodied the same life-enhancing principles. She abhors all destruction of life, all harm done to living beings, all pain inflicted. She loves the lame old man and he would know of her.

Leaving the old house with its un-ideological atmosphere of refinement, we enter the subtropical night. I stumble over a stack of bricks. The grounds are unkempt, full of holes, in disrepair. The people of the republic have little time to care for parks, though all China's parks became People's Parks after the revolution.

Flying across the Roof of the World

At 4 am anticipation is accompanied by a sense of unreality. Weather permitting, we fly to Tibet today. I recall a book by a Sri Lankan lawyer, disenchanted with the Buddhism of his native land, who with his wife visited Tibet in 1966 as a communist propagandist. They waited several days at Chengdu airport for a favourable weather report from Lhasa so the plane could cross the formidable ranges, finally dipping over a mountain wall standing at 20 000 feet to a runway lying at a mere 14 000 feet. Today we are going to make the trip and dip! The Director of Civil Aviation came to chat with those visitors, assuring them that since the inception of the Lhasa flights in 1960 no accidents had occurred, but regular schedules were not always possible. Nature being presently beyond their control, experiments to manage the dangerous passage were in progress. The director felt confident that, guided by Mao's thought, they would overcome these difficulties in the near future. Whether it was Mao's thought or modern technology, today the schedule is as regular as in most countries.

Clutching hotel lunch boxes, we farewell the bus driver and 'Call me Jack', the guide. Our appearance in the waiting hall causes heads to turn. No matter how many tourists come to China or take off from Chengdu for Tibet, there will always be Chinese who are seeing a foreign devil for the first time.

Backs turned to the audience, we eat our lunches for breakfast. This is the first of many meals consumed in public with people looking on — watching how we put our teeth into things, how we chew, swallow and discard. My famine-raised mind is acutely embarrassed. We can't assume that because people hold flight tickets to Lhasa, they have enough to eat.

We have heard that Chinese migration to Tibet is massive. Poor peasants unable to make it in the new free economy of China see Tibet as a last opportunity. There they can trade where none have gone before, or work for the government on triple the standard wage with subsidised housing. We travel with the hopefuls. Once a migrant sailing to unknown regions, I too hoped for a brighter future. Ironically I also went to a land conquered by imperialists, where native peoples were murdered, disowned or neglected to accommodate the newcomers' aspirations. I was then as ignorant of that history as these Tibet-goers are of Chinese imperialism. The mirror of history has double layers and a reverse image as well.

I become aware of how very large I am, feeling like a great panda in a zoo, slumped in a corner of this waiting room which fast fills up with cigarette smoke. China's tobacco industry is the largest in the world. Chinese males are continually lighting up, smoking, blowing, coughing, stubbing. I've seen only old women smoke.

Two Lhasa-bound planes leave ten minutes apart. We are on the second flight, leaving at 6.50 am Beijing time. When we land in Tibet two hours from now, it will still be Beijing time. Thus the republic unites its variously held dominions. It makes for internal telecommunications without errors of time and presumably it does not matter to clock-less people whether they go to work at ten or eight in the morning. But if the other major powers followed China's example, we would end up with three global time zones instead of twenty-four: Beijing time, European Union time and Washington time. The people of Sydney would dance to Perth time, just as the Tibetans have to pipe to Beijing's chime.

It's a sleek Boeing, smelling new inside. In front of us two Chinese men, one already smelling of beer, are ready for a session of foreign-devil bashing to pass the time. They seem as used to flying as to riding on a bus. Craning necks between seats, they peer hard, exchange remarks about our appearance and imitate the sounds of the words we speak. We are giant foreign pandas in a captive situation.

The woman occupying the window seat in front of me talks aggressively to the men. Staring at us between the seats, she delivers her opinion in harsh tones. Young, she does not look Chinese, could be Tibetan. And here, even before take-off, the enigma: a Mandarin-speaking Tibetan who is a citizen of the Chinese People's Republic. Born under the communist regime with education conducted primarily in the Chinese language, opportunities for her quick mind lie in China or in the world of Chinese make-believe that calls Tibet an autonomous region.

We stop talking, because such English words as 'okay' elicit a salvo of scornful laughter from the seats in front. Maybe the laughter is less derisive than it sounds. Perhaps it is an old Chinese custom to imitate honoured visitors, a very polite thing to do. Or are they laughing away bad spirits that possibly hang around us?

Two hours to contemplate cross-cultural behaviour patterns as we float silently above an endless quilt of snowy clouds. But suddenly, real snow appears atop a high peak jutting above the cloud deck. Floating over Tibet, I go hot and cold with excitement. Fifty-five years of wishing, and here, now, I am flying over the mountains of Tibet. There is no way a landing is not going to happen. Sun bright in the sky, weather perfect. Ten more minutes and I will set foot on Tibetan soil; I cannot believe that this is really happening.

Eyes glued to the scenery outside and then there comes that exciting moment when the plane shifts gears before going into its descent. It dives into the cloud deck and for some seconds we are suspended in vapour. Then we emerge, and with the view returns the sensation of moving. There, underneath the belly of the plane, lie the sepia mountains of Tibet, seemingly gliding as the plane circles down. I recognise the expected, yet the encounter with these mountains, so close I can see gravel on their slopes, takes my breath away.

A collective 'aah' soughs through the cabin. Tears roll down my face. The young woman in front is also glued to her window. Through the gap between seat and window our eyes collide. Seeing my tears, her eyes darken. Unexpectedly, she sends me a quick smile, friendlier now, before returning her gaze to the mountains and valleys beneath us.

We land after a perfect flight. As we shoulder our bags to leave the plane, the young woman nods goodbye before she follows the men to the exit. What a good omen. I would rush out and kiss the ground, but the tarmac covers the earth I long to set foot on.

I always find it exhilarating to step from an aeroplane, pause on the stairway and breathe in the air of another land. Sometimes it is a case of recognition, like the wet blanket of humidity forming a second skin at tropical destinations. But Tibet has the most rarefied air on earth. As my feet find the steps, I breathe deeply. Walking across the tarmac, the lightness and freshness of the air intoxicates — surely I can live on this stuff!

My greatest fear falls away. The great unknown has declared itself: I won't become a casualty of altitude sickness. And all around, the mountains. Slate grey, beige and hash brown, creased like chamois but elegantly solid, the mountains dominate and dwarf everything that humans have put on this pale stony earth.

The brand-new buildings of Gonggar airport look preposterous against untouched wilderness shaped by the elements. But what else should they have built for a terminus? Yet there is a great difference between a mountain man's dwelling in a landscape like this and a modern airport. This one is reminiscent of landings on other planets in science-fiction fantasies. Someone talks of lunar landscapes, but the lifeless desolation of moon pictures is not present here. These mountains are alive!

Despite the invigorating air, we are breathless before we reach the terminal. Jason warns: 'Move slowly, conserve energy. Stay together, we have a group entry permit'. But at customs other tourists push luggage and legs between ours in an effort to get there first. Where first? Within minutes of arrival one of us is having a heated argument with an aggressive Frenchman. One of the first signs of altitude affliction is irritability.

We meet the men we will spend several weeks with, our Tibetan guide and

Chinese driver. With relish Jason breaks out in fluent Tibetan. The joy of switching language, to speak again a tongue kept back for lack of other speakers. Wishing one of my languages was Tibetan, I filter out sounds familiar from listening to Tibetan lamas in Australia. When speaking English, the Tibetan guide's accent is similar to the lama's, mellifluously hesitant.

In the parking lot, backpackers run between buses begging rides to Lhasa, ninety-six kilometres to the north. The Chinese International Tourist Service (CITS) does not encourage individual travellers and planes are not met by public transport. Only organised tour groups find minibuses waiting. Drivers are instructed not to take hitchhikers. I cannot help but think of Mr Wu's invitation: 'Come and meet the people!'

Eating Tsampa
by the Tsangpo River

We will not drive to Lhasa today. First destination is the Yarlung Valley, cradle of Tibetan civilisation. The day is still young. The little bus turns eastward onto the dirt road for Tsetang, 170 kilometres south-east of Lhasa. There we will stay several days at 10 000 feet to acclimatise.

Driving through the great Tsangpo River Valley. Or Zangbo. Getting Tibetan sounds right in the Roman alphabet was difficult enough before the Chinese arrived with their Pinyin system, spelling Tibetan names the way they sound to them, which is not necessarily how Tibetans produce them. If the first letters contain a hiss, slosh or buzz, is it X, Z, Q or C, or old-spelling Ts? It depends who is in power and prints the maps.

Tsangpo means 'river'. Himalayan ecologist John Vincent Bellezza trekked on foot to the sources of three of the four great south-bound rivers that originate in Tibet — the Brahmaputra, Sutlej, Karnali and Indus. All have their source near sacred Mount Kailash. China's two biggest rivers, the Yangtse and the Yellow River, originate in Tibet, flowing through Kham and Amdo respectively. The great Mekong has its origin in the confluence of two rivers in Kham, where the Salween also emerges. Thus the Tibetan plateau provides practically all the river waters for Asia, north, south and east. All are controlled by China without international agreements for the protection of downstream users.

John Bellezza found that geographical and ritual sources apparently do not coincide, except in the case of one of the three geographical sources of the Brahmaputra, at Tamchok Kabab Kangri glacier, or Horse Spring. The other three rivers are attributed to the Lion's Spring, the Peacock's Spring and the Elephant's Spring, the sacred animals of Hindu–Buddhist mythology.

Thus the upper reaches of the Tsangpo are called Tamchok Tsangpo, Horse River. It drains into Tibet, following a west–east course on the northern side of the Trans-Himalayan range, becoming Yarlung Tsangpo before it curves south towards India to become the Brahmaputra.

Surveying at extremely high altitudes, with a summer lasting about one month is fraught with difficulties. The area of sacred Mount Kailash and Lake Manasarovar — believed to be an emanation of pure mind — is regarded by Buddhists and Hindus alike as the navel of the world and a sacred mandala of geographical features. The idea that there is one place retaining a measure of mystique by being unmeasurable is tremendously attractive.

Pilgrims find places of worship without consulting maps. They carry a map in the heart. In one possible world of all possible future worlds, peace will be every country's primary aim and the strategic knowledge necessary for wars will lose its importance, being replaced by ritual geography. Satellites will photograph the globe's mandalas and people will hang them on their walls to be reminded of what they innately know.

The road between the mountains is rough, but no worse than in outback Australia. Planting feet firmly on the floor and pressing my back into the seat, I feel all jolts and vibrations go right through my body without stopping long enough to cause disruption.

The Tsangpo's floodplains are inundated. It rained solidly three days, says the guide, most unusual. He adds that lately the weather is changing all over Tibet, as in all Himalayan countries. Annual rainfall for central Tibet is only between fifteen and eighteen inches. The countryside looks as if the entire year's ration dropped from the skies last week. Thousands of young willow and poplar saplings planted on the floodplains stand up to their knobbly knees in water.

On the mountainous side of the road, massive erosion is visible. Were these slopes once clad with forests? The river is a polished mirror for the backdrop of rising rock. I blink in disbelief at clouds hanging well beneath the peaks. Not much higher than the roof of the bus, real clouds float across the valley floor.

The mountains' colours are too subtle for words, but my word-bound mind, used to red and yellow ochres, finds caramel, beige and grey, styled like a Tibetan *chuba*, the wraparound sashed gown or coat. Near the peaks can be seen shades of bluish ice. Some wear caps of snow, like the cream on childhood birthday jelly puddings. Long white fingers slope down flanks. In the foreground an overwhelming impression of sage green, relieved occasionally by splotches of yellow mustard or the darker green of a copse of mature trees.

Signs of human habitation. Triangular stacks of mud bricks stand in orderly fashion on high ground, with gaps between the bricks for the wind to dry them. Small fields grow giant cabbages and Chinese greens.

Ratne D. Senanayake, the traveller whose book consists for a large part of statistical material provided by the communist government, reported in 1966 that Tibetans grew only six kinds of vegetables before the Chinese introduced forty-two new varieties. Margaret Williamson, who travelled Tibet in the 1930s with husband Derrick, a British political officer, noticed cauliflowers, cabbages, onions, carrots, lettuces, radishes and turnips of such remarkable sizes that they would have won prizes at English agricultural shows. That's only seven, but three crops a year were grown in Lhasa valley. Granted, the Chinese know their vegetables, but it is hard to swallow that a country has to undergo a Cultural Revolution and lose over a million people in order to obtain the seeds of forty-two new vegetable varieties.

A sigh of appreciation eddies through the bus when we pass a mud-brick house standing in a cloud of pink cosmos. At home cosmos self-seeds, but you suspect that here seed is carefully collected, stored during the long winter and re-sown every summer. Later we are to see them everywhere, these flowers of abundance.

We have an early comfort stop, as the driver feels unwell. He stands by the road lighting a cigarette, indicating a headache. There are stories of Chinese drivers managing to obstruct touristic aims and I wonder what we're in for.

In Tibet, Manhattan executives and Australian grandmothers alike return to nature at short notice. We relieve ourselves in a bushy ditch by the roadside and are noticed by Tibetan farm workers sitting in a circle on the earth some hundred metres inland, yaks parked nearby. Jason shouts a Tibetan greeting. The reaction is instantaneous. Arms wave invitingly and Jason bounds across reaped furrows to the group of about fifteen women, children and men.

We gallop after him, eager for an unscheduled meeting. Sixteen years ago in Dharamsala, Indian home of Tibetan refugees, I was struck by how close Tibetans stand and sit together. Forming circles to eat, drink, sing or pray, they obviously enjoy togetherness. Here that habit is at home: they sit elbow to elbow in the immense landscape, emanating ease.

Inside the circle stands a black iron pot, the ornamental handle of a spoon sticking out, and a large white thermos flask decorated with red poppies. The midday meal is just finished. But the moment I sit down on the ground behind the circle, a woman turns and offers a narrow cloth bag, inviting me with a nod of the chin to partake of what is inside. Several of these small bags stand inside the circle. I plunge my hand in and come up with a small amount of fine, cream-coloured flour. *Tsampa!*

Alas, not wearing a *chuba*, I carry no tea bowl in its folds. *Tsampa* must be mixed with butter tea to become the nourishing staple food Tibetans eat before anything else. To honour the hospitality, I take a lick of *tsampa* flour and, coughing a little, mix it with saliva and manage to swallow it. It tastes nutty. Jason translates that this *tsampa* is a mixture of barley and lentils. I continue to eat the rest, blowing some accidentally into my eyes, raising laughter. To be offered food by the first Tibetans we meet is a momentous experience. I have travelled in many lands and seldom have people spontaneously shared what they had at first acquaintance. All I have read about Tibetan hospitality has just been confirmed by this woman's spontaneous gesture. How I wish this Tibetan custom will one day become a global one.

Jason is thrilling the farmers with his knowledge of Tibetan. The exchange is hearty, quick, riddled with laughter. Faces frown in concentration, light up, break into smiles. The kids are a little spellbound having foreign visitors in their barley field. Shall I dare unwrap my camera?

The women are in Tibetan dress, but the men wear trousers, sweaters and zip-up jackets. Slouch hats or Mao caps cover heads, but several men and women wear braided hairbands. A boy, about ten with close-cropped hair, could be a little monk. He wears a hand-knitted, saffron-coloured pullover.

Everyone faces the lens as I operate the camera from ground level, framing the colourful group against a background of willows marking the field's boundary. The harvest has been removed. They are about to resume ploughing fields before the winter freeze, in readiness for spring. With such a short summer, Tibetans cannot waste time in spring on tasks that can still be done in autumn.

Three men pose with their team of *dzo* and *dzomo*, yoked together. Crosses between yaks and cows, the *dzo* is the female. These docile animals cannot reproduce themselves, but are the preferred working animal for the fields. They have the wonderful bushy tail of the yak, decorated by their owners with red woollen tassels. On their heads wave plumes of red and white wool, even the yoke is embellished. Although I wouldn't go near an Australian cow, I want to stroke that gentle *dzo*'s black glossy coat.

I gesture to a young girl that I would like to take her picture and wait for approval. She stops talking and laughing to look bemused into the lens. Her braided hair surrounds a pretty round face above a purple blouse and grey *chuba*, metal bangles on her wrists. She indicates permission.

A thin, wiry man wearing a huge cap on curly hair jumps forward to pose beside the girl. A salvo of laughter explodes in the group. The girl and the man punch and jostle before posing together, shoulders touching, producing beatific smiles. I gather he made a momentary claim on the pretty girl for the sake of being immortalised with her. 'They say he's a bit funny', says Jason. He is a wizened little man, laughter in his eyes, prominent nose and expressive bony hands.

Reluctantly we leave as the group resumes work. The driver has recovered sufficiently to continue the journey. The Tibetan guide has viewed our meeting in the field from a distance. If he doesn't know what we talked about, he doesn't have to report it.

Now I am smitten by *dzo*, calling them yaks for they look nothing like cows. Further along I request a photo stop to creep up on half-a-dozen magnificent black and white specimens, grazing free, red rosettes between their horns. In the background pleated mountain slopes, clouds hovering. Moving in on the sleepy animals it hits me that I am stalking yaks in a field on my first day in

Tibet. As docile as my dogs they are, although nomads say that the wild yak, twice the size of a domestic one, can kill a human with its tongue.

Tsepon Shakabpa has an interesting story of wild yaks. Nomads claim wild herds consist of about one hundred females and only one breeding male, because mothers castrate male progeny, leaving only the fittest able to procreate. Thus, fierce and bad-tempered sexually active males cannot upset the peace of the large herd. As yaks can't live in lower altitudes and have to maintain population balance for species survival, the practice serves as an effective birth control method. Tibetans limited population less drastically by means of polyandry and monastic life.

Russian explorer Nikolai Mikhailovich Przewalski (1839–88) and his men, penetrating northern Tibet in 1872, could scarcely believe that such vast herds of wild yak existed in what they deemed to be a sterile landscape. Like so many explorers, he could not resist hunting the beautiful creatures. In 1889 William Rockhill reported hills 'black with yak'. All twentieth-century travellers before 1950 reported abundant wildlife.

But when the PLA started marching into Tibet they shot mammals and birds everywhere to feed themselves. Between 1985 and 1988 naturalist George B. Schaller found the plains empty of yaks. He blamed the new road connecting Lhasa with China, allowing hunters easy access. He counted only seventy-three yaks in a remote uninhabited area of 3200 square miles. Another herd of over 200 yaks had no calves.

In 1984 the World Wildlife Fund warned that the wild yak (*Bos grunniens*) was: 'threatened with extinction ... as a result of uncontrolled hunting. Legal protection throughout its range, and the establishment of reserves are required to ensure its survival ... Effective control of military personnel within its area of distribution is essential'. It was thought then that the yak population had been reduced to the low hundreds. China had declared the wild yak a protected species in 1962, after the event, and belatedly established the Chang Tang Reserve in 1992, second-largest conservation area in the world. But enforcing the law in harsh, sparsely populated terrain is difficult when the will is lacking.

Numerous small herds of domestic yaks, cows, *dzo*, sheep and goats graze along the road to Tsetang. The mirror river takes my breath away. At every bend incredible views unroll, mountains present sheer endless variety of shapes and colours. Some peaks soar from a narrow base, others are summits of long folded slopes or gather more than one mount into a greater arrangement of rising rock and ice. Lit by sunshine, all hues between beige and grey alternate with black and slate blue in the shadows. The river reflects them to perfection. Clouds drift in pure waters before floating off into narrow gorges revealing darker mountains behind those lining the river. In this symphony of passing peaks, some close, some further, some far, I lose myself. Were I a flautist I could play these scales of near and far, low and high, as we move through a landscape made of mountains, where the great river valley is but a channel for melting snow. It spells a geography not designed for humans. I pinch myself — my first day in Tibet.

But humans have lived here for thousands of years. Passing a large mud-brick house with walled compound, we witness the intimately personal scene of a woman combing her long hair, because the height of the bus allows us to peep. Brushwood stacked against the wall, hay drying on top, prayer flags fluttering from the chimney. Another house opens onto the road, pink and white cosmos flanking the doorway.

The lines of Tibetan architecture are thrillingly unique. Walls, windows and doors narrow as they rise, creating an illusion of height. White cotton flounces are draped under lintels. A half-moon on its back supporting a full sun is painted on doors or above doorways, symbolising the union of wisdom and compassion that is enlightenment. Wisdom alone and compassion by itself are great expressions of humanity, but the art of combining them into a team that performs faultlessly in every situation was demonstrated by the Buddha in his lifetime.

Little houses appear on the far side of the river. In that valley across the Tsangpo the great Indian *guru* Padmasambhava, bringing Buddhism to Tibet in the eighth century, defeated local demons opposing the new doctrine. In sparsely populated countries, legendary and historical events are remembered as if they happened in living memory, having been passed on orally without a break. Knowing these stories, the traveller feels close to events that can still be read in the landscape. My heart yearns for isolated places. I want to leave this 'highway' for the other side of the river, where life keeps a very different pace.

The highway is yet to be paved. Electricity and telecommunication lines are strung from wooden poles. It is said the forests of southern Tibet have been clear-felled. Tibet is a big land, and if poles are going to little Tsetang, there must be tens of thousands of former trees, spaced at intervals along roads to Lhasa, Shigatse, Gyantse and Chamdo Golmud. But no poles march to villages sleeping in mountain valleys. What then is the purpose of this progression?

Tsetang in the Valley of the Kings

Things become clear at Tsetang, a huddle of earth-coloured buildings cut in quarters by two main streets, like a rotten apple. Next to the hotel are the army barracks. All wires gather here, as do petrol tanks, trucks and other hardware for a large military force. When the PLA came to the ancient royal village of Tsetang, it turned overnight into the fourth largest city in Tibet.

Close to the town rises the mountain where the *bodhisattva* Avalokiteshvara, of whom the Dalai Lamas are reincarnations, met an ogress who made him her consort. The reincarnation principle began to be adopted for spiritual lineages in the thirteenth century and worked back to earlier teachers and deities to establish unbroken lineages. Avalokiteshvara had taken the form of a monkey and the six offspring of his union with the ogress were half-human, half-monkey. From these children evolved the Tibetan people. Did Tibetans have an understanding of our noble ape ancestry centuries before Darwin developed his theory of evolution? Tsetang, where the first Tibetan children skipped down the mountain, means 'playground'. Now PLA children ride their bicycles between piles of rubble.

The first field cultivated by Tibetans also lies near Tsetang. Thus the area gave rise to the mainstays of Tibetan life: mythology, religion and agriculture. Traditionally barley crops from this field were presented to the Dalai Lama and if fields elsewhere became infertile, a handful of soil from this field was scattered across to make crops grow again. An early example of biodynamic farming? Wherever you turn here, you see legendary places where deities and culture heroes shaped the wisdom and welfare of the Tibetan people.

Clocks in the hotel's lobby tell the time in capital cities of Tibet's tourist countries, including Canberra. After an elaborate lunch — with thoughts of *tsampa* in the field — we rest our altitude headaches. By the time we regroup, it is too late to drive to Yambulhakang, the former home of the Yarlung kings. Tomorrow perhaps, after Samyé. Instead we drive south-west along a rough track to the tumuli. Here Songtsen Gampo, first king of all Tibet, lies in a prominent tomb amidst the last resting places of later rulers of a unified Tibet that existed from the eighth century.

Fording a flooded creek, our estimation of the driver climbs steeply. Calm and skilful, he manoeuvres the Japanese minibus in this treacherous situation as if it were a horse. Strange to be an idle passenger. In my road travels I usually held the wheel, crossing the Australian outback, fording riverbeds wet and dry, getting lost in deserts, camping in rocky gorges, doing the packing, driving and worrying myself. Bump! Another pothole the size of an outhouse!

More yak, sheep, cows, donkeys, geese and chickens. Now I record my first birds. One a small creature with curled white crest. The other brown and white, wings not flapping but rotating so fast that an imprint of concentric circles remains visible in the air for a fleeting moment. A magic sight.

In the wet fields people work with basic tools: hoes, rakes, carts. I ask the guide about the local agriculture. Barley is sown in March at the first sign of spring, wheat a little later. No second crops are grown in this region. After the September harvest, the fields are ploughed and manure is spread. In spring the fields are manured again before sowing.

Unattended donkeys carry bales of straw four times their size from field to compound, only ears and noses sticking out. Seen from the rear, two slender hind legs step precociously through the mud like a girl in high-heeled shoes.

Straw is stacked around houses, brushwood heaped against walls for winter's cooking fires. So scarce is fuel in Tibet that a family can scarce afford to boil the kettle more than once a day. *Tsampa,* already roasted, needs no cooking if mixed with butter tea, so barley is the ideal staple food for a country where fuel is at a premium. Mostly, Tibetans use dried yak dung for fuel. Large pats of dung are slapped against outer walls in regular patterns, drying in the sun. One of China's best introductions to Tibet has been the thermos flask that keeps tea hot all day. They could of course have traded them for wool, instead of invading the country.

When Mao Zedong ordered Tibetans to grow wheat instead of barley, it foundered not only because of climate but because of its unsuitability as a staple in a land with little fuel. Wheat needs more cooking and baking than barley to be palatable. It is now grown as a second crop in some areas, to sell in cities where Chinese bakers turn it into loaves, buns and cakes.

We pass large compounds with many long buildings and high walls topped with broken glass, sharp stones and barbed wire. Inside the walls stand beautiful mature trees of great height, obscuring virtually everything inside the compound. With a belated shock I realise this must be one of the notorious Chinese labour camps, built to house Tibetans who break the regime's severe rules or dare to call for independence.

Clusters of grimy tents house Tibetan workers who keep the road navigable. After recent torrential downpours they can scarcely be blamed for the road's condition. Yet a donkey, mule or yak would have fewer problems picking its way between boulders and puddles than a car. This land should be traversed on foot or horseback. So often when travelling I feel I was born too late. The

Chinese army introduced the transportation wheel to Tibet, last country on the globe to be motorised. Tibet had the wheel of life and the prayer wheel. The Thirteenth Dalai Lama possessed a Baby Austin, imported in pieces via Nepal. It remained in the stable until the Fourteenth — who would have loved to be a mechanic — got it going.

Mud-brick villages symbolise the essentials of living: shelter, warmth, storage for the food from the fields, nothing that has not come from the surrounding earth. A ruined monastery comes into view and nearer the road the buildings of a new one. Most monasteries in this region were destroyed during the Cultural Revolution. One may have been Chonggye Ruidechen, a centre of Khamba resistance, where the Dalai Lama stopped on his flight to India in 1959.

High on a mountainside we make out the pavilion of Weng Cheng, the Chinese princess who became one of King Songtsen Gampo's wives — some say the wife of his son. The communists make much of this connection, as if it proves that Tibet is part of China. But the girl was a tribute payment at a time when Tibet was Tibet and China her homeland far away. She came to foreign parts to appease.

The weather closes in when we arrive at the village of Chonggye beneath the mount of kings. An enclosing, drenching rain falls soundlessly. From swirling mists run children in long skirts to look at us with round eyes, followed by straight-backed, proud-headed women. Round faces, wide features, teeth sparkling, eyebrows finely arched, eyes clear. Their cheeks have the apple-red patches of people born at high altitudes.

The group slowly ascends the mount, accompanied by women and children. I close the ranks, elbows supported by two little girls. They pick me immediately as a laggard. A woman in folded headscarf and a *chuba* turned dark with grime, begins to pull me by the hands. Her grip is like a vice, its strength greater than I've ever met in human hand. I do not doubt she could carry me up on her back.

My breathing problems return some ten metres up. This is only our first day. I must make choices, save myself for Yambulhakang on the mount's high pinnacle. I can't ruin the whole journey by not allowing my body time to adjust. Looking up at the mount, hidden in mist, I mentally greet the kings and turn to descend. The children seem to discuss my decision with approval. The woman appears disappointed but helps me down, her grip on my arm guiding every downward step. One of the girls hands me a stick for support. My eyes suddenly fill with tears from disappointment and for their forthright, practical tenderness.

The driver sits in the bus, smoking. It must be a boring job. He opens the door. I don't want to disappear inside and be cut off from the villagers, but the driver's eyes warn me not to let them in. So I sit down on the doorstep, catching my frantic breath, willing my heart to calm down. The girls, the woman and a handful of youngsters group expectantly around me for a long wait. Were these villagers nuns and monks, things would be simple. We would smile, fold hands in laps, close eyes and meditate. Or if I had a *mala,* I would thumb the beads, repeating the universal mantra OM MANI PADME HUM, as many times as it takes for the others to come down the mountain.

The girls admire my Tongan shell earrings. I remove one and hook it in the eldest girl's left lobe. I hook the other into the smaller girl's right lobe, gesturing to them to stand together. A lovely pair of earrings! They gaze at me with clear disappointment. How easy it is to read their faces. How immediate are their reactions. I raise my palms, a universal gesture of helplessness. I came badly prepared. In my luggage in the hotel sits a small bag of Australian tumbled gemstones, purchased to give away in friendship.

The woman with the strong hands puts one between the folds of her *chuba* to produce a rough crystal, the length of a finger, as thick as two thumbs. Does she want to sell it? I brought no cash. Nor do I want to load the luggage with rocks. Not given to gazing, I admire the stone, turn it against the grey light of the falling afternoon and hand it back with a smile.

Two deep wrinkles form between her large, beautiful eyes. She shakes her head, takes my hand, puts the crystal into it and folds my fingers over it, causing a dilemma. Is this a gift? What can I give in return? Or is this her sales technique?

Once more I admire the stone, give it back and turn up my palms. She gets my meaning, but again puts the crystal into my hand, folds my fingers over it and presses my hands together. In accepting I hug her and her smile breaks through like the sun on a rainy day. I remain uneasy that something more may be expected, but her face returns to interested enquiry as to the nature of my being. She fingers my hair and her luminous eyes roam over every aspect of my appearance.

My eyes do the same to her and see a queen of the fields, a woman who carries loads on her back, flails the grain, rakes the hay, stokes a fire, subdues an unruly bovine or chases a man if she feels so inclined. She smells of earth and soot and there is butterfat in her black plaits. Her cheeks are red under a walnut-coloured skin. The strong features match her eyes. I think her exceedingly beautiful. We look into each other's eyes and I suspect that, despite age and disability, I too represent some remote dream to her, whether it is of apparent otherness or the strange lightness of my eyes. 'We have all been each other's mothers', so goes the Buddhist saying.

We are joined by a scrawny little boy in colourless jacket and trousers. Posing defiantly before me, he puffs grotesquely at a cigarette, looking barely seven years old, his nose dripping. He is probably ten. I have a dreadful sensation of watching a child written up for an early, preventable death. The Chinese import cigarettes into Tibet, where smoking used to be something only foreigners did. I gesture disapproval and it is immediately taken up by the woman and girls. They pour scorn on his clipped little head but he shrugs his shoulders, puffing away. A rebel will pay any price.

A tiny girl presses through the throng to repeat the woman's act of giving. A few small crystals, broken bits of earth glass. These mountains contain crystalline formations. She gently touches my earlobes, still showing tiny silver sleepers. But these I cannot remove. I repeat protestations, but she presses the crystals into my hand. In the end I accept, vowing to be better prepared another time.

Now that we are holding hands, I begin a game played many times with children whose language I did not speak. Turning over the girl's hand and holding up my own, I say 'Hand!' All the children look confused, so I take her finger, poke up my own and say 'Finger!' They grasp the meaning, eyes turn on and the game begins. They tell me Tibetan words for hand and finger, the head and parts of the face, the belly, legs and feet. When we have done with the body, we turn to trees, sky, raindrops, a gift of crystal, shell earrings and shoes.

The kids giggle or laugh raucously at some English sounds, leaving me guessing at their associations. But they turn deeply serious when correcting my Tibetan pronunciation until they are satisfied I will be understood should I speak the word outside their dominion.

Children's pride in their language alerts us to the crime of denying them education in their first tongue. Tibetan children are taught in Mandarin if they go to school at all, yet these girls are natural teachers. Members of an oral culture, they will probably remember every English word I give them, whereas I cannot remember one of theirs beyond the next one.

Our laughter attracts others. A young woman carries her baby in a back sling under a large black umbrella, snug as a bug in a rug. By now children and women are pressed so tight around me that I feel a kind of belonging. I stretch out a hand to the baby. The mother seems pleased, proud. The baby looks me over, round-eyed.

The girls begin the language game for the baby, the umbrella, the mother. They grasp new possibilities to extend the game to challenging abstract meanings. I am bound to fail them.

If they lived in Western countries these bright kids would head for university to study languages, cultures, concepts and scientific principles, under conditions a hundred times better than found in their mud-struck village in the shadow of the royal tombs. They might not count the losses, given that opportunity. Losses such as the difference between me and the crystal woman, whom I would choose to be if that were possible.

Filtered voices gurgle above us, shadowy human figures emerge from drizzled drapes. I'm sorry the group is returning, breaking up this intimacy. Sensing the end of the game the villagers fall away, allowing the tourists to enter the bus. I gesture to the girls with the earrings to pose for my camera. Obligingly, shy smiles on their lips, they look beyond the lens to something new that catches their imagination. I do not aim the lens at the crystal woman. She has looked so deeply into my eyes that I will remember her face forever.

Everyone clusters around the door to look inside as the crystal woman hooks her eyes into mine. She seems to make a silent request I feel helpless to satisfy. Then Jason, performing the ultimate American deed, starts handing out chewing gum and gets mobbed by children and adults alike, until the driver closes the automatic door and creates two worlds: theirs and ours.

Though responding to our waves as we leave, their faces smile no longer. This is not the Tibetan way to depart. Rich and poor in Tibet would walk or ride some distance with visitors before stopping for tea, then goodbyes, perhaps an exchange of gifts but certainly *kata,* Tibet's white greeting scarfs. The kids had hoped for a short ride in the bus. My heart cringes for being a disappointment to the woman who reflects the woman within me. Will this repeat itself day after day as we journey through this land of my longing? This feeling of being not just an intrusion, but a severe let-down?

But I must face my own limitations, personal, physical, financial. Isn't it better to come with a desire to make contact in order to tell their stories, than to stuff their hands with small money, their mouths with cheap lollies?

We are bouncing back along the wet track. Mountains, slate blue in daylight, appear a sombre bovine brown in drizzly dusk. The climbers talk of the tombs. I try to tell them about the children and the game. But talk of such different experiences cannot diminish our altitude sickness.

Only five appear at dinner, but my headache is gone. Am I conquering the altitude or is it the crystal in my pocket? Dinner is a plethora of small Chinese dishes, bits of meat and vegetables in piquant sauces. Rice and tea. Tibetan waitresses in silk purple *chuba* speak Chinese to each other — hotel rules. When Jason addresses them in Tibetan they become flustered, look over their shoulders, reply in Chinese. Jason doesn't understand Chinese, so then they speak their native tongue, one of them brokenly, forgetting they could have returned to English.

We debate whether to visit Yambulhakang tomorrow, before an all-day trip to Samyé monastery. Once the oldest dwelling in Tibet, Yambulhakang was probably a royal dwelling, possibly built by King Songtsen Gampo or by King Trisong Detsen whose tomb also stands above Chonggye. I would be sorry to miss seeing the old castle, although doubt I can climb the steep rock, not to mention five storeys and a tower, without suffering pounding headaches again.

But the altitude has taken its toll of everyone, including our leader.

The decision is given: we forego Yambulhakang, needing all day for Samyé. 'You don't want to see a Chinese copy anyway, do you?' says Jason when I voice regret. For Yambulhakang is actually brand new. The ancient building that stood for twelve centuries on the spur of a craggy hill overlooking the Yarlung Valley was entirely destroyed during the Cultural Revolution. The replica was built in 1982. But the place remains the cradle of Tibet's civilisation.

Comparing old and new photos of Yambulhakang there seems hardly a difference except that the new castle looks less crumbly. Apart from the building, I wanted to get the feel of a place redolent of early Tibetan history. This disappointment is the seed of a plan to return to Tibet to see places this group misses, perhaps at my own pace.

Sleep is an instant affair. I close my eyes. Thinking 'I am really in Tibet', I am gone.

The Coming of Buddhism to Tibet

In this rarefied atmosphere waking up is as instant as falling asleep. At 7.25 am, Beijing time, dawn is not even peeping in Tibet, but public loudspeakers at the barracks blare a clarion call, followed by revolutionary songs in breakneck tempo. I pull the blankets over my ears. But the loudspeakers are pitched to rouse all residents of Tsetang to a state of nationalistic vigour. The cacophony penetrates every nerve in the body. After ten minutes of crackling not deserving the name of music comes another trumpet call, followed by twenty minutes of entirely unconvincing passionate songs. Thankfully I can't follow the lyrics. Musical exercises follow and I don't need Mandarin to know the high-pitched voice shouts: 'Left up, swing your arms, right up, swing back, up and around, down and up again, aaaannnd repeat!!!' Dawn has not yet broken.

In the dark, memories are rudely awakened. Holland under Nazi occupation. The conditioning of a whole population to an unwanted ideology delivered at gunpoint. Soldiers marching to strident, approved songs. The hidden resistance, the secret ridiculing of official messages drummed day after day through airwaves and press — the lies. Will all of Tibet be like this?

At eight a female voice issues moral advice. Unable to escape, you begin to guess from the tone of voice what someone is implying in another language. I must not forget that this is due to our shared humanity. But the bathroom is fairly soundproof and for eight minutes I escape indoctrination. Do Tibetan houses have bathrooms?

Breakfast is at 6.30, Tibetan real time, daylight barely dawning. Chinese ladies open counters in marble corridors gracefully cluttered with souvenirs: fans, jade, lacquer, brushpaintings, small antiques. Resentment rears its powerless head, although I keenly bought such artefacts in China. But this is not China. It would be different if this were a Chinese hotel in free Tibet. With every step, around every corner, I fight thoughts like these, trying not to blame the people I encounter, for they are caught in a system imposed from above, taught that Tibet is an integral part of China.

The whole group including Jason admits to having been laid low by altitude yesterday. This morning I feel great, but we're all popping pills. Jason orders Tibetan butter tea to knead *tsampa* bought from the farmers yesterday. I try a piece. A nutty taste overlays basic blandness.

By nine o'clock the loudspeakers splutter unintelligible garble, radio waves from far away. News from Beijing. Someone lets off a round of fire crackers, or is it gunfire? Silently I panic as we board the bus. The driver looks no less indisposed than yesterday. The streets seem quiet. The morning is sunny, but Tibet sometimes has four seasons in one day.

Driving along yesterday's road it fascinates me to view the landscape from the opposite direction. Same landscape, same road, but another place altogether. In morning light, flooded plantations of yellowing poplar saplings pick up every other hue the landscape has to spare. Sky vivid blue, mountains muted walnut, deep folds of cinnamon. Long white clouds float below peaks, get lost in narrow valleys, hug lower outcrops for a rest. Pale green tree mops reflect in the river. Black water changes to tawny, then silver, as the light travels. Through the gold and silver runs barbed-wire fencing, keeping animals from nipping young trees in the bud.

When sheep, cows, *dzo*, donkeys and goats are not munching harvest stubble, they nibble saltbush stacked on compound walls for winter feed. Men and boys are cutting brush, bundling it onto low-slung tractor trailers. These versatile vehicles belch clouds of petrol fumes as they rattle past.

On the nether side the mountains seem rockier, more deeply folded, revealing one far valley after another, minute villages nestling in bowl-shaped saddles. In a rocky mud-brick ruin the outline of a house and compound can be seen. Were the massed walls behind it part of a destroyed monastery? Why would people leave a place close to the river, with run-off water and grazing? A few bends further a cluster of houses and trees, backed by terraced fields scaling mountains that arch protective arms around the settlement. My peasant sensibilities are aroused, but I must remain hunched behind my little window.

Dunes! Is there a landscape form this country does not have? Covering saddle and laps of two mountains, these are true desert dunes, sickle shapes blown by eastern winds. Not a footprint disturbs the perfectly sculpted surface. Not even the memory of a bird's evening trail or track of furtive mouse.

Samyé Dukou, the ferry crossing, is a bustle of comings and goings at ten in the morning. When yak-skin coracles were still in use, holding ten people, the Tsangpo crossing took two hours or more, depending on the current. Now the river is plied by motorised, flat-bottomed, wooden boats taking twenty people seated and unmentionable numbers standing up. It takes forty-five to ninety minutes to get across, depending on sandbanks. Across the road runs a long drystone wall, beautifully laid, disfigured by dense toppings of green glass shards. Poplar trees rustle behind it. Another prison?

Darting figures weave through a willow grove on the riverbank. Relieving oneself is public business in Tibet. Crowd watching requires new sensibilities.

Yet it does not bother Tibetans if you stand aside looking on, contemplation being an acceptable state of mind. Hundreds mill around the landing place, a low hum of conversation fills the air. Tibetan is a gentle language. Or are the speakers? Quiet voices direct where to place bundles, boxes, bags and bicycles, laced by the counterpoint of laughter. Luggage heaps up around a freestanding willow. Its bark is wounded from boats tying up.

Women without exception wear the *chuba*, but untraditional checkered woollen headscarfs are ubiquitous. All men wear shirts, trousers, jackets. There are a few Chinese caps, but mostly they wear wide-brimmed felt hats, introduced here a century or so ago.

Two boats arrive, unloading people, luggage and tree branches. I reflect on the scarcity of wood. And the mystery to be contemplated at all points of arrival and departure: what motivates people to move such distances? Some will be pilgrims bound for Samyé. Nothing is visible on the other side but a tiny hamlet. Yet Sarat Chandra Das's account of his travels in the late nineteenth century gives an impression that the area teems with settlements, monasteries and trading posts.

On this side there is nothing but glass-topped walls. The last village is half a day's walk away. Tsetang is thirty kilometres. Yet people disembark with a sense of purpose that hints of more life between these mountains than you could guess from here.

When in 1935 Margaret and Derrick Williamson arrived early for their Lhasa appointment with the Regent, they went for a cruise down the Tsangpo in yak-skin coracles. The boatsmen sang and whistled as they rowed. In every coracle travelled one sheep, because on the upstream journey the boatsman would carry his coracle on his back, while the sheep carried his belongings.

Two elderly Europeans depart in one boat with guide and boatsman — an elitist waste of fuel. We climb aboard the regular ferry full with Tibetans. The fare is two yuan for them, more for us. Prayer flags flutter from the stern. We bunch on the edge or lean against wooden panels that keep the freight from sliding.

Jason is soon engaged in animated conversation with a young monk of about nine. The boy, in trousers and windcheater, is being returned to Samyé by his farmer father. Not a simple monk recruit, he is a reincarnate lama who will spend his life at Samyé. His round face is lit up by a serene smile. Two adult monks wear heavily worn and patched robes. The younger one with the keen angular profile engages Jason in religious debate while the other listens quietly spellbound. Religion is the favourite topic for conversation here.

We start to absorb the presence of the river. Only our second day, and all this. On the river all colours assume a pearly sheen, clouds float upside down in quicksilver water. Nothing to do but look deeply into its swirls for the best part of an hour, the nicest of meditations, offering mirror-smooth peace of mind.

We need it when the other bank is reached. Sharp-eyed villagers have calculated the number of passengers while still midstream and are waiting with three cultivators. We climb onto the trailers and brace ourselves. This is a twelve-hundred-year-old pilgrims' route, but there is not really a road! The track shifting through sand dunes is fine for a pony picking its way between rocks and shallows, but hapless tourists bounce and vibrate another forty-five minutes. We laugh insanely each time we nearly tip. It's a game to keep upright: hit, miss, win, lose. But the boneshaking ride will be worth every moment when we reach Samyé, Tibet's first Buddhist monastery, established in 749 by the Indian sage Padmasambhava, who is to Tibetans what Saint Patrick is to the Irish.

There are correlations between the Irish and Tibetans that go beyond their love of a cup of spirits, ribald jokes and dancing to string music. Long ago the Irish invaded Britain and France in skin coracles! Both Tibetans and Irish were dedicated copiers and printers of religious manuscripts. While Ireland preserved many scriptures lost on the European continent during the dark ages, Tibet preserved what the weather and the decline of Buddhism could not maintain in India. Both Irish and Tibetans took to monasticism with zeal, men and women producing great abbots and abbesses. Both countries had their monasteries sacked by invaders time and time again, their monks tortured and killed, books destroyed, treasures looted and buildings burned down. And just as the Vikings established the first cities in Ireland after destroying much of the culture, so Chinese communists are turning Tibet's self-contained villages into Chinese satellite cities.

But Samyé will always be Padmasambhava's place. Tibetans call him the Guru or the Lotus-Born, who counts among his miraculous manifestations such mind-teasers as the fierce 'Adamantine Sagging Belly'. Such was his reputation that King Trisong Detsun invited him to introduce Buddhism to Tibet.

We pass two demure little stupas along the track, gleaming white against the dark mountain, marking the spot where the two met. The king was a local, born in nearby Drakmar village. This whole area still vibrates with remembered miracles in the wake of the Lotus-Born's passing. His lively, persuasive spirit still palpably abounds. Samyé has withstood plunder, earthquakes, fire and the Cultural Revolution, and rises again from the ashes.

Bön, till 749 Tibet's dominant religion, held that everything from a stone to a tree to a mountain and including humans, possesses spirit. In the Bönpo universe one negotiates with multiple surrounding forces to protect one's own existence in the scheme of things. Tibetan Buddhists still do. This worldview is familiar to Australian Aborigines and avant-garde physicists. Bön priests practised magic to continually restore the balance of power.

Although their beliefs and practices filtered into Buddism and on the surface Bön monasteries and priests became almost indistinguishable from Buddhist monasteries and lamas, Bön is still alive as an independent faith and said to be on the rise. When minding one's own business fails to stop invaders, oppressed people naturally look to religions that promise relief through magic. But it is also possible that a baby was thrown out with the bathwater — or a diamond with the rancid butter — when Buddhism came to Tibet. Bön, rarely studied outside Tibet, may harbour ancient knowledge not available in any other society now.

Buddhism introduced a more intellectual way of negating life's difficulties. It recognised the life forces in the universe under the collective name of *karma* and encouraged each individual to take control over his or her destiny through the practice of compassion and cultivating wisdom, thus building up good *karma* for this and future lives. The gradual amalgamation of Bön and Buddhism put the magic in the hands of the lamas, who consult oracles, perform esoteric rites, maintain secret teachings and grant special initiations. Yet every person remains responsible for his or her own life and decisions in the prevailing circumstances.

In the light of this past, it is not surprising that every Tibetan family strove to have one son or daughter in religious robes, studying Buddhist teachings. Religion is the axle on which the wheel of life turns and repeated mantras are the oil that keeps it moving.

Near Samyé is the cave where Padmasambhava meditated to gather strength to fight local demons opposing Buddhism's introduction. So successful was he, that at his bidding magical beings carried wood and stones to Samyé by night, as Tibetan building workers erected temples by day. Samyé was laid out like a mandala representing the Buddhist universe, modelled on Odantapuri monastery in India, no longer in existence. It has four portals, four great stupas, and four temples surrounding the central three-tiered temple. Eventually, Samyé comprised 108 temples great and small, the sacred number.

David Snellgrove quotes the king's minister waxing lyrical about the site and surrounding mountains 'raised in offering to the sky', comparing them with noble animals or sacred symbols. The plain is seen as 'an expanse of white silk' and the pool as 'a dish of melted butter'. The Tsangpo river is like a turquoise dragon and a nearby mountain called Tiger Peak is 'haughty as an elephant'. It makes me wonder when Tibetans first saw elephants. This song of praise for a very fine location imbued the place with sacredness from the start.

Indian sage Shankarakshita was Samyé's first abbot, but the first monks were seven Tibetans. Samyé's earliest beginnings represented an exercise in ecumenical religious activity, or a competition designed to get the best of Buddhism for Tibet. The main temple had its three levels decorated in Tibetan,

Indian and Chinese temple fashions. Indian and Chinese monks came to translate scriptures into Tibetan. Buddhism had come to China in the third century by way of the sea and before that in small doses down the Silk Road and flourished by the sixth century.

The Indian school held that all elements of existence of past, present and future really exist. And thereby hangs a great system of philosophy. Chinese pilgrim monks had returned home from India to develop that profound branch of Buddhism called Ch'an, later Zen. In short, Zen does *not* hold that all the elements of past, present and future really exist. And thereby hangs another great philosophy. Two halves of one supremely esoteric apple?

As Tibetan schools of Buddhism developed from this rich seedbed, they established temples in Samyé and to this day the monastery is not exclusively associated with any of the four main sects, although Indian Buddhism became the preferred source. In the eleventh century the Indian sage Atisha lived at Samyé, translating Sanskrit scriptures brought by Padmasambhava and no longer extant in their land of origin.

L. Austine Waddell, who once 'purchased' a Tibetan temple lock stock and barrel to persuade the monks to reveal their religious knowledge, published the first work on Tibetan Buddhism in 1885. He gives Samyé's full name as bSam-yas Mi-'gyur Lhun-gyis grub-pai Tsug-lug-K'an, or 'the academy for obtaining the heap of unchanging meditation', in other words: full enlightenment. Das claimed Samyé means 'three styles', after the main temple floors. But modern scholars translate Samyé as 'limitless thought' or 'beyond imagination' and its full name as 'Glorious Immutable Miraculously Accomplished Shrine Beyond Imagination'. Waddell found that Samyé was also Tibet's government bank for bullion and treasure, since it had a reputation of being safe due to Padmasambhava's spells.

Waddell and Das, these two great nineteenth-century Tibet scholars, lived contemporaneously in Darjeeling, yet never conferred because of racial and class barriers. Would Tibet's fate have been different had they met? Scholarly cooperation might have presented Tibet to the world in a different light than simply as a primitive country to be spied on for possible Russian interest in the Great Game of colonialism. Despite his genuine interest in things Tibetan, Das's survey work on the Lhasa route was sinister enough. It prepared the way for the British invasion of 1904, which in turn undermined Tibet's independent status in China's eyes, thus becoming the wedge that led to the 1950 invasion.

Buildings loom, the sand-gnashing cultivators calm down, lurching to a stop before a gateway in a high stone wall. Still vibrating, I tumble into the courtyard of Samyé, struck dumb with excitement at having arrived in the place where Tibetan Buddhism began.

Not that Samyé is the same as in 770. The iconoclastic King Langdarma, about whose life and death exist legends, songs and dances, destroyed parts of the monastery in the late ninth century, as did adherents of Bön. Earthquakes struck about 1749 and 1850, and a great fire around 1808 destroyed the main temple and library of Indian manuscripts no longer extant in India, a loss equivalent to the burning of Alexandria's library. Atisha had said that the library of Samyé contained more religious texts than the three greatest Buddhist temples in India together. These periods of destruction were crowned by the Cultural Revolution of the 1960s, when the monastery was severely damaged.

After each calamity the Tibetan people and government subscribed to have Samyé rebuilt — 100 000 ounces of silver after the great fire and almost double that after the last earthquake. In 1935 Derrick Williamson, British political officer for Tibet, was asked whether gold could be traded from India to regild the roofs — Tibetans not mining their own for fear of disturbing the earth. Today, pilgrims bring small banknotes and Samyé is being rebuilt again, stone for stone, wall by wall, temple after temple. And the gilded roof is back on.

Das, surveyor and spy for the British as well as Tibet pundit, mentions a prophecy attributed to Padmasambhava himself, that Samyé will eventually be engulfed by the sands on which it is built. Das thought the process well under way, but the winds must have blown from other directions, because Samyé sits defiantly upon the sands and the sound of singing building workers is heard on the breeze.

Samyé, Gracious Place
beyond the Imagination

On this journey I do significant things for the first time. Having visited monasteries and temples in China, Hong Kong, Nepal, India, Singapore, Malaysia and Australia, I am about to enter an original Tibetan monastery for the first time in my life. Having read detailed descriptions of Tibetan monastic life in a hundred books, I will now get glimpses of where that world began more than twelve hundred years ago.

Taking in the vast courtyard I prolong the moment. A horse, saddled with Tibetan carpet bags and dangling stirrups, stands tied to a pole. In the background thick layers of prayer flags in blue, red, white, green and yellow are strung between trees and a mud-brick wall. The little black horse has a white blaze and muzzle. He looks at me, cocking his intelligent head. Where did your rider come from this morning and what is his purpose? Or hers? In books Tibetan women ride horses on long journeys, but I have to see one yet.

The main temple, walls plastered white, russet upstairs with gold emblems, carries two *dorje,* sacred thunderbolts, on its gilded roof. Tibetans do things with cloth you don't see anywhere else. Curtains hang *outside* windows, doors, facades. Above the temple entrance stretch ten metres of white cotton, appliquéd with a *dharma* wheel flanked by eternal knots in blue. Red and white fringes fade to delectable pink in the hot sun.

Midday and the heat peaks between sandy ground and white walls. A monk rushes from the temple carrying a frying pan, jumping across piebald dogs asleep on the threshold. I touch the yellow tassel suspended from a brass ornament on the heavy door painted geometrically in red, yellow and blue, but mostly red. The tassel is saturated with butter. Excited I sniff my hand, touch the tassel again and the smell of rancid butter reaches my nostrils. The world I read about has come off the page!

I spend my life being exhilarated by exotic details, forgetting the spiritual essence of places like these. But the smell of rancid butter does more than remind me of books read. It tests the resilience of my senses. It is one thing to read and imagine, quite another to slouch through hot sand, touch, smell and risk being put off, having the story diminished. Some things only become accessible because I took the trouble to come and get rancid butter on my hands. Some things, but not others. The senses delude us, say the Buddhist scriptures.

Walking across broken pavers we send brass prayer wheels in red wooden racks spinning, touch red and blue pillars, fingertip ancient woodgrains. The pillars are covered with painted lotus flowers and stylised clouds. Seen from the dimness of the forecourt, blinding white light bounces off a wall and closed doors hung with flounces, in a passage open to the sky. All the time boy monks run up a broad wooden staircase, carrying empty frying pans, smiling over their shoulders. Going to roast *tsampa*?

Frescoes cover every wall, freshly painted. Primary colours and strong creamy pinks for faces and hands of *bodhisattvas* and buddhas. We are in a stone-paved alleyway open to the sky. Symmetry vanishes. Surfaces exist to be decorated. Boy monks peer from upper-floor verandahs, as in a neighbourhood street. Monastery dogs trot past on business.

Later I cannot recall how we found the main assembly hall, its atmosphere heavy with aromas of incense and butter. The huge dim space overwhelms before we see what appear to be huddled figures on carpeted benches, leading to a vast statue on a shrine. But the figures turn out to be thick russet monks' robes with yellow borders, draped so they appear to stand up. The monks wrap themselves in these when sitting in assembly. Robes and butter tea keep the circulation going. I rub the rough homespun between my fingers. How many weavers lost a livelihood when the monasteries were made to close and Chinese textiles flooded in?

Warm, glowing red dominates surfaces. Yellow, blue, green and white are complementary. The colours of prayer flags. Some pillars are covered with brocade patchwork in the five colours. New *thangkas* framed in red and yellow silk hang from the ceiling. Diffused light streams through high windows of twenty small panes each. Two young monks shuffle about, dusting brass objects, topping up butter lamps, lighting incense. Suddenly one of the heaped robes moves and rises. Inside it, a monk seeks healing for a fever at the shrine. Seeing us he smiles wanly, then lies down again.

Samyé's great Sakyamuni Buddha statue was decapitated during the Cultural Revolution but has been carefully restored. An elderly monk tells Jason that many smaller statues were spared. He beckons us to a sanctuary room where Padmasambhava's seal, his staff and five of his hairs are preserved. Awesome to stand before such deeply personal effects of a great sage across thirteen centuries of human endeavours. The monk relishes telling tiny details about the sacred objects under his care. Donated money, he assures us, is spent entirely on restoration work.

A circumambulation corridor surrounds the meditation hall. Two metres wide, the walls rise conically, painted with intricate frescoes to their full height, some ten to twelve metres. The light comes from just two windows and our eyes see little at first. Then the painted stories of Padmasambhava, Sakyamuni the historical Buddha, Tara the female *bodhisattva* of compassion and many others are revealed in the dim light. A Tibetan storybook that pilgrims came to read by the light of butterfat torches.

Many books speak loosely of Tibetan gods, saints and deities. In English, 'deity' can indicate a divine being such as a god or goddess, or a person deified. The *bodhisattvas* of Tibet were once people, but their lives were of such extraordinary sublimity, so marked by miracles, that they are credited with divine power. The dividing line between the divine and highly developed spiritual competence remains nebulous.

At Samyé, under the gaze of these benevolent faces, one senses that Tibetans never lost track of the knowledge that the *bodhisattvas* they worship started off as ordinary people like themselves, developing their minds life after life until their smallest gesture turned events for the better, their simplest words fell unforgettably on the fortunate ears that were present. *Namtar*, or life stories of these sages abound. None of this can be appreciated fully without accepting the principle of rebirth, although people can and do become enlightened in one lifetime by applying themselves unreservedly.

Padmasambhava sits on his golden throne bedecked with orange silks and white *kata,* the offering scarves for all occasions. Lighted wicks float in butter-filled silver chalices, lighting up his protruding eyes. He sports a handlebar moustache, this conqueror of spirits. Sogyal Rimpoche wrote that Padmasambhava's mantra OHM AH HUM — VAJRA GURU PADMA SIDHI HUM, is the most helpful of mantras when life becomes difficult. May its appearance on this page be of benefit to all who see it. His face means action — he was an organiser, managing not just humans but the spirits of the place, so as to quell greed and violence and establish the Buddha's Middle Way of peace and compassion.

Was Padmasambhava a missionary? There was a tradition in Asian countries for rulers to invite scholars and sages who could explain new religious doctrines and if these were acceptable they might replace older ones. Wandering sages were part of the landscape. But apparently Padmasambhava had missionary zeal and the local demons he fought at Samyé may have been of flesh and blood!

Jason talks softly with another monk, switching occasionally to English for our benefit. We gather before a simple wooden throne painted red and gold, heaped with brocade cushions. Incongruously, the throne is wrapped in plastic sheets across which pilgrims have draped many *kata*. This is the Dalai Lama's teaching throne waiting for his return, resting against a wall of tiny painted buddhas.

We stand around the throne, lifting our awareness to those people who have waited thirty-four years already and will go on waiting, placing fresh *kata* on their spiritual leader's empty seat. The throne looks old enough to be the same one Das saw in 1882 in the north-east corner of the assembly hall, where it still stands. What immense security people must experience when, even after destruction, objects reappear in the same patterns and positions as before. Could it be that inner change is more easily achieved if outer change is slowed down or not attempted at all?

Every so often I forget to breathe. On the ceiling above me is the amazingly intricate Kalachakra mantra, a universe in a wheel, surrounded by *bodhisattvas*. Did the painters lie on scaffolding like Michelangelo? Where in the world are ceilings still painted like this with thousands of shapes, circles and borders suggesting three dimensions? Getting dizzy, I lower my eyes to see more *thangkas*. Underneath a huge one of Padmasambhava hangs a fine small *thangka* of the Fourteenth Dalai Lama and the Tenth Panchen Lama seated together, smiling. The Panchen Lama died in 1989. The two only met a few times as very young men, because the Panchen was mostly kept in China, taken under the communists' wings as an eleven-year-old.

On the second floor, room after room proclaims its own purpose. Wonderful *thangkas* and statues, mostly new. But those massive doors have to be survivors. Walls running the entire width of the temple are painted with tiny White Taras, executed without duplicating methods as acts of worship! Another giant Padmasambhava inhabits his own hall, lit by butter wicks in a truly enormous golden chalice. All ceilings have mandalas.

We meet again the two young men from the ferry. They stand worshipful before a mural three metres high and maybe seven long. It depicts Tsongkhapa, the fourteenth-century reformer, surrounded by a stunning array of *bodhisattvas* and dignitaries in brocade finery, obviously from far-flung places.

A balcony on the first floor has a defaced fresco awaiting restoration. A shrine holds a large photo of the Dalai Lama, embellished with painted robes, lotus flowers and sacred objects. He grins joyfully. Beside him a smaller photograph of the Panchen Lama and a large one of the Sakya incarnate lama. *Kata* and money are heaped around their butter lamps. Elsewhere a large Panchen Lama *thangka* hangs from the ceiling. These repeating images are like an affirmation that Tibetan Buddhism is alive, receiving daily attention.

A young caretaker monk sits on a landing. He looks about fourteen, but as we've just learnt that the young incarnate lama on the ferry is fifteen instead of nine, this one may be a young adult. With prayer wheel and thermos he sits on a cushion under an open window. On his low table lie loose-leaved texts between wooden covers, wrapped in a *kata*, flanked by butter lamp and incense. If no tourists come, he continues his learning. When they do, he serenely accepts banknotes for the monastery.

Stepping onto another roof we enter chanting. In a courtyard below us, two incense vessels separate two rows of monks seated against the walls facing each other. Four monks listen on an upper gallery. A strong voice issues from under the overhang. The teaching lama is on his seat. Texts are in the monks' laps. They are not only learning by rote, but doing exegesis. For decades Chinese authorities disallowed teaching in Tibet's monasteries. But now there are only about 130 monks at Samyé to benefit from it.

The top floor is latticed but otherwise open to the elements. There is no evidence of Chinese decorations. The breeze has free play with *kata* draped on *thangkas* and painted pillars. A latticed gallery affords wonderful views of Samyé's ancient layout. Everywhere are structures in stages of completion to restore the original mandala. A hub of activity. But no nunnery exists at Samyé.

From this roof we can see the holy mountain Hepori where King Trisong Detsun once had a palace. On another peak a small hermitage. The mountains' outrunners from left and right meet in the near distance, creating a green oasis in an otherwise bare landscape. How I would love to trek to that far horizon where the mountains meet.

At lunch break, in courtyards and on lower roofs, clusters of young monks sit in circles playing cards! Do the cards bear faces of *bodhisattvas*?

We walk to the circular wall and the willows beyond. Das noted walnut, peach, poplars and flowers at Samyé. In his time the hills had stands of fine timber and were the haunts of deer and snow leopards as well as sheep and goats. He also met 'numerous woodcutters'. Today the landscape around Samyé is desert rather than the natural paradise Das describes. If the Tibetans managed to have fine stands of timber from immemorial times, what happened in the twentieth century that made them disappear?

We pass through a gateway in the wall that still surrounded the entire monastic complex when Indian explorer Nain Singh visited in 1873. The wall was then a mile and a half long, its four gates facing the four points of the compass. Now parts lie in ruins, but what remains is of great structural beauty. This wall you want to hug! Near the gate sits a massive boulder made into a grain mill. Too resistant and heavy, it may have lain here for centuries throughout all of Samyé's ordeals. The monks could always grind their barley.

Singh noted Samyé's altitude as 11 430 feet. We pant as we make for the shade of a willow grove by a picture-book babbling brook. Clear water streams across a pebble bed, taking small leaps where levels change or rocks cause little rapids, making the loveliest of music. I wouldn't put it past the monks of old Samyé to have arranged pebbles and rocks so that water music was produced, to delight those stepping from cold, dark meditation halls for a brief communion with nature.

But for us begins a traumatic incident that will keep occurring day after day, wherever we stop to eat. Half a dozen children from Samyé village come running up to sit with us. Three girls, three boys, faces awash with expectation, eyes laughing, their clothes mixtures of worn Tibetan garb and tourist donations, a cap, a denim jacket.

The group decides we shall eat first and the children must wait for leftovers. No sharing. The decision is conveyed. They sit down at a polite distance, staring at us. They still smile, eyes now glowing with anticipation. We live in the lap of luxury before their very eyes. All tourists in Tibet do. This rubs. I am terribly aware how much we pay to live in Tibet for one month of daily overflowing lunch boxes. It will take some of us years to pay for the privilege. And yet, what a privilege to be able to pay.

I don't take part in the decision. Once a hungry child myself, I am about to faint having had breakfast six hours ago. But looking from my lunch box to the children, my appetite wanes. My hunger is partly in the mind. Mentally I sit amongst them, aged ten and hoping. I leave chicken, apple, bun and cake, eating one bun and a pear to still my hunger. There are ten of us and the kids see their patience rewarded by a good amount of food. They go contentedly. But I remember the woman in the field who extended her *tsampa* bag the very second I sat down beside her. I would like to act as hospitably as she did, sharing my lunch with a child, eating together. But this would force the group's hand.

Slowly we walk back through gate and grounds, past temples, through the big courtyard to the track where cultivators wait to return us to the ferry. It is hard leaving Samyé. You can leave me behind, I tell Jason. In this special, gracious place. My feet drag through the sand. But I climb on board with the others and we shake away. Samyé's roofs are obscured by willows as we round the bend.

Later I don't remember much of the ride or the crossing of the silver Tsangpo. For ninety minutes I relive Samyé, anchor fresh memories forever. I wake up to the day when we slide up the landing place near the glass-topped wall.

Place of Perfect Imagination

Pilgrims disembark from other boats. Two men wear khaki *chuba* looking like army surplus cloth. But borders and cuffs are of colourful Tibetan weaves and the lining is sheepskin. Sleeves hang down to the knees for freezing conditions, but today the men have slipped their *chuba* off their right shoulders, giving freedom to one arm and cooling the body.

I feel bothered by the traveller's trappings: documents bag, camera, sunglasses, hat. But Tibetans wear three to four layers, held by belts, extra garments and bags tied around their waists. They are walking suitcases. The sun has become very warm. Two women pass in felt boots. It is good to see these boots are still being made, not all replaced by Chinese shoes.

A party of nomads has made a fire under the trees and enjoys a meal. The pace of life is utterly relaxed. We have heard that pilgrimages are increasing yearly. By 1995 this road will be macadamised. More pilgrims and tourists? More troops?

There's no time to drive to Yambulhakang. I'm disappointed and Jason offers to get me there on a bus. I decline, choosing to stay with the group. Samyé took everyone's energy. We've done well for our second day in Tibet. It is good to sit at a round table discussing the day with people who are strangers no longer. Two giant pandas look down on us from a giant mural. The Chinese have a way of expressing in art wonderful things that once used to be, seemingly denying that they are no more. These bears nibble bamboo in a forest eroded by people needing more land.

After dinner Kay and I go out, picking our way through dark streets by torchlight. Every fifty metres, loudspeakers blare revolutionary music and slogans. Games of chance are played in dark corners. In a teahouse, people watch cartoons on television. A few Chinese shops are open. One displays a rack of T-shirts bearing the word 'Beijing'. They look freshly arrived, folds still sharp. Chinese factories may have been ready to print '2000' on them, but parcelled them off to the colonies instead.

'How ya doing?' Kay asks from time to time. We breathe laboriously and our legs feel heavy, but walking feels good despite having to keep eyes to the ground to prevent falling into one of numerous gaping pits in the footpath. There is too much motorised traffic on the unlit road to safely walk there.

Abruptly the loudspeakers die. It is nine o'clock. Time for workers to retire, so they can rise at seven in the morning for communal aerobics before joining their work gangs. Or must they attend self-criticism meetings from nine to ten? The communist state aims to occupy the mind of its citizens all their waking hours. We return through obediently emptying streets.

In the night, which is spent wrestling with headache and breathlessness, there is no cold water in the bathroom. A glass is all that will fit under the hot tap. I fill the thermos to flush the toilet. Guests in other rooms are heard doing the same and soon cigarette smoke pours through air ducts. Nicotine addiction among Chinese men is epidemic. Take away the opium of the people and they choose another.

I toss and turn through the hours. Tonight the dogs of Tsetang are quiet. At 7.40 am a heaven-sent power failure kills off the public address system on the shrill note of a revolutionary ditty. A politically aware rooster takes the opportunity to announce the new day at the top of his glorious voice, knowing the dawn always belonged to roosters and one day will belong to roosters again. *Tashi delek,* rooster! Unfortunately the loudspeakers crackle into life soon after with morning exercises. Today we leave for Lhasa, via Mindröling monastery.

I take a photograph from the window to remind myself later that this hotel stands in Tibet. Through bars and across brick structures I snap a typical bare buff-coloured Tibetan hill. Only when I press the shutter do I realise that what I mistook for a patch of snow on a low ledge is a gleaming aluminium fuel tank. Yesterday we noticed many fuel depots in and around Tsetang. Troops stationed here can swoop on southern and western borders in a matter of days.

A flurry of newly arrived tourists takes off in the direction of Samyé. We were lucky having the company of Tibetan pilgrims yesterday. On our third day we are old Tibet hands. Nothing spoils a visit to a wonderfully remote place more than another bunch of tourists.

Following the same road, we turn left onto a rough narrow track after passing the Samyé ferry. Twelve kilometres inland lies the monastery of Mindoling or Mindröling, meaning 'Place of Perfect Emancipation'. The Nyingmapa order, or 'Ancient Ones', dates from the time Tibetan Buddhism diversified. The Red Hats resisted all reforms and kept to the *dharma* as introduced by Shankarakshita and Padmasambhava. They established monasteries far and wide, from the Himalayas to sixteenth century Sechen in Eastern Tibet, evocatively described in Chögyam Trungpa's autobiography.

Gradually the track rises through fields where yaks swing their gorgeous coats, sheep and goats graze, and people work the earth with slow, rhythmic movements. Farmhouses dot the landscape up to the village, where the monastery on the hillside becomes visible. A hermitage oversees all.

As we pull up at the monastery gate, more than a dozen children dressed in an array of Tibetan, Chinese and Western clothes, gather around. None are barefoot. The raggedest looking girl walks up to us in her grubby *chuba* with dark red sash, hair peaking in all directions. A beautiful face, open and trusting. And so pale. Many young Tibetan children look quite pale, having not yet been exposed much to the burning sun in the fields. She clenches two small fists to her mouth, looking up at us. Helplessness assails me again. It takes too long for tourist wealth to trickle down to the population. Some say it never reaches Tibetans.

The footpath to the monastery gate leads past a small house with two doorways. No need to read the carved signs — the smell advertises the purpose. How touching to find public toilets for ladies as well as gents, so far off the beaten track. Mindröling used to have a nunnery and marriage is not unknown among the Nyingmapa.

The spacious, beautiful courtyard is such a marvel that regret about leaving it again strikes instantly. Like yesterday in Samyé I want to stay, the pull is tremendous. Is this going to be my reaction to each monastery? What ties from a forgotten life tug at my heart?

The buildings around the courtyard are in a wonderful state of restoration. Destroyed during the 1959 invasion, most of the monastery was razed to the ground in the Cultural Revolution. Although the earliest building dates from the tenth century, Mindröling's great expansion took place in the seventeenth century.

Fresh ochre paint covers walls. Red pillars, floral capitals, blue, red and green friezes and pleated white fringes above every window. The stonework is so beautiful I must stroke its textures. Seen close-up the red ochre bands topping walls are made of bundles of twigs, laid face on, so that the cut ends of thousands of woody twigs are visible, piled half a metre high, coated dark ochre and held between layers of square-cut wooden beams. These eaves packed with brushwood are a feature of Tibetan architecture found from Lhasa to as far south as Dolpo in Western Nepal. This unique architectural design is a tribute to the ingenuity and artistry of Tibetan builders using materials at hand.

Windows in black-painted frames narrow upwards like the buildings. There is a delightful variety of levels, one, two or three storeys, with wide verandahs for little boy monks to look down at comings and goings. Balconies are fenced with rows of pots and tins of roses, geraniums and marigolds. What delight the monks must get from these potted flowers when they come inside for the long winter.

Freshly whitewashed walls, canary yellow window sashes, decorated wooden trellises and the steps to the *gompa* tomato red. The whole place is designed for enclosed living, protected from the elements, but welcoming visitors. The play of shadows from so many walls and levels is an aesthetic pleasure, enhanced by the feathery shadows of foliage from some elegant big trees where you can tie up your horse!

Young monks shout 'Hello! Hello!' from windows and doors. In the courtyard monks spread and turn bundles of fragrant grass on a groundsheet. Ground to powder, the grass makes incense. Tibetan incense has an invigorating fragrance.

In the small portal to the *gompa* a noticeboard gives the history of Mindröling in Chinese and English. It seems outrageous it is not written in Tibetan. It says:

A Brief Introduction to the Mindoling Monastery
Situated in the Mindoling village of Danang Township, Danang County, Ihoca Prefecture, the monastery is one of the three largest monasteries belonging to the Nyingmapa Sect, otherwise known as the Red Sect of Tibetan Buddhism with a total floor space of nearly 100 000 square metres it was rebuilt and expanded in 1677 by Terton Terdak Lingpa Dorje on the basis of the Tarpaling Monastery originally founded by Lumei Tsultrim Sherap, and it was renamed as the Mindoling Monastery.

The Mindoling used to have four buildings, big or small, two of which have been restored. The building on the southern side of the monastery is called Tsuklhakang. In the middle of Tsuklhakang is a sutra–chanting hall on either side of which there is a minor chapel. Behind the sutra-chanting hall is the assembly hall with a statue of Sakyamuni as the chief object enshrined. Tsuklhakang is the main building of the Mindoling monastery. The building on the northern side of the monastery is called Chokor Lhunpo Lhakang. In the front part of it is a sutra chanting hall where a goldplated statue of Terdon Terdak Lingpa and his throne are enshrined. Behind the sutra chanting hall there is a chapel with statues of Avalokiteshvara, Vajra-Pani and Manjushri enshrined inside. The monastery contains various kinds of statues of Buddha in different colours, postures and sizes. It has colourful murals with a unique style that present the images of the famous masters and disciples belong to the red, white, multicoloured and yellow sects. In addition it also possesses a hand-written volume of one hundred thousand Prajna and the life-long works by Terdon Terdak Lingpa. The Lamas of the Mindoling monastery are well-cultured in Sanskrit and in Tibetan language, medicine and almanac calculation. Their achievements of research in the fields of Tibetan medicine and almanac calculation are known throughout Tibet. The Mindoling monastery is one of the monasteries under the special protection of the Tibet autonomous region. In 1983, the state allocated a sum to repairing the monastery.

Such a factual description represses important religious information and we are to see many like it. Official Chinese histories ignore the ravages of the fifties and sixties.

Mindröling was the largest, most important of three Nyingmapa monasteries.

Dorje Drak and Nasi were destroyed, Dorje Drak being rebuilt by monks. Keith Dowman, who visited an incredible 170 monasteries, temples and meditation caves in the mid-eighties, took photos of Tubten Dorje Drak on the Tsangpo River. For every monastery on the tourist trail, there are dozens of inaccessible monasteries and temples in ruins or being rebuilt with only the resources of the local population. Although not on the trail, Mindröling has attracted government sponsorship.

The multicoloured sect intrigues, assuming white is Sakya and yellow Gelugpa. Or does the monastery have several colleges? The Nyingmapa have kept a teaching relationship with the reforming Gelugpa sect since the time of the Great Fifth Dalai Lama, Lobzang the Eloquent, whose teacher was the Nyingma abbot. Amaury de Riencourt — who travelled Tibet on horseback in 1947 and doesn't reveal how he obtained a permit! — writes that the Great Fifth forced Red Hat lamas to become Gelukpa by massacring the unwilling. Some escaped to Bhutan, starting the Dukpa Red Hat sect. But Rhie and Thurman write that the Fifth Dalai Lama 'was profoundly influenced by the Nyingma teachings' and 'revived the liturgies of various Nyingma deities in ... his personal monastery in the Potala'. Did the Great Fifth's change of heart come after the massacre, or have the Nyingma been existing on compromise ever since?

Monasteries are always the butts of foreign aggressors. Das writes that Mindröling never recovered from the pillage by the Dzungar Mongols in 1718, but 'the neatness of the stonework and the finish of all the masonry about the temple were very remarkable, and the courtyard was regularly paved with stone slabs'. Das and companion spent a night in the 'very large village' below the monastery, in the house of a well-to-do man.

Waddell wrote that the monks of Mindröling were celibate and the discipline very strict. But since the abbotship is hereditary, the abbot marries and so does one of his sons in order to continue the lineage. The present abbot lives in exile in India. Asked in an interview in *Me-Long* (1995) whether his son was being trained, Mindröling Trichen Rimpoche answered that he didn't know his son's whereabouts, as the young man was travelling here and there. Neither was he sure of his son's training, but he knew he had been studying for some years. The Rimpoche was clearly experiencing the agonies of a modern parent in the free world. But asked whom he regarded as his principle disciple, he replied: 'My daughter'. She acted as his interpreter.

Mindröling's main temple is a stunning building. Three storeys high, the third small and central like a penthouse, decorated with 'umbrellas' (for sheltering buddhas, one of the eight sacred symbols) in the five colours. A large portal hung with white banners with blue appliqué. Flanking the steps, two small walls with pelmets and flounces shade six *thangkas* of Mindröling's high lamas.

Walking up the steps we are met by that wonderful smell of juniper incense and butter lamps! Huddled figures crouch on carpeted benches. Once more they turn out to be cloaks — only fifty-seven. A monk — most seem young to very young — says the authorities allow Mindröling to have sixty monks. Elizabeth Booz counted only four monks and twenty novices in 1985.

There used to be 300.

The red pillars look so ancient, I stroke them to salute the magnificent trees they once were, now covered in brocade strips, ends turned back like men's ties. Small high windows enhance the elegance of wooden capitals as sunlight shines through appliquéd banners. Simple as Tibetan interiors are, details and colours are complex. The predominant use of primary red, yellow, blue and green, creates an astoundingly rich whole with white and black.

A junior monk with boyish good humour is keen to show us around. The Mindröling frescoes are impressive. Lama Anagarika Govinda, German-born Buddhist scholar and artist, travelled with his wife to Tsaparang in south-western Tibet to copy ancient frescoes in neglected *gompas*. He would have been happy to see what we are privileged to look at here. The monk says this building was used as a grain store during the Cultural Revolution and the frescoes whitewashed. This layer is now being carefully removed.

The number of images, *thangka* and paintings overwhelms me. I don't have a hope of identifying one tenth, but slowly turn to soak up the reverence in this sanctuary, bowing to a large Sakyamuni Buddha with bright cobalt blue curls, draped in orange silk against a flower-strewn background. On a string hang many *kata*. Silk flowers in porcelain vases and colour photos of the Dalai Lama fill up the shrine.

On a verandah protected from sunlight but still exposed to the elements, one fresco covers the entire wall. Some four metres high it has a stunning length of about sixteen metres. Yet the detail is pinprick small in the patterns of a brocade gown the Buddha probably never wore. Tiny painted stories emerge in 'blurbs' from the large-scale scene, like quick asides, a masterpiece of oral history alive on the wall! Unskilled attempts at restoration spoilt some small figures in the corner, but seem to have been discontinued.

In a dark stone room monks restore deities belonging to this particular temple room, mostly fearsome deities. But one monk works by the dim light of the only steel-barred window on a clay model of a seated Buddha, half a metre high. The others work by the light of a single electric bulb. Solar power, or is the monastery connected to the grid?

On the floor, bowls and tins contain cobalt blues, reds, greens, ochre yellows and whites, the traditional mineral and vegetable dyes of Tibetan art. Amidst the clutter a thermos, for without butter tea nothing is achieved.

This is the work skilled monks do, perhaps at the regime's bidding. Slowly and meticulously they restore everything that was destroyed, starting with fragments retrieved from the rubble. In the dark corners of the entrance hall sit three large decapitated hollow-cast images. One has sustained severe blows to chest and abdomen. The large Sakyamuni we saw was similarly mutilated, but the head was retrieved and the statue given a new body.

On an upper floor we are shown a small room with a low table and two small couches covered in plain yellow cloth. Here the Dalai Lama gave blessings when visiting Mindröling. He probably slept and meditated here too. Now his large portrait sits on the couch, a heap of banknote offerings before it. A nearby larger room contains his teaching throne, waiting under wraps for his homecoming.

In the next room we barely dare whisper in the presence of a hundred small statues of the finest craftsmanship, protected by wire netting. These, the monk tells, were buried by villagers as the Cultural Revolution broke out. When conditions were deemed safe again, they were returned. Undamaged they sit, an even greater treasure than before in the face of so much destruction — silent witnesses to a struggle between brutality and spirituality.

For Tibetans the monasteries must always have been their treasure houses. Not quite like our museums, which are secular culture places, but wellsprings of spiritual knowledge, worthy of offerings. Materially poor, Tibetans always offered their best to their monasteries. Nowadays there is no doubt they do so voluntarily, as the Chinese government remains quite anti-religious. We have seen that the pilgrim trail is trodden by Tibetans who support the reconstruction of their traditional treasure-houses.

It must be much more satisfying to donate acquired money or treasures to a local treasure-house which the whole community enjoys than to pay high taxes to a remote government. On the other hand, a government that does not levy direct taxes might insist it owns everything and exploit it accordingly, as in modern China. Tibetans used to be taxed by the Lhasa government, but saw few benefits for it. However, grain taxes to the monasteries would feed them in times of crop failure. Even the poorest villages had their treasure-houses right in their midst, although dwellings contained only the basics.

Hiding our puffing breath from each other, we climb a staircase to the roof. The bare hills slumber under white puffy clouds. Vertical silk banners flutter in the breeze. An incense burner stands near the edge of the roof. Imagine lighting incense here in the crisp cold of morning, to appease the spirits of the place! The valley lies green and lush below, watered in another season by now-dry rivulets that carry melted snow from the hills.

Jason is eager to get on the road to stop at another monastery before reaching

Lhasa. We thank the young monk, clamber down, wave to the monklets playing in the courtyard. Walking out past two containers, one growing a beautiful strong pink rose, the other pink dahlias, it feels to me like leaving home by the back door. I am surprised at my strong sense of arriving and reluctance to leave places like Mindröling and Samyé, about which I have only read snippets, whereas of Lhasa and Shigatse I have cultivated layers of preconceptions.

Our guide says not many tourists come to Mindröling because the road is a boneshaker. That's saying something in a land where every road takes its toll from vehicles. Strapping trekkers sometimes hike up here, but in the absence of well-to-do householders in the village, they have to camp out. We rattle and bounce a few kilometres, past a white stupa garlanded with prayer flags near the village whose people saved the statues. Whose relics lie in the little stupa? It may contain funerary ashes, a robe, book or other possession of a renowned lama.

The village, looking relatively prosperous, nestles amongst willows and poplars. On a little verge well beyond the houses we stop for lunch under some trees. But no sooner do bottoms touch grass, than children's voices carol across the fields and voices in the group sigh: 'Heavens, here they come again!' as if *they* were the aliens! Perhaps the kids yell to each other: 'Foreigners! Race you for them!' They come bounding down the mountain side, through the fields, bursting with curiosity, leaving the herds they were tending to fend for themselves.

Watching the children running towards us, it doesn't strike me that they come just in the hope of getting food. We are curiosities. Not many creatures like us come this way. What a diversion we provide! As a kid I used to run along with my friends behind fire engines, drums and pipes, the clatter of horses' hooves. We'd run several streets for the excitement of a fire, a musical march or a police posse. Compared with that, tourists are but a poor offering!

Abiding by the group's decision to eat first, I again have little of my lunch. From a distance the children watch every bite. Two women approach, one young and exceedingly beautiful. She is married, wearing the striped apron. Her round face and glittering dark eyes open up to us, laughing. Her beautiful skin has a rosy glow, white teeth sparkling. Carrying a leather whip in one hand she suddenly cracks it like Buffalo Bill! I gesture, asking her to do it again for the camera. Slightly puzzled she obliges, but is so lightning quick that later, when the negative is developed, the whip hangs already slack by her side. But we laugh together at the sound of it.

Imagine her life. Working in the fields, among the herds, in the homestead. Strong, confident, happy. That is not to say her life won't have its share of woman troubles, but she seems unlikely to suffer from stress!

The older woman hangs back, but when she catches my eye she sticks out her tongue in greeting. So infectious is this old Tibetan greeting that my tongue curls out down my chin before I know it. We wordlessly beam at each other. But when Jason addresses her in Tibetan she steps forward. He presents her with food and a particularly beautiful Dalai Lama photo. Reverently, she presses the image to her forehead. Before we climb into the bus, the children receive their share.

All the time Lhasa beckons, but my thoughts cling to Mindröling. I have never travelled like this before. A woman of the road all my life, putting up with staying in one place only to raise children, I have always looked forward to the next destination. But something else is at work here. At least one ancestor galloped west from Central Asia centuries ago and that drop of blood may be speaking up. Madly I wave to the women.

Temple of the Twenty-One Taras

Beyond Gonggar the road is new to us, following the *Kyichu* that flows south of Lhasa until it meets the Tsangpo. A distant snow-peaked mountain looks like Everest, or Chomolongma the Mother Goddess as the Tibetans call her. It can't be, but the sight is hypnotic. Eyes rove across every patch of snow that reminds us we are on the roof of the world, for midday temperatures on the plateau are in the twenties and we are peeling off clothes.

Almost imperceptibly the landscape changes. There are still sand dunes, tufts of tough grass and large pockets of sediment filling aprons of mountains, meeting in valleys. Still the mountainsides are bare of vegetation. Not an imprint of bird foot is to be seen on these sandy flats. But more tilted rock strata appear. Enormous boulders overhang the road, OM MANI PADME HUM carved on flat surfaces.

Suddenly, around a bend, people. Two men, one woman, a few children. Propped up on sticks by the road are two yak-skin coracles. The family seems excited to see us and talk to Jason. I am excited at seeing a yak-skin coracle in the skin. To travel in one, you put your feet gingerly on the thin frame of willow branches — so say the books. But the family turns out to be undertakers, so you're likely to travel toes-up in their coracles. Up the hillside stands a mud-brick dwelling. A small herd of cattle grazes in the gully beneath.

The men do water burials. The older one points to a stake garlanded with prayer flags on a small dot of an island in the river. There they feed corpses to the fishes, just as in sky burials the body is fed to vultures. Lamas attending the deceased will advise what type of burial is best. Of the four types of burial — earth burial, cremation, river burial and sky burial — the feeding of birds is the most common in Tibet. The body returns to earth, fire, water or air, but in Tibet earth resists and fire is a rare luxury due to shortage of fuel.

Undertakers were, with butchers, regarded as the lowest class in old Tibet's stratified society, presently more stratified than ever. Perhaps the undertakers' eagerness to talk is because no barrier exists between us. They are Tibetan and we are thrilled they speak to us. The men ask for cigarettes, but our only smokers are driver and guide. The guide parts with six cancer sticks and they light up with relish. The children happily accept a few health bars. They are poor people, their clothes threadbare, yet self-sufficient enough to have sheepskin *chuba* for winter — but not keeping up with fashions.

We travel on until the driver stops at a large complex of identical barracks in a mud-brick walled compound. The rough ride has massaged my back. This is a middle school, built in the middle of nowhere. The driver's sister teaches here and he goes to check whether she wants a lift home. Both children and teachers board. The sister has already taken a bus. Damned tourists delay drivers by talking to undertakers. The sun beats down on stark surfaces, no trees or flowers. Lhasa is coming closer but I still cannot believe I will be there tonight.

Villages are getting larger. In the fields people thresh and winnow grain, donkeys carry big loads of straw to compounds where haystacks build up for winter. Bundled grass dries atop mud-brick walls. Despite daytime warmth, winter will soon be here and this dawn-till-dusk activity is preparation for the long freeze.

Beside a shallow stream groups of women wash clothes, another activity that comes to a natural stop in winter. Much scurrilous writing has painted Tibetans as an unwashed lot, but coming from a cold country, growing up in houses without bathrooms, some with only an outside pump or well, I sympathise with the measure of reluctance Tibetans must feel to bare all and wash in winter. It is evident they wear their clothes day in day out, and yet in close encounters I find no smell barrier as some travellers have described. My sense of smell is quite alive. I just put this on record.

We pass what's left of Gonggar Dzong on its steep hillside. These *dzong*, always built in high places, are like old castles in Europe. Mostly ancient, they were in full use as administrative centres, treasuries or monasteries until the Chinese used them for target practice. Now most are deserted ruins. Every *dzong* used to have its *dzong-po*, a military man, bureaucrat or scholar who acted as governor for the area.

We cross a large modern bridge where the old road continues to Shigatse and we turn north on the other bank. Sentry boxes at each end. In this deserted landscape there is one river, one bridge, and one small Chinese soldier with a gun on each side.

'Why the soldiers?' I ask.

'To guard the bridge', says the guide.

'From what?' I ask.

'From the local demons!' laughs Jason and we leave it at that so as not to compromise the guide.

I frequently swallow questions or cringe at remarks, because we must not compromise the guide. Just as guides get accused of passing on 'state secrets', a term covering a multitude of perceived sins, it is dangerous for them to hear what foreigners think about socialism in Tibet. As all people must serve the state in communist China before they serve themselves or their communities, even simply speaking one's mind can be deemed revealing state secrets, if what one said does not uphold the party's image of China in the face of cold reality. Being a tourist guide in Tibet must resemble Scheherazade's job, telling stories just so that you don't lose your head or your freedom next morning.

About twenty kilometres before Lhasa stands a small monastery on a hill on the left, near the village of Nyethang. Its claim to fame is due to Atisha, renowned eleventh-century Indian sage, who stayed here to teach tantric Buddhism. He is credited with renewing monasticism and the teacher-student bond, and his teachings were marked by austerity. His main disciple, Dromtön (1005-64), established the Kadampa order.

Atisha died at Nyetang in 1054 and he remains much revered. Many stories circulate about his practices. One I heard from a travelling lama is of Atisha having too many students when he was an old man. He was so busy teaching that he didn't have time to go to the toilet. Rather than interrupt the teachings, he squatted more or less where he sat and defecated. Dromtön would scoop it up and carry it away above his head. When he went outside to dispose of the sage's faeces, he suddenly acquired clairvoyancy, being able to see things that existed or happened far away, an ability normally acquired only after long years of meditation. This was the result of his devotion to his teacher.

Atisha's cook never had a minute to himself to meditate. Being a cook was no sinecure. He had to find food, wood and water. The cook was reputed to be a much more highly realised person than all the meditators who had sat for years at the master's feet, even though he slaved over a hot kitchen fire. These true stories are told to show that devotion to one's *guru* is the first requisite for learning, and that practising the teachings counts for more than meditation alone.

Nyethang's temple — called Drölma Lhakhang or temple of Dolma — stands a few metres off the road and escaped damage in the Cultural Revolution. Gyurme Dorje writes that the government of former East Pakistan (now Bangladesh) petitioned that the temple of their famous countryman should be spared. Whatever political benefit the Chinese saw in appeasing the Pakistanis, compliance preserved one of the finest little temples remaining in central Tibet. Drölma Lakhang was spared, together with some other sacred buildings, through Zhou Enlai's interference.

It is a lively complex of small buildings. A tiny corner shop faces the road, young people hanging around. The stone gateway is flanked with brass prayer drums in a rough wooden frame, giving access to a homely courtyard dominated by a bulbous freestanding chimney. Juniper branches lie smouldering in the open hearth. To the left and right stand mud-brick dwellings of four monks who maintain the temple. Between these two oil drums, firewood bin, pump and drinking ladle by the well, a patch of self-seeding flowers and weeds growing lustily between broken paving. Atisha's ashes were returned to his birthplace in the 1960s, but his robe remains in one of the little stupas in the courtyard.

Tara was Atisha's personal tantric deity and he came to Tibet following a prophecy made by her. The temple contains twenty-one statues of Tara, one for each verse of the tantric hymn of praise to this female *bodhisattva*. She came from India or Nepal, legend says as the wife of King Songtsen-Gampo, others say as Weng Cheng the Chinese princess, a link to Kuan Yin. Her name means 'the one who saves'. Tibetans call her Dolma, spelled Drölma, sg-Rolma, or sGrolma. Whereas most Tibetan names, like Dawa, Pema, Tenzin or Tashi, have auspicious meanings and are used for boys and girls alike, it seems Dolma is reserved for girls.

Tara is also my special deity. Although I am without tantric training, she forced my attention in her direction in such subtle ways during a period when conflicting forces played havoc with my life that I was guided into clarity and into a direction that led me to this little temple seventeen years later. I think her powers considerable. I want to leave a home-sewn white silk *kata* here for Tara. We wait in the courtyard, discussed by local youngsters, while our minders negotiate with the temple keepers about our contribution and photo permit.

I started life unbaptised and was an early sceptic, but later became convinced that all people have a desire for a spiritual dimension to life. It is the one area where we have complete freedom. Although many feel restricted by the religious expectations of family and society, and others sell spiritual freedom for potage, fellowship or love, religion is a thought process as much as a doctrine and set of rituals. If we cannot realise that our thoughts are our own if we want them to be, then we probably don't stand much chance of finding harmony in life's other departments. I once met a Muslim who was delighted to meet someone he assumed to be a Christian, but turned out to be a Buddhist. Unbelieving at first, he tested me with one doctrinal question after another and I stood his test. He was widely read in other philosophies. Although keeping Islamic custom, he used freedom of thought to investigate what inspired others.

I had the good karmic fortune to be born in a family of unaffiliated seekers. When I was eight, grandfather wrote a few lines from the Dhammapada — the Buddha's collected sayings — in my poesy album. Mother gave me her little books of aphorisms by Krishnamurti and Rabindranath Tagore when I began to take an interest in things spiritual. As a teenager I was free to seek out churches and sects, finding the former too restricting, the latter too personally intrusive. After a brief and disappointing affiliation with a mainstream church I made my own religion. Sometime later I began to recover the markers in my life that from the age of five had pointed toward Buddhism.

In the early sixties in southern Australia, Buddhism did not hold a promise of fellowship, let alone guidance. I became a Buddhist fully knowing it would be a lonely row to hoe and I shall never forget a visit by another lonely Buddhist in the middle of that decade. We exchanged discoveries as well as frustrations about having no community with which to share our better insights. To some extent this has changed. Australia now has many Buddhist communities, some based on ethnicity, others on specific schools or gurus. But for me the search has long been over, the solitude accepted as a plus rather than a minus, and with the publishing boom in translated texts, commentaries, biographies and spiritual reflections, I am content to spend this lifetime acquiring knowledge, quieting my mind and training myself to be compassionate.

Although the main Tibetan tradition holds that one cannot progress without a *guru*, it has to be remembered that this tradition grew in a not fully literate community where books were mainly kept in monasteries. But Tara used the medium of a book to become my teacher and I her devotee, when I realised I had already identified with her before I'd even heard her name. Much as Tibetan Buddhism is about worship of great teachers, it is also about identification. In many practices the meditator visualises the deity to acquire her or his powers of wisdom and compassion.

One day, in the depths of misery, when no book could console me, I felt the need to draw, hoping to stave off insanity. Having no natural talent I looked for something to copy and came upon a minuscule black and white line drawing of Tara in a book of Buddhist reflections. I had never heard of her, hadn't read the book, but my eyes stopped at the tiny image. Taking paper, pencil and magnifying glass I drew this Tara line by careful line, about ten times larger so that I could look at her. It took all morning of a miserable day. The image needed colour. So strong was the creative momentum set off by this unknown deity that I took a bus to town, bought coloured pencils and rushed back to my room to apply light tintings of blue, yellow, green and orange to the copied image.

The next day an artist called, a friend of a friend, needing information. Enthralled with my newly discovered drawing ability, I showed him my Tara portrait. First he remarked that all the proportions were wrong, but then to my astonishment he did a double-take and said: 'But that is your face!' My turn to be astonished. There indeed sat I in the lotus position wearing flowing light blue robes, holding a lotus flower in my left hand, the other extended palm-up, indicating generosity in wisdom. Especially the eyes, mirrors of what we call our soul, were mine. The recognition lit up the dark centre of my being.

After the artist left, I rushed to the university library. I was living in Papua New Guinea, where libraries tended to have more books on science and agriculture than on literature and religion. So what made me hope to find information on a Tibetan deity called Tara? I did not really think something so elusive would be on the shelves, but hoped for a tiny reference in a standard tome on Buddhism. Who might this female deity be? She had stopped me in my tracks of self-pity and despair, inspired me with her image only marginally bigger than a matchbox, and coaxed from me a humble drawing skill when words failed to guide me. Yet all I knew was that she stood for compassion. Buddhism had provided many answers until that year, but could easily atrophy in my life if it shed no light on my newest predicaments. Would Tara be the catalyst?

The library was quiet that afternoon. There was little light in the corner where a small collection of religious books sat on a low shelf. I bent through the knees, eyes peering at spines and suddenly TARA beamed from the gloom. Unbelievable! My hand stretched and picked up a tome entitled *The Cult of Tara: Magic and Ritual in Tibet*, published barely three years earlier. I checked how many times it had been borrowed. Once. A lecturer must have ordered it when library money flowed more freely than by 1976, Papua New Guinea's first year of independence. The Department of Religious Studies taught no Buddhism at the time.

I sometimes wonder what happened to that book, or to that friend of a friend. Both turned up at a crucial moment in my life, moved there by positive forces. As indeed did my Muslim friend, who made me recite the central creed of my life at a time I badly needed to hear it.

I borrowed the book and learned about identification with the *bodhisattva*, the enlightened person who out of compassion for the world's suffering has vowed to return to the human realm life after life, until even the last blade of grass has reached enlightenment. Tara is a *bodhisattva* of compassion. To identify even once with a *bodhisattva* means one's life must serve her cause.

A few weeks later a concerned letter arrived from Tibetan friends in North India. The writer had heard I was not well, they had offered prayers for my health and invited me to come and stay with them to recover. These generous friends were refugees. The letter was dated the same day as I had been moved to draw Tara's picture. Having read the book, I understood they had offered prayers to Tara for me.

Although Tara was a historical person, be that a king's spouse or a nun, legends and myths have grown up around her. The most widely held mythological account tells how Avalokiteshvara, the *bodhisattva* of compassion, emptied all the hells and lower states of existence to end the terrible suffering there. But looking back he saw how all those realms filled up as soon as he emptied them. This so aroused his compassion that he shed tears for all suffering sentient beings. From one of those tears Green Tara was born and she manifested twenty other forms of Tara. One of them is the White Tara of compassion.

In another version Avalokiteshvara shed tears and the peaceful, compassionate White Tara was born from his left eye while the fierce Green Tara, who dispels dangers that might prevent one following the Buddhist teachings, emerged from his right eye. These two Taras are in perfect balance. So that compassion remains well-directed to be effective, Green Tara makes sure that White Tara's efforts are not wasted, while White Tara sees to it that Green Tara's fierceness is always tempered with compassion.

Being thus the consort of Avalokiteshvara — who is Chenrezig, the father of the Tibetan people reincarnated in the Dalai Lama — Tara is one of the most popular deities in Tibet, known as the Great Mother. Historians see a connection between her and Kuan Yin, the Chinese *bodhisattva* of compassion and protectress of life. Kuan Yin is sometimes depicted with a newborn baby in her arm and Chinese women pray to her to beget children. Observing them doing so in Chinese temples, I have wondered whether they now plead for a boy, because of the one-child policy. Maybe they always did.

Western missionaries in China thought Kuan Yin statues were oriental representations of Mary with baby Jesus. Even missionaries to Tibet wondered whether images of Tara were based on the Virgin's statues, traded along the Silk Road or by seafaring merchant ships. All it probably proves is that the need for a female deity is keenly felt in all religions. She is kept alive despite male dominance in the divine stable, and once arisen becomes extremely popular. Witness the return of the Earth Mother or simply the Goddess in our times.

In one myth Tara is a Buddhist nun having a dispute with some monks, whereupon she vowed to achieve buddhahood — which is enlightenment — in female form. It's probably the same story as Tara being asked by a devout Buddhist whether she hoped at last to be reincarnated as a man in her next life, as if that was something one had to earn! Early Buddhism held that only men could reach full enlightenment. Tara replied: I think I have done very well in a female body so far. Therefore I will continue to return as a woman. Or words to that effect.

Deals have been struck in the temple. Cameras will be allowed. The verandah walls are covered in very fine frescoes dating from the eleventh century. Kings of the four directions guard the temple entrance, their mythology reaching back to prehistoric times. Eight cobalt blue medicine buddhas live in the first chapel — must find out about blue significance. Among them sits a little bust with the unmistakable features of Atisha. Where Padmasambhava is the one of the bulging eyes and curling moustache, Atisha has the chiselled face of the ascetic, long eyelids and a shadow of a smile. The practice of creating statues in the exact likeness of revered persons has preserved some great portraits of Buddhist teachers. Even the historical Buddha's features are recognisable, although his garb may differ from culture to culture.

Therefore, entering the inner sanctum where twenty-one Taras reside in the company of buddhas and other *bodhisattvas*, we behold Tara's true face. Her features clear and serenely beautiful, her ears large but shapely, her serious eyes almond-shaped. Eyes that know all suffering and although she alleviates some of it, people always create more. Eyes shaped by the shedding of tears. On her forehead she displays the third wisdom eye.

Tara's twenty-one almost life-size images, dating from the seventeenth century, sit in tiered rows on golden lotus thrones along the walls, robed in red and green brocade silks with large golden patterns, red silk veils covering golden crowns, cobalt blue bands high on foreheads and necks, bead necklaces. Each Tara presents different hand gestures, explaining her particular concerns.

First impressions of these golden faces are shadows of sadness, overlaid by the emanation of active serenity issuing from the images. Slowly turning on my heels, it is as if the Taras beckon. Some statues lean forward with hand gestures. Tara is also the *bodhisattva* of activity, she gets things done, forging miracles in a world of people who would not see a miracle if it happened right under their noses. How is it that someone dead a thousand years and more can affect circumstances today? Maybe chaos theory has the answer. In a universe comprised of energy, a person exuding great quantities of positive energy will exercise influence long after her body has gone. From powerfully good energy, good things happen in connection with that person's memory, as will evil things occur in the name of a powerfully evil person long since gone. The Buddha, all *bodhisattvas* and other spiritual teachers, were inspired butterflies flapping their wings, causing storms of goodness to occur in space and time. I sniff up spicy incense mixed with the gentle dust of centuries.

Despite physical distress due to rising altitude, in the heat of day almost more than I can bear, I experience an inner peace for being here. I move sideways in the cramped space between offering tables and a low table with 107 small butter lamps — there should have been 108. As I move away from the group around Jason and the monk, I quietly slip my white silk *kata* over one Tara's bare golden foot and speak her *mantra*. It looks outlandish. All *kata* here are blue, turquoise, green, red or pink.

When the group reaches her, Jason wants to know the significance of a single white *kata*. The monk smiles sheepishly. He saw me drape it on her foot. Jason translates his mumbled reply: 'He doesn't seem to know', and shrugs his shoulders. Tara smiles. Perhaps the keeper of the temple will remove the foreign *kata* after we are gone, restoring a harmony of significances. Or he may wonder how a foreigner chose that particular Tara to honour and leave the scarf to disintegrate with other sincere offerings.

After paying homage to some large, more ancient *bodhisattva* statues we move on and out. Too short, this visit. But everyone feels the effects of altitude and try as we may it is difficult to concentrate. We say goodbye to the monks to drive the last twenty kilometres to Lhasa, once the Forbidden City.

Approaches to Lhasa and the Ghost of the Western Gate

Shortly before Lhasa we glimpse huge rock carvings in a perpendicular mountain wall, reflected in a pool of water. The images are painted bright orange and cobalt blue. Jason promises a photo stop another day. Dead tired, no-one objects.

Ponies graze in fields belonging to the Dalai Lama's former country estate. This Lhasa valley is a perfect little world between its high mountain walls. The land looks flat and fertile, there always seems to be a river, stream or pond, and the warmth of the sun is trapped between high walls of rock. I recall the many 'approaches to Lhasa' I have read over the years. But communism has changed the entrance to the holy city, once so beautiful and symbolic. The great Western Gate stupa through which all travellers entered Lhasa, has been destroyed. The Tibetan medical college on Chakpori Hill was blown to smithereens. That the Potala palace still towers over Lhasa is thanks to Zhou Enlai. It seems inconceivable that within the hour I shall lay eyes upon the Potala. But I also feel like someone going home after a long absence, knowing that something tremendously important is no longer there and never will be again.

My discovery of Lhasa's Western Gate had similarities with the discovery of Tara. I was in my late twenties, none too happy, seeking outlets for dreams of another existence. A neighbour suggested drawing sessions. I searched for something to copy. Thumbing through a *National Geographic* I found Heinrich Harrer's account of his seven years in Tibet and a photograph of the Western Gate, a red-robed monk framed in its portal. I drew and painted that scene maybe half a dozen times, getting drawn in deeper, yearning to walk through that gate one day like that monk. I did not know I was trying to recreate what had already been destroyed in a frenzy of brutal force. The year must have been 1963.

In those years scrutinising a photograph of Lhasa meant ecstasy and agony. Sometimes the impossibility of ever going there, locked up as it was, became so intense that I would cry hot tears over a picture or book on Lhasa. I did not know why I felt for Tibet, and Lhasa in particular, what no other place on earth instilled in me. The world then knew nothing of the murder of hundreds of thousands of Tibetans, the destruction of thousands of treasure-houses. Perhaps I cried for what my deeper consciousness sensed. I do not know. I cried for Tibet all through the 1960s. After that the intensity faded. Reality decreed I could not travel to Tibet. Growing older and tired of dreaming, the longing for Tibet was suppressed, although not the agony for what had befallen its people. I started to aid Tibetan refugees in the late sixties. Sometimes I dreamed of approaching Lhasa on foot.

Now I ride towards the city of old dreams. The group is talkative, discussing hotels, hot showers and faxes that may be waiting from frantic bosses who can't find a program or key. I focus to catch a first glimpse of the Potala, remembering other travellers' first approaches to Lhasa. The first map of Lhasa was made in 1880 by Kishen Singh. Nearer and nearer and still no Potala, the view blocked by endless barrack-like structures along a wide dusty road. It is said that Lhasa now has 300 000 Chinese inhabitants and only 100 000 Tibetans.

Disappointment rises, turning to alarm. The group also stirs. The whole approach to Lhasa has been desecrated. The Potala on its rock used to be the great edifice in the sky that every pilgrim beheld as the gate of the city loomed up. Abbé Huc wrote in 1846:

> The sun was nearly setting when, issuing from the last of the infinite sinuosities of the mountain, we found ourselves in a vast plain and saw on our right Lha-Ssa, the famous metropolis of the Buddhic world. The multitude of aged trees which surround the city with a verdant wall; the tall white houses, with their flat roofs and their towers; the numerous temples with their gilt roofs, the Buddha-La, above which rises the palace of the Tale-Lama — all these features communicate to Lha-Sa a majestic and imposing aspect. (Huc, *Travels in Tartary and Thibet,* pp. 286-7)

Another traveller, Alexandra David-Neel, was afraid of being unmasked, but so preoccupied with being the 'Only White Woman Who Succeeded in Entering the Forbidden City' that her description of the approach to Lhasa in 1924 falls rather between the river Kyi and a furious dust storm that helps her to enter undetected. But she mentions the Potala looming larger, its outlines and golden roofs glittering in a still blue sky.

Passing as a Ladakhi and fluent in Tibetan, she picks up remarks from 'countryfolk' that things were better under Chinese suzerainty and concludes that Tibetans have lost much in parting with China, whose rule she deemed to be relaxed. She is scornful about the Tibetan government's taxes and statute labour and plundering soldiers, judging them to exceed the extortions of the Chinese. It probably gives a pretty realistic picture of the times in Tibet, extortions being committed by both Chinese and Tibetan officials, but Chinese rule has been far from relaxed since 1950. Countryfolk anywhere always tend to suffer from the bureaucracy.

However, David-Neel's intimation that Tibet's independence was not based on political reality is far off the mark. She may not have had access to the historical sources available today. Many educated people in her time — and even today — believed China had a right to rule Tibet because Chinese and British sources proclaimed so, while historical records on Tibet's independent existence over the millennia were not widely available.

Alexandra David-Neel was the first Western woman to have an audience with a Dalai Lama — the Thirteenth, in 1912 at Darjeeling, India. Impressed with her understanding of Buddhism he told her 'Learn the Tibetan language!' Little did he realise she would not be satisfied to practise it just in Darjeeling!

Still the bus rattles on towards Lhasa. Ilia Tolstoy arrived in 1942: 'we rode through the little wooded parks that surround Lhasa'. Heinrich Harrer, escaping with Peter Aufschnaiter from a British POW camp during World War II, 'struggled and bluffed' his way across Tibet to the capital to see the Potala golden roofs ablaze in the January sun from eight miles distance. He felt a compulsion to sink to his knees and give thanks like the Buddhist pilgrims did. They had walked more than 1500 miles and climbed 62 mountain passes, some as high as 20 000 feet. He watched the Kyi River flow through fields, marshes and parks and the plain running to a towering wall of naked, sloping mountains. In the crystal air he found the scene perfect beyond reality, with the Potala crowning one of two jagged ridges rising like sentinels from the valley floor. He thought it had an air of supernatural grandeur, as if it welled up in massive slabs of stone from the earth itself.

Amaury de Riencourt, arriving in 1947, noticed the zigzagging battlements of the Potala, the gardens and parks, woods and lakes spread out between him and the Forbidden City. He is the last to write about the approach to Lhasa as it used to be. We drive through ugly concrete suburbs. Gone are the little woods and lakes. One hopes these apartments are more comfortable inside than they look, built as they were for Chinese soldiers' families not used to this climate, come to this outpost at the state's behest.

There are more migrants in Australia than Aborigines, which wouldn't matter if this was Aboriginal policy. There are more Chinese immigrants in Tibet than Tibetans, which wouldn't matter if this was Tibetan government policy. But it is Chinese government policy and didn't happen two hundred or even a hundred years ago when the world was in a frenzy of colonial endeavour, but 'yesterday' in 1950, when other countries were sorting out their colonial messes after World War II, returning independence to people who never asked to be ruled by others. China went against the global grain, becoming with Russia and the US the new post-World War II colonial powers.

I understand all too well the drive of wanting to go places on promise of economic progress, which is what Tibet holds out for the ordinary Chinese person. A chance to make good, set up a little business, work for the government or the army on excellent pay with a free apartment into the bargain. For that you'd brave a lot of cold, wind and isolation if you hail from a polluted Chinese city of millions or a poverty-stricken village.

Finally I glimpse the Potala in the distance, but we never come closer. The familiar shape hangs in the air like a mirage above an unfamiliar huddle of progress, expressed in jerry-built structures. The route into Lhasa is now lined with Chinese shops and the Holiday Inn. We have arrived and yet we haven't. No sinking on our knees to give thanks for the privilege of being here. Instead the opulent hall of the Lhasa Inn with marble fountain, Chinese tables and fake Tibetan decorations.

I take an unreasonable dislike to the jet set crowd in the lobby, to which we temporarily belong. Female joggers in shiny pink-blue-green outfits show off brand-name running shoes by hanging slim tanned knees over brocade couches. They belong to a sports group testing themselves on the training ground with the mostest, the roof of the world. I drag my bags to the desk. You can rent a 'real' Tibetan room at a price, with television set. From our standard room we view a pool courtyard. A pink man lies sunning himself. I feel lost beyond words. But breathlessness is worse and it is all I can do to hold body and soul together, postponing my despair about Lhasa until my lungs adjust to this altitude.

Pre-1950 travellers were well and truly acclimatised when they reached Lhasa, travelling on horseback or on foot. Zany Zen monk Kawaguchi Ekai rode into Lhasa on a borrowed horse in 1901, after traversing Tibet on foot. He studied Tibetan for one year in Darjeeling and another year in Mustang, where every Sunday he carried rocks up and down mountains to condition himself. The Loba people thought it a religious act. Maybe it was, for Kawaguchi's main reason for penetrating Tibet illegally was to study Buddhist scriptures unavailable anywhere else.

We missed out on a lot by having wings and wheels spirit us to this holy city. Only fit trekkers, able to outpace authorities off the beaten track, enjoy the best of Tibet nowadays.

In the dining room, with view of Chinese art gallery, Tibetan waitresses dressed in purple silk *chubas* speak Chinese with each other. House rules. I look so much like other diners that it bothers me. Western dream-chasers decked out in tough outdoor gear and mountain boots, New Age facial expressions, brushed with Buddhism. Here and there women in lurex evening blouses, old enough to have read Somerset Maugham. In empire's outposts one always dresses for dinner. Some appear wealthy, but most seem to be on the once-in-a-lifetime journey. So what are pilgrims doing in this tourist trap? Should we dig into white rice, Chinese greens and pork under electric chandeliers, or should we be lodging in what's left of old Lhasa town, eating *tsampa*, rinsed down with butter tea, maybe a tot of *chang*?

An elderly American joins our table. A one-man tour, Harry has a guide, car and driver at his beck and call every day. He tables his credentials in a fast rap. Been teaching some branch of science in a Chinese university and taking the opportunity to see Tibet before leaving. We nod approval. Retired, he takes on temporary casual jobs and consultancies, like setting up a medical insurance system in a Middle Eastern country after its liberation by the US of A. And things in Geneva. Airtight alibis. He's a big man and very much out of breath. I can almost feel his lungs labouring in my own chest. How will he make it up the Potala steps?

Suddenly Kay looks intently at me, chopsticks halfway her mouth. Lowering them she says: 'Baby, your lips are BLUE!' All eyes turn on me. It is after all my own lungs I feel heaving.

Kay has been hoping for an opportunity to visit the Tibetan doctor holding clinic in the hotel, once the Panchen Lama's doctor. The Panchen Lama died under suspicious circumstances. I have no breath left to argue. Kay drags me off to lower regions, cursing Chinese numbering systems and getting lost in three corridors. I sink exhausted to the floor outside the doctor's door.

Typical of me! Not coming down with preliminary symptoms of irritability, loss of appetite, vomiting and sleeplessness, but only breathlessness and a feeling of fullness in the chest. All that is still called benign AMS (acute mountain sickness). But malignant AMS — often fatal — is pulmonary oedema. The lungs fill with fluid, one is breathless even at rest, coughs and has blue lips or cyanosis. Just a step away from cerebral AMS and death in Lhasa. The ultimate destination of all life coincides with the ultimate travel destination.

When my turn comes I feel too dreadful to take an interest in this new medical experience. The room is decked out in Tibetan rugs. The doctor, in white coat, pats the couch and takes my hand between his. They are warm and soft, like the hands of high lamas who do no physical work. 'You have been in Tibet already three days,' he says in Tibetan. 'You should be used to the climate by now.'

His elderly translator in Western suit speaks English with a refined Anglo–Indian accent. He must have been educated in a North Indian school and may be of the old aristocracy. He has a finely chiselled face and strings his phrases with unhurried detail.

A young, round Tibetan woman looks after a medicine cupboard with five stacks of drawers, painted red and gold with lotus flowers. Pills are stored in little brocade drawstring bags. She talks with the men as they treat and translate, laughing a jolly laugh while wrapping pills in white paper. Sickness in Tibet is something you chase away by stroking, smiling, laughing and patting rug-covered couches.

Back in our room I soak one special pill for two hours, as prescribed. It resembles a goat pellet. So do the morning and evening pills. I add a diuretic from my kit and aspirin for a splitting headache, resigned to death by acute toxification.

So glad I rang home before dinner, when still sounding normal. 'Hi! This is me! I'm in Lhasa!' I chirped in high spirits to my daughter. 'Do you know what time it is here?' she asked in a lolling voice. Tripped up by Beijing time! But she was nice enough to rejoice in my arrival and obvious well-being on the roof of the world. Let it stand as my last message from Lhasa.

Nicola, most caring of room-mates, orders oxygen pillows, regulation khaki army bags with knotted plastic tubes. Later I learn to hold the oxygen flow under my nose. But lacking directions, I suck oxygen like a baby at breast, thinking of the Red Army struggling up these mountains all the way from China, oxygen pillows atop their rucksacks. They were often defeated by Tibetan fighters, until the Tibetan army was sold out by their own general one fateful day in Chamdo, and Chinese aeroplanes started bombing.

Kay comes in to check my progress. Jason checks up on his bedridden charges, for Peggy is also down with symptoms. The doctor ordered us to stay in bed tomorrow morning, but I want to visit Sera monastery in the afternoon. He thought it possible. Nicola wakes me at eleven for the evening pellets. I sleep and wake through the night, marvelling at a body evidently alive and breathing, no matter how rustily. The oxygen is soothing, though not supposed to be of any real benefit at this stage.

Breakfast in bed and of course my appetite is good. Some people die between two courses of a hearty meal! While the diminished group huffs and puffs up the steps of Potala palace, Peggy and I, 'having waited all our lives for that moment' as she puts it, loll about in bed, willing ourselves to recover.

A Peasant's View of the Potala

When we rejoin the group, worn out from climbing stairs outside and inside the Potala, they still have breath to tell what they heard. Since the infrastructure of monastic life has been destroyed, monks now 'earn' a government salary of 105 yuan per month in lieu of their traditional support system — lands and properties, trade, tenants and donors — less than any labourer and approximately what tourists pay for one day's food. No wonder so many have thin arms and gaunt faces. They do duties in temples and monasteries, guide tourists around, perform some rituals and rebuild, restore and repair the damage of the Cultural Revolution, maintaining the impression that they are still part of a functioning institution.

Wild horses can't keep me away from Sera monastery. Our Australian Rimpoche did his monastic training here towards a *geshe* or doctor of divinity degree. I will shoot an entire roll of film to show him how it looks today. Jason promises we shall see monks debating in characteristic Tibetan style, taking giant steps, bodies bending and twisting to underline their arguments, clapping hands when correct answers are delivered.

We drive along Dekyi Shar Lam, first renamed Xingfu Xi Lu or Happy Street, then Beijing Lu to show Lhasa pays tribute to the Motherland. Duplicity of names bedevils Tibetan towns. The road is lined with jerry-built shops and concrete buildings guarded by soldiers. Tubular steel fences separate footpaths from the road for crowd control. Green soldiers' uniforms are everywhere, usually in pairs.

When the Potala comes in sight, another steep rock rises on the right: Chakpori, where used to stand Tibet's Medical College. Between these two bulwarks of Tibetan culture, travellers used to enter Lhasa by the Western Gate. Now, across the street from one rocky outcrop to the opposite one, thousands of prayer flags flap *mantras* into the wind. Thus Tibetans honour the sacred spot where it was said the relics of the Buddha Mindukpa protected the entrance to the holy city. Only now do I feel I have entered the Lhasa that I came to see.

Through the Western Gate, flanked by two small stupas, pilgrims would enter a broad earth-packed road, passing the medieval village and monastery at the foot of the Potala, festooned with old willows. Somewhere here was a lake. Now the Potala rises from behind a row of shopfronts. The ancient village lies in ruins, but for one short street. Lhasa has become a network of Chinese shops. A Chinese shoemaker rests against a tree, his savings sunk into toolbox, last and stool for fashion-conscious women to sit on while he repairs their heels. Only Chinese women wear high heels in Lhasa's broken streets, stumbling across boulders, falling into cracks. They must be a symbol of immense social standing to risk breaking leg or neck!

The Potala's whitewashed facade with the red ochre central palace unexpectedly produces a lump in my throat. This one-thousand-room palace must be the most extraordinary building in the world. The inward-sloping walls make it look higher than its 110 metres, accommodating thirteen storeys rising from the rock. With straight inner walls, outward slope adds strength. At 4000 metres above sea level, the Potala is probably one of the highest buildings in continual use in the world. Being 320 metres long and 200 metres wide it has a total floor space of 130 000 square metres. The walls are built of rammed earth and stone and some are almost wholly constructed of packed cut twigs. It simply has to be the biggest mud-walled building in the world. Eight golden tombs on the roof contain remains of previous Dalai Lamas.

This is the wonder of the unknown world that Younghusband and his general MacDonald would destroy with artillery in 1904, unless the Tibetan regent signed an 'agreement' opening Tibet's borders for British trade. And but for Zhou Enlai, the Chinese army might have done the same. Although spared, the Potala is rumoured to be badly undermined by tunnels and bomb shelters to protect Chinese cadres in case of enemy attack. But Tibetans say the Chinese were digging for treasures! The official Chinese Potala guidebook belabours the significance of Chinese treasures in the palace to support the view that Tibet was an integral part of China during the imperial dynasties.

The reduced group that climbed the many steps to the main assembly hall where the Dalai Lama's throne stands empty, speaks of hollow rooms filled to the carved wooden lintels with art treasures and unused ritual objects, carefully numbered and documented. The Potala, they say, has become a lifeless museum. Once the centre of government and Tibet's parliament, it housed monks and its rooms were filled with treasure, stores and supplies for the Tibetan army. It was the centre of government as well as the centre of Tibet's religion.

Looking through the guidebook's photographs I wonder at the irony of years of longing and coming so close, but never seeing the walls painted with scenes from the life of the Buddha and Tibet's history, the Dalai Lamas' lives, great lamas, kings, queens, ministers, even the actual building of the Potala and Lhasa monasteries, scenes from daily life through the ages, sports and religious festivals, and the great Kalachakra or Wheel of Time.

I will not see the Potala's antique artefacts — now dated according to Chinese dynasties — of jade, crystal, enamel, pottery, precious stones and metals, wood and humble clay, such as the statues of Songtsen Gampo and his wives made during their lifetimes, golden faces touched up where the passing of centuries dulled them. Nor will I marvel at painted and carved doors, columns, beams, supports, lintels, wall panels, niches, furniture and figures and pillars wrapped in silk or Tibetan carpets.

What I'd most wanted to see were the yak hair curtains eighty feet long and twenty-five feet wide hanging down walls, covering sacred images, seen by Sir Francis Younghusband and his officers as they entered the Potala in August 1904 to force their wretched treaty on the Tibetans.

A great library of Tibetan books on Buddhism, history, geography, biography, architecture, medicine, literature and astronomy, plus full sets of the *Kanjur* and *Tanjur* are kept in the palace. There are over 10 000 *thangkas*, including a gallery of lifelike portrayals of historical figures. *Thangkas* and frescoes are Tibet's documentaries of historical events recorded in minute detail. They are Tibet's television, for even now news value can be had from contemporary *thangkas* featuring memorable events, culture heroes and heroines, or divine interventionists.

The Potala is Tibet's art gallery supreme, housing the most precious art, ritual objects and paintings of the last thirteen centuries. Songtsen Gampo built the core of the palace in the seventh century and the Fifth Dalai Lama greatly enlarged it between 1690 and 1694. Explanations for the origin of the name 'Potala' vary. It may refer to an island off the southern Indian coast where Avalokiteshvara once dwelled. Professor Tucci thought Potala was located in Madagascar. The rock outcrop on which it stands is simply called Red Hill.

For thirteen hundred years Tibet's best craftsmen worked in this palace. The most beautiful of treasures were presented and stored here, gaining meaning by interconnecting rituals, ceremonies, audiences and personal devotions by Dalai Lamas, monks and those received in the ruler's presence.

There may be no museum or art gallery in the world that has such a continuous tradition of collecting integrated art without disturbance or destruction until the Chinese captured the building in 1950. Rome's Vatican may be the only comparable site. That was also started by secular rulers before it became a religious enclave. The basilica preceding St Peter's was built in the fourth century and the next century saw a monastery erected. The first papal palace was erected in the sixth Century. There was much piecemeal demolishing and raising up until the present buildings were constructed in the sixteenth century. The Vatican suffered pillage by the Saracens in 846 and its archival holdings now only go back to 1200, whereas the Potala probably harbours older manuscripts and certainly held carved edicts from earlier centuries. But it is thought that many Potala treasures were destroyed or found their way to international art markets via China.

We turn into a muddy rock-strewn track that gives access to one of the grandest of world heritage buildings and the remains of Shöl village that served the Potala population. A primary school on the left. There used to be a printing house that published the entire *Kanjur* and *Tanjur*. Stopping short of the access lane, we order lunch in a Tibetan eating house, in a simple stone room decked out with Buddhist banners, women in *chuba* speaking Tibetan. No doubt it is bias that makes this meal taste better than hotel fare.

I resolve not to constantly see Chinese and Tibetan ways as opposites. In some ways they are not, as they were neighbours for thousands of years. But the fact that one is under the boot of the other creates situations where differences speak loudly. Who would deny the Chinese shoemaker his dream of making a fortune on the streets of Lhasa even though Tibetans don't need his trade? He followed PLA wives and Chinese immigrants. Why should he keep digging mud and pigshit if there are easier pickings in the Western Treasure-House, as the Chinese enticingly call Tibet?

But why shouldn't these Tibetan women and excellent cooks get a major slice of the tourist trade that comes to see *their* cultural heritage? Incongruities throw themselves up between rational thought and one's sense of justice at every turn in Tibet.

We finish the meal with pourings of butter tea. Pilgrims of old must have enjoyed their first meal in Lhasa here. When we leave I crane my neck to catch every aspect of the Potala. As the bus turns north towards Sera, the sun plays shadow games on the east wing's white walls of stacked halls with rows of tall windows and levels connected by broad outside staircases. Inside, the Potala may seem dead, barely 10 per cent being accessible to visitors, but the impact of its architecture on the living is a powerful antidote to the ghastly modernisation Lhasa is undergoing. Next week when we return from Shigatse we will see the rear from Dragon King's Lake.

As we pass under the massive walls I feel like a Tibetan peasant in Lhasa for the first time, fated only to see the great Potala from the outside, marvelling at its austere sublimity, praising the day I first set eyes on its cloud-gathering golden roofs.

Sera Monastery At Work

A mass of low stone buildings spreads across foot and apron of a bare pink mountain. Green trees sprout between rose buildings. Some places you have read about don't resemble at all what your imagination constructs.

Much learning came out of Sera, much politicking too, and its influence on governments of the past was great. Yet, from a distance, it looks like a deserted nineteenth-century mining settlement in outback South Australia, heaps of stones flung by a mighty hand out in the middle of nowhere. Such is the impression of isolation, one forgets Lhasa is only five kilometres away.

East of Sera lies the execution place where Tibetan counter-revolutionaries were put to death in large numbers in 1959 and during and after the Cultural Revolution. All Lhasa would have heard the shots reverberating between the mountains, as one Tibetan life after another was snuffed out. Just south of Sera is Drapchi prison, notorious for torture of Tibetan political prisoners, including nuns and monks. Gutsa prison east of Lhasa is no better. In these schools of torture, Tibetan officers are taught the latest cruelties to practise on their fellow humans. This goes on a few kilometres away as we approach, putting in stark perspective the individual's lack of power to oppose cruelty and injustice, except perhaps in the long term.

Sera comes into focus. The monastery was set up in 1419 by the principal disciple of Tsongkhapa, founder of the Gelugpa or Yellow Hat sect to which the Dalai Lamas belong. Tsongkhapa would meditate in a small hermitage on this craggy mount, where he wrote *The Essence of True Eloquence,* a study of two schools of Buddhist philosophy. The hermitage was destroyed during the Cultural Revolution. A replica has been built on the spot and meditation caves dot the hillside. In one, behind a green bush, our Australian Rimpoche used to meditate.

Japanese monk Kawaguchi, pretending to be a Chinese pilgrim monk, was allowed to study at Sera. Although he had believed Tibetan scholarship to be far inferior to Japanese erudition, he soon found he needed two tutors to keep up with studies for the entrance examination. But he passed as one of only seven candidates out of forty, indicating how tough the selection was. During his stay he became known as the 'Doctor of Sera' who administered herbal treatments to sick monks and poor people. His fame led the Thirteenth Dalai Lama to invite him for a consultation.

Sera is divided into four colleges but has one main assembly hall. As in other monasteries, colleges went by district. A monk from Tsang would join Tsang *khamtsan,* a monk from Kham the Kham *khamtsan.* Sera also had a Dya *khamtsan* for Chinese monks, as did Drepung. But Sera had a particular tradition of teaching Mongolian monks. Monthly debates were held in the debating courtyard, where one day Kawaguchi heard a 'mystical voice' telling him to leave before his disguise was discovered.

When Kawaguchi's identity became known after his departure, those who had befriended him were imprisoned. Even his old lama teacher at Sera was incarcerated and tortured, for the Tibetan government was as suspicious of foreigners who might be spying as were all governments in the region. A Tibetan porter who led Kawaguchi out of Tibet was on his return put in chains outside Lhasa's courthouse, tortured and interrogated, yet unable to yield any incriminating information. Such tales are unpleasant to the ears of Tibet admirers, but these events did take place.

Upon his return to Japan, Kawaguchi wrote a book about his experiences which became required background reading for London's War Office personnel, who tried to make sense of reports from British forces invading Tibet. They would have learnt a lot about monastic life! Kawaguchi was not impressed with the religious attitudes of Tibetan monks, finding the majority ignorant, cruel, dirty, lazy and dishonest. They fought over young boys. In a meeting of 20 000 monks he saw them pushing, making obscene jokes, quarrelling, and filling their stomachs. Kawaguchi hated the squalor in streets and houses, the tempers and infidelity of Tibetan wives. He abhorred public floggings, manacled people, mutilation, gouging out of eyes, amputations, and execution by drowning or heaping stones on the victim's head. In all these respects, except the status of women, Tibet's customs were in line with China, Central Asia, medieval Europe and the Middle East. Sadly, 'liberation' brought far worse excesses.

When Derrick Williamson became fatally ill in Lhasa in 1935, British trade agent Captain Keith Battye wanted a Royal Air Force plane to collect him for treatment in a Calcutta hospital. Battye found a suitable landing site in fields near Sera and went to the *Kashag,* the Tibetan cabinet. But the ministers regretfully refused permission, afraid that if one plane landed they would have to agree to an air service between Lhasa and China, for which the Chinese were lobbying even then. Battye suspected they also feared monks might stone an aircraft landing near their monastery. But the air force telegraphed that landing was one thing, but taking off at an altitude of 12 000 feet technically impossible.

Some of the monks and lamas who then lived in Sera have since flown around the world to teach Tibetan Buddhism. In exile they ride in cars, watch television, wear wristwatches and sunglasses, but may still dream of when they galloped on horseback to Lhasa and Samyé or climbed mountains gathering medicinal herbs between studies and meditation retreats.

Five thousand is the figure quoted most for Sera's previous population. But de Riencourt reports 7000 resident monks just before the Chinese invaded. His Tibetan host would not accompany him, since lamas of Sera-Che college had recently murdered their Mongolian abbot, put up armed resistance against the government and for a short while controlled Lhasa. Evicted in the end, they were still seething.

So de Riencourt visited Sera with a Sikkimese companion. They were met by two proctors in charge of internal security, wearing toga-like robes with padded shoulders, yellow-crested 'helmets' and carrying iron cudgels. Together they walked the deserted avenue to the great temple. He noticed crowds of lamas in side streets; others peered from windows or roofs. He drank fourteen cups of butter tea while talking religion, philosophy, politics and economics with four abbots. At their request he inspected Sera's dry well, but was unable to advise ways to make water rise again. As the sun set on Sera's golden roofs, the light turned to a veil of blue, as recitations sounded from every temple hall. A picture of serenity.

The troubles between Sera and the government centred on the personality of the regent who ruled while the Fourteenth Dalai Lama was a minor. Sera also maintained a lively rivalry with Drepung's equally militant monks. One can only guess how these internal conflicts played into the hands of the Chinese communists so soon afterwards. With attention turned inwards at factions in conflict, there was no cohesive force to defend the country. Many of Sera's buildings were destroyed in the Cultural Revolution and there are now only 300 resident monks.

Today the atmosphere is festive at Sera, a large fortified village. People throng the main entrance or sit in clusters under trees along the main avenue. Jason talks to someone the instant he leaps off the bus, getting the news that a *lung* is in progress, a reading of the *Kanjur*, the complete Buddhist scriptures in 108 volumes, as well as the *Tanjur* or commentaries, comprising many more. The reader is Kundar Rimpoche, Sera's renowned present abbot. The *lung* has just begun and will take twenty days.

Chögyam Trungpa, growing up in eastern Tibet as the reincarnated Eleventh Trungpa Tulku, wrote of attending an 'authorisation' or *kalung*, a reading of the entire *Kanjur*, at the age of seven! That one lasted three months and technically speaking he henceforth was qualified to teach those texts. He remembered it as a great experience. It is very propitious to hear even a part of such marathon readings. We are fortunate to have arrived on day one. As everyone is in the assembly hall, we can't tour the monastery, but will see it as a functioning institution, rather than a relic from the past.

The day is hot and dusty but the trees lining the avenue are tall and leafy. Families rest in the shade, eating, talking. You can't listen to scriptures continually, children get restless, legs needs stretching. Being in earshot of the *lung* is blessing enough. Mingling in the Lhasa crowd are nomads in sheepskins, country people in rough homespun, Khambas, visiting monks and nuns, and a handful of tourists.

There are so few tourists that I feel we enter Tibet afresh, after traversing Lhasa's ugly Chinese streets. Low drystone walls border footpaths. Lining the streets are multi-storeyed buildings of mud and the pinkish beige stone of the hill. Doors and windows set in black wooden frames, solid red doors with yellow edges, thick plaited cords hanging from solid brass rings, pelmets and white cotton flounces. Tibetan architecture, grown from the mountains, is never less than handsome. On roofs golden pillars rise into a sky so innocently blue it is as if it never witnessed anything but piety.

Wherever time has been immaterial, the environment always yielded enough to make pleasing habitats if built with love. Never before have I seen an architecture born of love. Some of Sera's destroyed buildings are being restored. Women labourers sift through a high heap of rubble in a cloud of stone dust, perhaps hoping to find fragments of old statues. Men hammer away on the roof, breathing fresher air. But all sing as they work.

Tibetan women don't appear to have benefited from socialist equalisation. They are pressed into work gangs. They sing, but how long will their lungs stand this work ten hours a day? Young strong women carry baskets with stones or single boulders on their backs, only a cloth cushioning the weight. Can they leave the job when they've had enough? Too little is known about working conditions for Tibetan peasants under Chinese rule. Wherever the work is hard, heavy, dirty, conditions harsh and facilities nil, we see Tibetan workers.

A loudspeaker crackles. Not here too! But it is the *lung,* broadcast from the assembly hall for everyone outside. It is just as it was when St. Xavier's Cathedral in South Australia was festooned with loudspeakers in May 1992 for the Dalai Lama's inter-faith meeting with leaders of all religions, when thousands of people stood in the rain listening to his words. Through red doors we enter a compound. I clutch butter-soaked plaits. In a sunken garden people cluster under broad-leaved trees. Families picnic, mothers feed babies, old men catch forty winks. A large Khamba in red turban stands motionless, absorbed in the words of the *lung* ebbing down the flagstone courtyard.

There, in the hot midday sun, hundreds of people sit cross-legged in orderly rows, under straw hats or just manes of glossy black hair, listening to sacred words. In the shade of a building sit another thousand, packed knees to chins, facing an exquisite banner featuring sacred symbols: wheel, lotus, vase, conch, umbrella, over the temple entrance.

I search for an opening on the edge of the crowd, having lost the group. Turning, I see the last two members disappear up the temple steps. Jason is bold! I dash after them as fast as breath allows, dodging huddled figures on stone steps, repeating 'so sorry' to red-robed monks.

Inside I am blinded by semi-darkness, assaulted pleasantly by the fragrance of incense and butter lamps. Keeping my big mountain shoes in focus, I watch them stepping along a foot-wide path kept open in a sea of monks and lay people packed like sardines. Bemused faces look up without rancour at the stranger barging through their holy space.

I trust Jason knows what he is doing. Maybe the shrine is of unusual significance. He may know the abbot, or want to show us a mural at the rear of the hall. The narrow path turns right and I continue stepping high, avoiding limbs, listening enthralled to the Rimpoche's clear voice reciting from a high platform. Never catching up with the group I turn right twice more, smile back at smiling upturned faces. This hall was built for 5000. With the people outside, there could be double that number gaining merit from hearing the *lung* today. This is how Tibetans spend a holiday!

As suddenly as I entered the half-light, good smell, sanctified space where sacred words flow, I tumble into the sunlight, blinking. The others saunter about the courtyard and I make for Jason.

'What was all that about?' I ask. 'What were we supposed to see?'

'You just did a circumambulation of the *gompa* during a *lung*! It's a great blessing!' He grins.

Now I understand why the people were so tolerant, keeping open the narrow path. May the blessing preserve my life for the duration of this tour. Selfish? But I am no longer touring simply for my own enlightenment. Walking back to the gateway I furtively press the camera shutter, recording Tibetans on holy holiday. For Rimpoche.

High above Sera, just over the mountain crest, prayer flags flap in a stiff breeze at the sky burial place. The custom has suffered disrepute from foreign writers and sensation-hungry tourists going to any lengths to witness what they regard as the ultimate in ghoulishness. Sky burials are conducted by professionals who dispose of a body in a few hours with the assistance of the birds of the sky. It's alright by me, should I die here. Sky burial places are not tourist attractions, but the equivalent of crematoria. You pass with a respectful dip of the head. Farewell to you up there who finished the earthly journey, keep track of the clear light in the *bardo* and happy rebirth!

Although the bodies of Dalai and Panchen Lamas, as well as high reincarnate lamas, are preserved by an embalming process using spices and oils, the ordinary Buddhist is not as worried about what happens to the body as to where the spirit goes. Having one's body fed to the birds serves to gain merit on the rebound, while the spirit — without going into Buddhist notions of non-soul and what the continuing entity should be called — journeys into the *bardo* before taking another birth, for this is the fate of the unenlightened still bound to the wheel of life.

We walk the main avenue in reverse, having seen no images, libraries, debates or retreats. But we experienced Sera during one of its rare open days. I'm glad to be alive and wander among happy people, running children, singing labourers, chattering monks in clusters of maroon. The skies are overcast with large white clouds and the mountains across the Lhasa Valley begin to take on that dark look of late afternoon.

Half a dozen vans are parked near the gate house. Administration and catering for three hundred monks is still a feat, but easy compared with the foot and mule traffic of earlier days, when food — and water when the well dried up — had to be brought in daily for five to seven thousand men. That Tibet could maintain Sera and other large monasteries on frugal fare indicates how rich the land was. Tibet only came to grief when having to feed an army as well. Effectively, the monks had to make way for the Chinese army. But the army is much larger, more ruthless, and more useless than the monks ever were.

A sleek white sedan car is parked in front of a small building. Groups of people stare and whisper. Jason learns that inside is a high lama who recently disrobed. The people speak of him with awe. Not because he disrobed, which to them is an incidental fact of life under Chinese rule, but because he remains for them the incarnation of a renowned line of spiritual teachers. Chinese authorities boast when high-ranking monastics turn civilian. It is equivalent to becoming collaborators and denouncing religion. It does not happen often. There is a growing tendency to enter religious life, despite strict monastery intake quotas. But a high incarnation may experience such external pressures that by seeming to comply he may hope to do more for his community. I wonder why the ex-lama visits Sera during the *lung*.

A small, slender woman in torn black T-shirt, shabby grey jacket and russet trousers approaches, carrying a black woollen wrap and a tin with wire handle. Her hair forms a wild halo around a shining, beautiful face. She is all smile, hands outstretched. I take them in mine. She is a beggar. Jason would say she is probably a prostitute. She dresses unconventionally. But at monastery gates it is meritorious to give to those less well off than ourselves. I press a banknote in her hand and read in her face that it makes her day. Quickly she hugs me, then steps aside to allow another woman to approach.

This lady wears a *chuba* and has the round figure of one who has borne children. Ye gods, I had to work hard to bring up my kids, even go from shop to shop selling things from my basket, but I never had to beg! I give, and her grin stretches from apple cheek to apple cheek. Both women now hug me and, laughing, we hold hands. The group isn't around. This is just between three women, so could I please take their picture to remember them? They hold up the money for the photograph. Never, in all my travels, have I met such civil and delightful beggars as in Tibet.

'*Tudeche!*' I say, bowing. '*Tudeche,* thank you!' for being extended the privilege of giving.

It has been hard toil to take my body for a walk today, but invigorating to be in the sun amidst a crowd with a purpose that harmonises with my own. Beggars, labourers, travellers, all are pilgrims here and have walked to the rhythm of sacred words. Behind us the mount of Sera turns a rosy pink.

A Summer's Afternoon in Lhasa

In Old Lhasa's south-east quarter we find a *thangka* factory housed in a two-storey villa, perhaps previously a noble's house, reached as it is through a narrow street, opening into a courtyard formed by surrounding buildings. The stone steps to the imposing entrance are shaded by an upstairs room with eight windows jutting from the facade. Two wings, four large windows on each floor, pleated flounces peeking from pelmets. In front, an appliquéd cloth fences off a number of picnic trestles. A woman sums us up from the flat roof.

Inside, marvellous murals, a house decorated like a temple. Upstairs a long corridor at the rear gives access to all rooms. The manager appears and apologises that he can't show us around. There's a wedding on. Can we return another day? Pretty women in silks and jewellery jostle, giggling up the backstairs. We have arrived at the very moment when it is all about to happen and promise to come back. Outside, women cover tables with platters of festive food as children shoo away dogs who come running, noses and tails in the air.

The Williamsons lived in a big house like this, set in a walled garden called Dekyi Lingka, 'Garden of Happiness'. Thin gauze on wooden frames covered their windows at night and by November hardy Margaret felt the chill. Most windows are glazed now.

The warren of narrow streets draws me. Let me loose here, let me roam! So much to follow up, but there's a program. Organised tours are good for a first visit. Then, knowing your way around, you must come back to do it on your own.

A Red Cross flag hangs from a house, a medical clinic. A courtyard full of washing, food drying on round trays. How Tibetans must love the short summer, when everything can be done in the open air! A little girl in red cardigan and trousers hoists a plastic jerry can up the steps of her house. Hardly tall enough for the task, she labours on, big eyes fastened on us, a shy grin splitting her round face when I wave to her.

In the nearby busy thoroughfare of the Muslim quarter, lined with traders, you can buy rusty spare parts, vegetables, and amazing odds and ends. There is time to visit the mosque. But for the minaret, it looks like another Buddhist monastery. The entrance has Chinese pagoda roofs, but the tiny courtyard looks like any village *gompa*.

Muslims first came from Kashmir via Ladakh to set up butcher shops in

Lhasa. Tibetans dismember dead fellow humans to feed birds or fish, but killing animals for food sits uneasily with their Buddhist precepts. Yet survival in Tibet was never possible without eating meat. Although *tsampa* is the staple, during winter there is no additional food but dried cheese and strips of yak and goat's meat. Like North American Indians, Tibetans carry jerky as they travel.

Recently Muslim traders from what is now western China have settled in Tibet. Two cheeky boys and a girl frolicking in the mosque's courtyard may be Uighurs. An ancient woman wrapped in black lace headscarf hobbles in, leaning on a stick. The mosque's keeper steps from a door to greet us. Jason converses with both. From a distance we look politely around. We can't enter the mosque itself.

Jason translates the old lady's claim that there are about 3000 Muslims in Lhasa. Traditionally there never was a problem for other religious groups to fit into Lhasa life. This still seems the case. Considering Tibet's past this is amazing. Waddell, in an appendix to *Tibetan Buddhism,* mentions the discovery of a book by Mirza Haidar, dated 1546. This Muslim general from Kashgar invaded northern Tibet to sack the fort of Mutadar in Nubra — names not to be found on modern maps — killing all the lamaist men and building a minaret with their severed heads. There are other stories like that.

Signs here are written in Arabic, Tibetan and Chinese. A two-storey pile of timber from demolitions is for sale. The Chinese methodically demolish houses in old Lhasa, for they cannot control people living in warrens and medieval courtyards. This wood stood as doorways, had thousands of elbows leaning on it through centuries when still windowsills, held up roofs and as staircases felt the bounce of people's feet. Now it's sold for firewood. Tibetan houses are replaced by Chinese flats, their layouts having no secrets for the secret police.

A short ride brings us back to the park behind the Potala, cordoned off by a horrid white wall carrying red slogans for the commemoration of China's 'liberation' of Tibet.

At the rear of the Potala, the feeling of being at home returns. The whitewashed towers and walls, topped with maroon, exude a tremendous sense of stability. In their shadow the park is a safe playground. Families drink tea in groups on the grass, separated by picnic cloths strung between tree trunks. Children play and musicians break into sound and song to earn a few yuan.

We meet a musician from Sakya playing the *drumying,* a string instrument with disproportionally long neck and enormous tuning pegs hung with *kata.* With his young male companion he will do us a song, sitting cross-legged on the grass as we form half a circle. I find I can practically hum along with the tune. Karmic memory, or does the melody meet up somewhere with an old European song? They perform another song, then break into a side-stepping dance. The musician's expression turns to rapture as he gives life to an old love song. On the last note he throws us the happiest of smiles and another when the hat goes around. I hope his sweetheart is in Lhasa.

Next we meet two sheep with black faces, like Suffolks. They graze untethered, bought and set free by someone hoping to earn merit in this life, to gain a better rebirth. Red bows festoon their necks for protection. To interfere with another's merit brings double calamity on oneself!

Hollow slapping sounds come from small groups of men throwing dice onto heavy leather pads, playing a game of chance called *sho*. Winning or losing, they are in high spirits and not drinking tea!

I was introduced to *chang,* Tibetan barley beer, at a picnic in Dharamsala, on the lawn of a former British official's summer house. Although the women drank tea, the foreigner had to taste the traditional drink. Young men refilled my glass after every sip. I realised that if I drank at their rate, I would soon stagger over the nearby precipice to become a bony feature of the brilliant Kangra landscape, a thousand feet below. I remembered my brother, a drummer, accepting drinks from customers, then discreetly emptying them into a potted palm. The palm had to be replaced often. So I quietly watered a tree in that Dharamsala garden, perhaps leaving a reputation for holding my *chang* remarkably well. Unless that tree gave me away.

We walk through a grove of ancient trees. Gnarled and twisted branches intertwine, forming an unbroken canopy filtering light. These trees have seen centuries of festivities, ceremonies and terrible fighting, surviving all change. Young trees in the park are planted in straight rows — for crowd control, one imagines. The lake of the mythological *naga* or dragon king was formed by a large depression left after making mud bricks and mortar for the Potala. On a man-made island stands the Lukhang, or Naga temple, built by the Sixth Dalai Lama as a retreat where he rested from palace politics. The Thirteenth Dalai Lama came here to meditate.

You reach the Lukhang via a stone camel's-back bridge, overhung with willows. Underneath its arches young people row little boats, playing peek-a-boo around pillars, laughing hilariously. In a Tibetan grammar book I came across a conversation exercise between two young Tibetan men contemplating whether to cross to the Lukhang in a skin boat, or to pinch a nearby attractive girl. Some things don't change.

The caretaker monk is home and will show us the entire temple. Until recently the upper floors were closed. The frescoes of yogis and deities going through stages of death and the *bardo,* as described in *The Tibetan Book of the Dead*, are amazingly detailed. They are protected by chickenwire and after a while I only see hexagonal shapelets.

I am interested, but the long day is getting the better of me and I forego the top floor. Three of us descend, note in passing carefully tended pot plants on the verandah and sit down on the temple steps for as long as it takes. Above flutters the wheel of life on a verandah curtain; prayer flags stream through the willows by the shore. The Potala's stark walls gleam through the golden leaf lace of a copse of trees. Craning, we can just see the golden spirals of Dalai Lamas' tombs on the roof glitter against a sky turned vivid blue. Amongst them the tomb of the Ninth Dalai Lama, who died aged ten in 1816. In 1812, Thomas Manning met him in the Potala and wrote:

> The Lama's beautiful and interesting face and manner engrossed almost all my attention. He ... had the simple unaffected manners of a well-educated, princely child. His face was, I thought, poetically and affectingly beautiful. He was of a gay and cheerful disposition; his beautiful mouth perpetually unbending into a graceful smile, which illuminated his whole countenance. (MacGregor, *A Chronicle of Exploration,* pp. 221-222)

That the beauty of the child was not skin deep is evident from Manning's confession:

> I was extremely affected by this interview with the Lama. I could have wept through strangeness of sensation. I was absorbed in reflection when I got home. I wrote this memorandum: 'This day I saluted the Grand Lama! Beautiful youth. Face poetically affecting — could have wept. Very happy to have seen him and his blessed smile. Hope often to see him again. (MacGregor, *A Chronicle of Exploration,* p. 222)

He didn't. The little Dalai Lama died a few years later. After the death of his previous reincarnation, aged forty-six, there had been fierce demonstrations in Lhasa against the Manchu emperor. Some Tibetan officials were accused of collaborating with the Chinese and such angry crowds rioted in the streets that the regent had to call out Tibetan soldiers to protect the *amban*, the Chinese representative. When Manning was in Lhasa, a Chinese mission of mandarins was still investigating the cause of the riots. The Ninth was the first of four Dalai Lamas who did not reach the age at which they customarily ascended the throne. All four died of suspected poisoning, leaving power over Tibet in the hands of regents under the influence of one Chinese *amban* after another for nearly a century. This dark chapter in Tibet's history is clearly related to the present situation. Manning left when the *amban* accused him of being a spy. That pattern also repeats in modern times.

History notwithstanding, a feeling of serenity here in the shade of the Potala has not left me. Laughter echoes across the water as boats with boys or girls row to the bridge for an exchange of bawdy jokes. Older people stand talking on the banks, soft voices murmur across the water. Slim spirals of smoke rise as picnics resume. It is a brilliant late summer's afternoon, the temperature perfect. We find ourselves talking of inner feelings and the way we try to mend our lives, strive for peace and balance, speaking of this while looking up at the Potala as if we do this every Sunday.

We are almost sorry when the others join us after an exhaustive examination of the unusually fine paintings in the Lukhang. If I came back another year, would I make more of that opportunity? Or would I join the Tibetans near the water, breathe in the stillness and listen to the music of thin sounds reverberating through the valley, happy for the sunshine and the loveliest of views across the lake mirroring willows, snow-topped mountains, white clouds and blue sky? In this place people unwrap their happiness at the picnic cloth, whether for a labour-free day, for making music and song, or for the setting free of captive animals.

Crossing the bridge we are stopped by Kham traders, he wearing a homburg hat, she resplendent in turquoise and coral coiffure. The woman carries a bucket in which swim a strange sort of eel. She bought them as an act of merit and will sell them to anyone who wants to share in that merit by setting the eels free. Just like the black-faced sheep. I should have bought the eels and poured them into the lake, but only think they will be caught again. I sit on the stone bridge beside the Khamba man as his wife trades with the group. They have to make a living. I buy their necklaces, nice presents. Merit of a lesser kind.

Dozens of young Tibetans come to watch the trading. Their laughter echoes across the water, faces beam down on us who sit. How to describe Tibetan women's voices when they get excited? There is laughter in their voices, energy and an indomitable spirit for taking life by the horns. They are strong as *nak,* the female yak, and just as elegant. I don't want to get up. The altitude has me by the frontal lobe, I am very happy and don't want to move. People die in snowstorms in states of utter bliss, entertaining visions.

Finally the group moves and somehow so do I. Shutter instinct keeps my finger working as we wend our way through the park in its mountain setting, Potala reflected in the water, gentle willows and happy people at the end of a perfect holiday.

But when Nicola, Kay and Donna decide to visit the market in front of the hotel, I revive. Every evening traders display jewellery and artefacts on cloths spread under old trees. Most are Khamba women from Derge, once an independent kingdom with a highly developed civilisation and a printing press famous for its Buddhist texts. The press is working again after years of interruption. I'd love to see it, but Kham is not open for tourists, although some individuals managed to get past controls.

Derge women wear the most colourful of outfits, hair and clothes hung with chunks of turquoise and coral set in chiselled silver. Notoriously tenacious, they grab potential customers by an arm, hand or finger, lead them by the nose, drape them with beads, laughing and talking their strangely vigorous English until the smiling victims buy or shake their heads.

One old man doesn't push. Leaning against a tree he polishes and fixes, lets you rummage as you like. He sells more. Could someone tell the Derge women to stop their forceful play? Some tourists buy their wares to be released. Then again, should their lust for life be tailored to the needs of trade? I am led by a strong hand from Derge, examine all her offerings and buy a trinket box and a prayer wheel that doesn't spin properly. Appeased, she gives me a necklace of what seem to be Tiny Tim tomatoes, for I paid the asking price and she's too honest to pretend it wasn't too high. But in my currency it is reasonable. The real rip-off occurs in the monolith behind us, the Lhasa Holiday Inn — the consciousness bind of the packaged tourist.

Three teenage boys are selling statues and I give myself away by stroking a Tara image with no other intentions. I shake my head. They plunge the price from 3000 RMB to $US 30 dollars among shouts of mirth. I turn up my palms. They hold no rancour and when an American tourist approaches they start again at 3000, winking at me over their shoulders.

Two sad-eyed boys under big caps come begging. How is this possible? One of the statue boys explains: 'He very poor'. The bigger of the two claws my hand. Another bind. If I give them money, will the trading boys who are trying to make their living feel short-changed? Unable to solve it, I walk away, feeling despicable, trinkets rattling in my pockets. Why are Tibetan kids begging in Chinese-ruled Lhasa?

During dinner I fret whether the sad-eyed boys are eating tonight. If they don't, it may be because of my indecision. Is it the altitude that makes me so? Isn't that why politicians visiting Lhasa for a one-day officially guided tour, meekly mouth everything the Chinese communists tell them to say when they come home?

From the contemplation of a beggar boy's fate and Derge women's hands-on communication, we plunge into the ridiculous world of tourism as we eat our soup. To promote a fashion show, a beautiful Tibetan woman, traditionally gowned, winds between the tables accompanied by a black yeti. The yeti clowns and grimaces, but suddenly grabs a Chinese diner who has shown no interest, embraces him and plants a firm kiss on his cheek. A stir of giggles ripples along the tables and the Chinese man wipes his face, which is lost for the remainder of the day. The revenge of the yeti!

In our room, Nicola and I wash our hair, and order hot drinking water to keep up the fluids. I take Tibetan and Western medicine, imagine I feel better. Jason couldn't resist consulting the Panchen Lama doctor himself. If we still felt ill, the doctor told Kay and me, we should come straight to him, not bother going through the administration. Everywhere these tiny acts of getting around Chinese overlords. We are never sure when to aid and abet them or when to abstain, keeping the Tibetans' interest in mind. I suppose the doctor is able to look after himself. He has been a man of power.

Over dinner we discuss how Tibetans are outnumbered in their own land. A 1981 Beijing publication gives the population of Tibet as 1.8 million. But that is the Tibetan Autonomous Region, not including Amdo and Kham, made part of Chinese provinces. It is hard to conceive how Tibet can maintain a larger population than it used to. It presently imports food from nearby Chinese provinces to feed 6 million Tibetans and 7.5 million Chinese. The Chinese reduced the Tibetan population by executions, fatal incarcerations and war casualties — over one million since 1950. It seems well documented that Chinese gynaecological clinics subject Tibetan women to forced abortions and sterilisations and have caused Tibetan babies to die. Case histories circulate. Earlier genocidal methods included forced marriages of Tibetan women to Chinese soldiers. Now Tibetans are a minority in their own country, the ratio being one Tibetan for every 1.25 Chinese.

A similar ratio of 7 million Han Chinese constitutes over half the population of East Turkestan, now called Xinjiang. Inner Mongolia, after a much longer occupation, is thought to have 2.5 Mongolians to 8.5 Chinese, although some sources quote as many as 35 Chinese for every Mongolian, the same as in Hawaii, where there is one native Hawaiian for every 35 Americans of sundry backgrounds. In Manchuria there are 50 Chinese for every Manchurian, while some sources claim only 2 to 3 million Manchurians survive in a sea of 75 million Han Chinese. In Australia there are about 90 people from all over the world for every person of Aboriginal extraction. The longer the occupation, the more indigenous people are swamped by their invaders.

There are only 4 per cent of indigenous people left in the whole world, including six million Tibetans inside Tibet. The other 96 per cent of us do not live in the place of our ancestors or have mixed ancestry, belonging nowhere or everywhere. Like me.

Jokhang, Beating Heart of Tibet

In the lobby stands a row of pots with hydrangeas, asparagus, wandering Jew (symbolising survival and vigour), small-leafed bamboo and a jade tree. I miss my garden. The group gathers to pay our respects in Tibet's most holy temple the Jokhang.

Through the morning streets of Lhasa we go, so familiar as if we had lived here a lifetime. Tinkling of tools in cool thin air. Later it will grow hot and noisy. Near the Jokhang, remembered pictures clash with what meets the eye. What terrible changes! Tibetan houses and shops used to cluster before the temple. Now a vast Beijing-style plaza has taken their place, fences everywhere. Ideal for crowd control and shooting straight at dissidents, who tend to pledge loyalty to an independent Tibet at the temple's door.

The Jokhang has been the scene of many a protest by monks, nuns and lay people against the Chinese occupation. People have been shot dead here in numbers no-one is sure of. In October 1987 unarmed demonstrators were shot with AK-47 assault rifles, beaten with electric cattle prods and blunt spades. Monks were killed, nuns arrested. Children died. Tourists were hit and hurriedly bundled out of the country. To the left is the infamous new police station. Surveillance cameras hang from buildings lining the plaza and narrow streets leading into the Barkhor.

This Orwellian world terrifies. The killings are immeasurably more terrible than the destruction of ancient Lhasa, but regret for both surges with dread of the stone-hearted powers that overtook Tibet.

Today is the second of a three-day holiday commemorating the Chinese Revolution. Will there be demonstrations? Crackdowns in March and May were vicious. Hence the menace of soldiers walking around in pairs, cigarettes between their fingers. Smoking in public was forbidden in the time of the Dalai Lamas and tobacco regarded as a harmful drug. In this, Tibetans were ahead of the rest of the world, but Chinese cigarette imports induced widespread smoking. The soldiers do not come close to the Jokhang.

Nothing can keep Tibetans from streaming in thousands to their holiest of all holy temples. Built in the seventh century by King Songtsen Gampo, the Jokhang's construction heralded a golden age of Tibetan culture. Legend speaks of a lake underneath the building, a sacred goat who filled it in, and the king throwing lots with his ring. It is certain that the temple was built for one of the Buddha statues brought by his foreign princesses.

Margaret Williamson wrote: 'Lhasa seemed pervaded by a spirit of happy contentment which seemed to me to be the product of the Tibetans' Buddhist faith'. Not only in monasteries and temples, but in homes and streets she saw people tend shrines, fly prayer flags, count prayer beads, prostrate and circumambulate, just as they do today.

A stele erected in 823 in front of the Jokhang has an engraved treaty in Tibetan and Chinese, between King Tri Ralpachen and Emperor Wen Wu Hsiao-te Wang-ti. Today a wall surrounds the stele, but the message it bears is widely recorded:

> Tibet and China shall keep the country and frontiers of which they are now in possession. All to the east is the country of Great China; and all to the west is, without question, the country of Great Tibet. Henceforth on neither side shall there be waging of war or seizing of territory. There shall be no sudden alarms and the word enemy shall not be spoken. This solemn agreement has established a great epoch when Tibetans shall be happy in the land of Tibet, and the Chinese in the land of China.

The preceding peace treaty was signed in 821 with the taking of oaths in China's capital Chang-an (Xian), the next year in Lhasa. Three stele bearing the text were erected in Chang-An, Lhasa and at the border dividing Tibet and China, probably Ya'an. Only the Lhasa stele survives.

No doubt the Chinese insisted on oaths because Tibetan armies often seized Chinese territory and were to do so afterwards. But when in recent centuries the power balance reversed, the treaty proved to be worth less than the stone it is chiselled on. The surrounding wall is thickly hung with prayer flags, hiding a low door behind which the violated text may still be legible.

A nomad family has made itself at home against the wall, resting from their long journey to the holy city. Their beautiful children of the great silent plains run around soundlessly. The three red-cheeked women wear their hair parted in the middle, draped like cafe curtains across their foreheads, gathered over the ears and plaited in two thick strands tied together. They wear sneakers and identical blouses, red with pretty cream chrysanthemums. Nearby an old man in dark glasses, Mao shirt and wine-red *chuba*, carefully unwraps something from yellow silk inside a white bundle. Watching Tibetans at their sacred business is an absorbing interest.

Thousands mill around the plaza. From this crowd an unbroken stream peels off to enter the temple's left entrance, while another stream emerges from the right, dissolving back into the crowd. Pilgrims, monks, women and men, pray or prostrate on leather aprons with knee and hand protectors. Large flagstones carry impressions from centuries of worship, but no marks were left by the blood that flowed. Old people finger prayer beads in the shadow of temple walls — to be here is bliss. Children weave between adults, not disturbing, nor shouting.

We shuffle along in the stream under white and blue banners with wheel and four eternal knots symbolising the interconnectedness of everything. On the roof the golden *dharma* wheel held by two deer is flanked by giant golden bells. There are signs of damage in the portal. An improvised workbench stands between fluted pillars, a pull-and-push saw hangs from a nail. There are stacks of planks, wood shavings, repairs in progress.

A few more steps in the dense crowd and we are in the entrance hall, causing an obstruction as Jason starts his morning ritual of explaining frescoes in unbelievable detail. His knowledge of Tibetan Buddhism seems as much internal as acquired. His eyes sparkle and his face glows as he discovers one old acquaintances after another on the wall. His enthusiasm infects the most jaded travellers. Other Westerners start hovering, lapping up Jason's erudition. As the press of people builds up, Jason moves us on with the flow. The Tibetans have borne the delay with customary patience and fascination.

Sweet smells of incense and butter lamps join pilgrims' prayers and *mantras* chanted by the monks' deep voices sound in the depth of the temple. Where else on earth can this be witnessed? Through a courtyard and dark corridor we enter the main hall where Maitreya's statue takes our breath away. Donna gives me her bag and camera. She is going to fulfil a promise of three prostrations for her exiled Tibetan nun friend in America. As I hang the equipment on my frame, a beggar lady prods me. I struggle on, holding her gaze, intending to get to my pocket to give her money, when she spots Donna on her knees going into full-length prostration. The expression on her face changes to deep recognition. She retreats one step, casts me a quick furtive smile and nods at Donna's prone figure. Then she disappears into the crowd. She only begs from tourists, not from pilgrims. That's class!

When Donna is done we swap luggage and I go down for our Australian Rimpoche. Bending my head to ancient flagstones, I think of the sweet sadness in his always smiling face, of his thirty-four years of exile, of the great horseman he was when still a young Sera monk, and how our hot climate and harsh civilisation affect him. Will he ever see the Jokhang again? I pray for it.

We rejoin the clockwise procession behind a nomad woman in grey skin *chuba*, white fur inside, bordered with chintz in the colours Tibetans love: coral-red and turquoise. A pink sweatcloth is looped into her silver-studded belt. One sleeve dangles on her back, revealing a blue and gold brocade blouse. Her waist-length hair is plaited with beads and turquoises. She looks stunning, wearing the very best she possesses on the most important pilgrimage of her life. Raising hands, she bows like a pocket knife in front of a giant statue of Padmasambhava the demon slayer, his face lit by the glow of butter lamps. Her plaits whip up and down like skipping ropes as she pays her respects.

Once again we are swept up in the throng, moved along by the press of pilgrims, weaving in and out of small chapels lining three sides of the hall, gazing at images familiar and unknown, silenced by the collective purpose of so much devotion. It is happiness to be part of this throng of devotees. The burden of personality falls away and I become one with the purpose of paying homage to keep alive the only hope Tibetans have: the spirits of the ancients, the birthgivers of their astounding civilisation. Carrying packets of hard yak butter, people cut off small amounts to feed butter lamps at the feet of all deities. Some carry their own lamps, lit from the shrines. A few bring *kata* as offerings, but most push small banknotes between fingers and toes of statues or throw them in the lap of the gods.

One hopes the money goes toward repair of these ancient shrines. For here are gathered all the personalities that make up the pantheon of Tibetan Buddhism. Apart from Sakyamuni the historical Buddha and Padmasambhava who brought Buddhism to Tibet, here are the *dharma* kings Songtsen Gampo — with wives Bhrikuti and Weng Cheng — Trisong Detsen and Ralpachen. Then Avalokiteshvara the lord of compassion, also called Chenrezig, father of the Tibetan people, reincarnated in the Dalai Lama, and his consort Tara, born from one of his tears. Also Palden Lhamo, protectress of Tibet, who seems to personify the complicated life most women lead by sheer virtue of being female. Apart from the Kings of the Four Directions there are the protective deities Hayagriva, Mahakala, Yamantaka and others. Also the great Gelukpa reformer Tsongkhapa with his main disciples; medicine buddhas, and Amitabha the Buddha of infinite light, incarnated in the Panchen Lama. Overseeing all is the buddha-to-come, Maitreya. Each represents an aspect of a faith that is perhaps more than most in tune with humanity's experience of life on earth as she is, with natural forces beyond human control and inner demons trying to spoil people's best intentions.

Even Westerners are imbued with reverence. The pilgrim mood determines the atmosphere even more than the sonorous chants of monks, who are after all doing their daily dozens. But the mood of the pilgrims carries urgent undertones. You begin to perceive they not only bring personal grievances and hopes to the Buddha and deities, but solemnly though urgently plead with and admonish their divinities to turn around Tibet's plight. The Jokhang equates with Tibet's national identity. All attempts by the Chinese to destroy it, make it a pigstye, a guesthouse and then a museum for tourists, have failed.

Children have the best views, carried on men's shoulders or women's backs.

In some chapels we stand pressed together like one body and with people carrying butter lamps the air stifles, the heat oppresses, the fire danger becomes real. I shudder to think of black tresses catching fire, but Tibetans in crowds move with beautiful circumspection.

The group soon proves Western inability to stay in a throng for long. Peggy and Nicola can't see over heads and mainly face elbows. Donna hates the crush, Kay objects to open flames that might set her own magnificent mop alight, Ben is put off by being shoved and I, delighted by moving along minutes ago, am feeling dizzy. Only Jason has what it takes to reach the end of chapel row, while we drop-outs wait on the cool floor of the hall.

Here the *dob-dob* monks, traditional keepers of order who used to wear huge shoulderpads to make them look impressive, are patrolling the crowd. They used to make up from 10 to15 per cent of the monastic population and by 1950, when the three monasteries around Lhasa were overflowing, it meant that *dob-dob* monk numbers exceeded Lhasa's official army of 1000–1500 soldiers. This put the balance of power in the hands of the monasteries when a conflict with the state arose, such as in the appointment high officials.

Suddenly a sturdy young *dob-dob* steps forward, grabs a teenager by his black leather jacket and marches him and his weedy companion out of the temple. The grins on their faces die. They were out for mischief. Warnings against pickpockets abound.

All the time I stroke wood. Stephen Batchelor writes that some carvings around doorways and the ends of beams and capitals may date from the seventh century, as does the Jowo for which the Jokhang was named. But he estimates that many of the statues were replaced after the Cultural Revolution. That is an awe-inspiring achievement, seeing that it took place under the eyes of a devastatingly hostile regime. Yet the feeling of ancient treasure remains, because the temple is still the holy sanctuary that always was.

Rejoining the throng where it thins, we gaze at the fabulous Jowo, studded to the last millimetre with jewellery and gemstones. So dazzling is the statue in the light of butter lamps that details lose significance. In this ocean of adornment the face is an island of peace, though it speaks of past suffering. Yet it portrays the Buddha at the age of twelve. According to legend he remembered many lives before the one we know, some ending in horrendous deaths, borne willingly. The Jowo was already ancient when it came to Lhasa from China. Made in India during the lifetime of the Buddha, two and a half thousand years ago, it is the most worshipped statue in Tibet. Anyone who casts eyes upon the Jowo is struck by the accumulated reverence paid to it over the centuries. Recent destruction and suffering gets gathered up in the people's unstoppable devotion.

Percival Landon, accompanying invading British troops as correspondent for *The Times,* saw the Jokhang filled with chanting monks in August 1904. He described the Jowo as the most famous idol in the world. Idols were a fad then with the groovy, but a devilish horror to Christian missionaries. Landon wrote: 'From its murky recess the great glowing mass of the Buddha softly looms out, ghostlike and shadowless'. This started a rash of mystery novels set in the idolatrous east, adventurous heroes hunting treasures hidden inside gigantic statues, tales dripping with blood behind altars, disaster-wreaking emeralds and deadly rubies.

An old monk shuffles past muttering a mantra, twirling an enormous wooden prayer wheel and carrying a khaki sack. His tattered robe is covered by a patched fuchsia-pink sleeveless jacket. Thick veins stand out on bare arms and bulging biceps. He may be rebuilding his monastery, wielding needle and thread at night to mend his only clothes. Are there people like him in Western societies? Renouncing ambition and possessions to devote a lifetime to a spiritual quest is anathema to rational economics, the ideology that first terminated true folk craft in Europe and is now engaged in destroying the global ecology. Old Tibet's economy prevented over-exploitation, over-grazing, over-production.

A pillar by the stairs to the first floor supports a stone with a hole in it. Jason talks to a monk who gestures for us to put our ears to the hole. Anyone who can hear the sound of water in the underground lake has merit. I listen as I used to listen to the seashells Grandma would press against my ear to let me hear the rushing of waves. Like then, my eyes grow wide when I hear it. Sure, there is water down below there, unmistakably! I grin at the monk.

The crowd thins as we climb to the first floor, where there are more chapels. A man in black trousers wears a short Mongol coat, gold-trimmed high across the chest. He carries a blue-flowered silk dillybag in one hand, a packet of butter and teaspoon in the other. From a chapel steps a woman in pink blouse, long black skirt, black and white cardigan, high-heeled shoes. She looks more Chinese than Tibetan, but carries a lit butter lamp while murmuring prayers. Would a Chinese woman in Lhasa dare worship publicly? Not likely. She has to be Tibetan, perhaps the daughter of a Tibetan woman and a Chinese soldier.

You don't hear about Tibetan men being forced to marry Chinese women. China has a shortage of women. Men of opposing nations tend to see the others as barbarians. No matter how they treat their own women at home, they won't have them touched by foreigners. But to have an army of hundreds of thousands of young men permanently stationed in a foreign land, getting sexually uptight, puts the indigenous women in peril. I know what I'd do, given half a choice between marriage to a stranger, or sterilisation at the hands of enemy doctors. I stare after the Chinese-looking woman who raises her lamp in homage between folded hands before entering another chapel. Some mother's treasured daughter.

I suddenly have a vision of future Tibet, its people looking somewhat more

Chinese due to intermarriage, filing in and out of temples on special days, paying homage to ancient traditions that never lost their relevance for life in any age, under any regime. The people here today are all ages, but the majority are young. The really old, shuffling from chapel to chapel, have survived indescribable times. The upper middle age range seems to be largely missing, as in China. Lost in the Cultural Revolution during the prime of their lives. The young adults seem very mature. They carry the responsibility for the continuation of Tibetan culture and identity. This sheer unending stream of worshippers is evidence of their determination.

On the first floor we look into Sakyamuni's eyes. He rises two floors up. We find a lovely chapel of King Songtsen Gampo *en famille* and discover he had a Tibetan wife, Monsa Tricham, who bore his only son. She was one of three Tibetan wives. Weng Cheng was a peace offering from the Chinese emperor and may have been his son's wife rather than his own. Princess Bhrikuti may have come from Nepal for similar reasons, as the Tibetans were fierce warriors then. But Bhrikuti has been dropped from the official Chinese history of Tibet to strengthen the Chinese connection. The rewriting of Tibet's new socialist history continues.

A row of carved white monkeys holds aloft the ceiling of the main hall. They sport yellow headdresses, green beards and wicked eyebrows. On the ceiling turquoise and coral red contrasts with green and gold. Intricately decorated friezes line the wall above a border of golden *mantra* and cameos of deities. Colours are fresh and bright, all spaces filled with religious imagery.

On the central floor, fenced off from the gallery with red fluted pillars and stone balustrades, stands a superb wooden cabinet, a row of tin cups on its shelf. Painted in gold on brown door panels are the eight sacred symbols of Buddhism: lotus, conch shell, vase, fishes, parasol, banner, wheel of *dharma* and the eternal knot. Golden flowers adorn a sculptured pelmet at the top. In any home this treasure would be proudly displayed, fondly polished. Here it stands covered in dust, splattered with paint. Underneath sit bowls and tins of the same mineral paints seen at Mindröling, that bring a civilisation back to life. The old cabinet, whatever its past, has a new destination.

Next to the cabinet a folded quilt hangs over the balustrade. Nearby a young monk recites, textbook in hand, at a green and gold lectern, his sturdy body swaying to and fro. Does he live on this floor? Working magic with his paints, sleeping in his quilt, drinking tea, taking breaks for religious duties? As I take photographs from a distance he looks up, throws me a quick smile, without interrupting his recitation. I respond by throwing my hands together in a Buddhist greeting and move on.

Before 1959 parts of the Jokhang were used as meeting and reception rooms by Tibet's cabinet. In the thirties Derrick Williamson met here with government monks and ministers, while the Jokhang experienced a mouse plague. So tame were the mice that he could stroke them and Margaret saw them stand on their hind legs drinking from offering bowls. Amaury de Riencourt had the privilege of being received in the reception area on the roof by the *kalon* lama, or president, and the two highest *shape,* or ministers. He sat on a purple cushion, exchanged *kata* and put questions of a political nature to the three cabinet members. Not getting very far, he remarked that although the Tibetans brought a greater feeling for sincerity and truth to the discussion, they engaged in hair-splitting and shilly-shallying, habits he thought they had learnt from the Chinese. He felt irritated that they would not inform him in the least about Tibet's position in the regional politics of the time. Many officials of most countries shilly-shally over tea! Amaury's main gain from the rooftop reception was an acquired taste for butter tea, despite having to discreetly remove floating hairs and live flies. In Waddell's days the Jokhang had a cauldron big enough to brew twelve thousand gallons of tea!

The Jokhang was sacked during the Cultural Revolution. Giuseppe Tucci writes that parts of Sakyamuni's statue were smuggled to India. After the sack the Chinese converted this holiest of temples into the Lhasa City Municipal Hotel, with living quarters for members of the Lhasa Chinese People's Political Consultative Conference. That they used the inner courtyard as a cafeteria was somewhat in character, for in earlier days the monks would have their butter tea poured here. But raising porkers for Chinese woks in the inner sanctuary was a deliberate insult to the sensibilities of the Tibetans.

As a special privilege we climb to the highest roof. Several roofs at different levels look like so many balustraded courtyards. Each has *lhakhang,* small temple-like structures with gilded roofs, images, *dharma* wheels and gilded bells. De Riencourt spoke of roofs 'with glittering sheets of solid gold!' It is hard to know how much gold is left. It used to be routinely stripped and transported as bullion to China. Today's scene doesn't have as many glittering roofs as old photographs show. But the Jokhang's was saved from Red Guards by Zhou Enlai, who ordered its preservation.

Other tourists are having a special privilege on a lower roof. No doubt privileges correspond to the daily rate paid for transport, guide and driver. The views are stupendous. The Potala rises above all clutter in glorious majesty. From a distance the palace is even more imposing than close up and the absence of detail enhances the grandeur of its lines. An upsweep of walls like a colossal white wave, cascading staircases, the set of thousands of windows like so many eyes. To the left, Chakpori's radio mast incongruously rises where once stood a fitter counterpart to offset Potala's splendour.

Looking down the temple walls we see what is left of the Barkhor, famous circumambulation path and Lhasa's main market. Inside the Jokhang is a circumambulation called Nangkhor, accessible only through certain doors now closed. The outermost circumambulation, Lingkhor, embraces the whole of Potala and old Lhasa, now interrupted by Chinese constructions. This threefold devotional walk with the Jokhang at its heart forms a mandala. Devout pilgrims used to prostrate along the Lingkhor on hands and knees. Sometimes you see a prostrating nomad proceed along the Barkhor, departing from and returning to Jokhang's portal, on a pilgrimage perhaps never to be repeated. Shoppers gently weave around the crouching figures. There is one story of a violent circumambulation. During the March 1959 uprising, a Tibetan collaborator was killed and his body dragged around the Barkhor by an angry crowd.

Robert Ekvall, born among Tibetan tribes in Chinese borderlands, lived for many years in eastern Tibet. He writes that foreigners do not perceive the significance of circumambulation in the life of all Tibetans, although they mention and describe it frequently. He calls circumambulation the pivotal activity of Tibetan life, ceaseless, universal. Even when swirling tea in a bowl, they watch the liquid circumambulate!

It is true that, as if tuning into a cosmic pattern they alone understand, Tibetans spin their tea bowl in a clockwise fashion when kneading *tsampa* into their butter tea. From this basic daily necessity, they circumambulate clockwise around the village stupa and *gompa,* until pilgrimage to a regional sacred place, or eventually Lhasa, absorbs all these circumambulations in the Lingkhor, Barkhor and Nangkhor, spinning the merit right up to the heavens. Mount Kailash on the border with India is the other supremely sacred place for circumambulation. Children the world over practise this cosmic way of moving in their games. Turning clockwise you advance, penalties send you anti clockwise. Children who don't play games except on computers lose touch with circumambulatory magic and perhaps the greatest balancing factor in life.

Not going clockwise is what may be wrong with the world, but in the pre-Buddhist Bön religion circumambulations are done anticlockwise. One can hardly settle the blame for the world's ills on so small a group of people. Yet here in Tibet we are consciously turning right and it builds a feeling of rightness. Semantics? Will turning left do the same? What about leftists and rightist politics, water swirling down plugholes? Is a little ritualism all we need in life to make us virtuous? Or is there virtue in clockwise motion? Yes Mr Eliot, we have arrived at the point we started from.

From the temple heart of Lhasa the old streets fan out, flat roofs stretching to the foot of mountains, like stepping stones in a delta of people. In the sharp light of noon the mountains appear like sitting giants comfortably wrapped in beige robes, waiting for the cool of evening. The noonday sun beats down through the thin ozone layer. We peel off jackets, put on hats.

The Dalai Lama's throne-room is also on the roof. From wrap-around windows he could overlook courtyards, Lhasa, the Potala. Looking past the golden bird on a roof corner into the courtyard, as I do now, he would have seen a monk contemplating in full sun, part of his robe flung over his head, barely casting a shadow. Galleries on lower levels are hung with Tibetan curtains, large pieces of white or brown cloth, contrasting bands making crosses, strengthening seams. On the cross an appliquéd diamond shape. Small seats and pot plants under a white awning. A few monks live at the Jokhang, but no monastic routine exists here now.

In the corners on the roof are closed chapels, one featuring a wall painted with Taras. The upper halves are made of the now familiar bundles of ochre-daubed twigs. A red wooden door framed in turquoise and gold has long iron hinges and an enormous brass ring knocker under a fluttering white curtain. Such combinations of solidity and the ephemeral stop me in my tracks. On the brush walls hang plaques featuring gilded replicas of human skulls. The whole Jokhang roof is a magic statue garden. On golden rooftops ride golden dragons, mythical birds perch on red and gold purlins, engraved stones guard chapel doors. One is supposed to resemble Tsongkhapa's hat.

Meanwhile a thin monk has been talking with Jason, speaking bitterly of Tibet's plight. He and his fellow monks live with one foot in prison, he says. The magic is only for tourists.

Belief, Practice and Politics

In Tibet you learn about meaning. Somewhere in the middle of my lifespan I discovered that determinists, who hold that all phenomena were predetermined by pre-existing conditions, thus rendering action meaningless, sounded as plausible as those who believed that each of us can change any course of events. This offered a choice: where you want meaning you put it in, and where you don't you don't. Life seems to lumber on regardless, like a juggernaut set in motion long ago, gathering up all that comes before its grinding wheels. To be persuaded by the juggernaut to give up all hope of personal satisfaction goes against most people's grain. But meaning in life is as much an internal personal creation as an external phenomenon we have to search for. It grows happiness or cultivates unhappiness. You can successfully create deep meaning from next to nothing and lead a glorious life dripping with significance. And when you get to higher Buddhism, meaning melts like snow in the sun and pure bliss takes its place.

Tibetans put meaningful images on everything they use, from buildings to the tiniest artefacts. Decorations almost invariably include the lotus, symbol of purity as it rises from its murky habitat — the pure state of mind Buddhists strive for. Although I don't know the meaning of skulls, ochre, or diamond shapes on curtains, these are bound to have specific meanings in Tibetan lore.

By apparently never applying meaningless decorations, or never decorating unless meaning needs to be given shape, the Tibetans have built themselves a civilisation consisting of meaning, relevance and dynamic interactions. I'm becoming aware that the uniform peacefulness visitors sense in Tibetans, even under the Chinese yoke, arises from being in their own country surrounded by known symbolisms they understand better than any foreign scholar does, just as they understand much else in the universe. Tibetan deities represent cosmic forces and psychological states of mind, whereas the Buddha, Dalai and Panchen Lamas, teachers, sages and kings are not only the bones of Tibetan history, but form an unbroken network of human endeavour towards enlightenment, accessible to everyone.

Australian Aborigines are also linked to their land and the images it yields. They and American Indians, whose culture similarly provided them with a spiritual existence richer than their descendants can hope to achieve, have had the landscape of their times overrun by another people's dream that has in so many ways become a nightmare. But like them, the Tibetans are not giving up their culture.

Tibetans not only worship and petition their deities, but identify with them in times of crisis. To act in the spirit of Avalokiteshvara, Tara, or Padmasambhava means rising above petty human concerns. The ability to do this comes from frequently reciting the deity's mantra, daily worship, visualisations and meditations on the truths the deity symbolises. It makes Tibetan people just that little more noble, courageous and compassionate than the rest of us. This is what I come to believe, standing on the roof of the Jokhang as pilgrims wend their way through the chapels below.

As we are leaving I almost stumble over a small stele. A pinkish stone no higher than my knee bears the gargoyle face of a little sprite. Knobbly nose and bulging eyes, it looks frightened or frightening. It reminds me of Sepik ancestral carvings. Two sets of upward strokes on either side seem to indicate wings. It is nothing like any images we have seen and doesn't look Tibetan. Could it be a relic of a pre-Buddhist era? When I ask, neither Jason nor the monk knows.

Lama Anagarika Govinda believed that stone engravings depicting the eighty-four *siddhas* were brought individually to Tibet and installed in monastery courtyards. The *siddhas* were religious wanderers and ascetics who walked the Indian subcontinent, holding to no monastic rules, but converting experiences into the stuff of meditation, believing that experience converted to spontaneous consciousness alone can lead to enlightenment.

Siddha comes from *siddhi*, 'gaining the goal' or 'perfection'. The word appears in the given name of the Buddha: Siddhartha. The Indian *siddhas* — also known as *sramanas* — led a revival of this Buddhist principle about a thousand years after the Buddha's departure. Monasticism evolved because the great numbers of Buddha's followers necessitated setting rules for communal living. But eventually monasticism shut out many people and rules meant to keep order were elevated to doctrine.

In the Tibetan tradition the enquiring mind is still a focus for religious training. Monks debate hours each day to sharpen each other's minds, provoke deeper thought, stir doubt about doctrine. New teachers rise from the ranks with new methods, keeping philosophy alive. Yet, monastic life has also created doctrine out of ancient rules.

In China religion had become atrophied and the communists called it opium for the people before trying to eradicate it. They never understood that in Tibet they were dealing with a living religious tradition, where twigs broke off only on becoming obsolete. It is like a giant tree that sheds dead branches while growing new ones and giving food, shade and shelter to sentient beings.

The *siddhas* had been the first to write about religion in the vernacular languages instead of Sanskrit, the language of priests and scholars. According to Lama Govinda some of these writings were preserved in an old language called Apabhramsa and in Tibetan translations. Since translation of scriptures into Tibetan started in the seventh century, the translators tapped into a rather recent revivalist movement.

Today Buddhist scholars go to Tibet seeking texts that have long disappeared in India, where climate, the Moghul invasions and a more volatile society have been less conducive to the preservation of fragile pages, whether palm leaf or paper. It is atrocious that Tibet has for thirteen centuries been the keeper of rare wisdom texts of great antiquity, only to see most of them destroyed since 1950 as the world looked on. Tibetan culture areas of Ladakh, Sikkim, Bhutan, Mustang and northern valleys in Nepal and India may still have texts awaiting translation from Sanskrit or Tibetan. Through printing and distributing multiple copies, their contents could be protected from humanity's violent impulses.

Would the face on the stele be a *siddha*? No image in this temple is without meaning, without a link to past events.

The monk's English is carefully elegant. He speaks caressingly of Tibet's history, explaining that Songtsen Gampo was Tibet's first great *dharma* king, but the second was the thirty-seventh king and the third the forty-second king. After the fourth, the Fifth Dalai Lama assumed secular leadership to establish the present line of religious rulers.

The monk's arms are thin sticks. His face is lined, yet I sense he is young. 'May I ask how old you are?' I ask politely, fearing this is not done, but wondering where he fits in. 'I am twenty-four years old,' he says, staring away to the Potala shimmering silver in the afternoon light. Born in 1969, at the height of the Cultural Revolution, he grew up during the period of slow liberalisation that followed. But he was an adult monk when the 1989 demonstrations for Tibet's independence were bloodily crushed at the Jokhang, when on these very roofs and stairways where we talk, monks were chased, clubbed to death or taken prisoner. More than forty lost their lives, hundreds were imprisoned, most still are. Tibetan New Year celebrations have been banned from the Jokhang ever since.

We stand among the ghosts of his murdered friends. The ramifications of the story are contained in his silence. Perhaps he hopes that, among all the tourists he meets, some can do something in the outside world that will help turn Tibet's fate around. Most tourists are professional people, able to afford the trip, but perhaps too busy to work out reasons and causes of what they saw unless something touched them indelibly.

When important politicians visit China, Beijing officials love hauling them off to Tibet, to show so-called progress made and peace in the streets. UN officials, Jimmy Carter, Helmut Köhl and Australia's Tim Fischer all went for the one-, two- or three-day trip with banquet, saw Lhasa, saw streets emptied of people and nursed their altitude headaches until they were mercifully flown out again. Recent delegations to Chinese prisons in Tibet suffer similar drawbacks and can never investigate freely.

'China is doing all it can in a difficult situation', politicians say, brainwashed into thinking that China did *not* get itself into the Tibetan situation in the first place. Patting a new trade contract in their briefcase they observe, 'China is making progress in Tibet', having been shown a hospital clinic and primary school, believing there was no medical system in Tibet prior to 1950 and that learning Mandarin ought to be more useful than learning Tibetan.

'China is making a lot of effort in Tibet', they say, brainwashed into thinking that what China puts into Tibet is not being paid for in human life and forced labour, sacked art treasures sold on the international market, logged forests, mined gold and minerals, space for surplus Chinese peasants and nuclear test sites. China's major nuclear base is in Tibet and all of Tibet's airfields, roads and electrifications were built for military purposes.

'We didn't see any disturbances in Lhasa', visiting politicians say, having forgotten the names of other places they saw, brainwashed into thinking there were no arrests before they arrived, no armed police placed strategically to suppress attempts on the part of Tibetans to throw a message to the foreign visitors.

The young monk must be depressed at the slow trickle of accurate information to the outside world. He probably thinks we won't do much either. I want to make a promise, but don't know what. Some of my acquaintances don't quite know where Tibet is, or think Tibet has always been a province of China, or worse, that Tibet is still independent. We take leave of the sad monk, old before his time, aware of our shortcomings.

Talking to Strangers Now

Stepping back into the life of the plaza requires mental adjustment. The Jokhang experience has been incisive. The group splits up, some go shopping in the Barkhor. As we must drink three litres of water a day to keep altitude sickness at bay, Ben, Kay and I walk back to the bus to fetch our waterbottles.

At the bus I decide to rest, while they go looking for a *thangka* shop. The driver stands under a tree, smoking, bored out of his mind, a condition many of his fellow Chinese find themselves in. Would he know that things could be otherwise? To be given a job by the state, knowing that's what you will do for the rest of your life unless the powers that be decide otherwise, must kill all initiative. He looks a nice enough man, but his sad eyes and placid face express no interest in anything. Sometimes he hangs around for hours while we are immersed in Tibetan iconography. Given a job like that I would bring knitting and a book, but all he carries is his bottle of green tea and cigarettes. I sit on the bus steps, clutching my waterbottle, watching life in the street.

Lhasa streetlife seems already so familiar that little causes surprise. I like the quiet hustle and bustle, the smell of dust and ozone, but cannot help noticing that all commercial transactions seem to be in the hands of Chinese settlers. Across the street is a market for clothing, shoes and plastic goods, the merchants mostly Chinese women. Only at the Jokhang and in the Barkhor a few Tibetan traders sell religious paraphernalia, *kata* and prayer flags.

Slowly I wander down the street. Although the only tourist in sight, I am somehow so used to being in Tibet that I tend to lose myself. Yet this is only day six. There is a timelessness here that lulls me into the illusion that I shall be staying. I mingle with the crowd. Suddenly something extraordinary happens. I find myself in conversation with a Chinese man. A passing glance, a nod exchanged for a furtive glance, a sudden daring and we are talking. He has little English but asks where I come from. I don't think he understands the reply. I produce a tiny album with photos of home, family and friends, a collection compiled to explain my rank in the family and my work, to answer obvious questions with pictures that say more than words.

He looks in some amazement, comprehending that I am a grandmother of grandsons, a grower of formidable squashes and pumpkins, wearer of blue overalls and a weaver. But when he sees a picture of Chinese friends he is speechless.

Finally he points and asks, 'China?' 'Yes,' I nod, naming the province they hail from. If he had a notion they were overseas Chinese, seasonally returning to the great motherland from Hong Kong, carrying consumer goods for lucky relations, he now understands this not to be the case. The idea that Chinese Motherlanders have left permanently for faraway lands to live in wide-roomed houses, wearing shorts, eating food fit for banquets from laminex kitchen tables, must be hard to take for a blue-collar immigrant in Lhasa.

I change tack, ask where he comes from. Same province! Change tack again. When? That long ago? He was only a little boy. One of the blameless ones. With parents and siblings he crossed the infinite highlands of Tibet in the midst of the Cultural Revolution, to settle on the roof of the world. I dare not ask the reason. His father must have been more than a foot soldier to be able to bring his family. He grew up here and now is married with a child. All siblings married Chinese settlers. No forced marriages with Tibetan women in his family. I gather that the idea of marrying a Tibetan is repugnant to him. Maybe Chinese soldiers had no choice, but married for the glory of the Motherland. Maybe only horny ones were selected. Who knows whether there was a norm at all?

One sister is a teacher, his brother a driver, his wife works in a department store. One summer they went back for a holiday, packing the family into two trucks, men taking turns at the wheel. Sleeping at truck stops, they reached the ancestral city after one month. They visited all the relatives and drove back before winter closed the passes. Home again. Is Tibet home to him? He hardly remembers China. He learnt some English at school from a Chinese teacher, but our conversation remains monosyllabic. Carefully he gropes through the meanings of remembered words: 'No good speak English', as I select short nouns and verbs of concrete meaning, discarding articles and prepositions, but using the occasional adjective to good effect. Amazing what you can convey with 'big', 'far', 'longtime' and 'very good'.

The exchange has been stimulating. We part when our cache of useful words dries up. 'Goodbye!' Goodbye!' There goes a blameless one, primed with his own set of cultural prejudices. A nice man you'd like to have as a neighbour. He got what I dreamed of: a childhood in Lhasa, although not a Tibetan. A lucky man?

When I return to the bus Mr X, the driver, is about to go in search of the group. It's past his lunchbreak. He returns in five minutes with Jason's happy shoppers. Throwing his latest cigarette half-smoked in the gutter, he climbs behind the wheel and starts up the engine, meaning business. Always mild-mannered, this is as threatening as he gets.

We rattle back to the hotel to catch a late lunch on our date-stamped meal tickets. No ticket, no meal. Thus only *bona fide* tourists staying in the hotel eat here and organised tourists don't have to mingle with backpackers or other lowly species fancying a posh dinner. Packaged tourists are discouraged from eating out where they may talk to all sorts of people, for instance Tibetans. Thus everyone chatting here at table has been vetted by a regime mortally afraid of minor spies. The packaged tourist fathoms this after three days in Lhasa. But the hotel shapes part of our Tibet experience, for we become statistics in the food politics of an occupied country.

Breakfast is a fantasy land of mountains of gold, snow white, crispy brown and juicy red. Between hills of watermelon and Danish pastries I glimpse the street below, wondering what passers-by had for breakfast. *Tsampa* and butter tea for Tibetans, a bun and plain tea for the Chinese. But I'm hungry and they charge for this meal like wounded bulls. So I eat these delicacies, as I need the energy of a yak to put one foot in front of the other.

Lunchtimes, on some days, I find a small platter of yak cheese. Ye gods, do I love cheese! Yak cheese tastes just like the best Dutch farm cheese before cheesemakers began messing with chemical rennets. Yak cheese brings back forgotten childhood impressions, aromas in cheese shops selling nothing but cheeses great and small, and the return of cheese after the war. One more slice of yak cheese will render me quite emotional.

Dinners are fairly indescribable. They vary between a semblance of offerings from good Hong Kong hotels to mother's hotpot with side dishes, or yesterday's disguised rehash. Package rate for a share room and this daily board of surprises is several hundred US dollars per day. But this is Tibet. Some of these foodstuffs are trucked in from China along the most difficult roads in Asia, or flown across the most intimidating mountain ranges in the world. Between 70 000 and 100 000 tonnes of wheat or rice are flown in annually to feed Chinese immigrants and foreign tourists. Across the Kyu river stand rows of greenhouses where Chinese immigrants grow Chinese vegetables, supported by the United Nations World Food Program. Tibetans remain largely untouched by aid programs, although on paper they are no doubt named as recipients. 'The people of Tibet' are Tibetans in foreign perception, but Chinese in Chinese perception. Tibetans eat *tsampa* with vegetables and sometimes meat, dried meat and cheese in winter, other foodstuffs on special occasions.

Propped up in the little bus for a long haul I try to work out how tourists affect food politics in Tibet. Crates of beer, Coca-Cola and mineral water are being delivered to shops and hotels and there's a landfill of plastic and glass just outside Lhasa. Nicola and I bought one bottle of mineral water each and daily refilled these with boiled water provided in the hotel. Not just to save money, but to leave only one bottle to pollute Tibet. In the event we carried our bottles to Kathmandu and polluted Nepal.

We may eat frugally at home, but the difference is we have that choice. Tibetan lamas coming to Western countries sometimes become overweight in a short time. Some have died too young of heart attacks. Hard-working Tibetan women hide very slim waists in bulky woollen clothes. There could be hungry stomachs under those striped aprons.

Food politics in Tibet have not yet been the subject of an independent international study. Nuclear capacity, human rights and environmental pollution cannot be studied in countries controlled by China and neither can food production, export and importation in Tibet. The great hoo-ha accompanying the Great Panda Conference in Chengdu was a symbolic openness to cover up closed closets.

The temple forecourt at Samyé with rows of prayer drums

Samyé Temple — the first and oldest surviving monastery in Tibet

A small monk at Samyé monastery

A mural at Samyé monastery, Central Tibet

A Khamba trader in Lhasa

Farm girl, Central Tibet

The Potala Palace, Lhasa

Here stood the famous Western Gate, entrance to Lhasa, destroyed by Chinese troops. Prayer flags have been strung across the emptiness that remains.

Chinese authorities erected this statue of two golden yaks at a busy intersection in Lhasa to commemorate their takeover of Tibet. Chinese inhabitants like to take family pictures here to send home.

Tibetan houses (now demolished) in front of the Potala Palace, Lhasa 1993

Monks in a courtyard assembly. Sera monastery, Lhasa, 1995

Monks debating, Sera monastery

Door in the first floor courtyard of the Dalai Lama's mother's apartment. Norbulingka Summer Palace, Lhasa.

The orderly kitchen at Ani
Tsangkhug nunnery, Lhasa

View of the village and Kyu River from Ganden monastery, Central Tibet

Norbu's Park and
Talking to Strangers Then

In brilliant sunshine we walk the stone-paved road to the Norbulingka summer palace in a parade of people in holiday mood. Frugal snacks sell from wheelbarrows and stalls. Families drink butter tea in the grounds in outdoor 'rooms' made from floral cotton stretched from tree to tree, a place to be private in public and keep the dust at bay. Children tie their balloons to the strings.

The idyllic scene is framed by aluminium crowd-control barriers around the lawn. Norbulingka saw the first mass demonstration against Chinese rule in March 1959. Five thousand Lhasa women surrounded the little palace to protect the young Dalai Lama, when it became known that the Chinese had ordered him to come alone and unguarded to a 'special theatrical performance' in Chinese headquarters. Assuming the young ruler was still inside, Norbulingka was shelled by the Chinese on 17 March 1959, leaving little doubt about their intention to kill him. The Dalai Lama, with family and retainers, had fled two days earlier in disguise under cover of darkness. Also shelled were the Jokhang, Potala and other important buildings and thousands of Tibetans lost their lives in the bloody massacre that followed.

We come prepared to see considerable damage, although restoration is proceeding. But first impressions on entering Norbulingka's grounds are the enormous height of the trees and the cool dappled shade they afford. Tempered sunlight spreads a golden glow over brightly painted gateways. Never have I seen such huge birches, poplars, willows and apple trees.

Norbulingka is a collection of mainly twentieth-century Tibetan villas, summer residences for the Dalai Lamas, although the first pavilions and chapels were set in a walled garden by the Seventh Dalai Lama. Here in Jewel Park, the Dalai Lama and his family would have holidays away from the sombre, dank Potala and its ritualised existence. Open-air performances of Tibetan operas were a summertime highlight. A travelling all-male troupe performed three days annually for the Dala Lama to pay their tax.

No less a highlight for Lhasa people were the Dalai Lama's processions to and from Norbulingka, at start and finish of summer, accompanied by monks, music and banners, when the entire population would line the road. Although Jewel Park has been renamed People's Park, Tibetans always had access to the outer gardens. Only the inner gardens behind the yellow wall, adjacent to the

Dalai Lama's household quarters, were closed to the public. In this inner garden the present Dalai Lama planted hyacinth and tulip bulbs imported for him by the British Resident.

Chandra Das, nearing Lhasa in 1881, wrote: 'Beyond a high sand embankment on our left was the park and palace of Norbu linga, and the beautiful grove of Kemal *tsal,* in the midst of which stands the palace of Lhalu, the father of the last Dalai lama'. He was referring to the Twelfth Dalai Lama, who died aged twenty in 1876. Das never visited Norbulingka, and just as well for those who ran the household. In 1879, on his first journey into Tibet, he stayed six months at Tashilhunpo monastery in Shigatse. He was the guest of a man the British deemed the prime minister of Tibet, a high lama scholar in the Panchen Lama's court who assisted Das in collecting and studying Sanskrit and Tibetan works from the monastery library. The editor of Das's journals, the Honourable W.W. Rockhill, comments:

> Not the least valuable result of this journey was, however, the friendly relations which the traveller was able to establish with the liberal and powerful Prime Minister, who, deeply interested in western civilization and its wonderful discoveries, of which he had learned much from the mouth of Sarat Chandra, requested him to come back again to Tashilhunpo, to instruct him further in the wonders of the west. (Das, *Journey to Lhasa and Central Tibet* 1902, 1970 reprint, p. xii)

It was a while before the Tibetan government realised Das spied and surveyed for the British, interested though he was in all things Tibetan. Thereupon Das's kind friend paid with his life for taking an interest in the wonders of the West. The man Das called 'the minister' in his journal was the Minister of Temporal Affairs of Tsang — the province where Tashilhunpo is situated. His name was Phendi Khangsar.

When, sixty-seven years later, the Italian scholar Giuseppe Tucci was officially received at Norbulingka to meet the fourteen-year-old Dalai Lama, he refers to the case:

> First to meet us was the Gronyerchenpo, His Holiness' chamberlain of the private household. He descended from one of the most noted families of the Gyantse area, the Palhas, most of whose goods were seized and most of whose members were executed towards the end of the last century because they had received and favoured Sarat Chandra Das, who was clandestinely touring Tibet at the time with a view to collecting facts for the *Geographic Survey.* (Tucci, *To Lhasa and Beyond,* 1987 reprint, p. 105)

Gyantse lies only a few hours horse gallop from Shigatse. The Palhas would have extended their hospitality at the same time, as did the minister, who may have been related. Cruel punishments like these were handed down for friendships with foreigners if they were not who they pretended to be. Yet a descendant of an executed noble once again fills one of the highest offices in the land. Compensation? Or was it expedient to keep an eye on families with foreign connections by having them at court?

Kawaguchi spent years lobbying for the release of his Lhasa friends incarcerated when it leaked out he was not the Chinese monk he'd pretended to be. Tibet's isolation policy, sometimes claimed to have been forced upon it by the Chinese who feared foreign influence in a neighbouring country, lured adventurous characters trying to enter in disguise. But many Tibetans were genuinely interested in foreigners and associated with them at great risk.

As they do today.

But some visitors were welcomed. Giuseppe Tucci repeatedly gained permission to do research in Tibet during the thirties and forties. He met the Dalai Lama and high officials, while other scholars must have been vainly knocking. Amaury de Riencourt was allowed to journey alone on horseback to Lhasa. Did some who penetrated forbidden Tibet have secret diplomatic links with the Lhasa government? Was that government becoming increasingly uncomfortable about its position between China, the USSR and British India — or were these visitors able to suggest that they represented foreign governments or influential, powerful interests in the outside world? Tucci mentions how he spent much time at Drepung monastery arguing with abbots, presumably about Buddhist doctrine. He said it was a test 'to ascertain whether I was not masquerading in borrowed plumes'. Although allowed access as a scholar, he was not wholly trusted.

Visiting Norbulingka, Tucci witnessed an ancient custom. In the throne-room a noble bent down before the Dalai Lama, drew his bowl from the folds of his robe and a monk poured tea into it. He raised the bowl up to the Dalai Lama, drank the contents, placed his hat on the ground and kneeled again:

> It was the survival of an ancient rite, when the officials had to taste in turn the food destined to the Dalai Lama in order to ascertain that it was not poisoned. In spite of this precautionary measure, after the first conquest of Tibet at the hands of the Chinese nearly all Dalai Lamas died inexplicably and at a very young age. (Tucci, *To Lhasa and Beyond*, 1987 reprint, p. 113)

Presumably the nobles gave no advance warning by dropping dead in front of these child Dalai Lamas. Either they were accomplices or other means of poisoning were resorted to.

Court physicians were often blamed when a Dalai Lama died, as much because they might have been implicated as for being a convenient scapegoat to cover up for the real poisoners. Yet foreigner Kawaguchi, who had herbal knowledge, was invited to administer to the Thirteenth Dalai Lama at Norbulingka. He nervously drank tea with the Dalai Lama, his physician and monk officials, hoping the ruler would not address him in Chinese, which the Great Thirteenth could speak but Chinese-disguised Kawaguchi could not.

But none of these encounters took place in what is now the main attraction at Norbulingka. A steady stream of Tibetans comes to see the Fourteenth Dalai Lama's summer palace, *chubas* hanging from belts around their hips or off one shoulder with one sleeve empty; youngsters in Chinese clothes. Some piggyback babies. The women stand out for wearing traditional dress, red wool woven into long plaits. To the yellow inner wall, through a gateway with three gilded roofs. Red doors with yellow hinges carry stickers with a message in Chinese and a picture of a saluting People's Armed Policeman. One imagines it says: 'We are here to protect China's heritage. Report any irregularities to your friendly PAP officer'.

In the inner garden the paved walkway is the original, edged with a low mud-brick wall. Birches stand thick like sentinels lining a short avenue opening up to the Dalai Lama's garden beds of massed pink and white dahlias. Lotus ponds glimmer in the sunlight. Climbing stairs to the Dalai Lama's quarters, I imagine robes and processions. No photographs allowed.

There is an Indian atmosphere here. It may be the use of space. Eight superb enamelled glass spheres, hanging from chains over the landing, may have come from Kashmir. Light hues and finely painted lines remind you of the Taj Mahal. No trace of the communist slogans and Mao portraits that covered the walls in the sixties. The crowd fills the suite of rooms from wall to wall. We shuffle in unison through meditation room, bedroom, sitting room. The sitting room walls are covered entirely with stunning murals depicting thirteen hundred years of Tibet's history. An old monk tells the stories. People cluster around him, drinking his words. This history is not taught at Tibetan schools.

Suddenly an old woman in a patched *chuba* comes charging through the rooms spinning a prayer wheel, wailing at the top of her thin piercing voice, hot tears streaming down wrinkled cheeks. The crowd parts to give her passage. I observe her passing, transfixed. Faces turn stony. Such public expression of wordless sorrow is as far as Tibetans can let themselves go before being arrested. The woman's wailing laments a beloved's absence keenly felt, here, where he would live but for China's 'liberation' of Tibet. Her voice echoes across the landing, cutting hearts. What can a regime do against a woman crying hot tears?

The yellow brocade sofa is roped off, but people make obeisance to the spot where the Dalai Lama used to sit. His portrait smiles at them from his seat. They bow touching the rope with their foreheads, throw money at the portrait. The heap of small banknotes almost tops the sofa's back. As if they are paying his fare to come home.

Behind us, some tourists get the Chinese history of this palace from a pretty Chinese tourist guide. 'This palace was finished in 1956 and the Dalai Lama only used it for three years.' Her voice expresses slight contempt at such extravagant abandonment. You can only assume she hasn't been told of the threats, the flight, the shelling, the uprising and subsequent desecration, nor about the removal of Norbulingka's cultural treasures to China. She is so young. All she needs to know to do her job is that the Cultural Revolution was a bad mistake by the Gang of Four, but that all damage is now being repaired.

The bedroom and meditation room are small and functional, with English club furniture, 1930s radio, and a sublime silk appliqué hanging that escaped the looting, depicting Atisha with two *bodhisattvas* .

In a small inner courtyard, open to the sky, the Dalai Lama's mother used to like sunning herself. The walls are a warm yellow above a metre-high frieze of red, topped with two bands of blue. Doors in primary colours and delicate Taj flowers on cream panels. Elaborately patterned architraves frame a symphony of plain wood and honest paint. Not the gold and marble of Chinese hotels, but the craftsmanship of folk artisans.

The Great Mother's apartment appears sombre in comparison, its novelty a bathroom with British plumbing. In the tiny sitting room you imagine her sipping butter tea while listening to her children play. The Great Mother bore seventeen children — fewer than half survived childhood. Of these, three were found to be incarnate lamas, one of them the highest in the land. Fond anecdotes exist about this shy woman, model of common sense, who fled into exile with the Dalai Lama. Her courtyard still has the feel of a quiet woman's private place of solitude.

Now a young monk sells souvenirs here: postcards, *bodhisattva* buttons, a few handcrafts and books. I buy a pretty little box of yak horn and brass, looking like a miniature stupa. A pin with a strange elongated symbol attracts the interest of Tibetan onlookers. Later I learn it is the Kalachakra *mantra*.

Lastly we enter the throne room to have our breath taken away by murals so elaborate that the eyes refuse to take in the details. It's called fresco fatigue. Here is the Fourteenth Dalai Lama's life until 1959, with tutors, officials, and ambassadors, all pictured on the walls.

Centrally stands the carved golden throne, one and a half metres high. It definitely lacks family atmosphere. Two uniformed Chinese men enter, caps off and looking furtively around before skirting us tourists and leaving hastily through the garden door. Unable to absorb more history, we also move into the sunlight to wait for Jason, who just found another knowledgeable monk to talk to until the yaks come home.

Later we walk through lovely gardens to another courtyard where the *gompa* stands. On its roof two ferocious dingo-like guard dogs snap and bark at anyone daring to come close. In the portal Chinese traders sell Tibetan artefacts. 'True *thangka*!' one offers. From the *gompa*? The *gompa* itself is closed.

Around these rear courtyards buildings are in disrepair, broken walls, sagging doors devoid of paint. One ancient tree clings to life in a quiet flagstone yard, its trunk mostly hollow, symbolising modern Tibet. Remnants of a wooden cart with shafts. A rusty bicycle, spade, brooms and washing line complete the picture of decay. *Hidden Tibet* shows a photograph of a Norbulingka courtyard after the Cultural Revolution, filled to the top of the verandah posts with flattened images, pillars, metals, wooden beams and rubble. That mood of destruction still lingers. What repairs we see on subsidiary buildings seem less than delicate. One monk remarked that all the master painters have left Tibet and restoration is carried out by people learning the craft anew.

We leave the inner gardens, crossing a park with ancillary buildings and houses lining narrow lanes, creating a village atmosphere. Grass and weeds grow lustily on doorway architraves. Shutters hang by single hinges, some windows are boarded up. One low structure, hung with the same white and blue curtains seen on the Jokhang roof, carries a red banner declaring 'restaurant' but the place is closed. A second red banner stretching along the facade reads in hastily scrawled black letters: 'THE VISIT KNOWS ABOUT TIBET LAND AND PEOPLE'. A cry through a tunnel, just unfurled by patriots mingling with the crowd? The scrambled message has an urgent undertone.

Outside the grand gateway the tiniest black and white puppy dog I ever saw sits forlornly in the street. It poses politely for the camera, quietly whining for its owners, divided over several groups. Undecided whom to follow, the pup embodies the fate of the Tibetan peasant. Whom to follow; what to believe; to flee or to stay put until the wheel comes round again and things perhaps return to normal?

That evening over dinner Donna tells how she thought she was about to witness the outbreak of revolution in the Norbulingka, when two Chinese soldiers entered the Dalai Lama's crowded sitting room where she had lingered. Suddenly two young Tibetan men spotted the Chinese, walked up to them, shook them by the shoulders, spat in their faces and spoke words which made the soldiers turn on their heels and leave immediately. We imagined what they would have said in that sacred space. Donna had stood there trembling, expecting imminent arrests. But neither she nor we saw subsequent turmoil. Such acts of defiance and resistance must be taking place all the time, especially in crowded places.

No wonder Chinese soldiers always walk in pairs. No wonder they seem apprehensive of burly Tibetans bearing grudges on their sleeves. Later I remember the two who scuttled through the throne room and how rosy their faces looked, as if they had rubbed them.

Harry, the solo American tour group, joins us for dinner in a mood of elation. Today he visited the Tibetan Medical School, where he was so struck by a quotation that he copied it. Pulling a piece of paper from his pocket, he irons it out with his hand on the table and reads: 'What a man is today comes from his thoughts of yesterday and his thoughts of today will shape his life of tomorrow. A man's life is the creation of his thoughts'. Joy of discovery rings in his voice. 'That's by Dhammapada', he says, stretching every syllable. 'And I want to know who he is!'

Jason and I recognise the opening verse of the Dhammapada, the collected sayings of the Buddha. We assure Harry he can buy it in any good bookshop in the States. This amazes him, but does not in the least dampen his enthusiasm for the wonderful insight he gained today in Lhasa, Tibet. In fact, a non-sexist translation speaks of 'What we are today ...' including the other half of humanity without violating the original Pali.

I go to bed surrounded by PLA-issue oxygen bags, courtesy of the hotel, fetched by caring Nicola. I hesitate to take my potions. The Panchen Lama's doctor's horse pills have brought no improvement. They upset my innards. I decide to discontinue the pellets and rely on nature taking its course.

Tomorrow we go to Ganden, about eighty kilometres north-east of Lhasa and the first Gelukpa monastery, also the first of Tsongkhapa's three monasteries around Lhasa. But Peggy must rest in the hotel on doctor's orders. It's like leaving one of the family behind on a long-anticipated outing.

Ganden,
Phoenix among Monasteries

The eastern route along the *Kyi chu* provides spectacular views. For many kilometres tall aspen line both sides of the road, each surrounded by a dry-stone wall like a village well, with 'breathing holes' at ground level. These guards protected the young trees from grazers, bicyclists, trucks, peeing travellers and the wind. Now they are the biggest trees I have seen in central Tibet outside Norbulingka, reaching six to eight metres.

In the fields villagers gather in the last crops and plough the land for the first application of manure. No time to lose with seeding next spring if two crops are to ripen in the short growing season. We pass a Chinese-run commune — ramshackle shopfront appearance, high compound walls. A Chinese woman carries a bundle of straw as big as herself. But most field workers are Tibetans. I'd rather walk behind a yak than roar along on a tractor, but few modern farmers would look upon this rural scene without pity. Yet for Tibetans a day in the fields between the mountains seems to give rise to more laughter than modern farmers muster on their techno-steeds. There is song in the air.

The day has an opalescent quality. It sits light as hoar frost on the tops of upturned clods of earth, shimmers down the slopes of mountains and shimmies up tree trunks. A perfectly blue sky reflects in the river, silver light enamels the water. The gold of autumn willows waves from copses on the riverflats. I sink myself into the beauty of the landscape to ignore my breathing. You have to die one day. To expire here and merge with the silvery blue river would be a greater reward for living than I deserve. Next time I take out a travel insurance I must add a rider: 'Don't fly my body home — I was a traveller. Let me go to dust where I stopped breathing'.

I am rocked out of my reverie by the sight of a *dzong* on a steep outcrop: Takste Dzong, formerly Dechen Dzong, an ancient ruler's seat. 'Stop the bus!' I squeak. The patient driver has come to fear my voice. I ask for more photo stops than anyone, but the others often avail themselves of the opportunity.

A *dzong* is usually on top of an outcrop. From it the *dzongpo* or local governor, or region's ruler, could see all comings and goings. He inspected sojourners' papers and for permit travellers arranged fresh horses, yaks, porters, guides and provisions from the village. For the villagers this was a form of taxation, in return for which they could claim shelter in the *dzong* during hostilities. Probably not a terrific deal, but where is taxation a good deal for the common people?

Chandra Das explains the place of the *dzong* in the complex government of a large country without modern telecommunications or transport, quoting from a handbook for *dzongpo,* entitled *Serab Dongbu* ('Bits of Wisdom'). The rules laid down by Tibet's government for its minions aimed to restrain familiar vices still with us, but were ahead of their time in warning the boss not to harass females in his dominion:

> Impartiality should be shown to all classes alike, to great and small, to lamas and to laymen. Uninfluenced by gratuities or the fear of criticism, the Djongpon should administer perfect justice ... Villages, houses and inhabitants should be counted and inspected yearly, and the numbers compared with those of preceding years ... Servants and labourers of the Djong should not be employed by him at his private work ... He should not allow the public lands to be encroached upon, nor should tenants on them be taken away by landholders ... No women should be allowed to loiter about the Djong, and the Djongpon should carefully refrain from any flirtation. He should see to facilitating the courier service, and he should see that no-one receives supplies for their journey unless they are bearers of passports *(lam-yig).* Frontier or foreign traders who cannot show a passport should be held, and any information he may obtain of affairs in other quarters should be transmitted to Lhasa. (Das, *Journey to Lhasa and Central Tibet,* 1970 reprint, p. 177)

A civilised and sophisticated government indeed. Adds Mr Rockhill in a footnote:

> Of course most of the Djongpon only attend to a very few of these duties. They squeeze the people under them, exact as much service as possible, and, together with the lamas, get everything they can out of them, and only stop when their exactions appear likely to cause serious trouble. (Das, *Journey to Lhasa and Central Tibet*, 1970 reprint, p. 177).

The peasants probably did all right out of their grain tax to monasteries, since these acted as granaries. Grain keeps for many years at high altitudes. In times of crop failure, barley was distributed to the villagers and no-one would starve. Tibet with its barely arable climate, knew no famines. The histories do not tell how mice and rats were prevented from consuming stored grain, since killing is forbidden in monasteries. Presumably they ate some of the surplus.

Warmer areas grow wheat as well as barley. Much of Tibet's grain crop now goes to China or feeds the Chinese army, administrators and 'advisers' in Tibet. In the new macro-economic system it is unlikely that local monasteries will be allowed to store grain years ahead to cater for local crop failures. If crops fail, food will have to come from China. But if crops fail in Tibet, they are likely to also fail in China due to wider weather patterns and it is anyone's guess who gets fed first.

Takste Dzong is a vast ruined castle with square corner towers. A small village straggles down the slope. Here our Australian Rimpoche made his first overnight stop on his flight from Sera in March 1959. 'It was deserted', he told me in whispers. 'I rested in the *dzong* that night, but there was no-one there'. Vague about his freedom road, he only remembered passing Samyé monastery. He probably rode from Takste to Ganden, crossed the pass and turned south, as experienced trekkers do today for the four-day hike from Ganden to Samyé. En route he gathered thirty of his students and led them to freedom.

On the right, set back, another building tops an outcrop. It could be Tselgung, a Kargyu monastery dating from 1175 — some books call it Gungtang. None of our guides is sure. Mapping is still an unfinished adventure in Tibet, although detailed maps exist in the minds of the people. We have the company of a retired guide, coming along to see Ganden. Perhaps our young guide wants to share the burden of our sometimes reckless conversations with a more experienced person, before deciding whether we fall short of proper socialist tourism. The elderly Tibetan engages Jason in spirited conversation, but he is less outspoken today. Me, I feel hackles rising.

These fortifications evoke the atmosphere of old Tibet as nothing else can. To build on such heights people had to use materials at hand. There were only riding paths in a country where wheels were used exclusively for prayer. Building materials from afar had to be hauled up on the backs of yaks and humans. From all accounts, *dzong* and monasteries had their share of wooden beams, brass doorknobs and teapots, gilded statues, carved furniture, shrines, carpets, cushions and *thangka*, all the material expressions of civilised life and monastic ritual. In a timeless land, all is possible.

This continues to astonish me. Not because I cannot visualise that people should be able to build such enormous dwellings without any of the half-million dollar machinery modern builders need to put a five-storey flat on a level block of land, but because today's builders would take one look at these outcrops and refuse to tender without a semitrailer access road. Modern builders could never build Ganden. But the imagination of Tibetans achieved it in the fifteenth century and again today.

Ganden gained more fame for its total destruction by Chinese mortars in 1959 than it enjoyed before. Although named as one of the three Geluk monasteries near Lhasa, it took a full day on horseback to reach it. Early travellers mentioned Ganden, but few actually went there, whereas Sera and Drepung were frequently visited.

We now pass the dark side of that mountain, untouched by the sun's rays.

Along one of the saddles can be seen the jagged remains of Ganden's highest walls, etched against blue sky. We are quietly awed. Like so many accusing fingers, those ruins are a terrible sight. How to comprehend the fanatic rage that inspired the destruction of a mountain city so close to the heavens? But the Chinese would have felt threatened by any fortifications overlooking their invasion routes. Moreover, Ganden is Tsongkhapa's place, the reformer who started the Gelukpa school of Buddhism to which the Dalai Lamas belong.

It is tempting to see a mountain-top city as impregnable, yet Ganden is extremely vulnerable. Its only feasible food supply route is through the valley below. When in 1871 the then treasurer of Ganden, Palden Dondup, set to scheming against the Dalai Lama, government troops cut off the supply line, whereupon the monastery surrendered. Palden Dondup fled, committing suicide when pursued, assuming his end was near. He had been a harsh though colourful figure. His procurements of funds for the monastery were so successful that they lasted until 1949. Meat being part of the monastic diet, he always kept a freshly skinned animal hide by the door of his office. He threatened to have anyone who incurred his displeasure sewn up in the skin and thrown in the river. This he reputedly did more than once. Although treasurer, he was virtually illiterate and perhaps benefited little from spiritual teachings at Ganden. But in monasteries everywhere the brightest novices proceed to scholarship and *Geshe* degrees, the rest train as administrators, artisans, cooks, builders, police monks or in any other capacity useful to the monastic community.

Although in 1871 Lhasa troops, with the help of hostile Sera monks, burnt and looted several Ganden buildings, the government later restored them. In this century Ganden worked for the return from exile of the Thirteenth Dalai Lama and he gave the monastery part of a district as reward for loyalty. Yet, with such a checkered history, nothing that ever befell Ganden reached the heights of terror and depravity of its destruction during the Cultural Revolution.

The local Tibetan population was led on by the Red Guards to dismantle what was left after the Chinese had removed all valuables. They took ancient wooden pillars, metal objects, shrines, book covers, kitchenware and musical instruments, but preserved some sacred items. Margaret Williamson had seen Tsongkhapa's gold and silver *chörten* containing his embalmed body, encrusted with turquoise, onyx, amber, coral and other semi-precious stones. Stephen Batchelor writes that when the Red Guards destroyed it, they found the body in perfect condition, hair and nails still growing. Incredibly, they then subjected Tsongkhapa's body to *tsamzing,* self-confession of crimes against socialism, before they burnt his body. Stupas of his closest disciples, Kedrub Je and Gyeltseb Je, often flanking him in *thangkas*, were also destroyed.

News of Ganden's destruction did not reach the world until a delegation from the Dalai Lama visited Tibet in 1979, the year China opened before it slowly closed again, finding the world too inquisitive. Accompanied by 7000 Tibetans, the delegation cried at the horrid sight and held a prayer service for Tibet's revival. After this event many Tibetans were arrested by Chinese authorities.

Turning away from the silver river we enter the valley that gathers outrunners from two brown mountains. Past the only village a narrow steep track climbs to the right, switching back sharply and repeatedly. It leads to the rear of the mountain that carries Ganden's peaked ruins. But here, beneath enormous rock folds, villagers and red-robed monks work between the boulders. In a landscape containing nothing man-made, they fashion things out of materials the earth provides, that will be of use in their dwellings wrought from the same. And whereas cars and buses have to grind up the switchback track, figures in flying robes clamber up the sheer mountainside, making a beeline for the monastery, carrying a load on their backs, arriving before us.

Our driver skilfully negotiates the hairpin bends, but halfway needs a cigarette. From here the sights are spectacular wherever you turn. Behind us the broad valley shimmers barley gold, patched with grassy floodplains where yaks graze. Beyond, the silver river streams are dotted with yellow willows jutting into the water. The sky azure, clouds puffy white and the mountains arranged in thousands of sepia pleats, grey-blue shadows down dark flanks. Ahead, a snow-covered peak shaped not unlike Chomolongma, rising above deep green slopes. With Ganden still hidden from sight, here is a picture of tranquillity.

Near the snowline the pass leads to Samyé. The Williamsons rode horses from there to Ganden, through fields of delphiniums, clematis, asters and other wildflowers the world first obtained from Tibet. High on a dark slope dotted with green bushes is Tsongkhapa's hermitage. Around our feet white alpine flowers grow between rocks and crags. I recognise a medicinal herb. Ganden had a medical school. In the middle of this grand design lies that little village. Above, still invisible, the monastic city.

When it does come into sight after a half-hour bus crawl, we fall silent. Charles and Jill Hadfield wrote in 1986:

> But the most shocking sight is Ganden ... Not a roof beam nor a wall was left intact, and our first horrified reaction to the ruins was that the monastery must have been bombed from the air, so total was the devastation. We later learnt that after the buildings had been dynamited, pickaxes and sledge hammers were used and most of the wooden beams, planks and pillars were taken down into the valley to be used for building elsewhere. It now looks like Warsaw at the end of the Second World War, really a most terrible, saddening sight ... Ganden today is a blend of past nightmares and future dreams. (Hadfield, *A Winter in Tibet,* 1988, p. 45)

And so it is still seven years later. Zhu Li wrote not an apology but a communist explanation in 1981, claiming that during the Cultural Revolution the Party's policies on religion and nationalities were trampled underfoot and monasteries and temples damaged or completely destroyed as a consequence. He names Ganden and writes that a lot of work is to be done to correct these mistakes.

From a vast ring of ruins rise pale pink new buildings around the giant red tomb of Tsongkhapa. Despite ten years of rebuilding by local Tibetans with the aid of a truck, there are vastly more ruins in this high amphitheatre than buildings restored. The Chinese authorities alternatively prohibit and support Tibetan volunteer efforts to restore Ganden. The Hadfields, counting ten restored buildings, two more than a year earlier, estimated Ganden would be rebuilt by 2006. Today I count about nineteen restored buildings, large and small. Ganden is rising from its ruins.

Ironically and yet not, Ganden means 'Pure Land' or 'Joyful Paradise', named by Tsongkhapa in 1409 when he built seventy buildings in the first year and filled them with 'costly images'. Tsongkhapa was born in Amdo in 1357. At age three he was discovered by a learned lama through dreams and oracles, and taken into the monastic life. For twenty years he studied the teachings of all Buddhist schools in existence. At barely thirty, he was an acknowledged scholar and spiritual master and soon after went into retreat for seven years, realising the teaching of Manjusri — the Wisdom Buddha — of cutting through ignorance with the sword of knowledge, a meagre description of all he realised. Emerging enlightened, he set about restoring and reforming Tibetan Buddhism, which had fallen into sloth and discord. He inaugurated *Monlam*, the Great Prayer Festival, celebrated annually at Tibetan New Year. Tsongkhapa founded his school on strong moral principles and discipline. This combination evidently appealed to Tibetans, for after founding Ganden, Sera followed in 1419 and Tashilhunpo in 1447. Tsongkhapa was also instrumental in the building of Drepung.

The abbot of Ganden was never a reincarnate child lama, as in other monasteries, but a scholar chosen from the best at Sera, Drepung and Ganden. So important was the Ganden Rimpoche, being the head of the powerful Gelukpa school, that he frequently became the regent of all Tibet, supervising the education of young Dalai Lamas — yet another political reason for the legacy of Chinese fury that stares down on us today.

The air is rarefied. Ganden lies at about 4750 metres or 14 000 feet, 2000 feet higher than Lhasa. Hence I decide on contemplation rather than circumambulation. But what a place to contemplate! Would that I could never sit anywhere else to clear my mind. Peace and beauty live between these ruins.

But first I walk with the group in the wake of three elderly monks, down the main lane, past a little shop and debating court, along walls dripping with woolly seedheads of *Clematis orientalis,* by a gleaming white stupa and to the founder's tomb. The new stupa contains the remains of scriptures, a few remnants of Tsongkhapa's skull and his carefully scraped up ashes.

Sensing the dedication that pervades Ganden's atmosphere, I become tearful. A young monk carries above his head — to show respect — a volume of scriptures wrapped in yellow cloth. Jason asks him about the book and is happily surprised to learn it's a copy of the very text he is studying. For a moment he seems torn between Ganden where the text lives and his home desk where his work on the text waits.

I am beginning to lose track of where I walk, want to sit and just be. Part of my brain tries to tell the other part I am sick. Life is impermanent, death a reality. I may not survive this journey. Shuffling through temples, I stop in front of a magnificent mural of the wheel of life in pictorial space filled with floating *bodhisattvas* and flanked by two bronze prayer drums. With a last effort I turn the drums, their prayers spinning to the heavens. By the steps an incense burner, above it a red fire extinguisher. Comic vision still functioning.

Restorations are visibly done on a shoestring. All roof decorations appear to be cut out of tin plate with tinsnips. Single coats of paint cover recycled wood. Salvaged bins and containers everywhere. On a rickety table in a sunny courtyard, fifty rinsed metal bowls rest one upon the other, drying. In old tins and pots grow lovingly tended marigolds, dahlias and shrubs.

The government of the Tibet Autonomous Region did not give monks permission to return after Ganden was destroyed. Yet they did. At first individuals and small groups of the original 3300 came back, many aging — 500 monks live and work here, many young boys who never knew Ganden in its fullness. Two hundred monks study and receive teachings.

At a junction the path rises steeply. I assure the group I'd better wait here until they return. I sit down on stone steps — tomb or temple. Passing monks greet me with open smiles, eyes taking in the appearance of yet another foreigner come to see the miracle of Ganden.

The poverty of Ganden passes by me. People in threadbare robes, possibly woven before the Chinese invasion, are picking through rubble to recycle whatever has any use left. Robes are neatly patched with new borders stitched on, many are three or four shades of faded maroon. Arms sticking out are thin and bony. No fat monks here.

Steam bellows from a door opening. Inside, the clanking of pots. Dogs lie in the sun on nearby steps. That makes it the kitchen. But the dogs' ribs stick out and all suffer mange. There can't be many leftovers here. Englishman Thomas Manning, who spent time in Lhasa in 1812, saw a city full of starving dogs gnawing on bits of hide, with dead dogs picked at by ravens. Tucci mentions dogs weren't allowed in Ganden in 1948 when he came here. Surely these dogs would try out the valley farms unless they received affection here.

Slowly two young monks, nine or ten, walk up the path bent under dented water cans on narrow backs. They carry them into the kitchen, returning minutes later, lighter, laughing. I might feel pity for their thin limbs, but if I ever saw happy children then these are. Mary Craig in *Tears of Blood: A Cry for Tibet* tells how on the day the Dalai Lama received the Nobel Prize in Oslo on 10 December 1989, Chinese soldiers were stationed at Ganden. When monks went out that morning to get milk, they were beaten with bars, clubs and belts. Yet they stayed. Still the young ones come. Still they smile, wisely, kindly. It breaks me up. Why won't the governments of the world *do* something?

I feel the need to write in my diary. A splash of water is thrown from the door and an old kitchen monk comes out for a stretch in the sun. Seeing me write, he comes over to take a look. Silently he sits beside me, watching my pen write words on paper. This is a land where writing and books are honoured, held sacred. He smiles. I smile. We watch the writing pen together. What can I write for him?

When the group returns we enter a small temple in the rocks. Here a spontaneous deity has emerged from the rock wall, paint highlighting outlines. The monk caretaker brings out the tooth of Tsongkhapa. It has healing powers and blessings are offered. A miracle, considering there was little left of Tsongkhapa's body. But this tooth was not in his tomb. It fell out shortly before his death. Because his disciples pounced on it, he placed it on the altar and after his death it was treated as a precious relic. Now, 574 years later, the tooth wrapped in bundles of grubby cloth is stuck on a wooden handle polished from centuries of handling by yak-buttered hands.

Donna pushes me forward. 'She needs it', she says. I bow before the monk and feel a slight tap on the head with Tsongkhapa's tooth. Affected by the ancient nature of the small ritual, I find a home-made *kata* in my bag to offer with a donation.

We flop down in the bus to have lunch. Several pilgrim buses have arrived after us and families are picnicking. Children come begging. We give away two-thirds of our lunch packets and when the children are gone I give a chicken leg to a starving dog at the end of the food chain.

Nicola is going to write postcards on a hillock. The group troops off to see debates and circumambulate the monastery's *lingkhor* to view the sacred places: hand and foot imprints of Tsongkhapa, deities emerging from the rocks, *chang* and milk flowing from another, *chörtens,* the spot where Tsongkhapa's mother died and his hermitage. I will stay in the bus to rest.

My eyes follow the route up. The driver sleeps. Feeling thoroughly sick I doze, but Ganden's generator starts up and noisily tears the peace to shreds. Just like home! After an hour it stops, bestowing bliss. Music and chanting washes down the hills as I doze.

I am woken by loud knocking on the door of the bus, closed against the chill breeze. A boy in skin *chuba* and felt hat, large black eyes burning in a brown face with bright red cheeks, indicates he wants food. Not a scrap of food left in the whole bus. I raise empty hands. He does not believe me. His eyes fixate me as his knuckles belabour the door. I close my eyes, feeling sick. He will go away. But he doesn't. He comes to knock at my window.

I raise empty hands. Puzzlement mixes with craving in his almond-shaped eyes. Finally the driver wakes from the din and what I least want to happen takes place. One growl of dismissal from a Chinese driver and the boy takes off.

He goes knocking on the last tourist bus. No pickings. Finally he ambles over to Nicola, sits down quietly beside her, looking at her postcards. She points things out to him and he bends over the pictures with the same total concentration that went into rapping the glass. Suddenly I recognise in him the child I once was. Ever pushing forward out of unprofitable situations into more hopeful ones, neither aggressive nor apologetic. Often hungry, but never without hope of a giant meal falling from the sky, always seeing other opportunities. There is something horribly wrong with an existence such as mine, having gone from hunger and poverty to the status of foreign tourist, yet unable to do anything for a hungry nomad boy. I grapple with it.

Shadows lengthen across the slopes. I have looked so long at Ganden that it will be imprinted on my mind until the day I die. Which could be soon. My heart races most inordinately. Deciding to fight for my life, I climb out of the bus for air, legs numb like stumps. The yaks are coming home, bells tinkling airily. On their backs they carry huge joints of freshly slaughtered yak meat. Dichotomies of a harsh environment. A few Ganden goats, giant long-haired beasts exuding powerfully rank smells, amble about butting unwary tourists. Like all animals here, they wander at will, looking too well fed considering these stripped hillsides. Monks fill containers at a huge black water tank. Powerlines are strung to some buildings, cutting incongruously across a timeless landscape.

A woman in black *chuba*, basket on her back, trips lightly along the rocky edge of the plateau, outlined against distant mountains as if she was the only person in this world. An ancient monk, grey and bent, shuffles home fingering prayer beads, patched discoloured robe wrapped close against the evening cold. He pauses in the last rays of the sun against lengthening shadows on the far mountain, as if he too inhabited this vast landscape all by himself. Such images re-occur in Tibet, whether monk on high mountain, solitary woman walking in endless valley, or a man riding a bicycle along a road beside a river where nothing reminiscent of humanity is in sight for as far as the eye can see.

The group returns, ending my contemplation. They tell of hair-raising precipices along narrow tracks, the views from the top and over the other side to the river. Nicola boards the bus and we discuss the nomad boy. 'He recognised the Potala and Norbulingka postcards', she says. 'He had been there.'

Shadows take on fantastic shapes. We are the last pilgrims to leave. At every bend we look back to Ganden, monument of Tibetan culture, now as ever. The last we see is Tsongkhapa's hermitage. Snowy peak behind us, we descend to the silver enamelled river, past the village stupa and a group of peasants fetching something amidst the rocks, past the last yak wandering home by herself along the stream lined with young willows. Again, I don't want to leave. If only my heart would quieten down and my breath stop heaving, I too could work the rocks and fields, gather and grind herbs, herd animals, carry baskets. It is so like my life on Australian hilltops that I ache simultaneously for home and for leaving the valley of Ganden.

As we descend my heart calms down. A giant headache I did not realise was there begins to lift. Barely a fit tourist and born below sea level, I should thank my stars I can travel Tibet but do my farming at lower altitudes.

In a settlement at the foot of an outcrop with ruined monastery, the bus undergoes a compulsory carwash prior to re-entering the city. We disappear under a curtain of water from scores of hoses, pumped from the river and flowing straight back into it.

The mountains change colour by the second as the sun dips. Now bluish brown, then charcoal. Yellow willows turn bright sienna and the ruins above are alabaster pink. Clouds gather, peaks disappear into their own world. People slowly walk or cycle up and down the road before the light fails completely.

In the hotel, Peggy has good news. The Chinese doctor gave her medicine for low blood pressure, saying it will fix her for going to Shigatse. I ring the doctor, as Nicola and I have low blood pressure too. Everyone is somewhat anxious about the high passes between Lhasa and Shigatse.

Dinner, so say our tickets, is served in the Hard Yak Cafe. Management moves groups from dining room to cafe to Chinese restaurant, keeping Chinese and foreign tourists separated. Today we waste a lot of what is put before us. Harry joins us and confesses that this morning, for the first time, he experienced a moment of guilt thinking of the resources he uses up. I am interested to pursue this, but as usual the conversation fizzles desultorily to other subjects. How does Harry manage to come up with some penetrating remark every evening, as if to draw us out? Is he engaging in counterespionage? Lhasa is getting to me. Or shades of childhood under the Nazi boot.

The doctor never comes. When I doze off, I smell yak butter in my hair from Tsongkhapa's blessing. My dreams take place entirely in monasteries. I have internalised a thousand times more than could possibly be recorded in a travel diary.

Drepung, Heap of Rice in an Apple Grove

Everyone has routine nosebleeds in the morning. Some Buddhist teachers used the blood from their nosebleeds to paint *thangkas*. I ring the doctor's office. He went to the wrong room last night. Now he arrives, tired and confused, looking about fifteen. He may be double that, but inspires no confidence. He was sent to Tibet by his work unit. 'Go west, young man, to Lhasa and administer to lucrative foreign tourist barbarians for the good of the Motherland.' I don't expect his impression of us is riveting either.

We explain our concerns. He says that if we have no headache, stomach trouble, cough or fever, it is alright to cross the passes. We have a bit of all these, but choose to ignore that. Nosebleeds are not mentioned. He must think us daft, since the Chinese at great cost built a low road to Shigatse to avoid the passes.

But today we visit Drepung monastery, passing by Tibetan tent slums on the river's marsh at the outskirts of Lhasa. Children play in filth and mud. Formerly Moslems used to butcher animals here for the meat market, building huts from horns and bones. In the thirties this was marshland with a profusion of waterlilies.

Drepung, meaning 'Rice Heap', is a compact white city at the foot of a steep valley formed by three mountain slopes. Peaks are shrouded in clouds this morning, but below them shines the sun. Turning in we pass the small village of Daru and a solitary house near a stupa, with windowsills full of geraniums, cosmos and marigolds. The appealing rural lane atmosphere makes me thirst to push seeds in the earth, tend plants, pick fruit. Torn forever between nomadism and a settled rural existence, humanity's prehistoric dilemma.

In a shady grove at the foot of Drepung, Lhasa people used to farewell travelling friends, sharing a picnic before parting. The road goes through a forest of low trees. Just visible is the roof of Nechung monastery, once the abode of Tibet's state oracle. Sometimes the oracle prophesised what eventuated, sometimes not. Before his death the Thirteenth Dalai Lama expressed his own vision of calamities soon to befall Tibet and turned out to be uncannily right. The oracle now practises in Dharamsala, India.

We emerge from the forest into a sunny plaza ringed by trees, at the foot of the staircase to Drepung monastery. Scores of Tibetans are feeding *tsampa* to fifty or sixty piebald dogs looking a blessed sight better than their poor kin at Ganden. Kindness to animals is religion in Tibet. A tiny monk sits by a bench of potted geraniums, taking donations. A mother lifts her baby to smell the flowers. Sweet peas, alyssum, carnations and marigolds abound.

Pilgrim buses are arriving, so we start our first climb of the day ahead of the throng. The rocky staircase hugs old sloping walls, on the left a low wall with overhanging trees, granite mountains ahead. A different kind of grandeur from the promise of Ganden. At a turn in the path an outcrop with a large portrait of Tsongkhapa on a slab of rock. Tsongkhapa and his main disciple founded Drepung in 1416. It became the largest and wealthiest of Lhasa monasteries.

At one stage Drepung housed 10 000 monks and was the domicile of the Dalai Lamas until the Fifth rebuilt the Potala. He also established the numbers of monks certain monasteries should have. Officially Drepung was to have 7700 monks, Sera 5500 and Ganden 3300, but in 1951 they respectively housed 10 000, 7000 and 5000. Drepung's highest lama would rule Lhasa for a month after Tibetan New Year, a reversal to old times when Drepung was sole ruler of the city and surrounding lands. Drepung also housed the Lhasa mint.

Drepung was the largest monastery in the world, a vastly more congenial claim than having the largest army in the world. Some think it decadent to have 10 000 monks in a monastery, studying religious scriptures and doing 'nothing useful' but making herbal medicine and performing rituals. Overlooking the fact that monasteries were Tibet's universities, some don't turn a hair at their own country maintaining a small army of 100 000 men in barracks, studying detailed manuals of how to kill, maim and put out of action their fellow humans.

Drepung had 6000 monks at the start of 1959, only a handful at year's end. Nine Drepung monks were arrested in 1989 for having translated into Tibetan the Universal Declaration of Human Rights, because they felt it addressed Tibet's situation. They also produced a draft constitution for a future free Tibet, combining Buddhist ideals with democratic principles. Ngawang Phulchung, who led 'The Drepung Nine', was sentenced to nineteen years in prison and became an Amnesty International prisoner of conscience in 1990. No democratic country stood up for him.

Today about 500 monks inhabit Drepung, work on the monastery's farm and sell apples from their orchard in town, to survive as monks and raise money for restoration. About one hundred monks are allowed to receive teachings. The monastery maintained five colleges accommodating monks in *khamtsen* according to province or country of origin. Monks came from as far as Western China, Siberia, Mongolia, Bhuryattia, India and Nepal. But in Loseling college almost 70 per cent of monks from Kham filled the most powerful *khamtsen*, according to the historian Melvyn Goldstein's informer, reflecting the demography of many monasteries.

Tucci said Drepung had more than fifty Rimpoches, learned incarnate lamas, who all fled to India in 1959 in the wake of the Dalai Lama. Also fleeing were 216 Loseling college monks, who re-established Drepung in Karnataka state, southern India, where they now teach 1500 monks, many recent escapees. Kham monks had been born under Chinese rule before, therefore many fled the country.

Tibetan architecture scarcely having changed for twelve centuries, buildings have an antique atmosphere. Drepung was partially destroyed and resurrected four times in six centuries. A 'mere' 40 per cent was destroyed in the Cultural Revolution. Peeling paint seems more attractive when a building is pre-Cultural Revolution. But the windows of four-storey Ganden Photrang are painted canary yellow, in black frames on white walls. There are gold emblems against maroon on top floor walls, golden stupas and pillars on the roof, a stunning example of Tibetan style. This was the Dalai Lamas' palace. Not capable of stairs today, I can't come to see the paintings inside. I'm having an outdoors day. There is plenty to see.

Any sizeable smooth boulder carries the mantra OM MANI PADME HUM in fine Tibetan lettering, painted in the five colours. There are deities on the rocks and a wonderful meditation cave with a spontaneously arisen Manjusri wielding the sword of knowledge that cuts through ignorance. A tiny Green Tara is actually in the process of emerging under a rock overhang. There's an outline for a mural in black on white, yet to be painted. I spin every brass prayer drum I meet, saying the *mani*.

Drepung's setting appears more dramatic when you are here than it does from a distance. A backdrop of massive black rocks is menacingly close. Yet curving lanes, alleyways and staircases cut into the rocks give the place an enclosed medieval atmosphere. Here and there footbridges span the air, connecting buildings. Green shoots sprout from walls. Views across the orchard and Lhasa to the mountains beyond are grand. I wander through courtyards overgrown with weeds and signs of domesticity: flour sacks, tools, wood stacks. Until the group turns up.

We meet at a blank wall in a gateway, a startling sight in a land where no wall is left unadorned. The wall is being repaired, cracks plastered and underneath ochre deities are visible, possibly painted out during the Cultural Revolution.

The kitchen of Drepung is the mother of all kitchens. It looks like a giant cave hewn out of the mountain, a deception caused by dim light and black corners. Colossal cast-iron ovens, imported from India, built in with bricks, flanked by blackened pots and steps to put pots down, or for kitchen monks to warm themselves. These ovens and monstrous cooking pots were carried over the Himalayas on the backs of yaks and men!

On the walls hang polished brass pans and on a wire twenty-four huge brass ladles. Gigantic tea churns lean against a wall. Thirty smaller wood and brass churns stand on shelves with half-a-dozen copper teapots. The amount of tea brewed here for 10 000 monks is incalculable, considering that Tibetans like to drink as many as forty cups of butter tea per day. Yet Goldstein explains that monks only received tea and some food during long daily prayer sessions, but otherwise had to prepare their own meals.

The catering is much reduced. Two young men in civvies chop red meat into fine slivers. A few kilos to feed 400. These young fellows are waiting to become monks. They won't be able to wear robes until two monks in the quota die or leave, thus have the Chinese authorities decreed. Meanwhile they work here so as not to miss their opportunity, taking part in monastic activities when allowed. They are so pleased that Jason speaks Tibetan.

A monklet in robes comes to listen. Jason asks his age. He turns out to be twelve. Does he get teaching? O yes, he does. Can he recite for Jason what he is presently learning? The small face under the cleanshaven skull glows, the clear high voice assumes volume and out rolls the formal recitation of a text. How proudly he shows his scholarship to a scholar from abroad. The kitchen monks look on fondly. We leave with praise and thanks.

I do breathlessly clamber to the wonderful temples where Tsongkhapa's 600-year-old collected works are kept. His astounding output lines several walls, some of it probably recorded by scribes as he lectured, carved into woodblocks, then printed for teaching. The stored original of one book makes a formidable pile of woodblocks, as each page is a separately carved block. It is said of some of his works that they encompass all there is to learn of Buddhism.

On a first-floor roof is a small bookroom where volumes are kept behind glass by a grey old monk with happy, lively eyes. He restores old works, handling his treasures lovingly. Tibetan books are loose-leaved between wooden covers, held with cotton tape. Many volumes here are swaddled in brocade with steel clasps or have carvings of tiny hands and faces on the covers. In a glass case a famous text is laid out, page after page, pure gold lettering on black. You shiver at the fragility of it, at the fragility of the keeper, at the thought that a hostile regime missed destroying this magnificent work of calligraphy but still threatens the very teachings it contains.

In Drepung, more statues line the walls than anywhere we have been so far: buddhas, deities, *bodhisattvas,* teachers, sages, abbots, Dalai Lamas and famous disciples. A great image of Maitreya, the Buddha to come, oversees the main assembly hall. Here Jason meets an old monk keen to tell his story. He involuntarily lived away from Drepung for twenty years, working the land in his village. Yet he always thought of the monastic life he had been expelled from. Now he is back, a happy, fulfilled man.

Critics of Tibet's monastic establishments never considered what alternatives poor countries have. Monastic life, even if occasionally militant, keeps up a moral standard, whereas standing armies naturally look for combat. Both live off the land. Every country has to find its own solution of what to do with surplus young men. But Western criticism levelled against Tibet's monasticism probably arose from disenchantment with Christianity. Such transferral of one culture's disillusion to a land minding its own business contributed to genocide in its ripple effects. Liberal-minded people agreed with the communists that monasticism bleeds a country dry. This was one reason why Western powers took no notice when China destroyed some 6000 monasteries, killing a million people and most wildlife as they spread across Tibet. It wasn't that the world couldn't have known. Governments didn't *want* to know what happened in Tibet. And still don't.

In the fifties and sixties many Western academics were still happy little Marxists on high incomes, preaching revolution. In their eyes Tibet was feudal, a European label that fitted oddly but one providing a glib excuse to let fate take its course. It was said Tibet was medieval, as if that was wrong. Yet the Thirteenth Dalai Lama encouraged modernity to enter Tibet: electricity, radio communications, English education and modern weaponry for Tibet's tiny army. More modern goods reached Tibetans than Australian Aborigines. The Fourteenth Dalai Lama was keen to import technological inventions to improve life in Tibet. He would have continued the opening up of Tibet had it been left unmolested. In exile, he has democratised the Tibetan government and lives a modern life, albeit it as a 'simple Buddhist monk'.

Imagine a Tibet still intact, without Chinese 'modernisations', using solar power and wheeled transport. Imagine an independent Tibet, communicating electronically with other countries, yet remaining the world's last spiritual bastion where plain dwellers might periodically seek refuge. A *Star Trek* scenario? But for Chinese 'liberation', this could have been today's Tibet. The Dalai Lama would have fostered education and health as he does for his refugees. Indeed, the Panchen Lama vigorously fostered education in Tibet.

Jason, translating what the monks tell him, attracts a following of other tourists, and Tibetan pilgrims crowd around to hear the Western man speak their language. When a monk explains eight images on pillars as the most important *bodhisattvas*, three nomad women exchange glances. Going from pillar to pillar, they reverently press their heads against them. Maybe inquisitive foreigners get more details from monks. Maybe Tibetans don't ask, though worshipping any depiction of sage or teacher and doing rituals.

Perhaps some stories get lost for lack of asking. Like that of the old teacher and his disciples rushing into Manjusri's cave, one breaking his leg and subsequently dying. To commemorate this, Drepung could never have 8000 monks, but only 7999! The monk tells the story, laughing loudly.

We all realise Jason is a gem-studded guide. A Belgian tourist says in Flemish: 'If only we had a guide like him, that would be such a privilege'. When I tell him, Jason checks whether his head is swelling.

Drepung is most scenic with its old courtyards, windowsills filled with flowers, ancient doors, handmade hinges, glimpses of mountains between sloping walls, goldplated pillars against sky. Leaking tea urns lie overturned waiting for someone to grow geraniums in them. Where to get soil? Carry it up from the orchard.

Nomad pilgrims smile fondly at Donna as she poses among them before they go off with packets of butter and Chinese teaspoons to scrape offerings at every shrine. In a lower courtyard we meet a lively group of Kham traders. The midday sun is hot, yet they seem comfortable in vast woollen robes, fleece-lined *chuba* over wool sweaters. Men and women are hung with turquoises and coral. One man sports a panama hat, the women red and blue wool in their plaits. Photographs of Tibetans and Peruvian mountain people show striking resemblances. An ancient link between them got lost in time. They press upon us, jostling, laughing with undamaged teeth, burnished cheeks — dangling necklaces before our faces. The smell of buttered hair evaporates in the heat of day.

Self Arising and Repatriating Deities

We return late for lunch and the hotel restaurant management is displeased. They can afford to with pre-paid guests. Food is forthcoming, but a request for desserts gets a disapproving look. The dessert cook has left. All of Chinese life seems permeated with disapproval for people who don't act to infinite sets of rules, don't arrive, eat, or leave on set times and don't do their exercises in the morning. So we lump our daypacks and take the bus to Chakpori.

At the start of the lane to Chakpori hill, remnants remain of the great Western Gate that was crowned with the Pargo Kaling *chörten*. Mere photographs of the Western Gate used to excite me. Now a white signpost declares in Tibetan and Chinese that bomb shelters are to be found in the caves beyond.

Climbing up the narrow path we pass three men carving *mani* stones. They chisel OM MANI PADME HUM in Tibetan script with small primitive tools in slivers of rock. Halfway up are the Palhalupuk and Tangtong temples, hewn from the rock. At the tiny monastery with its yellow window frames, three little monks and three youths in civvies are having an afternoon natter in the sun. Jason and Donna make their day handing out photos of the Dalai Lama.

It is amazingly peaceful. City noise grows dim up here. Prayer flags flutter gently. Rocks sprout greenery. By the abbot's single-window rock dwelling stand tins of pink roses. From the rock wall by his door drips a cascade of nasturtiums. And from the temple steps we get the most dramatic view of the Potala, one seen in old photographs. From here the Chinese desecration at street level is invisible. This is old Tibet.

An elderly monk leads us into the cave temple where spontaneous images protrude from rocks hung with *kata*, lit by butter lamps. Childhood's Aladdin's cave: little lamps, bending down through a passage, the old man's figure dimly ahead. He seems so tired. Too many tourists come to these easily accessible temples. So we thank him for the privilege and leave soon, after taking some magnificent photos.

The small monks wave us down past painted rock images of Songtsen Gampo, blue medicine buddha, a Dalai Lama, Sakyamuni, six-armed Avalokiteshvara, and an impressive figure in a white turban wearing huge earrings and a tightly fitting coat. He holds a sacred vase wrapped in white cloth.

The travellers are choosing *mani* stones. The carvers sit cross-legged between little pots with the five colours and slabs of carved rock, all orders. They have so few for sale that we place orders too for *mani* stones, to collect when we return from Shigatse.

We make a quick return visit to Thangka House. The entrance is adorned with flowerboxes showing a profusion of red roses, cornflowers and sweet peas, and a wonderful mural depicting a richly garbed figure, sleeves pushed up, pulling a growling tiger on a chain. It may relate to a story about taming the senses, or to a famous teacher taking risks pulling a complete doctrine into the phenomenal realm by tantric means, so that ordinary mortals may become enlightened. The tiger paws the ground to get away, cross-eyed with fury. The burly gent, dressed Mongolian style, calmly pulls in the chain, swinging the surplus across his shoulder. A pair of pheasants look on from a bamboo grove, peonies and zinnias flower in the foreground and four sacred symbols float in cloud-like formation through the sky. To find such art in suburbia!

The *thangka* painters are still on holiday, but the manager produces seven small *thangka* without brocade frames, costing from 600 to 1000 yuan. We nod seriously and examine the fine execution, but having seen old *thangka* in monasteries and temples, we not only quietly baulk at the prices, but sense a lack of life in these deities produced as a state enterprise. Real *thangka* art is a product of meditation on the deity portrayed. No deals are made. Outside, Jason says prices have doubled in three years. Then again, why shouldn't art pay even if *we* can't afford it?

Time left to visit Ramoche monastery in old Lhasa. Built by King Songtsen Gampo in the seventh century as a home for the Jowo Rimpoche statue, according to legend brought to Tibet by Princess Weng Cheng, it was called Ramoche, 'Large Enclosure'. Later the Jowo was installed in the Jokhang and Princess Bhrikuti's Sakyamuni Buddha statue took its place in Ramoche's temple.

In 1474 Ramoche became the Upper Tantric College of Gyuto, with 500 monks. They trained to chant tantric rituals in double- and triple-barrelled voices, and made coloured sand mandalas. These activities caused Waddell to call Ramoche a 'school of sorcery'. But Margaret Williamson, witnessing hundreds of monks chant with *dorje* and handbells, wrote: 'Their chanting set up a powerful vibration that I found thrilling'.

Until 1950 a yearly rain ceremony used to be held near Ramoche monastery. The governor would come in procession, handing small amounts of brick tea to the poor to propitiate the *naga* of the sky to send rain.

Although Ramoche was gutted in the Cultural Revolution, most Gyuto monks escaped to India, re-establishing Gyuto Colleges in Assam and Dharamsala, from where they tour the globe, giving concerts and performing rituals and sand mandala for the appeasement of destructive forces in this world. Ramoche was a Mao Zedong shrine until 1985. In 1986 a few monks returned to begin restoration.

We turn into the street of Ramoche. At a Chinese military corner post all vehicles must undergo security checks. In front of the low building two soldiers sit behind a wooden table, nothing to do. Across their laps lies a handsome Tibetan youth wearing red Khamba headdress, Chinese shirt and trousers. The soldiers fondle him while smoking cigarettes. From his prone position the youth stares brazenly at passers-by, none of whom pretend to notice. I catch his eye because of turning away too slowly.

It has always been women's problem whether or not to meet the sexual needs of occupying armies, if there is a choice. Some are raped, some fall in love, others make a living. But in Chinese society another factor lends a strange tilt to what a vast army in a strange land does about excess testosterone. In China the belief that only sons are worth having meant that girls were often neglected and died. With the introduction of the one-child law, girl infanticide increased. The introduction of ultrasound gave rise to gender-based abortions to prevent a couple's only child being female. These measures have resulted in 'unmarried' ratios of sixteen men to one woman in China proper. So what to do about sexual drive in the three million strong Chinese army is hardly a new problem.

The regime may disapprove of homosexuality, but no doubt it exists in the army as in society at large, just as it existed in Tibet's large monasteries. Certain Tibetan religious practices turn sexual energy to spiritual advancement, producing no secretions. But tantra is an esoteric knowledge that has been poorly served by centuries of sensationalist accounts of tantric practices.

This is a pretty neighbourhood of window boxes and lotus friezes. A typical old Lhasa street with Tibetan houses, prayer-flag-draped chimneys, backed by a snowy peak. We park opposite a whitewashed building with firewood stacked on the roof, lotus flower sign at the gate — perhaps former Gyuto monks' quarters turned into a school. Trading trestles display children's clothes in shocking pink, poison green and no-holds-barred orange. Two old Tibetans squat on the ground, teapot and cups between them. Another sits on a chair, a sleeping dog nearby. The three are in earnest discussion. The grey-haired one is chiselling a stone slab. A man wearing layers of torn and patched khaki clothes walks past, fingering prayer beads. A mother carries on her back a toddler in red and white checkered cap. A woman sells second-hand clothes spread on the ground. A bicyclist stops to look through the pile of Chinese garments. A two-stroke tractor ambles along, carrying eight men and women in scarfs and Khamba headbands, an agricultural work gang. And a little girl finds pebbles to play a game by herself.

In the forecourt of the monastery three children horse around dressed in colours of the devil's own fashion pallette. Otherwise the place looks grief-stricken. Dust, dirt and decay at every step. Padded curtains in the temple porch show ugly water marks and once-scarlet pillars have turned flaked pink. But new gleaming prayer drums wait to be spun and well-seasoned tree trunks lie stacked in the porch, waiting to be new pillars.

Inside you sense a change of energy. Seeing the results of loving tenacity in the face of official harassment, admiration soars for monks who return to their monasteries. A splendid rendering of Dorje Yu-dru-ma, protectress of Gyuto College, covers one entire wall. Against a dark red background sprinkled with gold flowers, tiny skulls, and pairs of blue eyes on red stalks, she rides her white horse through the clouds, waving a five-coloured banner. Above, a bold turquoise frieze of pink and blue lotuses. A wooden fence prevents pilgrims touching. The restoration is marvellous, proving there are new artists in Tibet.

Ramoche's inner sanctum arouses that gentle awe very old places elicit. A build-up of centuries of human endeavour, a concentration of intent that makes the place holy. Fittings so old that the touch of a finger may turn a faded brocade to final dust, a slight push collapse a fragile cabinet's legs. A monk emerges soundlessly from the shadows to tell the incredible story of how after the Cultural Revolution, half of Bhrikuti's Sakyamuni statue was found on a rubbish tip near Lhasa. The other half was located in a scrap metal yard in Beijing by the Tenth Panchen Lama, who saved it from the smelters and returned it to Tibet. We are shown the ancient statue, whole again. Who says there are no miracles?

In the temple's interior, a life-size portrait in flat bright paints of the Fourteenth Dalai Lama copies a photograph probably brought in by a tourist. In his early fifties, he sits on a throne upholstered in a brocade snow-lion pattern. In his lap lies a Tibetan text, left hand poised to turn a page in the act of reciting, prayer beads encircling the wrist. He looks at us with his familiar dimpled smile. In front of the portrait something lies wrapped in gold brocade.

Blinking at daylight we leave. An old Gyuto monk returning home exchanges greetings with Jason. He says Ramoche now has sixty to seventy monks, teaching and studying. Smiling, he goes in. Always they smile.

Workers are returning home. One man wears a fox-fur hat, bushy tail swinging across his back. Jason says Tibetans award a fox-fur hat for cowardice. The connection escapes me. This man seems to wear his as a proud possession. There can't be many foxes left in Tibet. Even if wily enough to escape Chinese guns, they would starve because Chinese guns eliminated all that foxes fed on.

Walking to the main thoroughfare we pass the Tibetan youth who lay spreadeagled across the laps of Chinese soldiers. He casts at us that sort of taunting look you meet with in back streets. I stare back, seeking to know what moves him to associate as he did in public with the oppressors. For gain? Or to do a bit of spying, wearing Khamba headdress for protection so that compatriots know he is no traitor? In an occupied country, all relationships between people become muddled and nobody can trust anyone. How I remember. How it hurts.

Tomorrow the big trek. In the evening Nicola, Donna, Kay and I stroll to the traders and I buy a wonderful old studded pouch, containing a tight wad of pages from a Chinese telephone book and two Tibetan coins. I already possess a pouch with tinder and flint, bought years ago in an Australian antique shop. Appealing to the old drop of nomadic blood, flint pouches call for a pause, a fire and a pot of hot tea.

Harry joins us for the last time at dinner; he's leaving tomorrow. He also visited Drepung today and, being sorely out of breath, took his pulse. This so intrigued Tibetan pilgrims that soon he was taking everyone's pulses. As Tibetan doctors take pulses for diagnosis, they took him for a medical man. Most pulses were very low.

In our rooms we pack and wash our hair. Women wash their hair prior to big undertakings. Filled with trepidation we try to sleep. Soon furious banging announces the lift is being repaired. Logically, lifts are repaired in the night when no-one needs them. Soon several floors are awake. Taps run, toilets flush, thermoses unscrew and cigarette smoke starts to drift through air vents. Towards morning the lift is fixed and we fall into an exhausted sleep. When the alarm goes off we are pooped.

Nicola and I have become addicted to cups of hot thermos water in bed. At breakfast poor Kay, suffering a head cold, asks for raw onion. Jason translates into Tibetan, the message gets passed on in Chinese by Tibetan waiters not allowed to speak Tibetan. Kay desperately chews the spring onion they bring, sending up antibiotic fumes.

Waiting in the lobby for the others, I grind teeth over sham decorations. The centrepiece is a large golden wheel supported by deer, traditionally only seen above temple doors. Pillars are decorated Potala fashion. A Chinese-made wall hanging of the Potala looks out of sync. So do waitresses' *chubas* of the flimsy satin adored by Chinese women. Name tags spell Tibetan names in Pinyin, so tourists will read them as Chinese names. The only jobs for Tibetans are waitressing and menial tasks. Above the Hard Yak Cafe hangs a giant stuffed yak head.

Colonialism underwent a cosmetic change in the middle of the twentieth century. Instead of imposing cultural values on conquered dominions, it began to appropriate the culture symbols of conquered peoples and display them in prominent places to declare government empathy with the vanquished. In Australia the appropriation of Aboriginal symbols and designs is almost total, with art dealers the new colonial masters. Many artists quite deliberately incorporate such design elements in their work to obtain the politically correct look. New Zealand's tourist industry leans on Maori culture. Thus it is with Inuit culture and with designs from native American life. In Hawaii, Americans are more Hawaiian than the few Hawaiians left there. Americans may be there by the power of the gun and the dollar, but living in paradise they feel bound to say 'Mahalo!' and name streets, shopping centres and schools after deposed Hawaiian kings and queens. And the Chinese in Tibet, realising tourists haven't come to see the triumphs of socialist architecture, gather symbols from temples, palaces and villages to feign authenticity.

Above the service desk bob well-coiffured heads of exiled Chinese employees, young and unsmiling. For every service you sign a rice-paper chit, which gets filed in the paper tower of China's bureaucracy. The fax service is operated by a woman who has no need to speak — all communication is done by slips and chits. You sign to pay for every fax that does *not* get through, which happens often. It's like gambling. A question gets the 'Be off with thee, barbarian' look or a finger that points at 'the answer'. She does understand the barbarian language. It is of course ridiculous to expect civility for a mere US$160 a day. We pay for marble floors and the Tibetan look, linen, hot-water service and the wages of an impeccable German management. After all, the Chinese employees are not playing hosts in their own country nor by their own choice, but in an outpost of empire where the regime placed them.

The End of Yamdrok Tso

We leave Lhasa along the road we entered, with Jason in an informative mood. He has at his command an amazing store of free-floating facts about Tibet and Buddhism that make the Tibetan guide's eyes pop. I try noting them in my diary, but road conditions make it a feat to put pen to paper. Passing through the outskirts we learn Lhasa had 40 000 people in the 1991 census, but with surrounding villages that becomes 120 000.

We pass a memorial honouring Chinese soldiers who in the fifties built roads across passes as high as 5000 metres, to Sichuan and Qinghai through former Kham and Amdo, costing the life of one person per kilometre. What ideological goal can justify such ghoulish sacrifices? Zhu Li explains: 'The Tibetans called the highways "golden bridges of happiness", for they linked Tibet more closely with the rest of China and hastened the economic and cultural development of the region'. Roll on Cultural Revolution.

The Lhasa–Shigatse route via the 4794 metre Khamba-La pass, and even loftier Karo-La is a mere 270 kilometres to be travelled in two days. Only the thought that some of my friends came back from doing this keeps me aboard.

But as we steadily rise my mood turns. I'm doing what I wanted to do all my life, so hang the consequences. Going to the Turquoise Lake, or Yamdrok Tso. And what if I die between the passes on the shores of that sacred lake? Death overtakes us all. I shed the last fears. If it takes me I shall be reborn in Tibet, cheating nationality and passport obstacles. Tourists usually die in Tibet from scaling mountains too soon after arrival, getting caught in revolts, or succumbing to altitude sickness. But I don't wish to die, preferring to see Gyantse, Shigatse, maybe Sakya. Fears gone, my delight in the visual increases by the moment.

But we are still in the Lhasa valley, taking photographs of the eleventh-century rock carving of Atisha in bright orange robes, cobalt blue halo and begging bowl, white scarf on his walnut skin. Flanked by three deities, he rises seventeen metres, facing the holy city above a muddy roadside puddle.

Turning onto the Shigatse road, we pass sand dunes and willow groves beneath mist-shrouded mountains, meeting little traffic as we zigzag up the mountain. Although the sun is rising, the air is cooling and the clouds are coming closer. Whitewashed villages nestle in fields of yellow rape. Fresh mud bricks are drying on the edge of a pit.

When Chandra Das came down the pass into this great valley, he saw a famous monastery called Palchen Chuvori, where a chain bridge spanned the Tsangpo. That bridge was built in the fifteenth century by Tangtong Gyalpo, who also built the monastery. He spent his life building 108 temples, 108 *chörten*, and eight chain bridges across the Tsangpo for pilgrims, sacred numbers all. His dedication appealed to the Tibetans' imagination and donations were always forthcoming.

Peter Fleming records that in 1904 British troops passing the village of Chaksam saw the river 'spanned by four huge chains, the durable and strangely rust-free remains of a suspension bridge erected in the fifteenth century'. Did anyone investigate that rust-free alloy hanging four centuries in a river?

Now the chain bridge seems to have gone and the monastery was presumably destroyed.

Suddenly a crunching noise and the driver stops the bus. The men pile out, finding a stone stuck in the wheel casing. We all get out. Gravity seems to be getting as thin as the air. My feet do not quite grip the ground, although I feel far from weightless.

On the apron where several mountain slopes gather, stands the last farm before Khamba-La, beyond which nothing much grows. It looks a huddle of ruins, but gradually various structures declare themselves as farmhouse and barns, brandishing prayer flags. It puzzles me that the main house doesn't appear to have a roof, until I figure out that my viewing perspective prevents me seeing a flat beam roof connecting the walls. I hope it exists, as this must be one of the coldest places on earth. Behind the clustered buildings rises a stone wall three times higher than the tallest building, breached in the centre and itself looking rather like a relic of a former fortress than a wall specially built to protect the humble farm. For that is what it will do when the snows start sliding down steep slopes in springtime. The only groundcovers are clumps of tough grass and low bushes, but between road and farm is a lovely hedge of wild clematis.

Like a space traveller I slowly turn to look at donkeys grazing in a meadow below the road. Beyond their antique heads the view sweeps down to the Tsangpo river below.

Amaury de Riencourt crossed Khamba-La in 1947 and traversed these bare slopes above me, emerging from the clouds to see Lhasa, enraptured. He likens the landscape to Colorado canyons, but was amazed to see a network of irrigation channels and canals, built hundreds of years earlier, regulating the flow of snowmelt. In the first village he saw well-paved streets, houses and gardens surrounded by poplars and willows. Both the village and the faces of the inhabitants speak of 'prosperity and contentment'.

Further down the shores of the Tsangpo he witnessed a flat-bottomed barge made of walnut planks, rowed by teams of men and women singing jolly tunes at the top of their lungs. The setting lies before me, but the singing is missing. Tibetan songs have a tendency to convey meaning and Tibet's Chinese gaols are full of Tibetans who have sung them in public.

Das exclaimed after crossing Khamba-La: 'From this point I enjoyed one of the grandest views I have ever had in Tibet — the valley of the Tsangpo was before me, the great river flowing in a deep gorge at the foot of forest-clad mountains'.

Not only the songs have gone, but so have the forests, although the view is still the greatest I have ever seen. Not often does a landscape have mountains, villages, fields, donkeys and a perspective created by a drop of 2000 feet. Altitude adds the dimension we lack on the earth's flatter surfaces and it changes everything. Slowly I stir my limbs, camera in hand, along a seemingly barren roadside. But in the crags grow bluebells, flannel flowers and ajuga. Das saw brambles, roses, evergreens and rhododendrons. There are none here now.

Across the road, terraced fields marked by low stone walls crawl up a crease between two mountains, catching run-off from a distant snow peak. This relentless effort of high-altitude agriculturists makes me quite emotional without knowing why.

From the last farm a woman emerges, children in tow. A girl about twelve, in light summer frock, breaks away from the mother to examine us more closely. Her face is screwed up from the intensity of looking. Peggy gives her a pen. The face of the girl tries to remind me of something, but all I can think is that thinking is becoming harder every minute. I don't know what it is I should remember.

Since the low road was built, this high road is mostly travelled by Chinese crews building the hydro-electric station on the lake's shore and mad tourists. Most traffic just flies past the lonely farm. But today, not only have we stopped, but below on the zig of the zag, a large bus of German tourists has sprung a flat tyre.

My eyes still function and cannot believe what they see. On the bank below the Germans are picking wildflowers. What the hell do they think they're doing? Can't they see how precariously these flowers cling to pockets of soil caught between rocks? Every flowerhead picked can no longer drop seed. And lots of seed is needed for some of it to find these pockets where growth is possible. I want to shout this out loud to the trespassers, but have no breath. Then Jason shouts. Mr X has dislodged the stone and we are off. I shamble to our bus, zeal extinguished by the effort.

The girl has put a hesitant foot on the steps, as if coming for the ride, her face still screwed up in silent astonishment. She clutches her pen, standing still in her thin frock, one foot on the cold mountain. Why doesn't she wear a *chuba*? She neither shivers nor looks blue, yet there's ice in the air. What is it in connection with her that I should remember? I feel very annoyed.

The door closes. We wave. The girl's eyes never leave us. She doesn't smile or wave. The engine pulls hard to climb and gain speed simultaneously. The roadside drops so steeply that conversation halts in mid sentence. The road circles so that we look down on the last farm and then Jason points to a pumping station for the hydro-electric scheme, high on a mountain crag, a narrow road snaking up to it.

Crossing a ford over a stream, we are jolted by the sight of human settlement in a gorge, if human is the word. A more miserable habitat I have not seen in my life. Shrivelled men, young and older, stand in rags by huts not deserving the name, possibly crates of hydro-electric plant parts. The days when the worst development work was done by Chinese soldiers are over, although still celebrated in monuments and books. These wretched men, standing in thick mud among collections of rubbish, are Tibetan roadworkers. Will these unfortunates, the new serfs of progress, be allowed to go home by summer's end? Without progress they would still lead the harsh but gallant life of high-altitude agriculturists, live in stone villages, enjoy family life, summer rituals and harvest feasts.

It has started to snow. Thoughts of roadworkers and farm girl plague me. No one speaks. Visibility becomes limited. Mr X drives with his usual alacrity, but the back of his neck seems strained taut. One little slip and down we go. Jason's blond face has turned pale, his brilliant flow dried up. The responsibility for half a dozen ignoramuses, who had little idea what they were in for, must weigh heavy. This is also his first trip over the passes. But our Tibetan guide, born to danger, probably traverses several times a month. Earlier meditations on death by breathlessness are abruptly replaced by the possibility of imminent death by plunging. It puts a different edge on life. But the difference hangs unchallenged in the air. Kay looks ill.

Suddenly Jason's cry. 'Khamba-La!' The vehicle rounds a shoulder topped by rock cairns connected by strings of prayer flags and stops. We tumble out and there, a few hundred metres below, lies a turquoise lake! It is shrouded in cloudmist, as are we, for snow is falling steadily. Jason leads a chorus of *'Lha gyalo'* to praise the gods. I manage the camera shutter while shaking with mountain sickness. Distances shift around, up and down. With supreme effort we pick up rocks to add to the cairns. Although travellers have added rocks for centuries when crossing the pass, the cairns are no higher than we are, evidence that fierce storms dislodge them. I say Tara's mantra in gratitude.

We struggle to the top, but the Tsangpo valley is hidden by veils of snow. A truck full of Tibetans roars up from the lakeside, rounding the shoulder. They wave, as people used to do in remote parts of Australia when meeting other wayfarers.

Descending to the lake's shore it doesn't seem a significant drop. Little hope of recovering my breath. The hotel allowed me an oxygen pillow after Jason signed pledges of return and promises of compensation in case of loss. I put the tube in my mouth. 'No, no', says the Tibetan guide. 'Not in the mouth! Under the nose!' Less chance of choking, he says.

Amaury de Riencourt climbed Khamba-La after spending the night at the lake village of Tramalung, 'Valley of Peas'. Peas are a good high-altitude crop. The village bathes in a patch of sunshine as we emerge from the snow. Half a dozen farmhouses surrounded by fields of harvested barley stacked in rows. Glossy yaks idle in a corral of stone walls. The village is a picturebook scene of pastoral bliss. Well kept, white walls, emerald-green grass, golden barley, the brilliant turquoise lake, red tassels on the yaks. The five colours could have originated here. The fields are stacked as marvellously as if the land were a canvas and the harvest a conscious work of art.

Just below the village fields the dream ends. Still between terraces lies a cluster of new buildings fed by a good road, electric wires and pipelines, housing Chinese personnel who construct the hydro-electric scheme. Not here the mud and rubbish of the miserable roadside camp of crates.

Work began in 1985 on the construction of four tunnels, each 6.4 kilometres long, to channel the lake's water into the Tsangpo flowing 800 metres below on the other side of the pass, producing 90 megawatts of energy to light up Lhasa hotels, factories and other Chinese buildings. The lake is expected to drop three inches annually, running dry in fifty years, even with reverse pumping during off-peak hours.

'No Tibetans are ever allowed there', says a voice. The tunnels are being blasted by Chinese soldiers. There is a prophecy by Padmasambhava that if ever Yamdrok Tso dries up, Tibet will become a wasteland. It is no wasteland now. Far from barren, Tibet is fertile and centuries of organic farming on the contours of the land have preserved its soils. In other countries big modernisation schemes have disturbed sustainable farming methods and it is about to happen here. Already farmers have been evicted, apparently without compensation, where fields are in the path of construction works.

Tibetan opposition to the hydro-electric scheme was led by the Tenth Panchen Lama, who had cultural and environmental objections. Environmentalists claim that turbulence caused by daily emptying and refilling of the lake will damage the lake valley's ecology. Refilling with the Tsangpo's far-from-pristine water would threaten fisheries adapted to the clear waters of this isolated lake, which has no inflow other than melting snow. Construction came to a halt because of the Panchen Lama's opposition. But in 1989 he died a sudden death, whereupon construction was hastily resumed.

Turbines, pumps and steering systems for the project come from Austria, where two construction firms make their money from setting up environmentally detrimental mega-dams, including a dam in Thailand which destroyed fisheries and displaced 20 000 people, a dam in Indonesia where the military displaced 60 000 people and a dam in Kurdish Iraq where the military cleared all life from the region prior to the start of construction. Critics of the Indonesian dam met with sudden death, like the Panchen Lama. The Dalai Lama, also highly critical of the hydro-electric scheme going ahead without a comprehensive environmental, economic and social impact study, was refused permission by the Austrian prime minister to speak at the Forum of Non-Government Organisations at the United Nations Human Rights Conference held in Vienna in June 1993. After a storm of publicity and support from NGOs and government delegations, he was eventually allowed to address the forum. The Austrian government supported export credits for the two firms' previous overseas projects.

You look at Yamdrok Tso with different eyes for knowing these terrifying facts. The water is so clear that cloudscapes mirror themselves to perfection, doubling their own beauty as Narcissus did. Below the surface reign the *nagas*. There is an eighteenth-century story of how a lama versed in magic, living in a Nyingma monastery near the lake, heard that Dzungars from Mongolia were about to invade the valley. He appealed to the waters' deities to make the lake look like a grassy plain. Snowfall and a slow drift of painterly grey clouds could do that. The army walked straight into the lake and drowned. Supporting troops, not finding the main army in control of the valley, turned on their heels and marched back across Khamba-La.

The turquoise water hugged by low chamois hills tinged with green flushes exudes an almost unearthly calm. Neither flow nor tide stirs it. The water has lain here like this for tens of thousands of years, snowmelt replacing evaporation. This last vestige of natural beauty on the world's roof will be destroyed for coloured lights, televisions and hotels, which could work on solar power, and provide electricity for Chinese military establishments and factories. This year's tourists may be the last to see the lake in pristine form.

Talk ceases as we drive along and evidence of destruction meets the very beauty to be desecrated. The absence of birds near such a vast body of water creates an eerie atmosphere. The road twists and turns, following the lake's octopus shape. Around a bend lies another large village, houses huddling shoulder to shoulder along main street, clustering up the slope behind. Children and dogs scatter before our vehicle. This is the sort of place where I would like to stop, but

Mr X drives as if passing straight through hell, foot down on the gas pedal. Maybe this is a village where dispossessed farmers would rather eat a Chinese driver than feed him. People turn to stare at us with closed faces. Not how I had hoped to travel through a Tibetan village.

I've always detested descriptions in travel books declaring, 'these wretched people in their miserable hovels' when describing peasant farmers. Yamdrok farmers wrest a frugal living from some of the highest farms in the world, the highest being in Dolpo, Nepal, also farmed by Tibetan people at 14 500 to 16 500 feet and up. But even here, at a 'mere' 14 000 feet, they have to be accomplished agricultural scientists to survive through the year. Timing different agricultural tasks must be first priority over all other of life's demands, if they are to grow crops successfully in the short growing season. Their one advantage: Tibet is geologically a young country where the soil is constantly renewed by the elements. Snowmelt carries minerals from the youngest mountains on earth, the opposite to Australia where geological activity is minimal, the ancient land worn out, the soil poor. In lower valleys Tibetans grow three crops between May and October.

This is no summer village. The thick house walls and dry fodder on the roofs mark it as all-year habitat. What moves people to these heights to till rocky earth and herd sheep? Persecution seems the only answer. Everywhere people settled in high places to escape persecution in populous lowlands. Thus in ancient times people may have come to these high plateaus and valleys, driven from surrounding plains by more aggressive folk. Features shared with people on Tibet's borders may indicate ancestral links rather than infiltration. Once Tibet's valleys were settled, even less aggressive people must have moved ever upwards to find a place to call home, until they reached the snowline. And now Yamdrok farmers are to be finally and completely disowned for the glory of Chinese modernisation and the pockets of Austrian engineers.

Once on the open road, again Mr X slows down and our Tibetan guide starts looking for a picnic place on the lake's shore. We pass a little boy herding sheep and stop a few hundred metres further on. The boy, looking about eight years old, comes running, then stops ten metres away. We put aside food. Jason talks to the boy, who is very shy, and packs two lunchboxes for him. His face has the high glossy sunburnt skin and almost closed eye slits of people of the snows. He wears dark trousers, plastic jacket, Mao cap and tennis shoes. On his back a handwoven bag.

The boy trundles off, lunchbox under each arm, to find his flock. But first he strikes down out of sight behind a large rock to inspect his windfall. We see him from the high bus window as we depart. Not many vehicles stop here. In some ways, he is a lucky kid. He shepherds his flock in a landscape of extraordinary beauty, although to him familiar as home. There may be no school in these parts, so that he spends winters learning from his elders: language, crafts, legends, songs, religion. Come summer, occasional foreigners bring surprises. But the hydro-electric scheme will change the rhythms of his life in ways as yet unknown.

The boy's ancestors saw the passing of quite a few foreigners, providing them with shelter and fodder, when this was the highway from Shigatse to Lhasa. The Williamsons trudged up and down to Lhasa many times, bearing presents of firearms and ammunition for the Dalai Lama. So fond was Derrick of *shikar*, hunting, that this was the finest present he could think to bring for the incarnation of Avalokiteshvara, the Compassionate One.

Britain was already then exporting arms and ammunition to Tibet on credit and Derrick advocated British army training. He felt continually frustrated being unable to hunt — forbidden in Tibet — while travelling amidst 'so much tempting quarry'. Along Yamdrok Tso's shores they came within fifty yards of gazelle and saw bar-headed geese, brahminy ducks and mallard in great numbers. Margaret observed Tibetan wild animals, never threatened by humans, to be very tame. She never saw a dog or beast of burden beaten or abused by adult or child.

Margaret Williamson is among my favourite Tibet travellers. She and Derrick rode horseback from Sikkim to Lhasa in seven weeks. The fourth Western woman to reach Lhasa (after Alexandra David-Neel, Lady Bell and daughter) she wore jodhpurs or tweed skirts. They brought their gramophone and records and were accompanied by fifty people and a hundred or so yaks, *dzo,* donkeys and ponies. Their dog Bruce walked from Sikkim to Lhasa and back three times, with side trips. Bruce walked beside Derrick's coffin after he died in Lhasa in November 1935. Derrick's pony followed fully saddled, stirrups turned. Margaret rode behind, widowed at twenty-nine after two-and-a-half years of married bliss in the mountains. After crossing Khamba-La and Karo-La and burying her husband in Gyantse, she rode in depth of winter across the bitter Tuna Plains to Sikkim to pack their things and return to England.

One keenly feels her loss when she writes that those few years were the richest of her whole life and that she would live them all over again if that were possible, despite the ending. Thus the man who loved Tibet and Tibetans and spoke their language came to rest among them.

In 1937 Margaret defied a British government ruling forbidding European women to travel into Tibet without a European man. She rode with Derrick's faithful servant Samdup, one Sherpa cook and five retainers to Gyantse to erect a granite cross and slab on Derrick's grave. But in 1954 a devastating flood washed away Gyantse's cemetery, taking Derrick's remains.

Margaret's rich memories included audiences with the Thirteenth Dalai

Lama, whose personality she found quite all-encompassing. Not only did he fuss over their personal comfort at Dekyi Lingka, but he begged them not to sail down the Tsangpo in yak-skin coracles again, as it was too dangerous. Margaret thought him 'a genuinely selfless person', who emanated something she did not define; but after the audience she felt strangely uplifted with 'every perception clear as a bell and the world around me radiant'.

The Williamsons discussed modernisations with the Thirteenth Dalai Lama. He wanted electricity and telegraph for Tibet, Western education, a police force and improved army. The telegraph line had been extended from Gyantse to Lhasa in 1923, young Tibetans had already returned from studies in England, and had the Dalai Lama not died in December 1933, no doubt he would have continued sensibly paced reforms. The regent governing after his death was a reticent, anaemic man. Soon World War II and the Chinese Revolution again cut Tibet off from the world, without an adult leader, although a young Fourteenth Dalai Lama approved of engineering works by Peter Aufschnaiter and Heinrich Harrer.

Left to itself Tibet would have absorbed modernisations at its own pace. The 1990s may then have seen a Tibet benefiting from increased trade like other Asian countries, instead of being China's bread basket, ore basket, timber basket and dumping ground for nuclear waste and millions of Han peasants. Although, perhaps the Americans would have lost no time trying to get a tracking station on the Chang Tang plains. Margaret Williamson reported innocently that in early October 1935 two American travellers, Suydam Cutting and Arthur Vernay, were the first Americans ever to visit Lhasa to spend 'about ten days sightseeing'. Sightseeing? The first Western tourists in Lhasa, half a century ahead of the boom?

At that time the Chinese government was so perturbed about British influence in Lhasa that it sent a condolence mission with lavish presents and gifts of money for the Thirteenth Dalai Lama's tomb, simultaneously checking out the Williamsons. Unable to refuse an invitation to banquet at the Chinese compound in September 1935, the Williamsons wielded chopsticks but hardly ate. Margaret was convinced the Chinese representative was about to poison Derrick. Soon after, Derrick developed a condition called uraemia, a failure of the kidneys to eliminate toxins from the bloodstream, a condition for which there was no cure. Two months after the banquet he was dead.

We still follow the lake's shore. A four-wheel drive passes, hooting. From the back wave two American girls who heard Jason's tuitions in several monasteries. With other travellers they hired a car to drive to Nepal.

I'll never manage to write all my impressions of this day sequentially in my diary. I seem to be reviewing my entire life while delving into Tibet's history.

As we leave the lake behind, we come across four bicyclists who have stopped for a rest on a sunny mini-pass. Two European couples. Three beam smiles, exchange the news of the road with Jason. But a young woman leans on her bike by the river with a face like thunder. Altitude? Or wondering whatever she saw in that guy to agree to such a journey? Amaury de Riencourt acclimatised slowly, travelling on horseback and resting in Gyantse before crossing to Yamdrok Tso, yet had trouble mounting and remaining seated. Bike riders must use their own legs to make progress.

The lake disappears and reappears along the route. On some hills the Chinese have laid out white rocks shouting revolutionary slogans at passing traffic. The Tibetans were quick to spell out OM MANI PADME HUM on adjacent slopes, giving travellers a choice. Sheep and goats dot the fields underneath the letters, but on the highest slopes graze yaks, like black beetles clinging sure-footed to narrow ledges, grazing what can be no taller than lichen.

Dorje Phagmo,
Protectress of Turquoise Lake

Jason shouts: 'Samding-la!' He points to a distant heap of ruins on a knoll jutting into the lake on the opposite shore. It is the monastery of Dorje Phagmo, reincarnating female deity who has led a monastic order since its inception in the thirteenth century. Traditionally, Samding had more nuns than monks.

The first Westerner to meet her was probably Alexander Hamilton, assistant surgeon with the East India Company, who stayed with George Bogle at Tashilhunpo on an official visit to the Sixth Panchen Lama. The Panchen Lama's brother, also a monk, had a daughter from a liaison prior to his marriage to a nun, for whom both left their orders. This daughter was deemed to be an incarnation of Chenrezig's consort, Dorje Phagmo, the Thunderbolt Sow, abbess of Samding monastery. She was about twenty-seven in 1775 when Hamilton was sent for to treat her melancholy. She was sickly and Hamilton paid her daily visits.

When Chandra Das travelled here in 1882, secretly mapping the Lhasa route for the Survey of India, he developed a fever and hacking cough. A Lhasa noblewoman to whose caravan Das had attached himself, advised him to go to Samding as the monastery had two physicians. She wrote him a letter of introduction to Dorje Phagmo, who happened to be her half-sister. Smallpox was raging in central Tibet and Das may have been afraid that he had contracted the disease. He had slept in houses where half the family was down with the scourge. Samding lies at 14 512 feet and only by resting at every turn did Das make it up the extra 300 feet of a flight of stone steps. The convent was closed to pilgrims because of the epidemic, but his introduction secured him and two companions hospitality.

Due to Das falling ill, we have vivid descriptions of life in Samding and the Dorje Phagmo of that time. Although he did not meet her until the end of his stay, she took a personal interest in his recovery. At first, all the doctors' attempts failed, as did her rituals. Das was so ill that he wrote his will. Dorje Phagmo then advised him to set free 500 fish. His men went to Nangartse village, bought 500 live fish from local fishermen and set them free in the lake. This was a marvellous conservation method, as were Dorje Phagmo's standing orders allowing no wild animals to be killed in the valley.

The doctor told Das not to drink the lake's water as 'it is injurious even to people in good health'. People here conducted water burials for the deceased. As a consequence, some fish in the lake measured seventy-five centimetres. Finally Das met the abbess in an elaborate religious ceremony. Later he had the privilege of being shown her living quarters, seeing 'a great store of handsomely carved and painted furniture, images of gold, silver and copper, neatly arranged on little altars'. He was also shown a library with 3000 volumes. All are gone now.

After his recovery, Das explored Samding's inner courtyard, numerous chapels, shrines and mausoleums of previous incarnations, all studded with turquoise, coral, rubies, emeralds and pearls. More than half a century later, Tucci writes of the large temple walls as 'bedecked with swords, spears and armour' captured from a Dzungarian army.

When Das took to the road again, villagers offered milk, eggs, water and firewood for sale. Where did they obtain firewood? There may once have been low woody growth, but now the land is denuded. People told Das's companion Ugyen that winter was the best season to travel. There would be no rain, hence no wash-outs. Feed would be cheap so soon after harvest, and meat, barley and wine could be bought anywhere. So this high valley was once a land of plenty.

Das was also offered fish, but devoutly refused because the Dalai Lama, on taking monastic vows, had declared a one-year prohibition on the catching of fish out of deference to sentient beings. He learnt that the inner lake of Yamdrok Tso is known as Demon's Lake, its waters held in place by Dorje Phagmo lest they inundate the whole of Tibet. So between Dorje Phagmo and Padmasambhava the lake remained just where it is and should be. So far. Das writes that Samding was built for this precise purpose. Dorje Phagmo never reclined, but rested in a chair propped up in cushions. But the Chinese needed the present Dorje Phagmo as a collaborator, so they could conquer the lake.

Her lineage started with Chökyi Drönme, youngest daughter of the king of Gungthang, Thri Lhawang Gyaltshen (1404-63/64), consort of Bödong Chole Namgyal, the fourteenth-century lama instrumental in establishing Samding. In 1440 she established a meditation place at Samding and became known as the first Dorje Phagmo. By the time Das writes, Dorje Phagmo is an incarnation of Tara-Dolma. And she is Vajravarahi the Diamond Sow — standing for transcendental wisdom or human delusion conquered — female partner to Shamvara who embodies compassion for all beings. In 1716 Dorje Phagmo and her nuns turned themselves into sows to repel a Muslim raid. Although she once had an abode in the stupa temple Mahadurkha of Nagarkot, near Padmasambhava's birthplace in India, she continued to reincarnate in central Tibet. The monastery's teaching rested on the Nyingma and Sakya schools which recognise marriages between clergy.

The Williamsons befriended her on their 1933 visit to Samding, finding 'a small, friendly woman of about forty with raven-black hair parted in the middle and fastened in a plait'. They invited her to the fireworks in the British Agency at Gyantse the next year and she travelled two days to attend. She must have died not long afterwards. The present twelfth incarnation was born in Lhasa. Tucci met her at Samding in 1948 'as a pretty girl of thirteen'.

In 1959 this incarnation fled before the pursuing Chinese army through Bhutan to India, in the same group as the Sakya party, settling with them in Kalimpong. Here Jamyang Sakya visited Dorje Phagmo, but suddenly the abbess and her relatives disappeared. The Kalimpong press claimed they were kidnapped by communist spies and forcibly returned across the border. Subsequently Dorje Phagmo turned up in Tibet, persuaded by the Chinese to lay off her robes and renounce religion. She has since lived a civilian life in Lhasa. This appeared to bring the lineage to an end, though it is doubtful Tibetans will let that happen. It is reported she again assists the training of monks, studying of scriptures and reintroduction of ancient rituals. The Chinese authorities do not allow her to return to Samding. She can only choose the road to freedom through rebirth.

Across the turquoise waters hovers the ruin. Samding was laid waste in the Cultural Revolution. Once the centre of civilisation between the high passes, its sacking must have had a devastating effect on the thirty or so affiliated temples dotting the countryside. Of the material losses, that of the library is perhaps the worst. Yet a few score monks, undaunted by mounds of rubble and a missing abbess, have returned to rebuild Samding. Alas, it's too late in the day to visit. Holding Samding in my view until it disappears, I resolve to return one day to see it risen.

We come upon a wash-out, the road blocked by large jagged rocks from the giant mountains on our right. Vehicles before us have just pulled through, each creating such impassable slush that following vehicles must seek new mud to break. The men start shoving and pushing rocks. I expect them to collapse in minutes so that we must camp here for the night, or until better acclimatised people come to the rescue. But most vehicles carry tourists. Sensible people take the low road to Shigatse.

The low road to Shigatse was built by the Chinese for the rapid deployment of troops and provisions. Under Tibetan rule the Yamdrok Tso and only route to Lhasa was forbidden to foreigners beyond the trading post of Gyantse unless by special permit, although Das heard that Nepalese artisans worked in monasteries in the lake valley, as they did in many places in Tibet. But this was a caravan route and the population would not have been as cut off from human traffic as now, when cars make the crossing in half a day.

Tibet had one of the most efficient postal services in the world, connecting

Lhasa with other population centres. Postmen would run a distance of about five miles, then hand over the mail to the next postman. The shepherd boy's grandfather may have been a postal runner from his village to the next. In parts of Tibet where habitation was sparse, mail was carried on horseback, animals being exchanged at villages.

Incongruously, there has been heavy traffic of elephants across these passes along Lake Yamdrok. The holiness of elephants is encased in myths from the beginning of time. Das mentions that the rajah of Sikkim sent a present of two elephants to the Dalai Lama. In 1901 a Bhutanese gentleman guided two elephants, two peacocks and a leopard to Lhasa for Norbulingka zoo. When British troops arrived in Lhasa in 1904, only one elephant was alive. Disguised, Alexandra David-Neel managed to photograph that elephant in 1924, wearing decorated cloth, taking part in a festival near the Potala. Sir Charles Bell stayed in a monastery called Lang Tang or 'Elephant Plain', twenty miles north of Lhasa. In the mid-thirties the Williamsons noticed the road along the Kyi *Chu* had been blasted out to let another pair of elephants pass. The trees were cropped where they fed. They were a present to the Thirteenth Dalai Lama from Nepal's maharaja. Later they meet the noble beasts near the entrance to the Lukhang, behind the Potala, where there were grass and trees to browse and the Dalai Lama could watch them from on high. In the early fifties, Jamyang Sakya found one elephant still living behind the Potala, drinking from the Dalai Lama's well, daily making three bows and offering water towards the palace.

Eyes squeezed, I imagine elephants shambling along this shore. A magnificent sight! Dark grey rippling hides against turquoise water and the lighter grey and fawn of rocks in daylight. Are stories still told about these giants passing through?

It has taken the indomitable Mr X about fifteen minutes to coax the bus across the wash-out, bucking and heaving. We clamber after it and board. Am I the only one feeling this sick? I can't even contemplate pushing a pebble into the water.

For hours we drive beside the lake between icy mountains, passing two fine old stupas, symbols of indefatigable faith in this overwhelming environment. Around villages peasants are busy harvesting, casting not even a furtive glance at the traffic. They may be fed up with tourist buses raising dust clouds, capsuled foreign worlds in which they have no stake. Not like the caravans of old. They may also be loath to speak to foreigners because of communists in their midst.

Nowhere are PLA soldiers helping with the harvest, nor are Han cadres in Tibetan costume gaily reaping barley alongside Tibetan farmers, as Beijing picture books have it. In 1981 Zhu Li wrote of Han cadres: 'these young people ...have helped to build a new Tibet. With the training of Tibetan cadres in huge numbers, the great majority of Han cadres will be transferred back to the interior provinces within the next three years'. The training of Tibetan cadres must have failed, for now the policy is one of massive population transfer of Han cadres and Han peasants into Tibet.

The views become ever more spectacular. Occasionally, on high mountains, we see ancient-looking towering structures with sloping walls, invariably in ruins. Our Tibetan guide thinks they could be 500 years old. He says that to offer an answer, but adds nobody really knows what they were built for, but people used to live in towers before there were villages. Occupants could signal from tower to tower and the whole population would shelter in them when the valley was invaded. This supports the persecution theory. It seems incredible that people in one of the highest and most hostile places on earth had to protect themselves against invasion upon invasion. It is even likely these towers date from pre-Buddhist times — when Tibetans were warriors — making them more than twelve hundred years old even though walls may have been rebuilt over time. When British troops first set eyes on Yamdrok Tso in 1904 they reported seeing half-ruined castles on its shores, which must have been utilised for other building projects. Peter Gouillart and A. J. Broomhall describe immense tower-like dwellings still in use by the fierce Nuosu, ethnic Tibetan people in Yunnan.

Poppies and blue myrtle were seen by de Riencourt carpeting the lakeside. No flowers now, but my delight in the visual symphony of mountains, ice and snow, clouds and crystal water reaches a peak. My eyes are the only parts of me that still swivel. My lungs are shutting down.

At the Samding turn-off rises the village of Nangkartse. One of its daughters, a princess, became the mother of the Great Fifth Dalai Lama, giving birth in Chonggye in the Yarlung Valley. Brides sometimes travelled vast distances to start new lives. Tucci saw a bridal procession bound for Nangkartse cross the Khamba-La. The bride rode a horse in a yellow silk shabrack, indicating high nobility.

Jason warns to look out for a massive glacier not far from the road. When it looms above us it takes my last puff of breath away. No ten volumes of Himalayan photographs or twenty accounts of high peak mountaineering prepare you for a first sighting of a whiter than white glacier hanging off a mountain right above you. Beneath it runs the blue-grey stream. Above, a pale mauve sky. A scene of stupendous beauty. Hauling up the camera I aim to capture the thrill of it. Photos my friends will flip over without stopping, because they will look virtually black and white.

At last Karo-La looms. Once we cross this formidable 16 500-foot pass, descent to the Gyantse plain will be rapid and all my troubles will cease. Just before the pass we meet more German bicycle riders with laughing tanned faces. Seven days out of Lhasa, they covered 180 kilometres. They hope to cycle all the way to Nepal, a distance of 800 kilometres in three weeks.

I feel slightly better on this pass, though unable to leave the bus. Still ninety kilometres to Gyantse. As the bus ambles across Karo-La, a forgotten childhood fear returns. From early years I had a revulsion of mountain landscapes in pictures and films. It was a strong emotion for one born below sea level, and it lasted until my teens before gradually abating. Not until I read Harrer's *Seven Years in Tibet* was I able to overcome a fearful dislike of stories about mountain travel, in order to read of his life in Lhasa. Where did these strong feelings about scenes never visited come from? An experience of mountain sickness or frostbite in a past life? Maybe they will be exorcised now, as we cross Karo-La.

The British Invasion of Tibet: Throwing Butter at a Granite Rock

Karo-La is higher but friendlier in appearance than Khamba-La. It may be the weather, cloudy but clear. An easy slope capped with snow-bound peaks, a scraggy pile of rocks hung with prayer flags, a comparatively easy track across the saddle.

Yet Karo-La was the scene of a far-from-friendly historical event that saw few Tibetan survivors and changed Tibet's fate forever. It was here in 1904 that Sir Francis Younghusband's British–Indian troops slaughtered 300 Tibetan peasants armed with muskets and stones. The farmers of Yamdrok Tso had once more been called to defend their valley, especially the road to forbidden Lhasa, but this time they stood no chance. The British tactic was to send small groups of Ghurkas, Pathans and Punjabis (Hindus, Muslims and Sikhs) up the surrounding mountains as high as 19 000 feet to pick off the Buddhist Tibetans below with modern guns.

The invasion was euphemistically called a 'trade mission'. Britain was one of the main players in the Great Game, translating as the carving up of the globe into spheres of influence between the big powers — it continues today. Britain was anxious to keep an eye on Russian influence to the north of their Indian borders and desired to establish trading posts inside Tibet to gain access.

About Chinese influence they seemed less concerned, except for Russo–Chinese scheming. The British cowed the Manchus into giving concessions on Chinese soil, including a hundred-year lease of the fishing island of Hong Kong in 1897. They appeared to see the Chinese as unequal trading partners but possible allies in the carving up of Tibet into zones of influence, to keep out Russians and Mongolians.

After invading Tibet, the British called a meeting of Tibetan authorities and the Chinese *amban,* as if he had any say in the matter. The Tibetans declined to come to the meeting. They had not asked to be invaded, nor had they requested trading posts or agreements.

This did not prevent the British and Chinese from forging ahead with their incursions into Tibet, and it is now accepted that the Simla Convention of 1914 gave China a foot in the door that eventually led to the full-blown invasion of Tibet in 1950. For it is well known that plans for incorporating Tibet into China existed during Chiang Kai-shek's reign as well as when the communists

159

came to power. Having been recognised by Britain as a legitimate signatory to an agreement that overruled the Tibetan government, China assumed that its alleged suzerainty over Tibet had been internationally recognised. Britain was in the early part of this century the most powerful nation on earth, with an empire on which the sun never set. All that remained to be done for the new Chinese leadership was to upgrade themselves to sovereigns and take possession of Tibet, which they called the Western Treasure-House.

Thus the battle of Karo-La became the most decisive in contemporary Tibetan history. Although not one Chinese was present, this battle enabled China to invade Tibet without Britain or the rest of the world lifting a finger or raising a voice in protest. Peter Fleming, himself a British colonel, wrote an exhaustive account of the 1904 British invasion, *Bayonets to Lhasa,* providing insights into the machinations, follies and failures of international politics, to which all subsequent writers who examine the British role in Asia must turn.

The main players in the drama were George Curzon, arrogant and highly strung viceroy of India; Colonel Francis Younghusband, a Central Asia explorer, later governor of Kashmir and president of the Royal Geographic Society with a special interest in Everest expeditions; and Yu-t'ai, the *amban,* demoted by the Manchu and packed off to Lhasa. Other characters, who did not want to play, were chain-smoking Brigadier General MacDonald who suffered dysentery and insomnia and had no desire to see Lhasa, and the Thirteenth Dalai Lama who fled to Mongolia, leaving the Ganden Rimpoche to deal with the evolving crisis.

For years Britain had fretted about Russian advances north of India's borders and now a Buryat Mongolian monk called Dorzhiev lived at Lhasa's court. This, in Curzon's eye, represented Russian influence. He could have known nothing of three centuries of religious exchanges between Central Asian peoples and Tibetans (especially since 1576) but Younghusband ought to have had an inkling. Dorzhiev commuted between Russia and Tibet in the cause of Buddhism — there still is a temple in St Petersburg — and if he traded information he did no more than keep ahead of the Game. Besides, Tibet, always bothered by China and now threatened by Britain, had good cause to look to Russia for help.

Britain had no representation in Tibet under the Thirteenth and previous Dalai Lamas, although Warren Hastings sent George Bogle to Shigatse in 1774 on the invitation of the Panchen Lama (called Tashi Lama by the British, after his monastery), to discuss border incidents and possible trade relations. In 1782 Captain Samuel Turner also reached Tashilhunpo but got no further. Although the Panchen Lama befriended Bogle, the Lhasa government did not encourage further outcomes of the visit. Not surprisingly, the Lhasa government thwarted all efforts by the British to get closer, seeing that Britain in its ignorance recognised Chinese suzerainty over Tibet and even went so far as to hold with China a Sikkim-Tibet border convention in 1890, followed in 1893 by the signing of trade regulations. Thereupon, the British told Tibet it wasn't keeping to those regulations made at a convention Tibet had neither recognised nor ratified.

The British had fought China to get a British minister stationed in Peking. They had a British agent in Kathmandu, Nepal, although he was not allowed to leave his garden compound. And although in 1879 their entire contingent of troops had been massacred in Kabul, Afghanistan, when attempting to beat the Russians to it, they now wanted representation in Lhasa, or at least in Gyantse.

As Lhasa officials were rebuffing all Curzon's efforts to get his way diplomatically, the viceroy seized on a pathetically futile 'border incident' to force the issue. Tibetans captured some straying yaks on the Sikkim border, whereupon Curzon ordered 1100 British India troops to advance into Tibet and exact a treaty. Carrying their supplies needed almost 11 000 coolies. Carrying extra supplies or coming along to be slaughtered to feed this huge army were some 2600 ponies, 7000 mules, 5000 bullocks, 4500 yaks, 138 buffaloes, six camels and two zebrules, crosses between zebras and donkeys. This herd of almost 20 000 had to try to find roadside grazing in Tibet! The army set out in the depth of the 1903 winter to cross passes as high as 19 000 feet, with men born in the Himalayan foothills and officers from the British Isles.

After four months marching and camping awaiting developments, they established headquarters in April 1904 at Chang Lo near Gyantse at 13 000 feet, two battles and 800 Tibetan corpses already behind them.

British engineers under Mr Truninger built a telegraph line to Gyantse as the troops advanced. When two lamas enquired about the purpose of the line, this gentleman replied that as the wire marked their way into Tibet, they would not get lost when they were leaving. Conceivably the practical Tibetans believed him. It also ensured they would not destroy it, lest they were stuck with the British forever! It is but a mild example of British arrogance regarding the Tibetans that took a more obnoxious form during the campaign. The permanent under-secretary at the India Office called Tibetans 'no longer stupid defenceless sheep, but ferocious determined fanatics' when they began to defend their country, while Lord Kitchener called them 'these absurd people' when they refused to sign a friendship treaty with an invading force.

The telegraph was used as much to play politics between one British faction and another as to relay information about advancing or holding back. Younghusband was in the habit of ignoring telegrams or pretending they arrived too late, in order to do as he saw fit.

There had for some time circulated a belief in Tibet that Palden Lhamo, the fierce protector deity of the Dalai Lama and the city of Lhasa, had reincarnated in Queen Victoria, assuring peace between Britain and Tibet. The queen of the largest empire on earth equated well with the deity who rode a white mule through a sea of blood, baring fangs at opponents. But when the queen departed from this earthly life the British invaded and the Dalai Lama fled north.

No foreigner was allowed to proceed beyond Gyantse. But the Tibetans suspected British intentions and just in case constructed a wall six feet high, four feet thick and 2400 feet long, blocking Karo pass. On 5 May 1904 the battle of Chang Lo took place and on 6 May the British attacked at Karo-La, breaking through one week after Curzon sailed for England. Friendly Gyantse had turned hostile. While the British wired for reinforcements and got a Pathan battalion to join their Ghurkas and Sikhs, some 5000 Tibetans were forced to abandon their normal way of life to take up arms. On 6 July the British blew up part of the Gyantse Dzong — Fleming calls it 'the key to Tibet' — and took it. On 14 July they began their march on Lhasa in a column seven miles long.

Years later Younghusband spoke feelingly at the Royal Geographic Society of marching and living at 15 000 feet, 'where the effort of breathing is a continued drain on one's strength, the mere weight of the clothes one has to wear is a strain in itself; any additional effort exhausts one immediately'. His troops marched three weeks in heavy uniforms, carrying packs and weapons, to cover a distance we drove in one day.

At Karo-La they had found a second wall erected behind the first, but fought their way through as before, clapping eyes on Yamdrok Tso on 19 July. A member of the *kashag*, the Tibetan cabinet, met them at Nangkartse to persuade Younghusband to turn back. He was ignored and they crossed Khamba-La on 22 July, taking five and a half days to cross the Tsangpo, where Tibetan officials again appealed for a halt to no avail, and marched into Lhasa on 3 August 1904.

The Dalai Lama and Dorzhiev had flown. A story from Kawaguchi (spy or gossip?) about a Russian camel caravan loaded with weaponry headed for Lhasa, turned out to be empty rumour. Yu-t'ai, the *amban,* was eager to ingratiate himself with the British, pretending he was in charge at Lhasa. *Ambans* often overstepped the mark, as do Chinese diplomats today. The *amban* did not enjoy a good name, as was the case with most Chinese officials exiled to Tibet. Moreover, as the Tibetans regularly intercepted his money cargoes, he had to borrow from the Tibetan government in order to eat. But by becoming chummy with Younghusband his prestige in Lhasa rose.

With the large military presence disrupting Lhasa life, a *dop-dop* monk attacked and wounded some British officers. As a prelude to the proposed British-Tibetan friendship treaty, he was publicly hanged.

Finally, on 11 August, the Tibetan national assembly discussed Younghusband's nine demands — including the payment of an indemnity — and turned them down. Instead they claimed quite logically that Britain ought to pay Tibet an indemnity. The *amban* rapped the Tibetans over the knuckles for such impudence. Meanwhile in London, Prime Minister Balfour and his cabinet had to miss the opening of the grouse-shooting season because of the Tibet crisis. This rather forced their hand and the prime minister stated with clattering ignorance of the effects of His Majesty's soldiers' progress through Tibet:

> The Cabinet decided that, if the Lama refuses even to consider our very reasonable and moderate efforts, we have no choice but to turn the expedition from a peaceful into a punitive one: and with every regard to the religious feelings of the Tibetans, to destroy such buildings as the walls and the gates of the city, and to carry [off] some of the leading citizens as hostages. This course is painful; but apparently inevitable. (Royal Archives of 15 August 1904, quoted in Fleming, *Bayonets to Lhasa,* p. 238)

Inevitable indeed, if they were to get to the grouse moors at all that year! The city whose fate the prime minister was sealing with the stroke of a pen was Lhasa. The 'peaceful' expedition had killed some 2700 Tibetans, blown up Gyantse *dzong*, 'cleared' Tsechen monastery for use as a lookout post, and taken over the strategic hamlet of Palla after killing between 300 and 400 inhabitants and defenders.

Not only had the countryside around Gyantse been scoured for grain, fodder and livestock to feed British troops, but villages were burnt for not complying. Wildlife was shot to provide meat for 1100 men, rivers were fished whenever there was no fighting. Younghusband believed that the Gyantse plains and the Lhasa valley could easily support a permanent British force of 1000 men. He regarded Shigatse valley as a potential breadbasket for British troops. No doubt at the point of a gun.

But negotiations in Lhasa kept faltering on the unwillingness of Lhasa officials to decide anything conclusive with the British in the absence of the Dalai Lama. Younghusband remarked that negotiating with the Tibetans was 'like throwing butter at a granite rock' but refused to acknowledge that he had come uninvited. The impasse was an ideal situation for the *amban* to step in. Through his mediation, carrying demands from British to Lhasa officials and probably adding his own interpretations, it came about that a 'friendship' treaty was finally signed in the Potala on 7 September 1904. In Younghusband's own words: 'I was able to ram the whole treaty down their throats'.

Tibet was forced to accept all nine points composed by Younghusband. Tibet was to respect borders — this was a justification for acting on the yak incident in a terrain where borders were notoriously hard to recognise and straddled tribal lands. Tibet had to allow trade markets in Gyantse and Gartok and keep

roads to those towns open. All fortifications between Lhasa and the Indian frontier
were to be demolished. Tibet was to pay an indemnity of 50 000 pound sterling
over seventy-five years, give the Chumbi valley near the Sikkimese border as
security, and have no dealings with foreign powers unless with Britain's approval.
But Chinese suzerainty was explicitly recognised in the treaty by Younghusband,
on no other grounds than that it suited Britain's divisive foreign policies and
despite Curzon's opinion that Chinese suzerainty in Tibet was 'a farce'. A separate
agreement allowed the British agent at Gyantse to proceed to Lhasa to discuss
commercial affairs should he not be able to get satisfaction at Gyantse.

To mark the signing of the treaty, the Tibetan government released two
Lhasa friends of Kawaguchi and two others imprisoned for inadvertently assisting
Chandra Das. This was possibly the only good that came out of the negotiations,
as these innocent people were incarcerated due to the Lhasa government's not-
unfounded paranoia about foreigners.

Three days after the signing of the treaty, wall posters went up in Lhasa,
signed by the *amban*, stating that:

> In future, Tibet being a feudatory of China, the Dalai Lama will be responsible
> for the yellow-cap faith and monks, and will only be concerned slightly in
> official matters, while the Amban will conduct all Tibetan affairs with the
> Tibetan officials; important matters will be referred to the Emperor ... You
> must all understand this and act accordingly, so that no punishment may
> befall you. (Fleming, *Bayonets to Lhasa,* p. 265).

In future ... because it never was so in the past. China now had an approved
foot firmly in the door. The Balfour Government in London dissociated itself
from the treaty when its full contents became known, although it said nothing
on the suzerainty matter. It more or less disgraced Younghusband, eventually
stationing him in Kashmir. But it was altogether too late to save Tibet from
foreign domination.

China asserted itself by paying the indemnity for Tibet in the short span of
four years. Britain did *not* refuse the money! In effect, China 'bought' Tibet off
Britain for 50 000 pounds sterling. During those years China embarked on a
series of brutal military campaigns to consolidate the empire's influence in the
mountainous strongholds of indigenous Tibetan princes and independent
monasteries. By 1908 they incorporated Tibet's eastern border territories,
incorporating Amdo into Qinghai province and turning Kham into Sinkiang.

The Chinese ruled with heavy hand. Monasteries were razed, monks killed,
indigenous rulers disempowered. Tibetan men had to shave their heads and
wear pigtails and all Tibetans had to wear trousers 'in the interest of morality'.
Officials had to learn Chinese, a land tax was imposed, and Chinese population
transferral became policy. This happened in 1908 under a Chinese emperor and

it happened again throughout the whole of Tibet after 1959. The only 'improvement' the communists introduced was the abolition of pigtails.

In 1910 the returned Thirteenth Dalai Lama fled to India as the Chinese marched on Lhasa. Here he befriended Britons in power at New Delhi. Yet they lost no time in officially recognising the puppet government set up by the Chinese in Lhasa. Only the 1911 revolution and dissolution of the Chinese empire saved Tibet at that time from becoming a Chinese province. From 1911 until 1950 Tibet enjoyed its independence without Chinese interference, although not in Amdo, or in Kham where Chinese warlords made regular brutal incursions. But Chiang Kai-shek as well as Mao Zedong had resolved to 'liberate' Tibet and annex it to secure what they regarded as China's southern borders. When Mao succeeded, it gave the People's Liberation Army a springboard for the annexation of South-East Asian countries that at some time in history had paid tribute to Chinese emperors. Lois Lang-Sims thought China was 'possessed by a colossal fantasy which includes the unification of their nation to incorporate every territory to which they had ever supposed themselves to be entitled'.

Because the British assumed in 1904 at Lhasa that China was an influential power, and the Chinese assumed Britain to be calling the shots, Britain's expansionist policy of the time facilitated China's expansionist policy then and in the second half of this century. Tibet paid the price.

In retrospect it is possible to think of small wisdoms that could have averted this outcome. Three things seem obvious. Had the Dalai Lama received Curzon's letters — his officials held them back — and had he opened dialogue with the British instead of going on a Mongolian 'retreat', he would have asserted Tibet's independence and himself as its ruler. He might have been able to strike the assumed suzerainty of China out of a treaty between Tibet and pushy Britain. And had his officials not used the excuse that they could not deal with the Britons for fear of annoying the Chinese, the British might not so readily have assumed Chinese suzerainty. And had the lamas near Gyantse not been satisfied with Mr Truninger's sick little joke, the Tibetans could have cut the telegraph line repeatedly to impede British supplies and advance, isolating them from New Delhi and London. Even though Younghusband chose to ignore telegrams when it suited him, to be stuck in Tibet without the telegraph would have meant that reinforcements could only start from India if a messenger rode hard for a week and came to no harm on the way. The telegraph gave the British a psychological and practical advantage that reinforced their sense of superiority. During the entire campaign at least 2700 Tibetans lost their lives and Lhasa had done nothing to assist these hapless ones. British casualties were less than a hundredth of that figure.

One day's march out of Lhasa on the return journey, Francis Younghusband, flushed with victory, stood on a hill along the road to Khamba-La, looked down on Lhasa and had a mystical experience :

> I was insensibly suffused with an almost intoxicating sense of elation and goodwill. This exhilaration of the moment grew and grew until it thrilled through me with overpowering intensity. Never again could I think evil, or ever again be at enmity with any man. All nature and all humanity were bathed in a rosy glowing radiancy; and life for the future seemed naught but buoyancy and light. (from his book *India and Tibet,* London 1910, quoted in Fleming *Bayonets to Lhasa,* p. 274)

Following this, Younghusband wanted to bring men of all religions together to break the barriers between them. In 1933 he founded the World Congress of Faiths. In 1942 he had a stroke at one of its meetings and died a week later. His coffin bore the image of the Buddha given to him on his departure from Lhasa by the Ganden Rimpoche. His grave bears a bas-relief of Lhasa. This is indeed the stuff that legends are made of. Until recently the push into Tibet remained known as Younghusband's mission or expedition. Only now is the event beginning to be called the British invasion of Tibet, which is what it was.

Gyantse's Three Buddhas

What followed was a plethora of books. Men and officers wrote letters and diaries during the invasion, but the next few years saw the appearance of books on Tibet by the troops' doctor, the leader of the mounted infantry, the *Times'* correspondent who accompanied the army and several others. Earlier books on the travels of George Bogle and Thomas Manning and works by Sarat Chandra Das, Sven Hedin and Francis Younghusband himself had lifted the veil that hung over Tibet. Only the incomparable Abbé Huc had a substantial tale to tell. But now Tibet had been penetrated. One cannot escape the sexual connotations of 1100 men without women, with 11 000 male porters, pushing into an unknown valley to gain the satisfaction of entering a Forbidden City. Western *tantra*, with Younghusband gaining the enlightenment?

From then on books on Tibet flourished, written predominantly by British authors who in one way or another became involved with Tibet. Some have remained standard reference works because they describe the country, its people, culture, religion, society and politics before Chinese communists changed Tibet forever.

A belief has been established through these writings that there exists between the British and Tibetans a very special friendship, but others have expressed surprise at this in the light of the brutal encounters of 1904. However, examined closely, the friendship was virtually restricted to, on one hand, the Dalai and Panchen Lamas, members of the Tibetan cabinet plus several noble families, and on the other, British India officials.

What these people shared in the first instance was an understanding of each other's high positions, power and influence. They belonged to the ruling classes and had servants. Subsequently, children of the Tibetan aristocracy attended boarding schools in India, absorbing English culture through learning the language. Some published their life stories. Poor Tibetans on the Indian side of the border sometimes had lasting relationships with British officials for whom they acted as servants. That is as far as the friendship went.

In seven decades of British book publishing on Tibet the same names keep turning up. Photographs of noble children complement photographs in other books where they are grown up. Even intrepid outsider Lois Lang-Sims, who went to India to do something for the Tibetan refugees in 1959 when the Dalai

Lama was in flight, meets some of these 'book characters' in the hotels and streets of Darjeeling, Kalimpong and Mussoorie in the course of her daily walks.

Literally speaking, to the British, Tibet was an upper crust, incestuous little world and contact with ordinary Tibetan people was not really part of that sort of Tibetan-British friendship. Ordinary Britons made contact only as soldiers. Since then the Americans have come in with scholarship money and publishers who publish nothing but books on Tibet, although even here the same well-known names of those who did it first keep being quoted.

Although British governments have never expressed any special feelings for Tibet and the Tibetans, British people have been in the forefront of studying Tibetan religion and assisting Tibetan refugees. It is as if the invading power in its decline turns to the gift Tibet now offers the world: an all-encompassing spiritual view of the universe. Will China be similarly affected by its occupation of Tibet? Generations of Chinese children are born on the roof of the world, growing up in rarefied air between peace-producing mountains, wondering about the meaning of prayer flags.

As we begin the descent of Karo-La it is not long before I feel lighter above the eyebrows. My voice returns. The stupefying headache I have nursed since Khamba-La begins to lift. Two mountain ranges meet at Karo-La, one from Shigatse, the other all the way from Chomolhari in the south.

On high slopes to the right appear the black tents of nomads. Although still inhabiting yak-hair tents, these are settled nomad herders. De Riencourt saw carcasses of dead animals along this route that would lie for decades without decaying, preserved by the altitude. They simply weathered away. None here now. Presumably eaten as soon as they fell. Tibet, locked into China's food production system, is constantly in danger of shortages and famine.

We enter a village where the harvest is in full swing, so we must have descended to 14 500 feet, the local limit for cultivation. Houses built into an aubergine-coloured rock wall. Traditional mud-brick dwellings with painted carvings atop doorways with the half-moon and sun representing compassion and wisdom. Dry fodder stacked on roofs. A young man holds the reins of two little horses, one brown, one white. Standing in the middle of a flattened heap of barley, he turns on the spot as the horses walk a circle, threshing the grain. A woman holding a pitchfork turns to smile at us from the centre of a great heap of stalks yet to be spread. Further on, women winnow grain on large round baskets. No machinery in sight. Agriculture Tibetan-style. The harvest looks good. A scene of pastoral peace.

Jason decides to stop to photograph the winnowing. Leaving the bus, shouting greetings in Tibetan, he runs towards the villagers. We see him give something to a young man and suddenly adults and kids come running from everywhere as if he wields some powerful magnet. He is being mobbed! Only then do we realise he is distributing Dalai Lama photos. He seems to be laughing as he holds his hands up high to save the small pictures from being torn apart, but is unable to keep his balance. He leapfrogs about as the crowd jostles him in their midst.

Peggy tries to distract the kids from Jason by waving photos from the bus door. In an instant the bus is being mobbed by scores of children. The bigger ones press down upon the little ones, who begin to cry and are in danger of being crushed against the sides of the bus. The children shout and violently push each other, the tiny ones scream with fright and pain. Everything happens in the space of twenty seconds.

Peggy has her photos ripped from her hands. Jason, freed by running out of pictures, comes running, shouting Tibetan words and suddenly, as quickly as they attacked, the children fall back. Jason jumps in and the doors are quickly closed. The driver steps on it and the village rapidly disappears behind us.

We are shaken by the scene and the realisation that the bigger boys could easily have killed little ones to lay hands on a Dalai Lama photo. It is hard to guess what aroused such aggression. Clearly Jason did not expect it. Distributing Dalai Lama photos is usually a quietly diplomatic event, accompanied by smiles, friendly words and the solemn touching of foreheads. Could it be that the photos have a certain currency, now that Chinese authorities have ruled that visitors may bring only one Dalai Lama photo per person into the country? Prohibitions encourage black-marketeering. Or does no-one stop here, do these villagers miss out on the treasured image?

Because the Karo-La to Gyantse road was forbidden to foreigners under Tibetan rule, this population suffered the length and breadth of the British invasion, defended the Lhasa route and was probably blamed for their defeat. It may have been a crucial factor in the population turning against the Lhasa government and accepting communist rule. Memories are long in Tibet. Now this is the reddest region of Tibet, as far as Shigatse. Yet the Dalai Lama seems to be above politics. The reason usually given for communism's strength here is that the Shigatse court had strong links with Chinese rulers, who tried to put a wedge between the Panchen and Dalai Lamas, succeeding with the Ninth Panchen and Thirteenth Dalai Lama.

We pass a string of villages in the throes of harvesting. One may be Gobshi ('Four Doors') a junction of four trade routes. From Gobshi, Tucci marched one day in a south-easterly direction to view the region's oldest monuments, including Nyinrodemogon temple with fourteenth century paintings. He found them not comparable with paintings elsewhere. In a land awash with religious murals,

Tucci could afford to be disdainful. In a nearby Nyingmapa temple at Kamodon monastery he found nothing of interest but the alleged stone foot imprints of Padmasambhava. Half his luck!

Peering between mountains in the hinterland, I wonder whether these ancient relics have been saved, though they would not be deemed important by a European art historian. I have a growing dissatisfaction with our manner of travelling on highways, unable to change plans and stop without permits to overnight here, unable to go for a walk into valleys beyond, see off-the-beaten-track monasteries, talk with people, buy *tsampa*. Of course it protects them from horrid Western influences, keeping them pure red.

At some places the river, now an impressive stream, runs far below us. The road merely clings to mountainous rock walls. The precipice is too close for comfort and we would be safer travelling these sections on foot, but I am beyond worrying. No sign of wildlife, although Das reported 'numerous flocks of cranes, and brown ducks with red necks … swimming in the river and the irrigation ditches' while the river teemed with fish. Margaret Williamson saw these hills green with patches of yellow mustard and in August the ground was 'enamelled with delphiniums, forget-me-nots and other wildflowers'.

The bus is bolting down the descent. Flying past a courtyard, I spot a solar disc. Agricultural fields are laid out on river flats and lower slopes. On very steep high slopes the incredible yaks make a dignified living, but sheep also browse in sheer inaccessible places.

My head is my own again. My energy returns as the landscape flattens out. We are traversing a fertile plain where the harvest is amazing. I come from dry South Australia, a wheat exporter, but I have not seen such bountiful harvests since my Dutch childhood when agriculture was organic, as it may still be here. There are plenty of animals to provide manure and no tractors except the two-stroke rouseabouts choofing along roads, carrying people, grain, building materials, anything. At this late hour the workers are singing in the fields.

In the distance a large outcrop and that telltale hush of green that hides the approach to a town. Gyantse Dzong. Half-destroyed by the British and more so in the Cultural Revolution. There are still old telegraph lines on mud brick pillars, the British wire to find their way out. Somewhere here must be the settlement of Palla, from where a road led to the British encampment at Chang Lo. Soon after entering Gyantse we turn left into a dirt track between houses and fields that leads to the Gyantse Hotel.

It is a quarter to six. Today I traversed not only two passes, but a mental plain of mere existence where I was entirely subject to circumstances, unable to affect my own life in any way whatsoever. I feel a different person from the woman who left Lhasa. Bounding from the bus I confront an elderly yak tied to a post and a raging monkey running screaming up and down a fence wire. Who in their right minds brought a monkey from India and for what purpose? Was it left behind by the last British leaving Gyantse ahead of the Chinese invasion? Monkeys live long. A sign warns in English: Please don't be near the monkey. Has it mauled a few guests' fingers?

The lobby is vast enough to host Olympic ice-skating competitions. Decorating the walls are the noble heads of two ibex sheep. A set of Lhamo costumes from Tibetan opera are displayed on dummies. Arranged around the seats in the atrium, flowerpots grow geraniums, snapdragons, fuchsias, oleanders, chrysanthemums and flowering cacti, all fertilised with sheep or goat pellets. It is the best indoor garden I have seen so far.

We carry luggage up the stairs and realise we are tired after doing nothing but sitting in a bus all day. Marvellous views of the *dzong* from staircase windows are all the sightseeing we are capable of tonight. We try to eat in the pleasantly old-fashioned dining room with high windows. Kay keeps to her room with a shocking cough.

In the evening Nicola and I amuse ourselves with the 'Directory of Services' issued by the hotel manager. As a migrant who came to Australia without English, I admire this effort to communicate:

'Please do not hesitate to contact me or one of my management team if we do anything at all to make your time with us more agreeable.'

Altitude makes me tearful again, not from callous laughter, but for that genuine wish to please when it states:

'You can decide your time for dinner and tell the Front Desk Staff, they will take the dinner table to the restaurant in time.'

All the dinner tables were in place when we went down for dinner and we can only assume this refers to a time the hotel had to manage with one dinner table for all guests.

'Our hotel provide you a yak service, for your tourist convenience. The yak place is on the right of the gate. Welcome you to ride the yak, the rate is five yuan.'

So that is the elderly bovine's function. She has a job, she is part of the work gang. If I could I would liberate her from the curse of having to carry foreign bums around the dusty courtyard for the rest of her life. She ought to be out in the fields browsing, fertilising the soil. But Nicola must have a yak ride and photo taken, as she promised herself this before coming to Tibet. We've learnt that most of the yak we see are *dri* or *nak,* female yaks, or even *dzo,* the crossbreed.

'Telephone service. We regret that at present the English level of our hotel staff can't be satisfied for you. Please speak a little slowly as you telephone that numbers, for that we can understand your requirement correctly.'

I empathise. Early years in Australia I would make day expeditions into the city on errands, for I could not understand spoken Australian on the telephone, or make myself understood.

The directory closes with a list of fines if you burn or break any item, and a plea to shake your ash into the ashtray. Messages directed at Chinese guests, whose cigarette smoke drifts through the corridors to enter any room. Cigarettes and liquor will be as capable of undermining the People's Republic as it leaps forward into the next century as opium was in the last.

Next morning I feel new buoyancy, having slept well. No headache. Yet Gyantse lies higher than Lhasa. After a bowl of *congee*, my favourite rice gruel, Jason orders a proper Tibetan breakfast: *tsampa* with lentil flour, mixed with dry goat's curds and butter tea. It is delicious and satisfying. But Kay is not well and coughs constantly.

The *dzong* pulls. After seeing her in evening gloom, I now climb from window to window to see her angles in the morning light. I see what seems a familiar landscape. Some places are like that. The *dzong* draws like a magnet, although no way can I climb it. The tree-dotted golden valley of the river Nyang is flat and picturesquely beautiful, hiding in a total embrace of large brown mountains. A natural amphitheatre rises at the end of the town, shielding what remains of Palkhor Chöde monastery and its famous Kumbum, the largest stupa in Tibet. In between that and the *dzong* and me lies the most Tibetan town I have yet seen.

Nothing in my reading prepared me for the responses Gyantse arouses in me. Dismissing it as a town that had suffered too much Western contact to be interesting, I was put off by British destruction and the ghosts that would abound. Pure Tibetan Lhasa was the place I longed to see. Never Gyantse. Now I find myself, a post-Lhasa tourist, falling in love with Gyantse, ghosts and all. The place smells of ozone, hot rocks and ripe grain.

Gyantse came to prominence in the fifteenth century and until the Chinese invasion was the centre of the wool trade, Tibet's main export. Indian traders obtained passes from British officials in Kalimpong to travel to Gyantse with tea, sugar, flour, cigarettes, cotton, kerosene and 'little wares'. Apart from wool they would buy carpets, musk and gold. Indian traders contributed to Gyantse's unique development for centuries, but this trade came to a complete stop during China's border incursions in 1962.

We walk the main street to Palkhor Chöde, the sky overcast and cloudy. On one side houses are built into rock that rises to become the *dzong* 's outcrop, some 600 feet above the plain. The *dzong* straddles the rock with a cluster of linked tower-like buildings. From it snakes a sort of mini Great Wall across the top of the amphitheatre, coming down on the other side and turning into a straight wall along the street that fronts the monastery, so that its only entrance is the main gate at the end of main street. Ugyen Gyatso measured the wall with his prayer beads and found it to be about two and a half miles long.

When the British under Younghusband stormed the *dzong* in 1904, shelled it, and finally occupied it, they found, according to Peter Fleming, not only storerooms containing thirty-six tons of barley, but one room crammed with the severed heads of men, women and children. I suppose he did not mean skulls, as it would have been difficult to know whether they belonged to men or women. Severed heads would keep as well at this attitude as does meat. Fleming points out that capital punishment was not part of Tibet's penal code, although severe punishments like cutting off a hand for stealing did occur. He found no explanation for the grisly find. Since the *dzong* was the headquarters of regional governors, it is possible that a particularly malevolent past governor resorted to a massacre and concealed the heads to prevent identification of the bodies. More Gyantse ghosts.

The Williamsons found the crime rate in Tibet very low and saw few draconian punishments meted out, reserved as they mainly were for serious political offences. But they were in Tibet when the aristocrat Lungshar lost the post-Thirteenth power struggle in Lhasa, had his eyes put out and was thrown into a dungeon. Reting Rimpoche, who discovered the Fourteenth Dalai Lama, also came to a sad end there. Earlier in the century, the head of the powerful Tarong family had been executed for collaborating with the Chinese.

The British eventually set up their trade agency near the foot of the rock near the wells, and a cemetery they shared with Muslim traders until the 1954 floods swept all away. The monastery raised funds by allowing the *tom* or marketplace on its premises, charging foreign traders rent. The large daily market traded from 10 am to 1 pm. Wool and a locally made woollen cloth called *nhamba* were the main products, but also cheap goods from Calcutta and China. Das counted fifteen to twenty Nepalese shops and half-a-dozen Chinese pastry outlets. Three hundred tombs in Gyantse's Chinese cemetery by the end of the nineteenth century were a measure of the Chinese presence.

You can only marvel at Gyantse's impressive ancient bulwarks. Every building or construction in Tibet impresses because it came about through the physical labour of man and beast without the cranes and bulldozers that build to block the sunshine from our cities. Gyantse is built like Lhasa, with a prominent outcrop housing the government, a monastery more or less in its fold, and the town clustering at the foot of the rock.

The rock is the most outstanding landmark in Nyang Chu valley that runs from Shigatse to fifteen miles beyond Gyantse, some sixty miles long and on average ten wide. In Das's time Nyang Chu — 'river of delicious water'— was alive with geese, ducks, cranes and kingfishers. Hares loped through the valley. No evidence whatsoever of wildlife now, a monotonous but frightening observation.

The rock and *dzong* were principally fortifications. Gyantse withstood attacks by the Nepalese, Ghurkas and Ladakhis before the British overpowered it. In 1882 Das reported a standing army of 500 Tibetan soldiers at Gyantse. These were paid by the Chinese emperor at the rate of five rupees per year — perhaps to protect Chinese citizens? — while the Tibetan government paid them forty pounds of barley each month. Landholders 'donated' one soldier per *khang* of land, one *khang* taking about 400 pounds of seed grain to plant. The soldier was really a farmer from an estate run on feudal principles. There were also fifty Chinese soldiers stationed at Gyantse, receiving family allowances of six ounces of silver per month, plus sixty pounds of rice per head, which seems considerably better pay. Elsewhere Das writes that Tibetan farmers were called out in emergencies at the rate of one man per family and one man per *khang* of land. But it seems that of the entire Tibetan army of 6000 men, half were on duty at two ounces of silver per month while the other half were on stand-by at home on half-pay.

A small boy of twelve or fourteen years of age, approaches holding up his musical instrument, a small *drumying*. Dressed in colourless pants and jacket, he tops it with the ubiquitous cap. His eyes are hidden between such thick lids that they are invisible. His cheeks are round and apple red. At a nod and smile from the Tibetan guide the boy begins to play and sing. It gives me a cramp in the chest. The sound is like nothing I have heard before, yet it touches a chord deep inside. The boy wiggles from one foot onto the other and back, in tandem with the rhythm. The song stops as suddenly as it began on a high sad note, leaving me in mid-flight while being transported to plains of great isolation.

Neither Jason nor the guide understand the words of the song. The boy may be a nomad. He certainly has fallen between the cracks of the system, earning his living by playing and singing in the street. His round ruddy face is different from the local fine-boned features of southern Tibet. He could be a child of the uplands of Amdo or Kham, a Ngolok boy perhaps.

We arrive at Palkhor's gate too soon. I would prefer to linger where Tibetans go about their daily business. A beautiful young woman with red cheeks, wearing a headscarf, clutches a listless boy of about two. She comes up to beg, her eyes penetrating. I wonder what her story is. It is meritorious to give before entering a sacred place. Other beggars flock around.

Through the gateway we enter a vast, unpaved forecourt where a work gang of women and old men chisel pavers out of large rocks and sift sand and gravel. The work is dusty and you fear for their lungs. Due to their efforts the forecourt may in time resume its former imposing appearance. On the left shines the Kumbum, white and gold. Rabden Kunsang, the king of Nyang, felt inspired by one of Tsongkhapa's main disciples to built Palkhor Chöde monastery and its Kumbum.

Palkhor Chöde was an ecumenical gathering place, with sixteen colleges for different sects from surrounding monasteries. Three thousand monks used to gather in the great assembly hall before us, but by the late nineteenth century that number had dwindled to 600. Above the entrance five sculptured lions, claws out, jaws open, sharp teeth and red tongues showing. In all their fierceness they look cute. Behind the hall, rocks rise naked to the rim.

Before entering I turn for a new view of the *dzong*. Snow-capped mountains in the distance. I want go back into that beckoning landscape an I promise myself to linger on the way back.

Inside, the hall and chambers are vast, dark and ancient. How to survive, after leaving Tibet, without a daily dose of this unique aroma of incense, butter, old textiles and surreal images gazing down from walls and ceilings? Tibetans are natural surrealists, having always known of other realms, never having been weaned off them by industrial revolutions or hair-splitting theologians. As Buddhism merged with ancient Bönpo, realm upon realm remained ritually accessible until the present day and Tibetans developed and maintained an art that represents the journey of the human psyche in all its divergence, from the grisly to the sublime.

Christianity, taking things so literally that theologians still debate whether Adam and Eve were really the first humans, has also taken Tibetan Buddhism literally. Christian writers wrote of devil dances because the masks they saw whirling around reminded them of their own devil, instead of their own mindscapes. It has fascinated many how easily Tibetan refugees acquire a familiarity with God as they acquire English, without for one moment relinquishing their Buddhist tenets. One suspects they simply recognise a divinity they know themselves when Westerners speak of God, albeit it in different aspects. They would have even less trouble understanding Jesus, a miracle worker like Padmasambhava and bringer of a new religion. Or Mary, resembling Great Mother Tara, protectress of life. Or the Holy Spirit, because there are disembodied emanations everywhere in Tibet. Most important to Tibetans is that one should have religion, that there be dialogue about things spiritual. Abbé Huc and other missionaries to Tibet thought that the Tibetans would soon join the Christian fold because their interest in doctrine, scripture and morality was at a high level. But when the Tibetans found missionaries vilifying Buddhism to aggrandise their own religion, they banned them from the country and no more were let in. Only adventurers like George Patterson, red-bearded Scottish missionary who entered eastern Tibet from China in 1947 when Lhasa had little control there, managed to stay, as did Robert Ekvall who was virtually born in Tibet.

Jason is talking to a knowledgable monk, getting a new date for the start of this vigorous monastic splendour. 'Lo. Lo. La-so', he says. 'Yes, oh yes.' The monastery's founder, he translates, came from Kashmir in 1201. So Rabden Kunsang's building program may have taken off from an already-existing monastery in this spot. But the images date from the fifteenth century. Ugyen Gyatso heard in 1879 that Gyantse's ancient history was recorded in a book entitled *Nyang choi jung Nyimai odser.* Could I but read that.

The monk says the monastery was not damaged in the Cultural Revolution. This seems extraordinary, as numerous buildings visible in old photographs have disappeared, leaving only the assembly hall, the Kumbum, and one large building between the hall and the *thangka* wall at the top of the hill. But there is no evidence of ruins, as there is at Ganden. Maybe the monk came here after the ruins were cleared and never saw photographs of old Palkhor Chöde. Or he is carefully treading the party line.

The benign faces of *bodhisattvas* tower over us. Dressed in beautiful old brocades, their very size depicts the stature of their personalities. Some murals depict tantric practices no longer performed and Jason takes a keen interest. This place is obviously a scholar's delight. We climb stairs to the chapels. Sometimes, when I have seen something especially superb, there is no room for further impressions. I tail the group, musing, inhaling buttery incense fumes, the smell of old textiles, and feel my skin come to rest in these dark halls. We shuffle silently, listening to Jason and the monk speaking Tibetan, Jason's frequent 'lo', the throat scrapings of old monks sitting in dark corners, see a thousand butter lamps flicker until we stand before Sakyamuni, the historical Buddha, flanked by Dipankara the Buddha of the past, and Maitreya the future Buddha yet to come.

According to legend Sakyamuni in an earlier life was Megha, a young Brahmin coming down from the Himalayas to the plains to find the fee due to his teacher. He already knew all existing mantras by heart and had studied the Vedas, India's most ancient sacred scriptures. As he travelled through villages and towns these became free of afflictions. Reaching the royal city of Dipavati he found it festooned for festivities. For a moment he wondered whether the kind people had heard of his coming and whether all this gaiety was to welcome him. But then a beautiful girl, carrying a water pot and seven lotus flowers, passed by. Megha asked her the reason for the festivities.

The girl told him he must be a stranger if he did not know of the coming of Dipankara, son of the king but also the famous Buddha of that era. Megha offered to buy five lotus flowers from the girl with all the money he had begged so far. But recognising the young man's superior mind and personality, the girl made him a counter offer. She offered him her lotuses if he took her for his wife for all time, through all their rebirths. Megha's quest was enlightenment and marriage did not fit into his plans. But the girl was persistent, pledging never to keep him from his quest. Megha then took her for his wife.

So it happened. Lord Dipankara entered the city, beautiful, graceful, his senses turned inwards, his mind calmed, 'transparent as a pool, clear and unperturbed'. Megha identified with the Buddha and vowed to become a buddha himself one day. When he threw the five lotuses at Dipankara they did not fall to the ground, but suspended in the air formed a halo around Dipankara's head. They stood for the five cardinal virtues of faith, vigour, mindfulness, concentration and wisdom. The girl's two lotuses also stood up in the air, perhaps symbolic of love and devotion, because she reappears some 20 000 years later — about 500 BC — as Yashodara, the wife of Sakyamuni Buddha. She finally loses him to the quest for truth, until she joins his order of monks and nuns. But it was on the day of their meeting in Dipavati city, that out of the compassion that had been awakened in him, Megha realised he wanted to turn the wheel of Dharma to set free all living beings.

Maitreya, the future Buddha, is expected to manifest roundabout AD 6000. He is the Buddha Tibetans pray to with particular fervency, to hurry his coming and be delivered. Maitreya is expected to come from the West and is by some scholars interpreted as female. There are pronouncements and prophecies by the historical Buddha and others as to these future events. In the light of Tibetan prophecies, such as the one made by the Thirteenth Dalai Lama about the calamities to befall Tibet, I am far from sceptical. But if Maitreya is to appear in 4000 short years, then s/he must already be amongst us. Just as Sakyamuni Buddha spent 20 000 years doing compassionate works on earth after being inspired by Dipankara, so Maitreya may have been inspired by Sakyamuni and has been perfecting his/her mind, wisdom and compassion ever since. It is possible to look around in this often horrible world of humanity and see luminous people who are able to cut through the dross of human defilements and bring light and hope in the most dreadful circumstances. They may be in all walks of life, but even when high-placed, they will walk where there is much suffering. They are today's *bodhisattvas* and one of them is Maitreya to come.

The bookroom is breathtaking. Stacks rise to the high ceiling, covering all walls. That this much was preserved, when elsewhere manuscripts were used to line soldiers' boots, is another miracle. Das wrote of his stay here:

We were conducted to the great library, the very sight of which filled my mind with feelings of awe and reverence. The books were all old, broadleaved, and some two to four feet long. I was shown the sacred scriptures, all written in letters of gold.

With what assiduity and devotion the Buddhists perform the sacred duties of their religion, the deep interest they take in the collecting of sacred books and images, and their zealous care in preserving them, can only be realized by visiting such places as this. (Das, *Journey to Lhasa and Central Tibet*, p. 90)

When we see daylight an hour or so later, we step onto a roof surrounded by smaller halls. A rough, wooden ladder leads to a newly built verandah with a signboard saying in Chinese and English: *'Now a days no open door. Beacouse the monastry is rebuilt'*. I delight in creative English.

Of course Jason bounds up the ladder, sticks his head around the door and speaks Tibetan. Soon he beckons us to come up. I'm not sure we should have such privileges, but change my mind when we enter the large empty room. Here Tibet's reviving religious art is in the making. By the windows sit two young Tibetans, shoulders touching, applying colour with fine brushes to Sakyamuni's lotus throne, delicately drawn in black and white. The Buddha's face and chest are still white, marked out with thin lines in the exact mathematical measurements underlying all Tibetan sacred paintings.

On the opposite wall a recently completed mural has a central yellow-faced deity I do not know. Tsongkhapa and his two disciples also figure prominently. The work is so new that light from the windows falls on the paint like a moving white splash, depending on where you stand.

The six windows in carved wooden frames have small panes of glass set in blocks of nine, like a quilt. They flank three larger panes in the centre, making the outer wall look like a pretty patchwork in glass and wood.

Cross-legged on the floor, with his back against the window, sits the master painter between two wooden boxes in which he keeps patterns and paper. He is a small, not yet grey man wearing glasses and a Mao cap. Before him a large wooden tray holds bowls with paints in the colours of the painting on his right. He tells Jason how he started young as a painter, during the Cultural Revolution. When hostilities reached a peak, he had to leave the monastery to become a farmer. He worked the land for fifteen years before being reinstated as the monastery's painter. He teaches two or three apprentices at a time. The fine lines are his, laid down according to tradition. Much of the painting is his too. But the apprentices learn their craft by painting in subsidiary motifs with colour.

'We are not very good', says the small master. We ask Jason to tell him these are the best new murals we have seen so far. He seems pleased, but unconvinced, carrying perfect images in his mind's eye. But we have seen so many well-intentioned but disastrous attempts at restoration. Of course we are no experts, yet we have viewed nothing but paintings, frescoes, *thangkas* and ceiling s for ten days. You might say we have a condensed acquaintance with Tibetan mural art. We express gratitude and leave him to his work. His must be one of the finest jobs to be had in communist Tibet today. Outside I spot ruined walls after all, outlined against the sky.

View from the Kumbum

From the painter's verandah we look down on the Kumbum, its top floor scaffolded for restoration, but the tower shining golden in the sunlight. What gods do we thank for the preservation of this incredible and most unusual stupa?

We clamber down to walk to the Place of a Thousand Images. It consists of an astounding 108 chapels, large and small, arranged in four tiers and topped by the traditional dome and spire. Although Stephen Batchelor could only view the first and fourth floor, the entire Kumbum seems to be open now. Alas, we do not make it further than the third floor because of altitude fatigue. Das and Ugyen climbed straight to the top floor, then circled downwards, because so many visitors wearied from the circumambulation and never reached the top. They refreshed themselves afterwards with copious draughts of tea.

We soon split up, viewing chapels at our own pace, lingering or passing on. Some images are so fierce that one look is enough, others so serenely beautiful you stand mesmerised. Jason goes around with a monk who knows the facts. But these images come so fast and furious that I do not care for detailed descriptions or even names. I recognise Sakyamuni in the larger chapel and further on Tara, Avalokiteshvara, Manjusri, Yamanthaka, Vajrayogini, Hayagriva, Palden Lhamo. I simply want to absorb the riches of form and colour, let myself be affected by the powers these images so obviously represent.

The works were done in the fifteenth century by Newar artists indigenous to the Kathmandu Valley, who were and are among the finest artisans in the world. Images and stucco work exude such vitality that sometimes I step back the moment I stick my head into a small chapel, overcome by the suggestive power of the figures. When I rest, panting, on the third floor, where Jason is still talking with the monk, I resolve I will I must come back here one day to do the circumambulations of the Kumbum in my own time, even if it takes a week.

The monk tells of an Italian crew who photographed every mural and image in the Kumbum in 1992, using powerful lights to illuminate the darkest of chapels. They plan to produce a book about the Kumbum and the meanings of its images. (And they did: *The Great Stupa of Gyantse: A Complete Tibetan Pantheon of the Fifteenth Century* by Franco Ricca and Erberto Lo Bue, 1995.) Gyantse's Kumbum ought to be on the world heritage list. There is nothing like it anywhere. Deep inside the stupa are relics not seen by anyone since they were deposited.

Turning to descend, my eyes blink in the sharp light reflecting from the long plain ahead. Gyantse valley is blazing with yellow mustard flowers. At this time of day the mountains enclosing the valley look like pink leather, dropped to crumple gently against a background of higher teal blue giants wearing snowy caps, surrounding Karo-La. The air is redolent of the fragrance of clean, sun-baked earth. The plain is dotted with trees, as is the town. There is not one mechanical vehicle visible in the main street. I can see people walking, a man leading a donkey, two women carrying baskets on their backs, children playing in the dust. The scene is biblical in a universal sense. Das counted some one thousand houses in 1878. There don't seem to be many more now, although I can't see around the rock. A wide and dusty cobblestoned street, lined with two-storey stone houses and tiny market stalls, leads from the monastery's monumental carved and painted gateway, its wooden posts polished from four centuries of devout touch to a smoothness resembling that of jade.

Once Gyantse was a thriving centre of Tibetan civilisation. By the end of the nineteenth century it was a bustling caravan centre and gateway to British India and the Western world, while the capital Lhasa — one week's travel across the high passes — remained the mystical city forbidden to most foreigners. To Westerners, Gyantse was the last Tibetan city accessible under stringent conditions, though Lhasa remained the goal. In 1993 Gyantse is a sleepy town, left aside by the progress imposed on Tibet by communist China. The new road from Lhasa to Shigatse passes it by. In 1993 Gyantse is the only one of Tibet's few cities that still looks and feels Tibetan, last pocket of a dying civilisation.

Descending the Kumbum stairs, I nearly stumble over a solar reflector, pushed in the sun by a boy monk. He smiles, noticing my appreciative glance for this appropriate technology, and puts on the kettle. It will boil by midday. Downstairs I admire a small monastery building, red-painted fluted pillars marking the entrance. Thickly plastered white walls. A balcony of carved wooden panels only one metre above the ground, two wooden ladders with railings leading up. Too dark to see inside, but what a gem of a place!

The heat in the courtyard is stifling. Once several thousand monks would sit here. The sun stands high in the sky. All you smell is dust, although the stonecutters have stopped for lunch. While Jason talks with a very elderly monk wrapped in layers of maroon as if it is close to freezing point, we seek the shade of the entrance gate to wait. Suddenly a tug at my sleeve. I turn and face again the young mother of this morning. Now she carries a recently born infant in her arms, points at it, makes high-pitched noises and holds out her hand. I take her hand, waiting until Jason comes. The baby looks pathetically thin.

'This morning she had a small boy with her and now she carries this baby', I tell him. 'Can you find out what her story is?'

'She's probably a prostitute', says Jason and walks on. But I am not satisfied. The plea in her eyes is too strong. So Jason asks our Tibetan guide, who asks local people standing around, and the story comes to us. She is a deaf mute and has to beg for her living. Crying inwardly, I give her money. I know her beautiful face and throaty sounds will keep haunting me as will the song of the boy musician. Who can tell the fathers of children of a woman who cannot cry out?

The main street has woken up while we were inside Palkhor Chöde. Market stalls appear in front of houses and people move about in that slow rhythm of those who carry loads. Framed by the monastery gate the scene looks even more archaic than from the top of the Kumbum. The man and his donkey are still there, the women are walking the other way. Now begins the slow walk I wish would never end. Soon I drop behind the others. I am possessed by that feeling children experience when they have found a place where they want to be and don't want to be hurried along. I don't look the part, but have a notion I once belonged here in a sense that happens seldom in a travelling life. Renewing very old connections, I stroll the long dusty street that has seen parades of potentates and princelings, high lamas and pilgrims, caravans of traders, invading soldiers from southern countries, Britain, and finally China.

Red-tasselled horses pull wooden carts on rubber tyres. Some steeds are tied loosely to hitching poles while their owners walk through the market. Vegetables lie spread out on sacks, healthy-looking giant turnips, Chinese cabbages, beans. A mule stands dreaming. Traders sit under sunhats on clumps of building rubble, a feature of streets where the Chinese rule. The autumn sun is blazing hot. The teahouse terrace, where rough wooden tables and benches are arranged under the trees, looks inviting.

The meat market is situated on a masonry platform under a corrugated iron roof. Skinned sheep carcasses and hunks of yak hang from hooks in the open air. Anywhere else there would be a buzz of flies, but here you hardly see any. High altitude preserves meat in ways we find miraculous. When Lois Lang-Sims visited refugee camps in Sikkim when Tibetans had just arrived, she found them stringing bits of meat rations on wire to dry as they used to do in Tibet, but the stench of rotting meat at Sikkim's lower altitude was overpowering.

Women sell vegetables and men sell meat — a mystery similar to finding that in the remotest countries women grow their hair long and men chop it off! Not only do men sell the meat, but other men stand looking at it, to buy or to chat. A few dogs sit around hopefully.

The textile market is disappointing, displaying mainly Chinese clothing. But I want Chinese pillowslips like the one I slept on last night. They come in bright satin colours with embroidered flowers; one of my daughters will like them. Trying a stall with household textiles, I gesture to the trader the measurements of a pillowslip, fold my hands on one side of my head, close my eyes and lean my head on my hands as if asleep. 'Lo!' he exclaims. He turns around and shouts into the open door of the house. A woman puts her head out of a first-floor window and they have an exchange. She pulls her head in again and he motions me to wait, things are about to happen. Down the staircase comes a rolled-up Tibetan carpet! I should have known! What Tibetan sleeps on a Chinese pillowslip? Carpets are for sleeping on! I am dreadfully disappointed to have to gesture 'no sale'. But I buy from him a nice walnut drinking cup for Tenzin, the young Australian monk who has never seen his homeland Tibet. We part smiling, mutually bemused. I have depended too much on Jason. A little Tibetan grammar book sits unused at the bottom of my luggage. But most likely there is no Tibetan word for pillowslip.

Wandering on I examine plasterwork on houses. Someone expressed a sense of joy by making upturned sweeping half-circles with a large brush in a nicely regular pattern, to good effect. Despite periodic whitewashing, there is a pleasing degree of neglect about Gyantse. Things get done, but not necessarily frequently. Windows have colourful but fading decorations and curtain flounces erode away to a frazzle in the ever-present wind of the plains.

Another horse on my path, its nose in a feeding bag, munching placidly. From a nearby house come laughter and men's voices. A *chang* house. The rider is surely inside, but has seen to it that his steed is content while it waits. As with the yaks, the horses are as tame as my dogs at home. This little one carries a beautiful saddle carpet featuring a large red lotus on a dark blue background in a border of stylised clouds. Further on I meet a brown cow, shambling along with nothing to do, while a man walks in the opposite direction carrying a heavy load on his back. This is Tibet!

Narrow side streets attract, but as I've fallen behind the group there is only time to look in. The houses possess architectural genius in the way light and dark contrast between walls, doors and window frames. Not a house stops at one level. There may be high walls surrounding a roof garden, a many-windowed room jutting out from a facade, or a tumble of apartments build on at later stages. All roof parapets and chimneys carry brush sticks with prayer flags, catching the breeze. The town seems festooned for a festival.

Sheets stretch across the footpath, from house to tree, providing shade for traders. Woven Tibetan horse trappings are on offer, but most goods are cheap imports and their tinselly colours clash with the mellow tones of Tibetan weaving. Two men on a donkey cart clip-clop past. On the backboard three children return home from school, one wearing the red triangular neck scarf of the Chinese Revolution.

It had to happen. I meet a truck, monster from an unwanted future.

Fortunately it is parked beside another horse, while the owners sit talking in the doorway of a house with half-moon and sun sign above the open door. Over the windows pyramids are painted with large dots, counting five, three, two and one at the top. Their significance eludes me.

The doorstep talkers look up and spend a smile. Smiles and nods in passing seem customary in Gyantse. But now it is a last goodbye, for at the end of the street stands the bus, waiting. The group is clambering aboard. We have to make Shigatse today. I turn and walk backwards to keep the street, market, monastery and the rock in one embracing gaze. But at fifty-nine you can't catch a bus walking backwards down a cobblestone street, so finally, reluctantly, I make speed, board, then turn my head in all directions at once as we slowly drive out of Gyantse. How many hair cracks can a heart stand before it breaks?

Tea Party at Shalu Monastery

We return to the hotel in the fields to collect luggage. The monkey runs up and down the metal railing. It is stark raving mad and screeches at us, dancing up and down.

She is chained up in full sun and her water bowl is empty. This I cannot stand. I make a dash for the bowl, retrieve it and run for a tap in a toilet. When I carry the full bowl out, the reason for it being empty becomes obvious. It leaks. I run to the monkey and it snatches the bowl from me and drinks. Then she throws it away. Kay retrieves it and volunteers to do another water run. By the time she returns there is precious little water in the bowl. But as the monkey snatches, she also knocks it over and scratches Kay's hand.

A Chinese policeman comes out of a watchhouse, waving his rubber stick at us, pointing at the sign. We cast him a scornful look and walk away, aching for that little animal brought from India for someone's profit, living out her life bereft of her own species, just an ancient yak for company. If it could but be owned by Tibetans, how different its life would be. The monkey keeps jumping and yelling. We sort of know what she is saying, but how should she understand we are powerless to help?

Before we leave, Nicola climbs the old dri's back to ride around the courtyard. We take the photographs. She is so thrilled, stroking the long black mane. Luckily she is a lightweight.

Soon we are among the fields, where the harvest still proceeds accompanied by singing. I am struck again by how prosperous Nyang Chu valley looks. Our Tibetan guide confirms that this is rich land and the farmers well-to-do. They plough in March, seed in June, harvest wheat in September, barley in October. He does not know how many crops they plant per season, but thinks no more than two. Presently they are winnowing. The barley stalks are rubbed by hand to release the grain.

Jason adds that during the Cultural Revolution the people in the Gyantse district were very strong on *tzamzing,* the infamous self-criticism sessions which led to the sentencing of former landholders, lamas and others disapproved of by the regime. Shigatse, not far away, is a notorious stronghold of communism.

Why such vehement resistance to Chinese occupation in areas closer to China, whereas Shigatse and Gyantse, of all Tibetan centres most in touch with foreigners, turned communist? Until the British invasion that contact was mostly on the Tibetans' terms. The clue for why this area and the villages around Karo-La are red may well lie in that fatal encroachment.

At the time the British were advancing to Gyantse, the Lhasa government was looking for scapegoats to blame for the intrusion. The Lhasa government had always put the responsibility for keeping foreigners out of Tibet on the inhabitants of border areas. There are countless travellers' tales of entering Tibet, usually in disguise, only to be discovered in some village not far from the border and marched back under escort. The punishment for failing to stop foreigners was severe, as friends of Das and Kawaguchi discovered.

So when the British advanced on Gyantse the Lhasa government was throwing people into gaol on mere suspicion of having been lax in preventing the approaching disaster. Yet Tibetans had bravely opposed the invaders at Guru, though their matchlocks stood no chance. Nine hundred survivors walked away through a hail of bullets, 'slowly and with bowed heads, as if disillusioned in their gods', so wrote Edmund Chandler, *Daily Mail* correspondent who lay injured himself with seventeen sword wounds and a severed hand.

Beyond Guru, the Gyantse *dzongpön* met the British to explain he could not surrender the *dzong* without risking execution. Yet the British eventually took it and proceeded to live off the countryside and the *dzong*'s store of barley. The farmers of Nyang Chu valley and the people of Gyantse bore the brunt of the battles, having to relinquish their hamlets and food stores, while the Lhasa government, unaware of the military power of the new invaders, kept looking for someone to blame according to the age-old method by which Tibet had been kept free from foreign influence. This time that method did not work.

When finally the treaty was signed in Lhasa and political 'friendships' cemented, the mood in Lhasa changed against the Chinese, who had taken advantage of the situation. When subsequently the Dalai Lama returned and a few years later fled to British India to escape an advancing Chinese army, the circle closed. From then on some members of the Lhasa government set their hopes on political associations with Britain, to get away from under the Chinese yoke which applied increasing pressure until the Chinese empire collapsed in 1911.

Meanwhile, no-one compensated the Tibetans who defended Tibet against the British, only to see Lhasa turn 180 degrees after the defeat. The 2700 dead were dead forever and there would have been not one family around Gyantse without someone to mourn. People's memories are long. Although life expectancy in Tibet is not high, there could be people alive today who heard of the 1904 invasion from old people who were young at that time. Tibetans are great oral historians and do not let many details slip in the telling.

Seen in that light, it would be understandable that when the present Dalai Lama fled southward, to the country from where since time immemorial the invaders of the Nyung Chu valley had come, the population decided to throw in their lot with the invaders from the north. *Tzamzing* sessions would have given them an opportunity to level old scores with landholder families who contributed soldiers for the defence force slaughtered so mercilessly by the British. Having been the 'Gateway to Tibet' brought Gyantse as much trouble as profit and in 1950 they may have chosen to look after their own needs rather than those of Tibet at large.

Since the Chinese have built the low road from Lhasa to Shigatse, Gyantse has become a quiet town. No longer a gateway, it lies sleeping in the sun, while farmers sing in the fields, harvesting bountiful crops. Although the main reason for their prosperity is the fertility of their soil, can one blame them for being red? It is easy to overlook that peasants anywhere became communists because no-one ever lifted a finger in their favour. It is chilling how the producers of food are pushed about by banks, multinationals and governments because they are not an organised political force, or mechanisation has so reduced their numbers that their voting power is negligible. No country can prosper without its farmers. No country whose farmers suffer from generation to generation can survive.

These thoughts are interrupted by the sight of tall ruins on a hilltop against a backdrop of mountains. Tsechen monastery. Taken by the British as a lookout post, destroyed in the Cultural Revolution. But the walls still standing are substantial, easily four storeys, and there is a hamlet at the foot of the hill. One day reconstruction may commence. These mountains have that crumpled look of cloth thrown in a heap by a careless hand. The ephemeral yellow of harvested fields is a stark contrast to their purplish-grey bulk. Yet on a thousand ridges and minuscule ledges grow tufts of greenery, giving the clifflike walls a festooned air.

At last it happens. Our first flat tyre. Mr X whips out a tool kit and sets to work. The other men lend moral support, but Mr X knows what to do. Willow trees line the road and the fields are dotted with farmers, yaks, children and wagons piled high with harvest. An agricultural scooter loaded with sacks comes choofing by. The men and boys riding it clearly think we're mad taking pictures of them. People here go extremely well dressed. The farmhouses sparkle with fresh whitewash and paint. Yaks are sleek and fat. Under the willows runs a little canal, like in the countryside of Holland.

Mr X packs up his tools and we are mobile. The road is remarkably good, graded so recently that we could imagine being on a luxury day tour. But suddenly Jason points and confers with the Tibetan guide. Mr X swings the wheel and we turn off into a shallow riverbed 'Shalu!' shouts Jason, excited. 'Can you see the Chinese roof?'

At this distance we cannot see anything very precisely and the little bus rolls and heaves like a camel crossing the Sahara, taking a zig-zag course through shallow patches and gravel beds of a meandering river that appears the only access to Shalu monastery. On low banks stand square mud-brick pillars, perhaps copied after the British ones, telegraph wires running over the top of them to the monastery. Like sentinels they guard the approach to Shalu, marching into a valley formed by an embrace of four mountain slopes.

While fording the river six times, Jason gives us the bones of Shalu's history. The monastery was founded in 1027 by Sherab Jungne, under the patronage of the princes of Shalu and with a donation by a Mongolian Buddhist donor from China, hence the roof of green glazed tiles. Though a Red Hat monastery it once had strong ties with Sakya, further south.

Shalu's most famous scholar lama was its eleventh abbot, Butön Rinchen Drup, one of the world's greatest bibliographers. He managed to put order in the multifarious Buddhist writings that had reached Tibet in ad hoc fashion over the centuries. His work resulted in the *Kanjur*, the collection of the Buddha's discourses, and the *Tanjur*, the even more voluminous body of commentaries thereon. Butön Rinchen Drup himself wrote out 227 volumes of commentaries by hand with a metal pen. Copies were made over the years and any monastery worth its salt would have the complete *Kanjur* and *Tanjur*. But the originals and the scholar's pen, kept in Shalu monastery, were burnt by Red Guards during the Cultural Revolution, as were his personal writings. Scholars' hearts and pilgrims' hearts break at hearing this.

Shalu attracted the best artists, specialising in mandalas and fine *thangkas*. Its murals are said to be not only the most ancient but the most beautiful in all Tibet. Butön Rimpoche, being a great art historian, recorded important mandalas in such detail that his descriptions have been used by painters for centuries.

San Francisco's Asian Art Museum has a superb *thangka* featuring Butön wearing a yellow hat. Red has faded to yellow? Or had the painter, centuries after the Rimpoche's death, forgotten he was a Red Hat abbot? Or is this a case of posthumous Yellow Hat appropriation of Tibet's foremost scholar? I have a lot to learn. The portrait dates from the late seventeenth century, when fine *thangkas* were being produced at Shalu, and shows Butön in meditation, hands in the teaching position and surrounded by fifty-eight buddhas, *bodhisattvas*, disciples and other historical figures, including Tsongkhapa and Atisha (who lived for a while at Shalu), the Great Fifth and the Sixth Dalai Lamas.

Shalu was severely damaged during an earthquake in 1329 and rebuilt under Butön Rimpoche, whose energy obviously matched his intellect. Ribuk hermitage up the slope behind Shalu was destroyed in the Cultural Revolution, as was a shrine to Rabtenma, a form of Palden Lhamo. The monastery, being on the tourist route, has been given money for restorations. I'm glad we will see it before it becomes an advertisement for paint.

Shalu was particularly known for esoteric studies and psychic training so attractive to early Western travellers. One hesitates to quote L. Austine Waddell because, expert though he was in his time, he could be so scathing and sceptical as to defeat the purpose of understanding the religion he studied all his life! On Shalu he remarks:

> Here instruction is given in magical incantations, and devotees are immured for years in its cave hermitages. Amongst the supernatural powers believed to be so acquired is the alleged ability to sit on a heap of barley without displacing a grain; but no credible evidence is extant of anyone displaying such feats. (Waddell, *Tibetan Buddhism,* p. 277)

What 'credible evidence' had he in mind? Surely not a painting or photograph? If anyone sat on a heap of barley without sinking waist deep into it, he would have used the sort of mindpower we accept today as attained by martial arts experts after years of dedicated training.

In his attempts to sort out which deity did what and how many emanations each might have, Waddell complained the lamas had not 'attempted complete lists of their motley deities'. Why did he assume that lamas, who knew their deities and their doings by heart, would make lists for Western scholars? A recent publication identifies over 3000 Buddhist divinities, not only Tibetan (*Buddhism: Flammarion Iconographic Guides*). Waddell wasn't the only one to treat Tibetan religion with arrogant scorn and lack of empathy, though one of the more liverish. Today scholarship has changed dramatically. Hundreds of bright young scholars devote their lives to the study of Tibetan Buddhism, recognising its highly developed psychological component, and Jason is a fine example of their enthusiasm. He bristles with anticipation as we approach the dark walls of Shalu.

Sudden coolness descends from tall, leafy trees as we step off the bus into the intimate courtyard of the assembly hall. Apart from the beautiful Central Asian roof, the buildings are Tibetan in every respect. Jason hopes to see some good mandalas, but the young monk meeting us says the abbot has left for a blessing ceremony at a new stupa, taking the keys.

However, the monk can let us into the south chapel to the right of the *gompa*. It has beautiful, almost life-size stone statues of deities in the verandah. The posts and elaborately carved fascia appear to have been repainted recently, but inside it's a different story. The chapel was used as a grain store during the Cultural Revolution and the frescoes in this first- floor room were painted out. The paint has been partly removed to reveal very ancient mandalas. At least the grain preserved them and restoration may be possible.

I photograph a beautiful *bodhisattva* holding a lotus flower, wearing golden ornaments, a finely patterned brocade scarf and rainbow pants. He stands on a lotus throne and the surrounding mountains are roamed by deer and tiger, while ducks frolic on the lake. A green halo surrounds his head and his entire body emanates blue rays. The sky is filled with cotton clouds and lotus flowers. A scene of almost romantic loveliness.

Shalu used to house 350 monks, but now there are barely 40, mostly invisible. Shalu seems spooky, with only the young monk about. He has pointed out details with intelligent fervour, but now asks us to wait while he gets the caretaker who, after all, holds a key for the *gompa*. Shortly he returns with an old man with wispy white beard, dressed in faded grey *chuba* of coarse homespun, carrying a large iron key. The old man leads us into the high, dark hall with an air of bemusement at Jason's ability to speak his language, albeit with a Kham accent.

We are still sceptical over missing keys and the old man's seeming reluctance, when he suddenly leads us into a dark passage. It turns out to be the beginning of an inner circumambulation corridor, about five to six feet wide, surrounding the assembly hall. High up in the 25-feet-high walls some openings let in light. Birds sit in one of these windows and I worry lest their devastating white droppings damage the precious frescoes, though there are no signs of this. By torchlight we pick our way across huge, worn chunks of stone, a floor probably over 900 years old. Jason is ecstatic!

The walls of this passage are entirely covered with frescoes. I imagine painters working by the light of butter lamps and the little daylight falling through those skylights. They would have built extensive scaffolding, working from the top down. There is so much we understand no longer. The work must have taken years, decades, even a century. The mind falls still.

The inner walls are covered with thousands of tiny Buddhas in endless variety of sitting positions with varying hand postures of specific meanings. The inside of the outer walls are covered in Newar-style paintings telling stories of Buddha's early life, the Jataka stories. Underneath each picture the story is told in fine lettering, so that it can be read by torchlight. Is this an indication of widespread literacy among the patrons, painters and pilgrims of the time? Why else paint all this lettering if only a few lamas were literate, and knew the stories by heart anyway?

The style dates the paintings to probably the twelfth and thirteenth centuries. Not all of Shalu monastery was destroyed in the earthquake. Jason is wondering aloud whether these paintings have been recorded anywhere. Perhaps the outer wall was built around the *gompa* at a later date, before the painting of the high walls could begin. It is a remarkable example of what an attitude of timelessness in a civilisation centred on devotion can achieve. Generations of painters may have worked in this very long passage. Their work is well preserved in the cool, dark atmosphere. It is hard to tear ourselves away, but the old man and Jason trudge on, pointing, talking, until we emerge from an ancient world into daylight.

The old man has so warmed to Jason that he makes a friendly joke when we are about to step outside. Wouldn't it be nice, he says, if he could invite us to tea and bake some biscuits for us? The way he puts it, Jason translating, excludes the possibility. But the idea being delightful, we gently chuckle along with him. Turning the giant old key, he saunters off across the blazing hot courtyard and the young monk takes over again.

Now we hear the old man's story. The caretaker was once the abbot of Shalu, although at the start of the Cultural Revolution the monastery was almost extinct. He was forced to disrobe and marry. He had a son. Now his son is the abbot of Shalu, who has gone to the stupa blessing, taking most of the keys. By forcing the abbot to marry, the Chinese begot another abbot, although in this area monks and abbots tend to be pro-Chinese and many do as directed. The old man's fantasy of serving us tea and biscuits has after all a place in his past, for it is what an abbot would have done when visitors arrived.

The courtyard bakes in midday heat and dust. But I register a thrill walking on cobblestones that are probably the originals laid a millennium ago! Left to ourselves we walk around locked buildings, admiring elaborate carvings and intricate paintwork. Much is fresh, but retaining the fine lines of older styles. Where a modern architrave may have lotus flowers and geometric borders, here we see a tiny but intricately carved seated Padmasambhava in a wooden capital. The windows are ten-pane panels, set in yellow-painted frames in long rows, reminiscent of a pretty country railway station. Entire tree trunks, faded to pink, stand unadorned except by prayer flags. There can't be white ants here, for wood appears to last forever in this climate.

When we hear another bus arrive, we make to leave. Having had Shalu to ourselves for the better part of an hour, we don't want the stillness broken. But the German tourists at the entrance are as quiet as we are at our best. Hopping puddles, they disappear into the courtyard as we board our van, wondering whether the old man will come out again with his iron key, dreaming of serving tea and biscuits to his guests.

The Big Rock

We leave Shalu valley through the shallow river, past a sleepy village. Soon after, Shigatse comes into view. Lying at 3900 metres it is Tibet's second city.

Tashilhunpo monastery has been the seat of the Panchen Lamas since 1570 according to Tibetan history; and 1385 according to a Chinese interpretation to prove that the Panchen Lamas were an older line than the Dalai Lamas. In the tandem rule of Dalai and Panchen Lamas, the oldest is always the teacher of the younger one. The present Dalai Lama was the teacher of the recently deceased Panchen Lama. But because the Chinese wanted to use the Panchen Lamas to overshadow or unseat the Dalai Lamas, in the past as now, it was in their interest to claim seniority of line for the Panchen Lamas by naming three earlier abbots of Tashilhunpo as first, second and third Panchen Lamas.

Hence, the last Panchen Lama, who died in 1989, was the seventh according to Tibetan history, while the Chinese chiselled 'Tenth' on his tomb. But Tashilhunpo is as Yellow Hat Gelukpa as the big Lhasa monasteries, established as it was by Tsongkhapa's nephew Gendun Drup — retrospectively named First Dalai Lama, for the Tibetans also adapted history — in 1447. At that time Tsang province was fiercely Red Hat, and Yellow Hats often had to flee from their fury. It took many years before Tashilhunpo built up a strong monastic community of 4000, making Shigatse a Gelukpa centre away from Lhasa's direct control. The city was also an important trading centre, close to India and Nepal. Now tourism is important, although there is still a wool and carpet industry. The town has about 40 000 inhabitants.

Before we can see the town, the first man-made shape looming against a mountain backdrop is the Kiku-tamsa, the white tangkha wall above Tashilhunpo. Reading about this giant structure is one thing, seeing quite another. It is awesome and built by hand. Actually, the wall is a nine-storey building without windows front or back, only in the narrow side walls and then merely for the five middle storeys. On religious feast days, appliquéd *thangkas* of a size covering the entire nine-storey facade are hung on the sloping front wall. The *thangkas* are stored inside the building, but when Tashilhunpo housed 4000 monks, much of it was storehouse for dried carcases of yaks, sheep and goats needed to feed them.

Although Tibetans are better than most at keeping the Buddhist precept of not taking life, they are not vegetarians. Das found people using the chapel room in their homes to store carcases without any sense of hypocrisy.

The unrolling of gigantic *thangkas* from the top parapet, several times a year, was top entertainment as well as an important religious event. Tibetans also enjoyed their indigenous opera, spectacular religious dance performances and a variety of quite thrilling sporting events, especially on horseback. Now they must do with Chinese television in the teashop. The *thangkas* are still unrolled once or twice a year, but most of the rest went by the socialist wayside as being potentially subversive, especially the opera.

Once Shigatse's own Potala straddled the high rock outcrop at the foot of which lies the town. It served as palace for the kings of Tsang and was built as a smaller replica of the Lhasa palace. The kings were unseated by a Mongolian invasion in 1642 and later the palace became the *dzong*, where the governor of Tsang oversaw the province. But in 1961, Shigatse *dzong* was destroyed for the sake of socialism. It must have taken some doing. To think the Chinese spent all their energy in Tibet on destroying the old in just a few years, while the little new they have introduced has taken them thirty-four years. Their new architecture is an insult to the Tibetan landscape that was so entirely complemented by superb structures like Shigatse's Potala.

Driving into a long wide dusty street, still no town. But a Bank of China and we need cash. Further on, the Shigatse Hotel. A real-life expedition has just drawn up. Three bronzed men and a bronzed woman clad in clinging khaki, emerge from two mud-spattered vehicles as if they've just come from King Solomon's mines. They are testing Russian-made Lada cars in Tibet. A friend in Australia owned a car of the same brand and tested it there to his grief. There must be a reason why tourist vehicles on Tibet's rough roads are Japanese minibuses.

A two-car expedition in a street so wide is rather drab compared with Das's tale of the arrival in Shigatse of the caravan of the Kashmir maharaja's envoy in the 1880s. Fifteen thousand Shigatsians dropped what they were doing to watch the pageant. The envoy rode accompanied by fifty uniformed men and another hundred mounted followers from all Himalayan states: Sikhs, Muslims in white turbans, Ladakhis in sheepskins, Murmis and Dokpas, Nepalis and Kiron Tibetans. As if that were not enough spectacle, there were merchants dressed like princes, whose servants wore silk liveries and whose ponies were decked with silver and gold brocade ornaments.

The Tibetan custom of providing travellers with fresh ponies and porters also applied to caravans such as these. Although the envoy came every three years to bring tribute to the Dalai Lama, the merchants and traders following in his wake merely availed themselves of an opportunity to travel in safe company.

Yet the people had to provide porterage and ponies to carry merchandise and personal property, while the Lhasa government accommodated and feasted the official party. Das heard the people of Shigatse speak critically of the passing splendour and begrudge this form of taxation. Yet the tribute arose from a disastrous war inflicted on the Tibetans by a Sikh general who, having already conquered Ladakh, Balti and Skardo, cast eyes on Tibet's woolgrowing districts. Times were often less than peaceful in Tibet, however hard the Tibetans tried.

In recent years Shigatse has also had its share of demonstrations and dissent. During a 1983 crackdown over one hundred demonstrators were arrested by Chinese police. About 3000 people were arrested all over Tibet and many executed before that year was over. It's one way of making a city toe the line. Historically, Shigatse could always expect attacks from any direction.

At first impression, the hotel is mostly lobby. A sweeping staircase with badly laid red carpet has us panting upstairs with the luggage. Today we are fit enough to dump the bags and go out to find the town. A long walk yields endless Chinese shops. I remember reading that Lhasa has 12 000 Chinese shops and only 300 run by Tibetans, but here shops seem 100 per cent Chinese-owned. They sell cheap Chinese consumer goods and much trash no-one can possibly need. Kay and I enter a textile shop to look for pillowslips. Chinese proprietors and Chinese customers are in conversation. We wait a long while before I step to the counter and they reluctantly interrupt their talk. No pillowslips. As we peel away, they close ranks, glaring over their shoulders. Perhaps they came from a province decreed 'no-go' for Western tourists.

I try one more shop where pillowslips decorate the walls. Pointing, I ask for more colours. Each one is more ghastly than the last one and I buy the lettuce green variety, best of a bad lot. The pretty ones in Gyantse Hotel resembled antique lace compared with these.

We look around while waiting for the woman to wrap them and fetch change. This must be any Chinese peasant's dream. A little nook of a shop stacked to the ceiling with every loud-coloured textile Chinese exiles might desire. My feelings about modern Chinese taste are as arrogant as Waddell's about Tibetan religion, although I realise that Chinese classical taste was supported by the sweat of common people. No doubt modern peasants like luminous textiles because they never had any colour in their lives before the revolution, or because satins and lace were once only seen in palaces. Or because they are sick of wearing blue and khaki Mao suits.

The woman is made up for the stage, dressed in a clinging red satin dress. Long lacquered fingernails show she is not a peasant. Her husband wears a more mundane sleeveless pullover and beams at us. How did they make a living in China? Neither looks strong, though still fairly young. Their parents may have gone hungry, unable to give their children adequate food. There is a baby in the back and a little girl, also dressed in lucky red. Have these young parents done what so many migrants do? Packed up without asking too many questions, to settle in a place where the future may be better for the children? Chinese people know no better than that Tibet is part of China. The woman smiles politely as she returns with change. Her teeth are rotten. I hope she can earn enough to buy a set of dentures.

We run out of streetlights without finding the real Shigatse and stumble back to the hotel. In the lobby I pick up a copy of a month-old *China Daily* carrying a report on the inauguration of a gilded stupa containing the body of the Panchen Lama who died on 28 January 1989. According to the paper he died at age fifty-nine of heart disease following religious ceremonies. For four-and-a-half years his body sat in the meditation position in which he died. Then on 30 August 1993 his remains were placed in the new stupa Sisum Namgual — 'Immortal in Universe' — in the presence of his 77-year-old mother, younger brother and Chinese official Luo Gan.

> In his speech, Luo Gan spoke highly of the 10th Bainquen [Panchen] Lama's lasting effort in safeguarding the unity of the motherland. Following the master's death, the central government dubbed him a great patriot, noted statesman, a true friend of the Communist Party of China and an outstanding leader of Tibetan Buddhism.
>
> Luo said that after the founding of the New China in 1949 the Bainquen Lama inherited and displayed the glorious patriotic spirit of all the previous Bainquen Lamas in various periods including those of the peaceful liberation, the democratic revolution and the social construction of Tibet. The Bainquen Lama accumulated indelible meritorious deeds under the new historic conditions, he added.
>
> The building of the stupa and the memorial palace is a symbol of the respect and esteem held by the Party and the State for the Lama's patriotic deeds, of the care by the Party and the State for the Zhaxi Lhumbo Lamasery and all the patriotic people in Tibet, Buddhist circles, and of the ethnic and religious policies of the Party and the State, the State Councillor pointed out.
>
> Luo said that the freedom of religious belief is one of the major long-term policies of the Party and the State.

No-one familiar with contemporary Tibetan history would hesitate for one moment in agreeing with the salient points in this statement! Of course the Panchen Lama's age is wrong. Born in 1938, he was only fifty-one years old when he died. But not a word about the fourteen years this great patriot was incarcerated.

'Discovered' by Chinese officials needing a candidate they could groom for the second highest office in Tibet, the Panchen Lama was not officially recognised until 1951, when he was thirteen years of age. The Chinese government installed the boy from Amdo, despite two other candidates being investigated by Lhasa officials. They arranged that he meet the young Dalai Lama, who at nineteen was barely three years his senior, in 1953 on his way to Beijing. There the two teenage monks represented Tibet in 1954 for the signing of the notorious Seventeen-Point Agreement, in which China demanded that Tibet feed the People's Liberation Army and see to their daily needs while they occupied the country, promising that in return they would not take 'a needle or thread' unlawfully from the population.

When the Dalai Lama fled to India in 1959, the Panchen Lama, then twenty-one, was made Acting Head of Tibet and in 1960 Vice-Chairman of the National People's Congress. This required him to live in Beijing. The Chinese no doubt wanted to prevent his popularity rising in Tibet, now that the Dalai Lama had gone. He was kept like a dog on a leash and allowed occasional short visits to Tibet and his monastic seat of Tashilhunpo.

The Panchen Lama showed himself indeed to be a great Tibetan patriot when in 1961 he complained to the National People's Congress in Peking about the plight of the Tibetans and asked for the following remedial measures:

- The persecution of Tibetans must end.
- The food ration must increase. The monthly ration of 22 pounds of grain per person is far below an adequate norm and has caused many deaths from starvation.
- Religious freedom must be preserved. The destruction of sacred manuscripts and religious articles etc., must be stopped.
- The aged and infirm must not be neglected.

(Thubtob, *Tibet Today*, p 16)

Although Mao Zedong promised that Chinese officials in Tibet would be instructed accordingly and pamphlets were duly distributed, nothing changed. Subsequently, the Panchen Lama showed himself to be a true statesman by using every opportunity to remind the Chinese in public that he did not regard himself as Tibet's leader, praising the Dalai Lama instead of condemning him as required by the authorities. In 1964, after religious ceremonies in the Jokhang, he prayed for the Dalai Lama's long life and early return to Tibet, thereby demonstrating his inherited glorious patriotic spirit regarding the peaceful liberation of Tibet from Chinese overlordship.

He was ousted from his posts in 1964 and labelled anti-party, anti-socialism and anti-people. When he was first arrested, Zhang Jinwu called him 'the big rock on the road to socialism'. He was kept under house arrest in Beijing as a true friend of the Communist Party of China until 1965.

In August 1965 the party and the state made clear the respect and esteem they held for the Lama's patriotic deeds and imprisoned him in a labour camp in Sichuan, where he underwent torture to reinforce his glorious patriotic spirit for the democratic revolution. He was twenty-seven years old. In 1969 reports surfaced of his escape from a labour camp and later of him being in a prison in Beijing, where he probably underwent brainwashing. Altogether the Panchen Lama was looked after in this manner by the Chinese government in labour camps and prisons for more than fourteen years, being 'rehabilitated' in 1978.

One of the 'alternative emanations' of the Panchen Lama was born in 1939 in Kham and recognised by Tibetan lamas. He was clapped in gaol in 1959, but managed to escape to India and now lives in Ireland, where he has established a Tibetan Buddhist centre.

On his release in 1978, the Panchen Lama immediately resumed accumulating indelible meritorious deeds under the new historic conditions. He requested permission to visit Tibet to see for himself. While waiting, he was reinstated as Vice-Chairman of the National People's Congress in 1980. He requested again and again to be allowed to go to Tibet until this was finally granted in 1982. Between then and his death in January 1989 he managed to visit Lhasa seven more times, as well as spending short periods at Tashilhunpo, where he conducted religious ceremonies and kept commenting publicly on the state of social reconstruction in Tibet, objecting to such projects as the Yamdrok Tso hydro-electric scheme.

On the day before his sudden and unexpected death, he was in great form. Having only just returned on 9 January 1989 to inspect the rebuilding of Tashilhunpo, he summed up at a religious gathering on the 27th what he thought of thirty-nine years of Chinese occupation in Tibet. He is reputed to have said that although the Chinese brought some useful things to Tibet and made a few favourable changes, on balance he had to agree with the Dalai Lama that the Tibetan people had lost rather than gained from the Chinese presence. He did not survive that statement long.

Thus 'the big rock' was finally removed. With the Panchen Lama out of the way, Tibet could be developed unimpeded according to Chinese pattern. Even though since his release the Big Rock's influence had been minimal, he was a critic of Chinese rule. The only way he could stem the tide of cultural genocide was to speak out, loud and clear, on those few occasions he was allowed to address the National Congress or a large public inside Tibet. His courage on that last occasion, knowing the possible consequences as keenly as he must have, was astounding. He was a rock indeed. A rock of courage.

Tomorrow we will visit his Tashilhunpo monastery. The care taken by the party and the state for the Zhaxi Lhumbo Lamasery and all the patriotic people in Tibet has also been vividly described by lama Ngawang Thubtob, a monk at Tashilhunpo for forty-three years before he fled to India via Nepal, taking 109 days to reach the Dalai Lama.

He tells of arrests, public torture and executions. In December 1960 all Tashilhunpo monks were arrested and accused of complicity in the revolt against the Chinese occupation. On 21 March 1961 all the people of Shigatse were called to a public meeting and surrounded, whereupon ten Tibetan prisoners were marched up for all to see. One of them, a monk, was shot dead on the spot and the people were told that this would happen to anyone who opposed the Chinese presence. Many monks committed suicide rather than be coerced. By these and other means the monastic population was reduced from 3800 to 800. No prizes for guessing which monks were allowed to stay on. That is how Shigatse became red.

Just when we doze off the phone rings. The desk clerk is checking that everything is alright. This late? At eleven o'clock the phone rings again. This time a Chinese man wants to know the number of our room. I give him short shrift and we are not sure whether we are dealing with a half-drunk cadre after a pick-up dialling the wrong number, or another check-up by the security police. I have a fitful sleep full of Nazi flashbacks.

Tashilhunpo and the Carpet Weavers

Breakfast becomes a group discussion about whether to go on to Sakya tomorrow, 140 kilometres west of Shigatse. A sixteen-hour bumpy ride, two passes, there and back in a day because there is no group accommodation in Sakya village, says the guide. That leaves an hour to view the remarkable monastery, dating from 1073. If we go, our guide has to chase permits this morning.

Sakya's history is bound up with the history of Tibet as a nation and particularly its relationship with China, as the Sakya lamas wielded secular power in the thirteenth century by virtue of being the Mongol emperors' religious advisers. The son of Sakya's founder was a disciple of Padmasambhava and among the first Tibetans ordained as a Buddhist monk. Sakya rulers marry and have hereditary ascendancy, similar to the Nyingma, so there is always a young Rimpoche in training while the elder one rules. This lends a cohesiveness not enjoyed by the Gelukpa in between Dalai Lamas or when the Dalai Lama is a child. The present Sakya Trezin and his family live in exile in Seattle.

Although Sakya's Northern Monastery was destroyed in the Cultural Revolution, the massive Southern Monastery stands and its library of handwritten books remains presumably intact. The first Westerners to visit Sakya were the Williamsons in 1934. They noticed tree trunks three feet in diameter, reputedly from India, China and Tibet itself, supporting the main temple roof. Jamyang Sakya, a Kham lady married into the ruling Sakya family, tells how her mother-in-law bought timber for the costly restoration of the Great Temple. Each year timber was brought on yaks from a place five days yak travel away, and in the 1940s the biggest logs were still 'more than a foot thick'. Such observations in Tibetan literature assume meaning in the light of the rapid clearfelling of all Tibet's forests for China's building boom.

Jamyang Sakya tells of life in the Sakya palace kitchen with its wealth-bringing knucklebone pole, where grandmother spun fine fleece dyed with wild rhubarb roots to weave monks' robes. I'd love to re-imagine them in that kitchen and touch the pole, yet the prospect of a one-day round trip does not appeal. Jason is keen as mustard but the votes go against this mad dash in favour of an extra day in Lhasa.

Today the sun shines as it does in Australia, fierce and glaring. The dusty street rattles with mechanised traffic belching clouds of smelly black fumes. We

199

spot a street market, but reach the monastery without seeing the real Shigatse. Jason thinks it must have been demolished. Jamyang Sakya observed in 1956 that about half the population of Shigatse was Chinese and there seemed little animosity between them and the monks, but rather a friendly attitude in contrast to Lhasa. Now the population seems to be mostly Chinese and Shigatse a Chinese city.

Chandra Das, who spent time studying in Tashilhunpo, came to know Shigatse in the late nineteenth century. The Chinese presence, traders and diplomats, was considerable. He witnessed a procession to the monastery on a Chinese holiday for the emperor's accession to the throne, when Chinese subjects offered homage. Tibetan government ministers participated. Chinese men carried boards declaring the *amban*'s titles and 'his commission to supreme authority over the whole of Tibet'. There's nothing new in today's assertions by China. Tibetan men carried similar inscriptions in Tibetan and one can only speculate how much they needed to placate the Chinese. There was a lot of flag-waving and throughout the march 'Tibetans occupied a subordinate position while the Chinese displayed their superiority in every possible way'. Yet a Tibetan official confided to Das that Chinese officials chosen to go to Tibet were known 'for their dissipated and licentious habits', being the worst recruits China had to spare. The same is said today.

When the senior *amban* left for Lhasa a few days later, people had their ponies seized for his caravan, while Chinese retainers took the best food from Shigatse market, mostly without payment, leaving little for the population. When the junior *amban* wanted to leave days later, 300 ponies, each accompanied by a Tibetan, had to be provided as pack animals. The *amban* ordered the requisition of all ponies in the province, 'no matter whether they belonged to subjects, traders, or pilgrims'. As the caravan got under way, Chinese on horseback whipped men whose ponies lagged behind, so that some disappeared, losing their animal. It was daylight robbery and the manner hasn't changed.

What has changed is the public practice of religion. Circumambulations of Tashilhunpo on the night of the full moon by the entire population could not occur now in this Chinese town. The monastery has only about 600 monks and the employment that used to be generated by the monastic community is drastically diminished. Das visited the nearby village of Tashi-gyantse, whose inhabitants all worked for Tashilhunpo as copyists, clerks, painters and artisans. The monastery created employment.

As we approach Tashilhunpo on foot, there is that sense of old Tibet so prevalent in Gyantse. Everything is Tibetan-style, not a Chinese shack in sight, a donkey cart lending a rustic touch to the foreground.

Jason tells us that the highest building with curved roof on the left contains a statue of Maitreya 26.8 metres high, the face four metres high and one finger 120 centimetres! Maitreya's hall was built in 1914 by the Sixth Panchen Lama (now the Ninth) and took 279 kilograms of gold to make. Our Tibetan guide says the people say that when the Cultural Revolution struck Shigatse, this statue bowed its head and wept and the curly hair on its head straightened. Now it is back to normal. Why?

The second gold-roofed palace of 1662 contains the tomb of the First Panchen Lama (Tibetan counting), Lozang Choekyi Gyaltsen, much revered as the Fifth Dalai Lama's teacher. And high above the accumulation of buildings gleams a new stupa decked in gold, protecting the remains of the Tenth Panchen Lama, consecrated just before we arrived. The abbot of Shalu and his small quota of monks must have been in attendance.

Tashilhunpo ('Heap of Glory') delights the senses. It spreads out its rose-coloured walls with black and white trimmings at the foot of Tara's mountain. Damage during the Cultural Revolution was mainly to monks' quarters. But the remains of the Panchen Lamas also incurred the Red Guards' vehemence, despite historical connections, so that the Fourth Panchen Lama's tomb now contains bits of relics from the Fifth to the Ninth Panchen Lamas, swept up after the ravaging. The interior of that tomb was entirely destroyed, but restored by the Tenth Panchen. Sacked in 1792 by invading Gorkhalis from the south, Tashilhunpo was already devoid of antiquities when the Cultural Revolution further diminished its treasures.

Tashilhunpo has had more written about it than almost any other monastery. It still is like a self-contained small town. Cobblestone alleys connect buildings, willow trees willow and sleepy dogs sleep. But monastic routine is not observable. It has been called a 'monastic museum' because its teaching practices are in doubt and it no longer represents a living religious tradition. Older monks have reinstated a teaching program and several colleges, but when Jason enquires from two young monks guiding us around what the mandalas mean, they don't know because their studies have not reached that level. Yet, until disbanded by the PLA in 1960, Tashilhunpo was a great Tibetan university, where scholars and monks from India and the Himalayan countries came to study. It maintained famous printing shops and the sutra hall still houses 10 000 woodblocks with religious texts.

Even Waddell was impressed with the religious atmosphere of the place. At about four in the morning, junior monks would chant from the temple roof, before stone bells were beaten to awaken the monks. They would emerge in procession, yellow cockscomb hats on their shoulders, carrying tea bowls and *tsampa* bags. They would bow in the court and circumambulate temples chanting mantras. Margaret Williamson saw tea being brewed in the monastery in seven gigantic cauldrons astride roaring fires. Four times a day they were emptied and filled again, for tea mixed with *tsampa* was the monks' food and drink. Sixty copper kettles went around at each tea break.

One December Chandra Das observed the anniversary of Tsongkhapa's death, a religious holiday called *Gadan Namchoi*. The government supplied butter to every house to illuminate the city. Monks arranged rows of butter lamps on Tashilhunpo's every roof, lighting up the tombs. Das watched for an hour, enthralled at this flickering tribute to a great man of religion. Then a gale struck up, the lamps blew out one by one and people went indoors to shelter. A century earlier Samuel Turner wrote of another illumination, the rising sun lighting up Tashilhunpo. He wrote that it left an impression 'which no time will ever efface from my mind'.

Today's Tashilhunpo gets money, because the Chinese regime still wants to build up the Panchen Lama office to replace the Dalai Lama. No costs have been spared on the new tomb for the Tenth Panchen Lama. The golden-roofed stupa is stupendously opulent, the forecourt incredibly ornate. The state financed this and pilgrims contributed. The freshly painted ceiling mandalas are truly amazing. There are still master painters in Tibet. Did they lie on scaffolding on their backs, like Michelangelo? How few still have the knowledge contained in those mandalas, expressions of the most esoteric tantric mysteries? We look, heads thrown back, mouths open.

On the walls, buddhas and deities. Pillars wrapped in the finest brocade. Hundreds of kilos of gold went into the stupa and the Panchen's statue. Behind the statue his remains still sit in meditation position, invisible to onlookers. I have such a strange feeling about that body, used all his life and now in death for political ends that his mind opposed. This state-decreed opulence is not religious piety but foreign politics. Why else should the plaque over the tomb's entrance state 'The Great Tenth Panchen Lama' in English?

We gape at eleven giant new chalices, one of gold, and watch a thousand butter lamps flicker in continual remembrance of this man, plucked from his village as a child pawn, always powerless, but beloved by the Tibetan people first for his office and later for his honesty. We file out past marvellous murals in the forecourt: the wheel of life and stories from the Panchen Lamas' lives. Tibetan pilgrims, carrying babies piggyback, come up the stairs to pay homage.

Between rose-coloured walls we walk, climbing staircases to the vast inner courtyard. Chinese soldiers parade in pairs, watching and spitting. We saw no soldiers in any other monastery or temple, except the two in Norbulingka. Monks, pilgrims and tourists mingle, but I feel uncomfortable. The boy soldiers are not here to pay homage. I aim my camera only at architecture. From here the heaping aspect of Tashilhunpo is abundantly evident. A two-storey temple with pillared verandahs carries several living quarters on its roof, above and behind which rise five storeys of a monks' house. Electricity poles spoil every picture.

Turning slowly on my heels I photograph Heap of Glory against the skyline, hoping one day it will shine again as an institute of learning and scholarship. Its teaching system was and remains esoteric and pyramidical compared with Western universities. One lecture a year by a Dalai or Panchen Lama, passed on by incarnate lamas. Incarnate lamas and other scholars also pass on teachings, but ritual and restoration take millions of monk hours. Yet the knowledge of a well-studied monk is said to be phenomenal.

We have been here a few hours. The group splits up, some roaming courtyard and alleyways, others 'doing' every temple open to the public. Lacking amidst the ostentatious new frescoes and statues is that happy devotional atmosphere evident in other monasteries. But Tashilhunpo has beauty. My eyes feast on whitewashed walls, painted windows, potted geraniums, signs of carefully tended life.

We leave alongside a Tibetan couple striding arm in arm towards the gateway, which is guarded by a large monk wearing a sunshade. He neither smiles nor utters a farewell.

It has not been the long absorbing visit we paid to other monasteries, so we stop at a Chinese department store. Another pillowslip, notebooks and diaries. Nicola tries on a Tibetan blouse and *chuba* in summery colours. She looks wonderful in them, with her petite figure and dark hair. Tibetan onlookers smile approvingly and she can't resist buying the outfit.

Next Nicola wants to see Tibetan handicrafts. We find a counter manned by a tall Chinese who lights a cigarette and blows the smoke straight in our faces while staring at us. I assume this is as much an insult as it would be back home and walk away. But Nicola persists to buy silk purses and a traditional striped apron. In this consumer palace the customers are mostly Chinese, like the attendants. Yet every propaganda pamphlet shows happy Tibetans in traditional clothing clustering at counters, buying electronic goods, textiles and food. Maybe Tibetans don't shop on Wednesdays.

We return through the wide blazing street, walking on the road as the footpath is broken up. One area between two blocks of flats is entirely obstructed by heaps of rubble, rocks and holes, a permanent feature of Chinese streets.

Over noodle soup we talk of visiting the carpet factory. Having dealt in Tibetan carpets I rave about quality, density of knots and the unique method of knotting a whole row over a steel rod, then slitting the loops with a sharp knife. Only Tibetans weave this way and I learnt it from a young woman at her loom in Dharamsala. Carpet weaving, mostly for local use, was one of Tibet's great industries. Refugees in Nepal and India have established carpet industries, ranking third as foreign currency earners in Nepal, after foreign aid and tourism. I can't buy a rug this trip because they are like pets. You can only maintain so many. Our household has its share of Tibetans and not a Persian in sight.

Where you round a corner just past the market, to the left of the monastery, is all that remains of old Shigatse. Some small Tibetan houses and in the grounds of the carpet factory low buildings with cotton valances over windows and doors. A young woman is hanging skeins of dyed wool on ropes running between wooden posts. Today's dye baths are indigo and black. I wonder what the main colours will be in this workshop. Each centre develops its own combinations.

An assistant manager tells us this centre was set up by the Tibetan who is now manager, to provide work for poor Tibetans, training them in spinning, weaving, dyeing, relief cutting and sales management. The rugs are made of pure Tibetan wool, with natural dyes and traditional designs. They are shipped anywhere in the world. Tibetans love trading and meet potential customers with all their knowledge and charm spread out before them. No sullen faces or cigarette smoke blown in your face here, no backs turned to shut out the foreign buyer.

To our surprise we hear that 70 per cent of the profits go to monasteries as the factory also aims to improve the living conditions of local monks. I've heard this factory was the Panchen Lama's idea. The government grants it tax privileges and the state bank backs it in times of hardship, so that production continues. Yet the workers are paid competitive wages. It's primitive. It's basic. And it works. In the weaving rooms, red-cheeked young women with sparkling eyes, wearing purple and teal blue summer *chubas*, let their fingers fly across steel rods, counting so many ruby knots, so many mustard, so many night blue at the end for the border.

The looms are made of strong steel frames, bolted together. The women sit inside the frames on cushioned scaffolding. Before them stretch the warps, behind them hang balls of wool. Warm and deep are the dyes in this weaving centre. Most looms have two weavers working mirror images of symmetrical patterns and most rugs are the commercially popular three by six foot single bed size, for use on the floor and on the bed as the Tibetans do. Dragons and lotus flowers dominate, but two experienced women are weaving a fine rug containing eight bright sacred symbols on a natural white background. A sample rug hangs over the top of the loom. Asymmetrical, each border has different symbols. I suppress rising desire.

Weavers want to be photographed, raising two fingers, pointing at each other. Two prints. It is no hardship talking sign language with people so forthcoming, so happy to see visitors, so eager to pose and show their skills. We get the feeling our coming is some great adventure for the women. Their happiness is infectious, dissolving our lingering altitude lethargy. We respond by taking a real interest in what they are doing.

In a corner a woman is cutting relief along pattern outlines in the pile of a finished carpet. It is breathtaking to see her take to a fine rug with a well-used pair of electric shears and zoom around a lotus, or zigzag up and down a border. The result is instant. The whole pattern begins to stand out and invites touch. The woman does not look up from her work. She does not smile. She is either concentrating hard, or shy, or cross. As I photograph her in action, I pick up emanations of anger and don't linger. Not everyone is thrilled to have a bunch of scruffy foreigners troop in and disrupt daily routine.

Outside, several men are laying out a double doorhanger. These two stunning rectangular rugs are still connected by warp threads, so they can be thrown over a door beam, one rug facing in, the other out. The field is a deep ruby red, dark blue cross and borders dividing it into four. Yellow diamonds highlight corners, centre and junctions. In each panel two symbols artistically combine: a conch shell balancing atop an eternal knot, and the two fish of spiritual liberation holding up the umbrella that protects the dharma. The wheel of life combines with the receptacle holding the hidden teachings, and the lotus flower, representing purity amidst defilement, carries the banner of victory. The rug is topped with black tiger stripes on green, picking up the colour of lotus stem, fish scales, eternal knot and segments of the wheel of life. The total impression is one of long-established balance. There is something mysteriously impressive about an identical pair of hand-knotted rugs that far surpasses the sum total of the two.

From the next building comes spirited singing. Some thirty women sit on cushions on the floor, spinning fleece on small whirlygig wheels fashioned with a few pieces of wood . The space is grubby, paint peeling, naked light bulbs hanging from the ceiling. There are gaps in the roof, providing fresh air today but what when winter comes? Window frames are painted a cheerful light blue, the spinners wear pink aprons over their *chubas* and the colours of their blouses run from turquoise and lemon to spring flowers. Their fingers roll the fleece into yarn to the rhythm of their song.

Some women card raw fleece into gossamer clouds, others wind skeins, but most make the wheels whirr. Without stopping work they gesture who wants to be in a picture with whom. Two or three fingers for prints. I step across heaps of fleece, worm between wheels, and manage to frame everyone. I long to sit with them and spin a thread, dip it in the dyepot, lay it in the weft and beat the loom.

But we are led to the salesroom, where the assistant manager comes into his own. The large room is hung and piled with rugs, woven jackets, bags and hats. Six very young girls sit on cushions, their legs under a rug they are finishing, brushing fluff from relief cuts. Dusty work. How old are they and shouldn't they be in school? But such questions make little sense to poor people. They are happy girls, giggling, making little jokes about our big shoes and appearances, clapping hands to mouths in embarrassment when I take their photo. I have never photographed as many people as in Tibet. Usually I restrict myself to scenery, not wanting to annoy people. But no Tibetan has been annoyed at being photographed, except the relief cutter who was cross about something else. I usually ask permission, but realised too late she did not allow that either.

The assistant manager presents several young assistant salesmen, speaking a little English. With carefully poised pens they write words they have learnt as pertaining to the sale of carpets. The group turns over piles of rugs, choices are made, invoices written. I buy a riot of a jacket with hat, and two woven straps to tie my Tibetan boots.

When the buying rage is over, the assistant manager confides in Jason. Never has any tourist group bought as many rugs. Perhaps my praise of Tibetan carpet craft has paid off for these lovely people, who create superb products in barely adequate conditions. A last walk past the whitewashed buildings huddled in clouds of pink cosmos and we are off, leaving behind days of work to pack and ship to America the biggest single order of carpets they ever recorded.

On the Streets of Shigatse

We are in high spirits. Maybe for giving the spirit of acquisition full reign. Maybe we are acclimatised at last. Or was it the singing? Charged with energy we head for the *tom* to look at artefacts, jewellery, *thangkas*. Also displayed are consumer goods, clothes, shoes, pots and pans. And there is a meat market. To get to see anything is the problem. Raucous, grinning tradeswomen pounce, pull us over, shout prices before we lay eyes on the wares. One gorgeous enchantress in a red blouse, hair and neck adorned with coral and turquoise, hooks her arm into Kay's to pose for the camera.

The competition is fierce but jolly, yet they would probably all sell more if they gave customers a chance to look around. I manage to buy five cloth print *thangkas* from a man who lets me select without interference. Sakyamuni, Tara, Padmasambhava, Tsongkhapa and a father-mother *thangka* of Samvara and consort Vajravarahi in the embrace of compassion and wisdom. It will be an act of devotion to frame these myself.

The beggars spot us. I furtively give some money to the first little kid holding up its little hand. The next moment I'm attacked by three bigger kids, one a boy in a straw hat who won't let go. They push and pinch me for over an hour as I walk between the stalls. I take their hands every so often to stop their pinching and finally two of them leave. I suspect the next shift is biding its time behind the stalls. Finally I take the persistent straw-hat boy by the hand and gesture that we are going for a walk. I will buy him something to eat. Chandra Das used to buy at this *tom* not only butter, salt and *tsampa*, but pastry and cake! But the boy's grinning face changes to an expression of amazement as we walk hand in hand through the market. People laugh and shout remarks. Suddenly he becomes suspicious. I might be taking him to the police, or kidnapping him. He starts pulling back but I hold his strong bony fist firmly and pull forwards. We are going to find him a feed. Suddenly he jerks and is gone. He looks back once over his shoulder, fear of devils in his eyes.

Begging is an old tradition here. Ugyen, Sikkimese travel companion of Das, found himself in this very same *tom* surrounded by two parties of beggars. Recognising a newcomer, they managed by 'alternate threats and solicitations' to squeeze several pieces of silver out of Ugyen. He also saw a fierce Khamba violently abuse a woman salt trader, spoiling her salt. He was 'greatly surprised at the lawlessness of the people in the market, their violence towards the helpless, and the absence of police supervision'. Ugyen's remarks sound uncomfortably contemporary.

Now walking in peace I feel a heel, a public child abuser. But the stallholders are laughing. The little titan met his match. At the meat market I am invited to take photographs. Four men sit on a low stone bench, behind carcases on crumpled blue plastic. The meat looks fresh. There are few flies. One man smokes. They may be Muslims, for one wears a grey fur fez, but also a turquoise in one ear. Another wears a Khamba headband. They laughingly gesture I should buy meat. For a vegetarian-when-possible, meat markets have a strange appeal to me. But I'm interested in the food logistics.

More Tibetan men than women inspect the meat from a polite distance. The Khamba picks up a small carcase by the hind leg. These are no yak. The legs still have skin on them. The distinctive black stripe on the front of white legs reveals they are Tibetan antelope from the Chang Tang plateau. These animals, as are the wild yak, ass (*kyang*) and gazelle, are being hunted to extinction since the introduction of motor roads, vehicles and guns.

Wildlife scientist George Schaller spent several months each year counting animals of the Chang Tang and the Arun Basin. He met nomads who reduced their herds to take up more profitable trapping and hunting. One bought a truck from the sale of *shahtoosh*, the fine antelope wool fetching fifty dollars per hide. *Shahtoosh* shawls cost thousands of dollars in Europe. The carcases remained frozen near the hunter's tent until needed or sold for meat. The male antelope's horns were sold in Lhasa for Chinese medicine. To buy gasoline for his truck, the nomad had to trap more antelopes than ever.

Although the wild yak and Tibetan antelope are protected by Chinese law, hunting parties of Chinese officials go in truckloads to the Chang Tang to shoot them, so the nomads see no reason to obey new laws. Laws were never necessary when there was a balance between grazing animals and wildlife, with herders hunting only for their own needs of meat and pelts. George Schaller, environmental evangelist, handed out cards to the nomads showing a kneeling hunter laying down his weapons before peaceful animals. The card carries the Buddha's message in Tibetan:

All beings tremble at punishment,
To all life is dear.
Comparing others to oneself,
One should neither kill nor cause to kill.

Schaller also wrote a book on pandas. There is a need for more knowledge among conservationists worldwide to lobby for Tibet's and China's wild animals and save them from extermination.

Turning away from the problem, I look at stalls selling bright hanks of wool. I could cheerfully sit down on the kerb and knit a hat, my fingers are itching for work. Another stall sells plastic bags of skin chips. Two tiny tots think them inviting, gazing at the chips as if mumbling a wish-fulfilling mantra. Should I buy them a bag? But what about the beggar boys? I still smart from having been suspected of being a child stealer or police informer.

The group gathers at the bus. Straw-hat boy watches from a safe distance while his young brothers cling to mother's skirt. She is young and pretty, but her face contorted into begging mode. She holds out her hand. Jason says behind me: 'She may be a prostitute'. It's a disagreement between us. She may have been, but now she has three growing children. And if she is, then business must be bad. She waits by the bus window. I give her money. On the other side of the bus straw-hat boy makes the sign of a Tibetan curse. Hand balled into a fist, his thumb points repeatedly at the ground as he pouts at me for the last time. Another year of demon diseases to fight off. I wave to him. Lost cause. His expressive eyes, still haunted by the fear of how I might have sold his freedom, stare darkly at me from a distance.

From the height of the bus we overlook the entire *tom* against the dramatic backing of rock outcrop on which once stood Shigatse's Potala. The ruins are extensive. Only a few towering but crumbling walls stand etched against the sky. Rows of small empty windows stare from the bastions. Prayer flags fly below, from the rooftops of what looks like a small monastery.

After washing off the dust in the hotel, we enter a dining room where a mural takes up the entire rear wall. It is a pretty picture of the white town of Shigatse, lying amid green bushes against the background of the rock, Tashilhunpo on the left, the Potala on the right. That is how it once was. Tourists will remember that Chinese hotels do everything in their power to pay homage to a Tibet that once was, by means of lavish simulations. We analyse the mural to see what is missing outside, while waiting for table numbers. Chinese hospitality runs on numbers and chits. Then we sit on straight green chairs eating noodles. Always hungry, we analyse side dishes, suspecting unmentionable ingredients. Dinner is jolly after the spree. We pumped some money into the local Tibetan economy, apart from paying dues to the Chinese at Tashilhunpo. The dining room looks out on two courtyards overgrown with weeds, storage for containers and blocks of cement. No one takes pride in the place. Tourists are trade. They are fed, bedded and sold souvenirs. That's all.

While packing, I remember deciding in Lhasa to give away my surplus white sweater. It should have gone to the little girl at the last farm before Khamba-La. Instead I give it to the Tibetan lady who cleans our room.

Afterwards we inspect goods in the lobby shops. I buy T-shirts for the boys back home, featuring Tibet, Potala, a noble yak head. At home these symbols take on a different meaning, make people ask about Tibet and how things are. I sleep the sleep of conflict consciousness. In a way it is sad to leave Shigatse tomorrow. Stressful as the visit was, today is a turning point. Once back in Lhasa, our days in Tibet are numbered.

The Low Road to Lhasa

We drive into a wide open plain down the low road to Lhasa. Not far out of Shigatse, we stop so Jason can talk with two monks walking along the deserted road carrying tiny shoulder bags. They have just started their pilgrimage on foot to Lhasa, their faces huge grins of pleasure, their voices buoyant. And it occurs to me that a pilgrimage is not just an act of worship performed at some sacrifice, but a walking into freedom, away from routine tasks, into a time and space where the mind becomes still and perhaps touches the infinite. In a way, that is what this pilgrimage by minibus does for me. Despite bus services between the main cities, there are still foot pilgrims in Tibet. We wish the monks good travels, wave goodbye and drive on. They were not interested in a lift.

In a broad valley stretching to the horizon, flanked by mountains reclining as if napping, we spot two moving dots. A woman and a man, carrying shoulder bags and herding five sheep. In that whole immense landscape no other people are to be seen. I shall always remember Tibet by the solitary figures that walk through its vastly grand landscapes with the dignity and trust of the indigenous human.

The mountains are packing together, row after row, still low and covered in green tufts down the runnels. But in the distance the first snow peaks glitter, sign of passes to cross. We catch up with the Tsangpo river. No birds to be seen anywhere. But on the river's pristine beaches, bird or animal tracks are visible. On an isolated beach across the river, ten *dzo*, who must have grazed down the jagged rocks until reaching the water, enjoy an afternoon nap on their feet or bedded on the sand. If I had not seen *dzo* and yaks clamber up and down slopes of 40 degrees I would have assumed this little herd had been brought to that beach by boat, to be corralled.

A Bön monastery sits high on a slope, looking no different from Buddhist monasteries. The old Bön religion is experiencing a revival— the West because of a rising interest in indigenous religions, and in Tibet because the people are under stress and Buddhist tolerance has not been able to stop the worst excesses of the occupiers. Neither has Buddhism failed, judging by the dignity of the Tibetan people under suppression.

Bön and Buddhism made compromises after initial skirmishes. Buddhists would circumambulate clockwise and Böns counterclockwise. The same applied

211

to turning prayer wheels and the swastika. The swastika, so bitterly misused by Adolf Hitler, is a Sanskrit symbol for happiness and well-being. In China it was *wan tze*, a symbol of long life and eternity, meaning 10 000 characters. When Jamyang Sakya visited a Bön monastery, a monk explained the counterclockwise tradition by saying they were going to meet the Buddha, not follow him! No matter how much Buddhism influenced Bön, it is inconceivable that the unique form Tibetan Buddhism has taken would have been possible without Bön preceding it.

Towards midday we see four small boys, naked above the waist, hacking brushwood. In these last days of summer, all hands are busy bringing supplies to village compounds before winter closes in. We have seen no villages for a while and the mountains are thrusting more steeply out of the valley, narrowed down to river and road. Sometimes the road is forced to cross a shoulder and precipices become a familiar sight once more. The landscape is a book. Its geological processes can be read from bend to bend, like turning pages. As the geologically young mountain ranges build up, weathering by the elements deposits fine layers of mineral-rich dust in valleys and rivers, creating tremendous fertility, compensating for climatic harshness.

The driver is due for a long rest and the guide knows a good spot by the river. When we get there, it is occupied by a small family. But we all need to stretch, so we scale rocks across the road to a level strip of grass. Above us is a herd of grazing yak, red tassels bobbing as they chew. Above them stands a great tumble of sepia rocks without a sprig of growth, as if the earth had just been turned over by a giant's spade.

The view is enchanting. Across the river in a valley squeezed between mountains lies a village surrounded by orchards. Terraces slope gently toward the river where narrow strips are dotted with barley stooks. Every metre of accessible soil is cultivated. Snow peaks rise behind the saddle, heads half-hidden in puffy white clouds against cobalt sky. Further on, the river broadens, flowing strong and making an elbow turn to disappear between green humpback hills. An idyllic enclosed world. If it were not for the Shigatse–Lhasa highway, politics and armies would scarcely penetrate here. But an army lorry roars past, two soldiers atop the tarp-covered load. Two more trucks. Then a truck from Lhasa whizzes by, laden with Chinese furniture.

We munch lunchbox delights, watching the family on the river ledge. A farmer, a young married woman wearing an apron, two boys of perhaps fourteen and ten. She may be the farmer's young wife, or his daughter. The boys could be her sons. In the midday heat she wears a long-sleeved Tibetan blouse, purple-striped, hand-woven vest and a jacket. A red woollen scarf matching the colour of her cheeks is wound around jet-black tresses.

The farmer is repairing something with string while the boys keep an eye on the yaks and sheep above us. But they and the woman creep gradually closer, until they sit five metres away from us. Jason addresses them and timidly they come towards us. We offer buns and their eyes brighten, although they look well fed. Finally the farmer walks across. Again we watch the delight of a Tibetan on finding that Jason, this strange agile creature with barley-coloured hair and sky-blue eyes, speaks his language even though the other strangers seem dumb.

The farmer points to the river bend. He lives a kilometre or so away, growing all his family needs, even peaches and apricots. This is orchard country. Nearby snow peaks assure a good run-off. These kids live on traditional Tibetan food: *tsampa* with vegetables, milk and cheese, fruit in autumn and dried meat and curds in winter. Buns are a great novelty.

The elder boy spots a yak drifting from the herd. He whips out a sling and shoots the animal's rump with a tiny pebble, ordering it back to the herd. Jason examines the sling, made by the boy of finger crocheted, twisted yak hair, leather patches, and red wool for decoration. Our Tibetan guide remembers his boyhood when he too herded animals in wide open spaces. A new concentration lights up his usually slightly bored face as he manipulates the sling and finds he hasn't lost the touch. It may after all be more interesting to herd animals day in day out, than ride from Lhasa to Shigatse day in day out with well-read foreigners who ask many stupid questions.

Remembering packing wool and crochet hooks to give to new acquaintances, I clamber down to the bus, rummage through my kitbag and find one ball of sky blue and a plastic hook. Conditioned by cultural trends in my part of the world, I turn to the woman to show how the hook makes a quick chain that turns on itself to make a patch. Timidly she tries, but can't get it right. After the third attempt the elder boy, muttering impatiently over her shoulder, takes wool and hook from her hand and within seconds is crocheting a chain. She looks on, losing interest.

The farmer scoots on fast-moving feet down the slope and across the road, sling in hand, to rescue a strayed yak wedged between rocks near the river. As the group packs up, another truck stops and the driver recognises ours. They chat. I use the delay to take shots of a yellow-flowering groundcover like the one growing in my home bush, a trail of moisture-loving plants in a mudhole under a rock, and delicate ground-hugging mauve primulas. Then we are off, waving to the crocheting boy, apple-cheeked woman, small guy clutching an aluminium can and the farmer's face creased by habitual smiling. Not a young man, yet the children are. Where was he during the Cultural Revolution — in hiding, with the guerillas, in prison? The eldest boy was born no earlier than the late seventies.

As we round the elbow, the landscape carries more meaning for having met the small family living a self-sufficient life in this river valley. When the village comes into view I pick a house I imagine is theirs. It has a small orchard. For a while there are orchards everywhere. This valley has a magical quality. The mountains are either what seem freshly turned-over slopes of pink barren rocks like orthoclase feldspar, or tilted striated layers, lying prone like sleeping humped giants covered with a blanket of greenery. On one rounded top sit two ruined square towers, fortifications rather than an old monastery. Our guide doesn't know how old they are. Charles Bell writes that these were forts of petty chieftains who ruled after the line of kings ended with the death of Langdarma in 842.

The valley is narrow and the mountains high. Run-off feeds perfectly into the orchards. Strips of barley rib higher slopes dotted with homesteads. Near the road, little brooks babble between the trees. Two girls are washing pillows in the stream by dancing on them in the water, bunching up their skirts. They pay no attention to the bus. I pray their lives are little influenced by the highway. But the road means opportunity for a man selling apricots along the roadside. This valley offers a picture of Tibetan summer life I haven't read about in books.

Then suddenly, as if it was a dream, all life and activity ceases. The valley narrows, mountains close in, snow peaks appear and the road rises. We part company with the Tsangpo and head for a pass. As a last sign of human endeavour, prayer flags fly on high peaks. We travel in silence. The views change at every bend. Precipices on the netherside of the bus do not induce idle chatter. Neither does traffic from the opposite direction, requiring the utmost skill from both drivers to squeeze past each other without wheels going over edges.

I have developed a probably unrealistic faith in our driver. He blasts the horn before every bend but does not slow down. At least he is wide awake, more than we are. Even Jason seems tired. It has been a hard trip and he has talked for hours each day, giving historical perspectives to places visited. No university lecturer works as hard, or would put up with the conditions, giving major lectures in a jostling minibus while consuming three litres of water to combat altitude.

The pass causes no discomfort. The land broadens out and after ten minutes, an hour, two hours, we drive through the wide Kyi river valley again, until we reach an official imperial rest stop. The driver pulls up and jumps out for his smoke. We can dive into the bushes or enter a splendid white structure with barred windows and an attractive squat tower with octagonal lookouts behind Chinese grilles. As an afterthought, Chinese ideograms for male and female have been sloppily painted beside two entrances. Inside it stinks. This official restroom, more spacious than the average Tibetan house, is a symbol, but no-one seems to have been appointed to look after it. The toilets are cesspits of disease, the bushes far preferable.

We stretch our legs to talk to a man who has nothing to sell. He just wants to show the buttons on his hat, collected from passing tourists, making him a tourist attraction too. Then the last stretch to Lhasa. Along the river people make mud bricks while the weather is fine. Row upon row of little grey pyramids line river flats. The bricks should be well cured by spring, when the freeze relents and people have talked all winter of building new barns and repairing old houses.

Lhasa appears on the skyline. Then the Potala. The familiar streets. We are coming home after a pilgrimage. Really, we haven't been away long enough to appreciate the moment — the curse of motorised transport.

The Barkhor

We book into the inn, then take the bus to the city's heart. Nicola and I follow the Barkhor starting left of the Jokhang; a scouting trip through the market. Tomorrow we'll return to buy small presents for relatives. Jason, Kay and Ben go shopping for *thangkas* in a state emporium.

When we reach the meat market and side lanes I walk straight into the scene of an old dream from which I woke years ago when I thought I'd never see Lhasa. These are the winding streets of that dream. From the lodging house the Potala was visible. I keep looking for that street, that house, where I camped in the front room with several people in sleeping bags, unremembered people I didn't know in my waking life. How powerful are the scenes of dreams.

The most amazing aspect of today's homecoming to Lhasa is that my head is my own again, my lungs are working and my energy is buoyant. Now that I feel on top of the world, where I am, we are preparing to leave the land of my longing. It doesn't seem credible because I feel right in the moment. Neither past nor future seem real, as if the one only mattered to bring me to this point and the rest of my life will follow on from this present.

We dine leisurely tonight. The group is a temporary family. I like each one for her or his own peculiar humanity, care for each and have been cared for by each. I have probably had the most trouble with altitude, Peggy has ups and downs and Kay suffers a fierce sinus infection that started between the high passes. But at Lhasa's relatively low altitude we can manage, enjoy dinner for the company if not for the food, even discuss the improbable fact that we will be dining in Kathmandu two nights from now.

Sleep brings a vivid dream of the Barkhor. I am being pushed about by droves of red-robed monks. Among them walks the Dalai Lama, doing the religious circumambulation around the Jokhang while explaining repeatedly to all around him: 'I am only a simple monk'.

I wake up exhilarated. If I dreamt of lodging in Lhasa and seeing the Potala years before I came, even if the details differ slightly, does this new dream mean that the Dalai Lama will one day return to Tibet and walk the Barkhor in thanksgiving? I have very few dreams as clear as these two have been. Those I remember were usually about individuals I was closely involved with and always carried a solid kernel of truth that would reveal itself, if not at the time, then later. We live in hope.

✦　　✦　　✦

A slow start to our extra day. Lhasa has become like the place where we live, so we are domestic, repacking, washing hair. I do them as a matter of habit, but departure remains unreal.

Nicola and I decide to walk to the Potala for a bit of street life. At an intersection two golden yaks hold court for Chinese immigrants having their photos taken for the folks back home. Teenagers and parents holding babies pose for the historic shot. The statue was presented to the Tibetan people to commemorate the fortieth anniversary of Tibet's 'peaceful liberation' by the Chinese. The nerve! They attacked from eight points, behaved themselves, then killed about a million.

Another old dream place is where the Western Gate once stood. I photograph it from all angles. New shabby buildings clutter the site. Once through the non-existing Western Gate, a lane leads to a street running along the Potala's rock. We walk in but find it is a dead end. A woman steps out of a house, calls to someone inside, closes the door and climbs on her bicycle. She peddles past unsmilingly. We are intruders, but take one photograph because the street is pure Lhasa with the Potala as backdrop.

A hundred metres further we turn towards the palace. I won't attempt the giant stairway; something keeps me from entering the place. Like a Tibetan pilgrim of old, I have come to the sacred city to walk around the Potala with awe and joy, except that everyone's joy must now be tainted.

Instead we turn into the destroyed village of Shöl at the foot of the Potala. There are no tourists about. A military jeep is parked in the middle of the space and an officer approaches. The military presence makes me jittery, but at least uniforms make them recognisable. However in any occupied country one fears the hidden enemy, dressed in civvies, smile on the lips, ears working for the regime.

People still live in Shöl. A woman labourer sifts sand through an upright frame. A man sorts through a pile of building blocks. Some houses have been patched up, rising from half-demolished walls and yards filled with rubble. Down a broken lane, the footpath a metre wide, a house flies prayer flags above pots of marigolds on a first-floor roof, closed in by second-floor rooms on opposite sides to make a sun-trap terrace. Turning to the Potala, I see it through the gaping windows of a single wall of a once-large building, left standing in heaps of rubble. Walking deeper into the village I see people living in the ruins. A small girl holds her grandfather's hand, guiding him between the rocks. Two old men stand talking on what was once a street corner. Where there are two sticks of prayer flags on wall or chimney, there people live. Once more I am an intruder and turn back to find Nicola in the T-shirt shop.

Facing the Potala opposite Shöl's entrance stand the remains of what must have been a great house or monastery. It has the fluted wooden pillars seen in monasteries, made up of many small trunks strapped together with iron bands. The colour has all but gone, bar traces of pink. Above the entrance flowered friezes. Double wooden doors and architraves are massive and skilfully carved. Inside we can see stacks of cement sacks. The wide verandah is filled with old beams, building blocks and rubble. Is restoration in progress or is this a building depot?

Nicola wants to go inside one more department store. Again we watch Tibetans looking at merchandise and Chinese buying it. We don't buy either, but stroking Chinese silks comes free. Riding the public bus we get closer to the people of Lhasa. We should have done this on day one.

The afternoon finds us near the Barkhor. I would like to enter the Jokhang, but today is a working day and it may be better to keep the memory of our inner circumambulation as part of that great throng of pilgrims. We roam alleyways before returning to the market to shop. Stalls are a mishmash of folding tables, trestles, sun umbrellas, poles, sheeting or the ubiquitous red, white and blue plastic. Clothing and textiles are Chinese, metalwork indigenous. The meat market is held in an open space where Tibetan houses have been pulled down. To one side looms a brand-new four-storey building, without many doorways, nooks or crannies — just concrete, steel and glass. This is what the regime intends to do to all of the Barkhor.

More interesting than the merchandise are the people, combining religious ritual with shopping. Quite a few Khamba youths, large sheathed knives stuck in their belts, red wool braided through great bundles of black hair. The first time I came across a Khamba, in Kathmandu, I saw a giant. I still think they are a last vestige of the original human race of prehistory. They are the only Tibetans who continue to wear their weapons in public.

A few nomad families are still in town, old grandmother carrying the baby. The women's dark *chubas* are bordered with striped hand-loom cloth, their blouses hot pink, bright purple, lime-green. Hair braided and chests hung with silver lockets, turquoise, coral and the ancient zebra beads called *zi*. The men have the bandy legs of horsemen, walking as if they've been at sea for months. One sleeve hangs down their back, for the sun is hot. They look at many stalls without buying.

I find a bronze Tara that fits the palm of my hand. I buy coral and turquoise, small silver lockets, and look for a ring like the one I bought in Dharamsala sixteen years ago, with the grey cloudy stone set in silver alloy with tiny drops of metal like minuscule ball bearings. I don't find one; it must be unique. At the stand of a sad-eyed Tibetan woman I purchase two metres of brocades to frame the print *thangkas* from Shigatse. The idea of sewing *thangkas* at home softens the pain of departure. There is an absence of manufactured kitsch souvenirs. All presents bought, like handsome inlaid teaspoons, are also used by Tibetans.

At another stall, a Khamba buys several metres of black felt and shorter pieces of red and green. He is a bootmaker. Despite floods of imported Chinese shoes, this man is going to make several pairs of traditional felt boots for himself and family. The uppers will be red and green, embroidered with lotus flowers. He will hand-stitch the soles of layers of yak hide.

One stall sells hides. Against the backdrop hangs the skin of a snow leopard. We stare. The merchant stares back with knowing eyes. Probably every second tourist points at that skin of an endangered and protected species, without spending one yuan at his stall. Snow leopard skin used to be worn on hats and collars, especially in eastern Tibet, but the animal is on the brink of extinction.

Against a wall there is a one-plank stall. A cheerful old woman trades bundles of red and blue silk to braid into hair. She motions us to buy. I finger a glossy bundle and wonder, but the old woman holds one to the side of her face and fully expects me to go so adorned from now on. Her appealing grin breaks the budget. Nicola also surrenders. Passers-by stop, adding advice. The old one chatters to us in Tibetan while wrapping our new ornaments, explaining no doubt on what occasions they should be worn. She is so lovely I could hug her. How I wish I could speak Tibetan. *'Tashi Delek, tashi delek'*, we say, bowing and grinning in parting. She cackles delight as we tear ourselves away.

Several times people have pointed at me during this circumambulation of the Barkhor. Some walk up to me for a closer look and discuss me. Nicola thinks it is the long brown woollen skirt I wear. People may wonder whether I am a foreign nun, although my hair is in a bun and my shirt looks far from ecclesiastical. I am taller than Tibetan women, but no taller than some men. Perhaps being as tall as a man attracts attention? Then a cluster of yuppie Japanese tourists point, laugh, and snap away at me with their cameras. What caption will they give me in their albums? Western nomad? Halfway nun? Very weird foreigner?

At the end of the Barkhor stand the religious stalls. Here you can buy printed texts, rolls of prayers to insert in prayer wheels, appliqué banners, valances in the five sacred colours, yellow cloth and bells and bowls for the home shrine. Three old nuns in brown robes shop for their nunnery, squares of green cotton on their heads keep the sun off shaven pates. An old lama in a woollen hat walks past, rapidly fingering beads, lips moving. A European considers buying a pair of *radong*, long horns, and the stallholder beckons a man to help blow them. They manage a considerable noise that in no way resembles the music of monks on monastery roofs. But the tourist is convinced he is buying the real thing, perhaps for his Buddhist monastery in Europe.

We have almost reached the end of the Barkhor before it opens out onto the Chinese plaza. Pressed between two stalls I linger to watch the passing parade. Rising above the crowd the Khambas, towering over little nuns, running boy monks, shopping old women in grubby *chubas* and worn aprons. The nomad family in pink, green and purple is buying ritual artefacts. A father, mother and three curly-mopped boys walk hand in hand, strung across the street. Young men in jackets and homburg hats pass the time of day. Where do you see a crowd so relaxed?

On the pavement underneath the temple wall a market of Chinese plastic goods, bags and textiles is spread out as if the merchants just stepped off a plane to sell this lot before turning back. The first may be true. But if they sell their wares they are not likely to waste the profit on returning to China, but will place orders for more and set up permanent stalls. In a few years the Barkhor will have lost not only her grand Tibetan houses, but the market will sell mostly Chinese goods.

Rounding the last corner we face Jokhang's entrance for the last time. How out of place the plaza is with its steel fences and glass balloon streetlamps. Turning, I want to enter the temple, but stop in my tracks for prostrating pilgrims. In the four spaces between pillars figures bend and bow, on kneepads or without. Monks and nuns, very old, poorly dressed, are praying. Two young women pray side by side, flower-decorated straw hats lie beside them with prayer wheels on top. One has tied a rope around her skirt just above the ankles, so she can only proceed with tiny steps. It will take a while before she reaches the shade of the portal. She hopes to earn a lot of merit. A trader quickly pushes a cushion forward as he bows and rises. He has to get back to his stall. A young mother with toddler on a bicycle stops, pointing to the holy space, telling the child about it. A Khamba decked out in layers of khaki trousers and jackets strides past, looks at the worshippers and smiles broadly at the sky, white teeth eating sunshine.

The Jokhang has remained at the heart of Tibetan life. I will not disturb this scene by walking in, having had the privilege of being inside with thousands of worshipping Tibetans. It should be enough. Silently I offer the Buddha's mantra OM GATE GATE PARA GATE PARASAM GATE BODHI SVAHA.

An old nun, slightly bent, walks up with a sweet smile, hand stretched out. She is dressed in faded robes, generously patched. I smile back and offer money from my pocket. But pushing my hand away, she shakes her head impatiently, repeating words I haven't understood. I bend towards her and make out: 'Dalai

Lama picture'. Turning to Nicola I tell her of the nun's request, regretting once more not having ordered Dalai Lama photos before coming here.

But Nicola, bless her, produces the last but one of her Dalai Lama photos and presents it to the nun, who presses it to her forehead, visibly overcome. She would have been a young nun in 1959 when the Dalai Lama fled, and may have seen him in large congregations or at ceremonies. Scenes from old Tibet spring to mind. Then I am rushed with such strong feelings that tears spring into my eyes. I cannot cope at this moment with the unjust irony that I, a non-Tibetan, have met the Dalai Lama twice, once in private audience, and again only a year ago at an inter-faith meeting in Australia. I heard his voice, shook hands with him, received his blessing, while this nun was waiting, hoping, praying for his return to Tibet so she can glimpse him, from any distance.

I turn to the old nun. We see each other's tears. And then we are holding each other, crying together for the terrible fate of Tibet. Crying together about the long, agonising wait for the return of the man of peace who had wanted to lead this country gradually into the modern world without crushing the Tibetan spirit. I want to tell her I saw him recently. But all I can do is stroke her back and gently rock her thin body until her sobbing calms down. Then she wipes her tears with the back of her hands, looks once more with wet eyes at the beloved image and places the photograph in the folds of her clothes, on her heart.

People have gathered around us. Nicola gives her last picture to an old woman. Now the small crowd pushes in, but I motion them back, still comforting the old nun whose tears flow again. I hear Nicola explain to a man who speaks English that I am a Buddhist. A sense of wonder ripples through the crowd. The tourist and the nun wipe their tears together. At last the nun smiles. We press hands before she slowly turns and walks away.

We walk to the *kata* stalls where I buy a good white one for Rimpoche, to go with the Tsongkhapa *thangka*. As we leave, a monk with a nice open face, looking dreadfully poor, keeps tapping my arm wanting to sell a tiny piece of inscribed bone. But I am out of cash, bar the bus fare. Maybe it is all he has to sell. Maybe it is very precious. How sad. Tears keep pricking at the back of my eyes. The emotions that just rocked me are ready to surge again.

Casting a last look at Jokhang, the heart of Tibet, we leave at last. The bus waits near another market. We check it goes our way by gesticulating to the lady conductor. We are the first passengers. The driver stands smoking outside as his wife cries out destinations to attract customers. Slowly the bus begins to fill, but the couple seem to have no plans of leaving until it bursts at the seams.

We sit on the first seat facing forward, knees pressed against a side seat, occupied by a gorgeously decked-out Khamba woman hung with strand upon strand of turquoise, amber, coral and worked silver. Her glossy black hair is studded with turquoise and moonshine jewellery. Her husband, wrapped in an enormous brown *chuba* of good fine cloth, wearing a homburg, carries a bejewelled long dagger stuck in his belt. They are as intrigued with us as we are with them. I think we have the better deal, but Nicola, on whose slender knees the solid Khamba woman has partly sat down, is in two minds. We manage an exploratory conversation about each other's clothes. They show us their silver Tibetan calendar and admire our cameras. We women appreciatively touch each other's earrings. It is great to be with people not afraid to speak to us. They are traders of course, swaggering about the city that they have made their home, as Khambas do wherever they roam.

The energy emanating from the couple is just what I need after the emotional depletion at the Jokhang. It balances. Perhaps in the end, balance is the essence of Tibetan life. Balance between emotion and laughter, hard work and leisure, rude jokes and religion, the material and the immaterial, this world that we see and other realms we sense to be around us.

We wave goodbye as we get off the bus, thank the driver's wife and carry their smiles as we report for duty in the hotel. Tonight we have a farewell banquet in a real Tibetan house, says Jason, adding that it is of course owned by Tibetans working for the Chinese International Tourist Service that has kept a tab on where we were and went. The banquet is included in the tour fee and is the sort of send-off supposed to leave a lasting impression of happy, well-groomed Tibetans living in nice houses, serving delicious food to honoured guests.

I feel intimidated by this set-up. But now that I am acclimatised, the altitude merely translates as healthy appetite. We sit on carpeted benches around a wooden table. The food is very good. Jason insists on learning the names of all ingredients. He decides we shall not eat fish as it is not a traditional Tibetan dish. Tibetans were forbidden to catch fish, except where the Tsangpo traversed a sandy desert where the people had nothing else to live on. Of course some did in other places, like Yamdrok Tso. The fish is returned to the kitchen. The Tibetan girls who wait on us are puzzled. What could they possibly remember of a decree from the Potala prohibiting the eating of fish?

Only Chinese tea is served. We have to ask for butter tea. It comes in a nice old Tibetan teapot and is satisfying in its own definitive way. Jason drinks it like a fine wine, sipping delicately. I drink my fill, cup after cup, to the surprise of the serving girl. Well, given more frequent toilet facilities, this tourist could drain as many cups of butter tea as your average Tibetan!

Visiting the toilet is a small dark adventure. In the tiny garden, tripping between tins of geraniums and marigolds, we find the outhouse in a corner where it usually is in Australian yards. But we didn't expect to find a mod-con flush affair behind the wooden door. Nothing is too good for CITS tourists.

The last supper over, we make to leave. Other groups have come in after us, familiar faces from the tourist trail. But especially now we keep to ourselves, rise, thank our hosts for a good meal, bow, smile and file out.

For the last time we drive through the streets of Lhasa. Tomorrow we depart at 5.30, Beijing time, probably three o'clock Tibetan time. We will drive into the dark countryside without seeing Lhasa or the Potala again, as it was on the flight of the Dalai Lama. We pack and go to sleep early. For a few days we shall be together in Kathmandu, before dispersing on respective flights home. Some in the group seem excited about moving on. I feel dull and empty. How can it be that the weeks went so quickly? I seem to have lived in Tibet much longer than the itinerary says.

Francis Younghusband, having led the British invasion that so disastrously changed Tibet's status in Asia, went alone into the mountains on his last night in Lhasa. Looking down on the city bathed in autumnal light, he was struck by the overpowering emotion that lifted him above all the destruction and misery he and his men had caused and showed him another way. He wrote in his book *India and Tibet* how this mystical 'exhilaration of the moment grew and grew till it thrilled through me with overpowering intensity ... That single hour on leaving Lhasa was worth all the rest of a lifetime'.

His life till then had been packed with adventures and journeys of exploration through Central Asia. Going into Tibet had been the culmination of his life as a soldier explorer. But on his return — after a spell in London — Younghusband was appointed British resident in beautiful Kashmir and on terminating his official career he devoted the rest of his life to the bringing together of people of different religions from East and West.

I lie awake this last night in Lhasa. I have not had a mystical experience here. But I am filled with a new understanding of Tibet as a physical country where real people live, rather than a geographical metaphor for the heights of spirituality humanity can achieve. I think I will spend the rest of my life studying its culture and religion and supporting its struggle for self-determination.

Last Day in Tibet

Up at 4.30 am. Quick breakfast, then the ride southwards through the dark night. The others rave about the stars, so clear they seem portals to heaven. I feel empty having to leave, but my heart is heavy. I may never see Tibet again. I try to make sense of my new perception of this country.

Tibet's case can only be presented to the world community by Tibetans and friends of Tibet living outside these barbed borders. Tibetans demonstrating for independence inside Tibet end up in brutal goals and labour camps or die of torture. Their removal deprives the whole society of energy and courage. In thirty-four years a people can be forced into meek compliance by a brutal regime. The women of Lhasa will never rise again as they did in thousands in 1959, now that they know the cost in lives that fateful year.

The morning star rises. Then the outlines of the mountains declare themselves darkly against an indigo sky. Pure beauty. Daylight is barely breaking when Gonggar airport looms. A few Chinese hang over the first-floor balustrade, chatting, looking down on the gathering of tourists for the early flight to Kathmandu. Buses drop off more travellers and we form queues. Chinese personnel walk to and fro without apparent intentions to process us. No seats. I sit on the floor. Two hours later the counter opens and four queues move like a snails' sack race. Only one Tibetan, a young woman in Western clothes, is among prospective passengers, talking with Europeans. Some Tibetan refugees return periodically to Tibet as tour guides.

Just when we sight the counter, a big European in expensive winter coat and hat arrives with a tall Tibetan youth and proceeds to push his way into the side of our queue. The man looks with distaste at the tourist rabble. He is clearly something else. For one thing, he seems to think himself a latter-day Svengali, who can force us to make way for him by casting his cold stare on our motley group.

But our queue is being held up by a Yugoslavian girl who was going to ride a bicycle across Tibet but became ill. Is she the one who stood forlorn by the icy stream? She has to pay a large sum she doesn't have, to take her racing bicycle out of the country, but claims it came in as normal baggage. She only carries a small backpack. It seems reasonable to count her bike as a suitcase, but the Chinese have their own rules and they've never heard of bending them for anyone but themselves. The argument rages on. Jason tries to mediate, but as other queues disappear into the departure lounge he advances the bicycle fare and swaps addresses with the girl.

We have been so preoccupied with her distress that we are surprised to find Svengali in the winter coat standing right by our side at the counter. He carries a hideous sort of *thangka* of the Potala on a plush background, the sort made in Chinese factories. We mumble politely. 'Interesting'.

'Where did you get it?' asks Jason, staring incredulously at this hybrid art.

'It was a present', the man replies curtly in a Middle-European accent. Possibly he came to do business, talk about the Yamdrok Tso project. An official visit rewarded with an official present from an appreciative regime, to hang in the boardroom in Europe.

Brazenly the Tibetan youth shoves Svengali's suitcases forward and speaks to the counter clerk. I lose my temper in the way I do when I am made a doormat. Trying to push the youth aside with my elbow I tell the man we have been here two hours and he can jolly well wait his turn after arriving at the last minute. But the youth takes no notice and the man's eyes of steel could not care less.

Suddenly there is a push from behind and Ben takes over, bristling with the same anger that has already run out of adrenalin in me. Ben lifts up my bags, pushes the man's suitcase sideways and firmly plants himself in between. His face is white with fury. I am desperately grateful for his intervention, feeling we acted on principle. But at the same time there is that overwhelming sense of powerlessness in the presence of a character who will stop at nothing to get his way. This is how Tibetans must feel.

The rest becomes a blur. The baggage is finally checked in, we hang around for what seems forever in a cramped lounge where all seats are taken, visit a stinking toilet and finally are literally horded onto the plane as if we are likely to escape. Deportation must be like this. It is this final experience, per favour of the Chinese tourist authority, that makes some people express volatile relief at getting out of Tibet, if so far they had imagined themselves exempt from oppression.

The South China Airways plane seems brand new, as is the flight from Lhasa to Kathmandu. Until recently the only connection was overland. We are led to reserved seats by unsmiling stewardesses who hand out salted plums, sweet drinks and luggage straps with the airline's name woven in lucky red letters. I sit next to a Chinese man. There are other Chinese on board looking like cadres. Going to do government business with the barbarians outside. I am a thousand times more cynical than when I flew into Tibet, when I thought there had to be redeeming features about China's position there. I saw none.

After take-off I look past my fellow passenger at the landscape. Snowy mountains come already into view as we rise. People shift seats to take photographs and videos. Crossing the Himalayan range we look down on this greatest of all mountain chains. I feel like an astronaut.

The stewardess brings tea as we glide over a mountainscape of indescribable beauty. Blue ice valleys and crevasses form pits of colour amongst the monochrome and brilliant eternal white of the highest peaks, rising row after row, ever higher and closer to the golden sun on this cloudless day. Some of the scenes below us have no record of human footsteps. Mountain climbers approach the high peaks from the outside of the range. But between the northern side in Tibet and the southern side in Nepal, there are vast folds of high peaks, pushed up 20 million years ago, still rising and not seen until recently, except by pilots straying during World War II. There's a catch in my throat when the familiar shape of Chomolongma, Mount Everest, passes by the window at not too great a distance. Yet she is merely taller than the others; seen from above she is not the isolated mountain of films and books, but one peak amongst countless high peaks.

Sipping jasmine tea above the brilliant, breathtakingly stunning Himalayas seems the peak of all incredible experiences. No pictures can ever convey what eyes see and mind registers. The camera stays in the bag. I want to discover this pristine beauty for its own sake. Looking down into these untrodden ice valleys, I am acutely aware of my love affair with the earth and how these weeks of traversing central Tibet have revived that love to passion level.

Only a few passes between the mountains make a land crossing possible. There is one official crossing into Nepal with customs, armed guards and prisons on either side. The others are too high and cold to be patrolled in winter. So every year when the weather turns fierce, numbers of Tibetan adults and children risk frostbite or losing their lives to cross into Nepal. If they escape Nepalese authorities who will sent them back, they join the ever growing refugee population in India, suffering unreasonably for their rightful freedom.

Cold shivers run up my back. I cross the border as a free person.

PART II

THE SECOND JOURNEY – 1995

Tsetang Revisited

Two years later I find myself in Chengdu again, ready to fly to Tibet. Going the first time settled nothing. On my return I combed obscure books and new publications to confirm my experience and to find answers, and urgently started to write up my diary. From thinking there were enough books on Tibet I changed to believing that could never be, for every traveller discovers Tibet anew. And Tibet may disappear. If not the mountains, then certainly the culture and ultimately the Tibetans. One day I tripped over a sandwich board on a city footpath. It read: 'Go to Tibet!'

Yes, I thought, it's time again. And booked a fare. In the intervening years I was diagnosed asthmatic, so this time I shall tackle high passes with puffers. No one recommends this, but as I have already survived one journey, I will be my own judge.

At five in the morning a bevy of travellers boards a bus. At the airport somebody takes a group photo. An official runs up indicating this is a forbidden site. He stops short of confiscating the guilty camera. In China you are not to take photos on or near airports, bridges and other strategic structures. Haven't they heard of satellites?

Third time in China and that straitjacket feeling is back. But it is not my business. I am returning to Tibet with a group of Australians and a Tibetan speaking tour leader. The thought lights me up, like sunlight breaking through black clouds.

Pressing closer to the exit for the plane, we rub shoulders with a group of Tibetan students returning after four years study in China. They still speak Tibetan, but look Chinese. Clothes, bobbed hairstyles, plastic trinkets and avoidance of eye contact mark them as un-Tibetan. Yet they are youngsters excited about going home at last, unaware of culture shock to come.

The planes on this route are still pretty good, the weather excellent and the flight smooth. But on my last journey to Tibet I could do without Funniest Home Videos, which has local passengers in stitches. It is followed by blaring China South-West Airlines promotionals. Why must they copy the worst of the West's novelties?

We fly over solid cloud deck for almost two hours until the descent begins. Then, camera ready, I see again the fawn saddle mountains of Central Tibet and once more tears trickle down my face. There is Samyé! Pang of recognition. The tender green of willows. And upon landing the thin air, so familiar it hurts. But the river is alarmingly low. In some places it looks like a rippled Saharan sandbank with only a few black rivulets snaking across. There has been no rain until last week and much more is needed, says the Tibetan guide who meets us with a driver. The young guide seems to have high blood pressure, his face is purplish. He also has a limp from falling off a yak, he tells us.

There is still no bus service from the airport. Apart from discouraging individual travellers it keeps local sightseers away. We give a lift to an anthropologist and her husband, dropping them off where some young nuns wait for them at the roadside, smiling a welcome. She researches Buddhism in Tibet, coming and going from Nepal.

Tsetang township looks as if it was bombarded last week. The wide street is entirely broken up in jagged pieces of masonry with potholes metres wide. Thick dust hangs over the quagmire. The explanation stands high at the main intersection. A giant billboard carries one of those images of exaggerated perspectives town planners are fond of, buildings rising cloudward like a space ship. Tsetang is being made over for the thirtieth anniversary of the declaration of the Tibetan Autonomous Region on 1 September. This is one of sixty-two development projects to be completed by that date. Once the playground of Tibetan gods, Tsetang is now an experiment in Sinofication.

At the Tsetang hotel Tibetan butter tea, *pö cha,* is produced on request for Tibet junkies. I drink three cups. Three of us go for a walk to inspect the devastated town and three Tibetan kids join us. They have a little English. 'Hello', 'goodbye', 'Your name?' and eventually 'Money'. We enter a Chinese lollyshop where the woman doesn't seem to want to serve. Sign language buys lollies anywhere in the world, but here you are extracting teeth. Finally she relents and sells me soft coloured wedges, like mini watermelon slices. Chinese businesses in Tsetang outnumber Tibetan ones by more than two to one.

The children suck the sweets but lose interest in us when no money is forthcoming. They tell us not to walk further in this street, for there are bad dogs. '*Tashi delek*', they shout, crossing the street and disappearing into a brick gateway.

We walk past a wonderful old Tibetan house in an advanced state of decay. A communist meeting house, confiscated from the family who once lived here. As we turn and pass again, the continuing drama of human society, the struggle between rich and poor, begins to shout at me from crumbling walls, bleached architraves, a hollow courtyard where decorated ponies once brought supplies: 'Why should the people of this mansion have been so rich, living so well, working so little? Was it not entirely because of the labour done by poorer people?'

I make comparisons. I grew up poor and mother cleaned the houses of wealthy people. Most were kind and generous with food, clothes and toys. In Holland the only destruction was caused by an invading enemy. After that — lasting five years as compared with forty-five in Tibet — reconstruction, democracy and social reform took off. There were still rich and poor people, but the poor were better off and social security improved. Now my mother enjoys a good old age. No-one had to be killed for the new prosperity, buildings destroyed or gaols filled with dissenters — there were not one million graves of the sacrificed to haunt the survivors. And those who went elsewhere to try to get rich more quickly by dint of hard but voluntary labour return at will to share in hard-won gains.

This I signal back to the sad house of disappeared Tibetan aristocracy. Not the only model, but the one I know best. When that rich Tibetan family lived here they engaged artisans, a gardener, cook, servants, stable boys. They bought goods from local and passing traders. They gave donations to monasteries and alms to the poor. No rich family in an intimate society like Tibet could be rich and not spread it around. But who is sharing now?

On the corner of this old street and the main street is a Chinese department store, a planter box in front. No flowers grow in the cement box. In it lies an elderly, naked Tibetan woman scarcely covered by a heap of rags. Neither food nor water by her side. Tibetans and Chinese alike walk past without taking notice. Could this have happened in the time when the rich house was inhabited, when the local monastery was not closed, when Tibetan society still functioned on Buddhist principles?

One of us slips the old woman money. With a dumb look of defiance her squeezed eyes gaze at us — three well-padded giants. Then a small hand, parched skin over protruding bones, appears from the rags and with a deliberate motion pushes the banknotes away, over the edge of the box and onto the street. We stare helplessly with our useless compassion, but her eyes close. The billboard of future Tsetang casts a chill shadow over the dying woman in her public coffin. The sixty-two development projects will, so the authorities claim, benefit the Tibetan population. Perhaps some even attracted foreign aid.

I am sickened by the knowledge that the woman wants to die and will die. Powerless, we walk away. Who is she, that no-one cares? A nun? Religious women have been dreadfully persecuted in Tibet. Any *ani* who ever sang patriotic songs or waved the snow-lion flag spends time in goal and may be tortured. Sentences run as long as nineteen years. If they survive until release, people are afraid to be seen with them. Their nunneries may have been closed down. They can disrobe and hope their families are not too intimidated to take them back. If there is no family left, how are they to make a living being *persona non grata* in a country where people are registered in workgangs? There are countless stories of nuns and monks refusing to give up religious vows even if forced to disrobe, although some nuns do so after being raped.

Coughing dust I deplore this new Tsetang. The oldest inhabited placed in Tibet and hardly a Tibetan house left. The town has doubled in size since 1993. Row upon stark row of concrete apartments, barracks and department stores, military offices and hastily thrown up video cafes are all that is visible. Two Tibetan restaurants try to compete with Chinese eating houses. Within a year a new rule will dictate tourists may only eat in Chinese restaurants.

The dying woman is amongst us at dinner. I write postcards before going to bed to think of her asleep in a street box a hundred metres from here.

Waking up at seven to revolutionary songs on tannoy loudspeakers. Just as I resign myself to two hours of bedlam, it stops. An improvement on two years ago.

Tsampa and *pö-cha* for breakfast, and toast with fruity jam. Would the dying woman accept food? Were we too stunned last night to try other ways of helping? Or is she determined to die so publicly? Is she signalling a message to anyone passing by? We board the bus. At the intersection there is no sign of the woman. The planter box is empty.

Our Tibetan guide tells us about the sixty-two projects, aimed at impressing visiting dignitaries and looking good on television. Hotels will be closed to tourists from mid-August till mid-September, as high Chinese officials fly in to celebrate Tibetan autonomy. We also hear Lhasa university has about 1000 students, teaches science and three languages and that Tibet had about six million people of whom there are some four million left, maybe. Usually the figure given is six million, but one senses conjecture in these figures. Tibetans have no access to their own statistics unless they serve the regime, in which case they have to manipulate them like public servants everywhere.

We drive through a hard, dry landscape and endless barracks before reaching rural land. No fields with ripening crops, but bony sheep grazing tufts of greyness sticking up between the stones. Walled plantations of young trees provide the only green. We stop and wander. A flock of sheep comes up the slope with three shepherds in dark homespun. I kneel for a good picture. Through the lens I see one skinny sheep break away from the flock and purposefully trot towards me. The shepherds look amused. I lower the camera and hold out my hand. She walks right up, meckering, nibbles my fingers for a moment, then turns to join the flock. She has made my day. But perhaps she hoped for a handout.

A little further on, Chinese men and a woman are planting trees in stony ground. Acre upon acre along this road is planted to trees, surrounded by low mud-brick walls to keep stock out. I ask whether I may take photos. They nod, but seem displeased and one of the men makes obviously derogatory remarks. Give me a skinny sheep any time.

We drive to Chonggye in clear weather through Tibetan villages with tidy yards where everything has its place and purpose: mud-brick stacks, thornbush, straw, utensils. Two women warp a stick loom on the ground.

Chonggye is a pleasant little town hugging a spacious square. A new monastery is being built. Beyond are the tumuli of the royal burial grounds. This time I hope to climb up unaided. It turns out to be unpredictably easy, thanks to my puffer. My lungs must have been in a sorry state two years ago. Snotty-nosed children, as young as three, and old women with sore red eyes, come running to sell crystals, but they are not the people I played language games with two years ago.

A pleasant monastery with a red *gompa* marks Songtsen Gampo's burial mound, against the dramatic backdrop of a dark mountain range. In front are the monks' quarters, curtained windows either side of the gateway with its white and blue cotton hangings. So poor is this monastery that instead of a gilded wheel with flanking deer on the roof, these are appliquéd on cloth. In fenced garden beds small trees struggle in stony ground and geraniums flourish in rusty tins. Inside the gateway there are new murals, one of the tiger being subdued, with gorgeous borders.

In the cobblestone courtyard a heap of dried juniper waits to be ground for incense. Ah, that familiar smell! In the porch even the ceiling is made of fabric, painted with lively dragons, flaming pearls and *torma* offerings. The prevailing atmosphere in the place speaks of loving care through recycling the most mundane materials into devotional articles. Although reconstructed, this tiny monastery dates from the thirteenth century and is kept by five part-time Nyingma monks. Main statues and *thangkas* are of Songtsen Gampo, his wives and ministers, the Buddha and Padmasambhava. It is an endearing place, sitting on this windswept mound overlooking the green Yarlung valley.

As we leave the fragrant hall, a familiar face appears in the shadowed gateway. The woman's eyes light up in recognition, growing big with surprise. She probably wonders how I propelled myself up this time! I rush to her, struggling with my pockets to produce a photograph of the two girls who shared my earrings in 1993. I wear the same jacket. She wears the same clothes. Seeing the photo she nods, accepts it and slides it into a fold of her *chuba*. Then she takes my arm and together we walk the king's mound, looking at each other, grinning. She picks up something from the ground and folds it into my hand, closing my fingers over it. A tiny tektite to remember her by. One of the travellers takes our picture. We walk the whole mound, talking, gesticulating about prayer flags, the view and our happy reunion.

Simultaneously I try to take in other burial mounds and the historical ambience of the place. Many Tibetan kings found their last resting place here, but the mounds are no longer clearly defined, though clusters of prayer flags stretch into the distance. One fifth-century king took his queen and personal belongings and retired into a royal tomb in the Yarlung valley, where they remained the rest of their days so that their son might reign with the help of the first minister. Now, only destroyed monasteries can be seen on surrounding mountains.

There is little time for investigation. The group is leaving. My friend points at the bus. She supports my elbow. I press her hands. She grins and starts waving. Perhaps she thinks I'll return periodically on pilgrimage. She will be looking out in vain. I wave as long as I can see her, standing on the earth, one arm crooked over her head, the other waving.

There are other burial sites in the valley, some excavated, revealing chambers and stone coffins. Chinese archaeologists may be having a wonderful time here, but what do Tibetans think? Will dating their ancient civilisation impress Beijing and lead to a restoration of Tibetan land rights, as Australian archaeology impressed upon Canberra that Aboriginal people had ancient claims on Australia?

At our collective request we have interrupted the ride to walk through a village, when a deafening explosion reverberates between the mountains like rolling thunder. It finds an exit and quiet returns. Chinese use of explosives to change the landscape is deeply offensive to Tibetans, who hold the earth sacred.

In a village you recognise that Tibet is best travelled on foot, passing gateways, glancing into yards such as this one, circling a resting donkey with a load of thornbush still on its back, avoiding dogs roaming little lanes, touching a wall plastered with a pleasing pattern. You finally understand what the colours of prayer flags do for the colour of mud.

The most extraordinary dog I have ever seen stands quietly on the path. As tall as a German shepherd, it has long black hair, square face, bushy tail, eyes hidden by hair. Its back sags like a saddle and the belly hangs down. I feel sorry for this placid creature, so sad, maybe hungry. It would be nice to feed her bread or *tsampa*, but we carry none.

It begins to rain. The road back to Tsetang is very rough but we are in high spirits, feeling good. At the hotel a waitress in red and yellow sash welcomes not us, but a party of Chinese teachers entertained by a Tibetan woman official. Sharing the dining room, we watch them lunch copiously before the handsome woman — in her forties or fifties — hands out presents to the teachers: woven Tibetan shoulder bags and *kata*. All the time she eyes the Tibetans in our party. Finally she sings a melodious Tibetan song in a beautiful voice, stroking the Chinese visitors with sounds and loving glances. I enquire what the song is about. She sings the praise of friendship with Chinese bringers of good luck. The teachers look nice chaps, slightly embarrassed.

Striking east, we travel through roadside villages and groves of pollarded willows. The people look extremely poor, many work in road gangs. It rains steadily, yet the sky is clear enough for us to see the impressive outlines of Yambalakhang on top of Mount Tashi Tshe Ri, a ridge standing astride the Yarlung valley like a statue in a pond. I experienced the thrill of at last seeing with my own eyes a building familiar from long-perused photographs, a relic of an older more warlike Tibet, when *dzong* with watchtowers like these were strung across the land.

Regarded as the oldest building in Tibet, Yambalakhang was completely destroyed during the Cultural Revolution. What we see today is a reconstruction dating from 1982. The golden roof added to the tower by the Fifth Dalai Lama, born at nearby Chingwa Ri ('Tiger Top Mountain') in 1617, was not restored, nor was the third floor of the chapel. Yet Yambalakhang looks as ancient as the legends suggest it. Twelve shepherds elected as king of Tibet a man who descended from heaven to build the fortified palace. The year 127 BC and the third century BC have been named, but Tibet's monkey ancestor, reincarnation of Chenrezig the *bodhisattva* of compassion, is also claimed as its founder. Successive kings and Dalai Lamas added to the complex until it became a wholly religious building. King Songtsen Gampo unified Tibet from this sacred place and declared Buddhism the country's religion.

At the foot of the ridge my heart sinks. Time to become a real pilgrim. Shouldering day pack and water bottle, locating my puffer in a pocket, I start the steep climb. Countless times I stop, heartened by the view of our diminishing bus until it is just a toy. The others are waiting at the top. Two travellers come to assist me, talking me up those last few switchbacks to a stone-walled platform with an entrance to what turns out to be quite a small two-storey temple. My heartbeat calms down, my breath behaves itself. Exhilarated, I touch grey stone bastions and sloping walls. Door curtains flap in the wind, plep-plep, a song of defiance.

Two women live here, looking not like village women but more colourful, even a little wild. Amazed at the sight of us, they come close to examine our faces, hair and eyes. Moments of mutual curiosity. As we fill up the little cave of a hall, they screech with delight at our invasion. Are they lama consorts?

Half a dozen Nyingma monks run the *lakhang*. Few tourists come up here. Perhaps Jason's view prevails that a replica is not worthy of a visit. That would be a pity. That the building is of recent reconstruction matters not to me, nor to the Tibetans, to whom Yambalhakang and all it stands for, including any scrap saved from the old *lakhang,* constitutes a sacred site. We meet the head monk, who is a wise elderly man. As with many restored religious buildings there is a vigorous feel about the place in this rarefied air.

Considering the site, it is safe to assume that reconstruction was done largely with the rubble from the old *lakhang*. This accounts for the missing storey, for new materials would have to be piggybacked up the steep rise. Outside and inside Yambalakhang looks as old as the mountains. A few repaired statues are ancient, but there are new images of Tibetan kings and their ministers. The main statue is Amitayus, Buddha of Long Life. The dark second storey houses scriptures on a wooden landing, allowing a view of the temple beneath.

Outside we circumambulate buildings and tower. Three men do temple woodwork under a feeble overhang at the rear. Life up here is down to bare essentials. Clothing, tools and materials are of the simplest. But there are dogs for company and the views compensate for many a hardship. Leaning on the stone wall, you get a dizzy view of a green valley dotted with groves of trees and villages connected by narrow footpaths. Seen through the branches of a tree clinging to the rock, hung with prayer flags, the view bestows a sense of wellbeing. There is something thrilling about dwelling at great heights. This then is the cradle of Tibetan civilisation. Here Chenrezig united with the ogress monkey and begot the first Tibetan people.

The other side has a view of bare mountains and a village verily swimming in mud with not a sprig of grass, yet abundant greenery grows across the road. Due to the rain, going down proves harder than climbing up and again I arrive last. But gazing up at Tibet's first building I am thrilled to have made it.

On the way back we stop in Trandruk village to see the oldest monastery in the Yarlung valley, dating from the seventh century. Songtsen Gampo built the first temple around a spontaneously arisen statue of Dolma, Tibet's maternal deity. Through meditation the king was able to clear the site of detrimental influences and have the lake that existed here, inhabited by a dragon, drained by a miraculous falcon. Trandruk means 'fossilised dragon'. Over time Dolma disappeared, but the story still lives that she consumed offerings put before her. Do they ever lose a story in Tibet? If ever a land was stitched together by stories it is Tibet. Songtsen Gampo lived at Trandruk and the stove of his wife Weng Cheng is reputed to be here. We don't get to see it.

Trandruk is laid out like the Jokhang, yielding wonderful views portal after portal, courtyard upon courtyard, even as we walk in the gate. Voices of reciting monks meet us as we step into an earlier millennium. Some buildings still have original seventh century wood in their structures, thanks to a preserving climate. Stone pavers are worn smooth from a millennium and a half of prostrations and shuffling footsteps. We add ours. Metalwork on thick wooden doors looks pre-medieval.

Although largely spared in the Cultural Revolution, Trandruk monastery was used by Chinese troops as quarters, storage and offices and fell into a bad state of neglect, still painfully visible. Here and there a mural is being repainted, hammering can be heard, cement sacks lie about. Some paintings of obvious antiquity are in disrepair. One wall has new Sakyamunis in outline, only the topknots coloured in with lapis lazuli. A mural of yellow line drawings on black, shows vivid masked dancers. So there must be a master draughtsman around. Blank walls still wait for the plasterer's trowel.

King Trisong Detsen established Trandruk as one of three foundation monasteries for Buddhism in Tibet during the eighth century BC. Destroyed during the turbulent ninth century AD when King Langdarma suppressed Buddhism and probably rebuilt in the fourteenth century, it was restored by the Seventh Dalai Lama as a Gelukpa monastery. In the hushed caves of dark chapels hide statues from the monastery's beginnings. Some plundered statues were sent back to Trandruk from China by the Tenth Panchen Lama, who worked for the restoration of damaged monasteries in the few years left to him between his release from a Chinese prison and his premature death.

One Trandruk treasure is the pearl *thangka* of Avalokiteshvara, stitched 900 years ago with 29 000 pearls. During the Cultural Revolution it was kept hidden in Padmasambhava's cave high on a nearby mountain, a climb of seven hours which our Tibetan guide once made out of devotion. The pearl *thangka* was retrieved in the 1980s and reinstalled. It is a miracle in more than one way. Padmasambhava lived at Trandruk with his consort Yeshe Tsogyel, an important yogic mystic in her own right.

In a courtyard stands an unusual stone incense bowl on a base of lotus flowers. Nearby huddle oil drums, implements litter the ground. This wonderfully ancient place lacks a firm hand to ensure that it will be fully restored, the possibility of which can be seen in many erstwhile ruined monasteries. Trandruk still looks as if the Chinese bivouac here. Bicycles lean against antique murals whose deities are hardly decipherable. Rubbish litters the forecourt. Centuries-old wooden pillars are stripped of paint, the grain open to the elements. A trailer is parked on a verandah. The upstairs monks' quarters seem uninhabitable: walls crumbling, doors missing, windows uncovered and roofs suggesting they leak rain and snow.

Things improve further into the complex. A long wall, freshly painted pale yellow and demure pink, with bands of pink, yellow and duck-egg blue, carries the eight sacred symbols in tender fresco colours. Two Kalachakra mantras flank the temple entrance. Inside is a statue of Guru Rimpoche, made in his lifetime and approved by him as a good likeness. Did he have a mirror? The eyes look straight at us.

Avalokiteshvara's statue is newly gilded, the shrine crowded with photographs of the Dalai Lama at various ages. *Thangkas* in blue and gold brocade flank the statue, butter lamps shed a golden light on a scene of lively worship. Despite distressing disrepair, at heart the monastery is alive.

We climb to the second storey to find young monks learning texts aloud. Two monks seated in an alcove practice horns. The three-metre-long instruments rest on a gilt wooden stand, inlaid with red and blue glass. The sound passes right through the body and you wonder whether the boys get lulled into a trance, but they stop eagerly to talk to us and take a breather. They look more like high-school students sent off to do homework than musical monks destined to announce the great moments of Tibet's religion through the years. But a life where all tasks, likeable or not, add up to devotion is enviable. Of course there is nothing to prevent me dedicating my own tasks at home to the wellbeing of all sentient beings. All it takes is awareness and a small private vow.

Around the upper courtyard are open verandahs where older men sit on long cushions, producing new silk dresses for statues, draperies and appliqué hangings. One operates a treadle sewing machine, another stitches by hand. So the monastery is restoring statues itself. These artisans wear lay clothes. They may be textile workers, or former monks returned to serve their monastery in this capacity. Each artisan has his own thermos flask, flanked by a wooden bowl. They seem shy when we make admiring noises and bend over the work in their hands. I long to embroider a lotus.

We peek into a smoky kitchen, soot-blackened corners, but the kettle is on. Burnished rows of polished copper tea urns glow in a wooden cabinet, a red thermos on top. I climb down a narrow ladder, clutching a butter-smooth railing, to take in once more the atmosphere of times gone in wide courtyards where shaggy dogs roam, snuffling for remnant offerings.

At dinner we discuss decorations in Tsetang hotel's guestrooms. Our guide points out that *thangkas* ought to be hanging above our head, not at the foot end of the bed, which is disrespectful. Neither should towels and cloths, used to mop up dirt, be coloured orange, the colour of the *sangha* or Buddhist clergy. One supposes people don't use purple bathmats around the Vatican.

Before falling asleep I muse about the tendency to deem traditional sensitivities nonsense, and the counter-conviction that anything non-Western societies hold sacred must be respected universally. Might we create a gentler world if we learnt more about each other's sensibilities, heeding them when appropriate? It wouldn't do any harm reserving a few colours for other-than-advertising purposes. Or are the *sangha*, the emperor's yellow robes and purple for cardinals the biggest advertising stunts in history? Sleep holds back the answer.

Samyé and the Hermit Monk

The bus nearly capsizes on excavations in mainstreet Tsetang. In the planter box at the junction now sits a homeless man. Where is the old woman? Old? Younger than myself, probably. She must have died. She seemed so determined. All that can be done now is pray for her advantageous rebirth, if she needs to return at all. On the next block a woman in sheepskin clothes dresses a child by a burning firepot. A man sits nearby, packs lie around. They camped in the street overnight. Pilgrims passing through or the new homeless?

Not illogically the conversation veers to restoration. Our Tibetan guide says that Lhasa's Western Gate is being rebuilt with all three stupas. I gasp. To have destroyed it was sacrilege. To rebuild it for Chinese army trucks and noisy diesel traffic to drive through is worse. The purpose of the Western Gate was to house relics of a revered lama and form the entrance to the holy city. The relics were destroyed and the city extended by several kilometres. What is the reason for this sudden restoration?

The poplars planted for flood control between Tsetang and Samyé have grown well in the past two years. New plantings are in evidence. The road is now entirely paved. But when we arrive at the ferry place, the willow grove is gone, the bank bare of trees. Only the glass-topped wall is still here. We board and settle down on the ferry's wooden partitions for the crossing. Everywhere sandbanks protrude above the water, due to the drought. The ferry has to steer downstream to get around them before aiming for the far shore.

When the rhythm of the engine becomes part of the heartbeat, a drowsy state of mind ensues and river magic takes over. From behind sunglasses I aim my camera at the shore, taking a frame of the passengers when I sweep to the other side. It is so rude to aim at people directly, yet I want to remember them. Some women and girls in Chinese clothes are not fooled. I am sorry. They look crossly or cover their faces with their hands.

The men in the stern are engaged in animated conversation. One monk whirls a prayer wheel the size of an outsize coffee mug. Before leaning overboard for a face and arm wash, he hands it to an elderly man who continues to spin without missing a beat or a word in the conversation. It is handed back in the same manner. The gods won't even notice the change of hands.

239

When my gaze turns to the boy monk I jolt in surprise. It is the face of the young incarnate lama, passenger on this ferry to Samyé two years ago. I took his photo and remember him well. Now he wears maroon robes, prayer beads on his neck. Could he have grown this much? But boys do between fifteen and seventeen. Leaning over the side, humming a tune, his hand trails in the water. The large eyes in the smooth round face stare dreamily upstream. He seems in a world of his own, in harmony with the river and the movement of the boat. Where did I last see an adolescent so contented that he sings to himself, forgetting all around him?

Snippets of conversation are being translated for our benefit. The adult monk with shining eyes and beaming face spinning the prayer wheel is going in retreat. He has done a long retreat before and is returning from visiting relatives and a pilgrimage to Lhasa. Tomorrow he climbs the mountain behind Samyé to enter a cave where he will live for the next eleven years. The only human noises he will hear are those of people who occasionally bring food. He will re-emerge in 2006. You couldn't meet a happier man. I know I will often think of the monk meditating in a cave for the benefit of all sentient beings.

Although in isolation, he will not be alone. On Samyé Chimpu, twelve kilometres from Samyé monastery, Keith Dowman found more than fifty yogins and yoginis in 1985, who had restored caves and hermitages destroyed in the Cultural Revolution. Some years later Victor Chan made the five hour climb and found more than one hundred hermits meditating there. Chimpu is again a place of pilgrimage.

Our Tibetan guide says Samyé literally means 'think' (*sam*) 'better' (*yé*), appropriate for the first Buddhist monastery on Tibetan soil. But the compound word means 'better than the imagination' or 'beyond imagination'. (I am indebted to scholars who discussed on the internet complementary translations such as 'limitless thought' and 'beyond imagination'. Kunga Sanggye wrote that the full name of Samyé monastery is 'Glorious Immutable Miraculously Accomplished Shrine Beyond Imagination', which fits the place to this day.)

At last the other shore and trucks to transport pilgrims. Luxury indeed. The two oldies will ride in the cabin. We are not slim, but the young driver good-humouredly presses his thin frame in a corner. Worried that we may not know where we are going because we do not speak Tibetan, he uses his little English most creatively to explain that Samyé is a place of worship. 'OM MANI PEME HUNG', he says, taking both hands off the wheel as we plough the familiar rutted sand track, placing them reverently on his forehead. We hastily nod complete comprehension! On we hurl, past the little white *chörten* hewn from the rocks. He then treats us to Tibetan music on his tape-recorder, jigging in his seat to the beat in his jolly efforts to Tibetanise us in half an hour.

Ruins on the left and at the rear. Ganden monastery was shelled by Chinese military
during the Cultural Revolution.

Woman walking. Ganden.

An elderly monk at Ganden, restored buidings rise from the rubble

This stele in front of Jokhang, Lhasa, records the treaty of 821 AD between King Tri Ralpachen and Emperor Wen Wu Hsiao-te Wang-ti:

'All to the East is the country of Great China; and all to the West is, without question, the country of Great Tibet. Henceforth on neither side shall there be waging of war nor seizing of territory.'

(ref. Batchelor p. 82)

Identical steles originally stood on the border and at the Chinese capital.

The *Dzong* at Gyantse

The Kumbum in Gyantse undergoing restoration in 1993

Harvest time in the Gyantse Valley

View of Gyantse's main street from the gate of Palkhor Chöde monastery. The *dzong* is on the left.

Above Shigatse's market, selling Chinese goods and illegally shot antelope meat, towers the ruin of the destroyed Shigatse *dzong*

Dying wool at a Shigatse carpet factory

Tashilhumpo monastery, seat of the Panchen Lamas, Shigatse

One of the twenty-one
Taras in Drolma
Lakhang

Monks practising *radong* at Trandruk monastery near Tsetang

Abbot's house in the rocks at Chakpori

Pilgrims leave money at a shrine bearing portraits of the Fourteenth Dalai Lama and the Tenth Panchen Lama. The Dalai Lama's portraits are now forbidden in Tibet.

After a vigorous jolt rounding the shrubberies, Samyé appears. The new golden roof on the temple blazes brilliantly on the boundary between emerald green fields and slate grey mountain. My heart jumps. To come here a second time — what happiness!

There is a kind of rapture in revisiting beloved places, knowing the way, recognising smells. Samyé is livelier than ever. Rows of small *chörten* on the elliptical wall have been painted white. The roof over Trisong Detson's stele has been painted green and gold. It has stood left of the temple entrance since 779, proclaiming Buddhism as Tibet's religion, where its temples shall always be maintained, so may the gods be witnesses. There are bound to be other stones in the building used in the first temple. Older writings mention a bronze bell donated by Trisong Detson's queen having survived the centuries, but we don't see it. The Tenth Panchen Lama gave much money to restore this temple. On the steps six dogs sleep in a row, one in the portal, while number eight sits up like a snow lion, keeping watch.

I touch again the butter-greased plait hanging from the bronze doorknob, before climbing all floors. The top floor, open to the elements in 1993, has been enclosed. I note again that peculiar Tibetan ability to make a place look venerably ancient in a matter of years, with the paint still fresh. Partly this is because sacred places get painted frequently, maintenance being an act of worship, partly because materials from holy places are always recycled.

More restored murals. A new Sakyamuni outlined in red, only the blue topknot coloured in. It seems important that the blue topknot is coloured in first. There's a lovely White Tara.

A particularly gorgeous mural takes up a portico's entire wall. It depicts a company of people in Indian or Chinese silks and Mongolian fashions. The textiles have been painted deliciously: muted shades of sienna, moss and rust brown, intricate florals and diamonds of gold. The faces are portraits, skin colours vary from pale or tanned to brown. The variety of headgear might indicate who these people were if I knew its history. Some carry *kata* ready to present. All eyes seem fastened on a figure in monk's robes who appears to address them. A deity in yellow hat, flanked by numerous others, floats above the crowd. Something to look up at home. The guides are ahead, hurrying because we need to reach Lhasa and the river crossing is long.

Samyé, sacked so many times, destroyed by earthquake and fire, is rising again. After being used as a collective farm during the Cultural Revolution, signs of which were still plentiful in 1993, the mandala of its buildings is visibly regaining ground. At least four temples were destroyed, together with four large *chörten* denoting the four directions of the Buddhist universe. Today the *chörten* are restored. The moss green, white and red ochre ones are of similar shape as the Western Gate, with a thirteen-ring golden peak. But the black *chörten* has no bulbous middle, looking rather like the gold and black skirt of a temple dancer.

From the roof we take in the sheltered valley, the majestic mountains where the monk will meditate from tomorrow until mid-2006. Compared with many other landscapes Samyé has no obvious beauty in a country of stunning vistas. It is one of the very few monasteries that sits on level ground instead of straddling an outcrop in the clouds or clinging to a sheer rock wall. But it has an intensity of magic and light. Tibetans claim the magic is Guru Rimpoche's, who put his indelible stamp on this place; it was chosen by him as the launching pad for Buddhism in Tibet. But there is a more homely magic, a welcoming mystery about Samyé that makes me want to stop here — like last time. Since my first visit I have learnt Guru Rimpoche's mantra and read stories from his life, but it was the place he chose that first caught my imagination.

Tucked away in a covered verandah is a sewing room, one man treadling while another looks on. An old monk sits deep in thought at the cutting table. Padded brocade bands wait to be stitched. The view from this roof mesmerises. The sacred mountain Hepo Ri rises nearby and in the distance, Chimpu.

On level ground, walking within the elegantly towering elliptical wall, we find one of the original courtyard *ling* — a garden. *Ling* also means 'island' or 'continent'. There were four *ling* representing the four main continents of the Buddhist universe. After its completion Samyé was the scene of ecumenical debates between Indian and Chinese Buddhists. These discussions were scholarly and amicable at first, with projects such as the teaching of meditation and monastic ritual and the writing of grammars and dictionaries to enable Tibetans to learn Sanskrit texts. But eventually the Indian system of slow and systematic learning over many lifetimes and the Chinese (Ch'an, now Zen) system of enlightenment in one lifetime clashed. King Trisong Detsen chaired the Great Debate and the Indians had majority support. Yet the attraction of Samyé is that it has remained open to all schools of Tibetan Buddhism until this day.

We move through a gateway, onto a verandah surrounding a small courtyard. 'Aaaah!' sighs the company. Raised flagstone beds surrounded by river-stone paving barely contain masses of nasturtiums, mallows, double pink and wine red hollyhocks, flowering broadbeans and juniper. Climbing a bamboo pole to a balcony is a hot pink Dorothy Perkins rose. Would her name be Dolma Tsering here, or do Tibetans know their flowers by face rather than by name? It is a scene romance writers from the time of *Lost Horizon* would have bribed to see. This gorgeous hideaway reveals the hand of a plantsman, but the place is deserted, the little temple closed.

Someone decides to have lunch here and we sit down on smooth pebbles, close to the entrance. I am not sure this is good form. Soon the local children find us, staring at our plenitude. I prefer to share as I eat, others want to eat first — majority wins. Eventually a big boy comes to wait patiently on the verandah. When he gets a share of food he passes it to an old woman by the gate and some little kids who would have missed out. He takes nothing for himself. He will be a great lama one day. The children eat more ravenously than the frolicking bunch by the willow creek in 1993. There is a shift in the eyes of hungry kids when they bite into offered food that does not occur when they are well enough nourished to see lunchbox food as merely a desirable novelty. Birds fly in and out, cleaning up crumbs. Nothing wasted.

When we are nearly finished, an elderly monk arrives, somewhat bemused at the intrusion. We stand up and introduce ourselves, ask whether he is the gardener. His face lights up, arm sweeping to embrace the flowers, the cats he feeds, the birds. Yes, he tends all this and the temple. Would we like to see inside?

He opens a heavy door. It is darkish, tidy, clean. The butter lamps are burning. We stand in quiet respect in this tenderly tended home of a deity restored, set in such quietude and beauty. Outside again I look up. A second floor, set back on the flat roof, has two big windows and red doors with wooden steps to the roof. Below the windows rows of clay pots and shiny tins with pink and crimson geraniums. Birds peck between the cobblestones while a cat licks its paws. Friends, not enemies in this peaceful *ling*. Paradise restored.

Faded murals on the walls of the covered verandahs are protected against the sun by white and blue curtains. Young trees wave green plumes. Beyond, not far away, the ochre and gold of the red *chörten* stands out against slate grey mountains and gathering clouds. This then could be Aryapalo Ling, the oldest temple at Samyé, built even before the great temple.

We take our leave of the smiling monk, removing our too boisterous presence from his haven of peace. As my feet move the thought arises: 'I will never see this place again'. It lodges as a small pain. Goodbye Samyé, beautiful beyond the imagination. We climb on the truck for another joyride to the ferry.

At the river there are troubles with a boat stuck in the mud, but solid Tibetan swearing and muscle strength get it afloat. On board I sit in the stern, legs stretched out, beside an elderly couple. Behind them, a young woman with a fat baby hands the old man some snuff. His daughter. 'Ama-la', I greet the older woman. She hugs me and gestures I must sit closer. She begins to tell me something about her husband, winks at me woman-to-woman-like, shaking her small fist at him. He, under his felt hat, looks uncannily like Einstein complete with his wispy white hair. He shakes his head, protesting his innocence of whatever she accuses him. His eyes look droopy, intoxicated. The snuff may not be the first drug of the day, because Einstein is a little off the planet.

Ama-la dips into the folds of her *chuba* and hands lollies to three of us. I reciprocate with the last of the watermelon sweets. Daughter refuses, looking displeased with mother's new acquaintances. She scatters wind horses upon the river, tiny squares of handmade paper printed with the winged horse that carries prayers to the gods. The gossamer squares float in the boat's wake, messages to an invisible rescuer. Ama-la dips into her folds again to produce cubes of *chugum*, dried yak cheese. I suck one contentedly for the best part of an hour.

When we reach the other bank my face is fiercely sunburnt. My hat was in my pack. Ama-la and Einstein reluctantly pose for the camera. I thank them profusely, wishing to convey this is not for publication, lest they worry. Their daughter will tell them off.

At Daga, where the bridge divides the roads to Gyantse and Shigatse, a monstrous roundabout is being constructed. It is one of the sixty-two projects to benefit the Tibetan people. Roads are being paved and guttered. Hundreds of road workers include Tibetan women loosening gravel with pickaxes and Chinese women in city slacks, sun hats and dust masks carrying rocks in gloved hands. Everywhere tent camps, bulldozers and dust. This is the Friendship Highway, connecting Lhasa to Kathmandu.

At my request we stop at Dolma Lakhang and light a lamp for the speaking Tara. The others are pleased not to have missed this little treasure temple from Atisha's time. Nothing much has changed, though the porch is freshly painted. My plain white silk *kata* with the unravelled fringe is still here. All the Taras wear orange *kata*, but mine is knotted around an old metal Indian stupa.

We are told a good story. When Zhou Enlai visited India he was approached by a scholar requesting that Atisha's ashes be returned to his homeland Bangladesh. Zhou Enlai agreed and they went home from here.

I notice that the mural on the porch is similar to the one of the great procession in Samyé. It may be Atisha's welcome by the grand lamas of central Tibet. He was perturbed at their rich festive clothes and trappings. It is like coming across a familiar reproduction in another book. Monastery murals are Tibet's storybooks.

White clouds are massing on top of Lhasa's ring of mountains in the distance, wild fairies dancing. Lhasa means 'place of the gods', but once it was Rhasa, 'place of goats'. At some time in deep history a political decision changed Capricorn's stamping ground into a holy city. When Tibetans say Lhasa it still sounds like Rhasa, the 'L' aspirated with a backdraught in the middle of an open mouth.

We pass Atisha on the Rock, reflecting in the shallow pool. Then more projects: a formal park being laid out, building construction, a boulevard, lotus lamp posts, a pink stone statue of Tibetan giants commemorating Tibetans who lost their lives to enable progress to come to the Tibet Autonomous Region. All to be ready in less than two months to impress Beijing delegations. No press are invited, tourists are banned. Xinhua News Agency will portray the celebrations to the world according to party lines.

Closer to Lhasa hundreds of trees are being planted to hide living quarters of 30 000 Chinese troops. The new road is still a long wading pool. The approach to Lhasa now looks much like the approach to Chengdu: kilometres of jerry-built structures, dust and debris. Societies that have destroyed their own past cannot live alongside another culture's past. They want the world to forget what they themselves try to forget. The Chinese are covering historical places in Tibet with icons of a communist future that must compensate for the loss of past civilization; a future that must blot out Tibet's past so that the world may forget it and allow China its prize of conquest.

The corridors of the Lhasa Holiday Inn sound hollow, the staff is frigid. We get rooms on the fourth floor, drag in the luggage, go to where food is served and eat. Afterwards I go to bed, too depressed by the new Lhasa to go out, although being in Lhasa for the second time in my life is fortuitous. You firmly remind yourself of miracles in fake surroundings like these.

Lhasa on the Dalai Lama's Birthday

Today is Tenzin Gyatso's birthday. The Fourteenth Dalai Lama was born on 6 July 1935 and celebrates his sixtieth birthday today. And so does Lhasa.

At the Jokhang clouds of fragrant juniper smoke, *samgbum,* billow from large cement incense burners. People crowd around *kata* stalls. Pilgrims do prostrations. The women tie their skirts around the ankles, making them look like packages folding up as they bow heads between raised arms. Surveillance cameras point from both sides of the plaza. Chinese police conspicuously patrol in pairs.

The celebrations are low-key because the Chinese are conducting a campaign against 'the Dalai and his clique'. He was accused of trying to split the motherland when on 14 May he announced the new Panchen Lama, six-year-old Gendhun Choekyi Nyima from Lhara district, north of Lhasa. This child is held to be the reincarnation of the Tenth Panchen Lama by the monastic committee appointed by the Chinese government themselves. But the chairman, Tashilhunpo's abbot Chadrel Rimpoche, required the Dalai Lama's approval, as all Dalai Lamas and Panchen Lamas give final endorsement to each other's reincarnations. The Dalai Lama then chose to do his duty and the Chinese authorities have been breathing fire ever since. There are rumours that Chadrel Rimpoche has been arrested.

There is not the crush of throngs in the Jokhang as in 1993, although the bottleneck is still choked with people. A file of elderly Tibetan men see me hesitate to join the crowd and spontaneously make room for me. I fold myself sideways into their queue for the slow shuffle of chapels. How fortunate to do this a second time in my life. If I lived in Lhasa I might do it every week, in old age every day. Hundreds of butter lamps flicker before the main shrine, reflections dancing upside down in brass counterpanes. Grandmothers hold little kids with one hand while pouring butter into burners with the other. Shouldering travel bags, many pilgrims have come from afar for this day. A large photograph of the Dalai Lama looks down from a gilded frame wreathed with *kata*.

On the first floor a line of traditional *chang* women — ladies who pour beer at official functions — dance and sing for Songtsen Gampo and his wives. Since my last visit I have learnt he had two Tibetan wives as well as the princesses Weng Cheng and Bhrikuti who are now regarded as embodiments of Green Tara and White Tara, the most important of Tara's twenty-one forms. Historian Christopher Beckwith thinks Weng Cheng may have been a bride for the king's son, demanded from the Chinese emperor in the course of neighbourly politics when Tibet was more powerful. Her coming was not proof that Tibet was part of China. Folk stories have it that during her long journey Weng Cheng fell for and became pregnant by the king's envoy who fetched her. Stylishly the *chang* women step sideways, forward and backwards before the royal chapel, singing what sounds like a dirge but for their bursts of laughter between lines.

Two painters, not in robes, painstakingly put colour on new mural designs. This is one of the few jobs that allows a religious-minded person who did not obtain a placing in the monks' quotas to connect with a temple. A painting brown with the grime of ages has a top corner cleaned, revealing six delicate *bodhisattvas* in creamy dull gold. Another wall has minute cameos of the building of the Jokhang.

From the top floor come sounds of chanting, long horns and the boom of drums. A long-life prayer for the Dalai Lama is being delivered to the gods. We form a half-circle around a dozen monk musicians. When Tibet was independent, this ceremony would have been performed by tens of thousands of monks all over the country. Considering the 1988 invasion of the Jokhang by Chinese troops, when monks were beaten and imprisoned, these monks are brave hearts.

A monk guide takes us to the roof where Tibetan pilgrims may not go. Over the balustrade we watch them in the street, burning incense, prostrating, clutching packets of butter and *kata*. Even a youngster of barely four prostrates between women and old men, as naturally as a he would kick a ball.

Today the Potala looks sublime. Small white clouds float beneath the ramparts, the sunlight a diluted gold, bordering on platinum. It is a vision of breathtaking beauty, this beacon of Tibet's uniqueness. Behind us, the balcony where the Dalai Lama would watch Jokhang ceremonies is festooned with flowerpots, windows draped in saffron, waiting for the day. As we descend to the courtyard, throngs of people carrying butter lamps snake through the temple, praying, touching foreheads to the hems of statues embodying their deepest hopes and wishes.

We circumambulate the Barkhor around the Jokhang. Because of the birthday, pairs of People's Armed Police sit ready for action on wooden chairs every twenty metres in the middle of the roadway. People weave around them as if they were invisible. The PAP talk only to each other, furtively viewing the crowd from beneath large visors on their green caps.

Completing the route, we buy dried artemisia from a little woman so shrivelled and thin, yet not old, that I fear she lives in constant starvation. I tower more than two heads above her, an overfed giant from a world that doesn't manage to reach people like her. Diving into the smoke clouds around the big burner, we place our offering on the charcoal and I pray something will happen in Tibet that improves the lot of the poorest.

In the plaza four young women walk arm in arm, strung out, their hair, faces and clothes dusted with white flour. Two tourists and a Newari come from the same direction, also powdered. Flour throwing is a traditional blessing on the Dalai Lama's birthday and it takes place by the river.

After a Tibetan lunch we go shopping in the Barkhor. We buy a Tibetan prayer book each, the length of a forearm, wrapped in yellow cotton and held with red ties. I buy a printed Tara and Buddha for *thangkas*. It's not easy to find Tibetans selling brocade. Most traders are Chinese or Newaris from Nepal. The sad woman of my last visit is no longer here, but toward the end of the Barkhor is a shop run by Amdowas. They are interested in my *thangka* project, tell me which colours and patterns are right, and give generous measure.

Skins of snow leopard are still on sale. The PLA has a large stall selling sneakers as part of economic restructuring. I am all in favour of armies earning their crust, it could diminish wars. But the PLA runs the vast prison camps where so many of China's export goods are being manufactured.

In the plaza Derge women, arms hung with jewellery and determined to sell, pursue struggling tourists. So determined, you cannot see their wares until, having battled through a hedge of strong hard bodies, you have safe viewing from the bus. We escape to Norbulingka.

On this special day the summer palace keeps severely restricted hours. We form a majority in the grounds, where Tibetan workmen are laying drainage pipes. Where are the pilgrims? Norbulingka was the stage for the great Lhasa uprising of March 1959, mostly by women, trying to prevent the Dalai Lama going to the Chinese camp alone, as he was pressed to do. Earlier a lama from Amdo had accepted such an invitation, went alone and was never seen again. A Tibetan who collaborated with the Chinese tried to shoot his way through the crowd around Norbulingka but was hanged by the angry people.

Ten days later, when the Dalai Lama's party was secretly fleeing south, the Chinese shelled Norbulingka, thinking him still inside. By the time the uprising subsided, dead bodies were stacked to the tree branches, doused with petrol and burned by the People's Liberation Army on the lawn where I saw people picnicking in 1993. Catriona Bass relates the account of someone who saw it happen when he was a boy. Chinese documents record 87 000 Tibetans being wiped out in the eighteen months that followed.

This is a sad visit, remembering the hundreds of people who two years ago pressed through corridors and rooms, now empty. The authorities are obviously clamping down on visits to what has become a shrine to the Dalai Lama's early life. Fruit ripens on the gigantic apple trees in his orchard. You shudder to think what caused such fertility. I have never seen apple trees this high.

Inside, on the first landing, is a fresco portraying translators as birds with two heads. A striking image. You use two heads to translate; the sound of each language must be heard in isolation. The *bodhisattvas* Vajrapani and Avalokiteshvara are sometimes portrayed as a twin-headed parrot and a twin-headed duck. Together with Manjusri, the *bodhisattva* of wisdom, they stand for action, speech and thought, hopefully not in that order.

In empty rooms photographs of the Tenth Panchen Lama feature prominently, a political statement. When will his young eleventh incarnation be brought to Shigatse and Lhasa to begin religious training? As we stand in the throne room, dazzled by detail on ceilings and walls, a group of Chinese people enters. They respectfully walk through the room and out into the courtyard. Many Chinese are still Buddhists. I remember the old woman wailing, the Chinese soldiers beating a hasty retreat.

Only one barking watchdog sits on the roof of the Seventh Dalai Lama's palace. Inside, a special red butter *torma* for his incarnation's birthday. Chinese peddlers offer unrelated merchandise in the portico. Trailing to the exit, I feel a little overcome by a mural proclaiming the context for significant ceremonies whose celebrants are absent. Tired out by the fatigue of a place that has seen so much suffering that only throngs of hopeful worshippers can diminish the effect on the casual visitor. The sound of laughter falters here, absorbed by those immense trees of death.

We walk back to the hotel. Once Norbulingka stood well outside Lhasa. This used to be countryside. Meals in the inn are served in a room seating seventy. This looks better when there are only forty guests at the height of the season in a hotel with hundreds of rooms.

After dinner I walk the gauntlet between two rows of traders spread along the footpath. Hands behind my back, I indicate 'only looking'. To touch is as good as a sale. But after much shaking, smiling, nodding and shrugging, I return to a Tibetan copper teapot. The trader quotes his price. I could never afford one in Australia and nod acceptance. So amazed is the man that he nearly loses his hat as he gets up to give the pot a final brush. He assures me it is the family teapot, which makes me feel ignoble, but the price I pay without bargaining obviously fills him with ecstasy. He pumps my hand, other traders look on. A tourist who does not bargain? You should be so lucky!

A filigree oil pot joins the teapot, also without detested bargaining. Only then I wonder how to transport the pair over mountain passes without denting, not to mention train journeys and four aeroplane flights. I stuff the pots with socks, wrap them in trousers, savour the unwrapping at home.

The sky over Lhasa is black with rain-bearing clouds. Soon a thunderstorm breaks loose, followed by a blackout. It doesn't last long. I shower and turn in to dream of butter tea at home.

Drepung, the Nunnery and the Barkhor

A morning ride to Drepung, the white riceheap on slate-dark rocks. At its foot the remains of a village where outcast butchers lived, slaughtering for Tibetans wishing to eat meat without being party to killing, much like a modern consumer's idea of buying meat. The dogs of Drepung still look well fed, but the forecourt is full of Tibetan beggars, from one-year-old to aged. We are distressed to see these kids. There are also too many persistent Derge women who will not let go of our arms until we buy jewellery. With tourists so thin on the ground, they are scratching for earnings.

We escape up the staircase hewn in the rocks, climbing to the forecourt of Ganden ('government') palace, built by the Second Dalai Lama. He was a retrospective Dalai Lama, the title first bestowed by Kublai Khan on Sonam Gyatso, now recognised as the Third Dalai Lama, in the sixteenth century.

The palace is open. A ground floor has deities in dark niches, the ferocious protectors Yamantaka, Mahakala, Palden Lhamo, and buddhas in the hall. A Maitreya looks down with the beginning of a smile — the future holds peace. Shuffling in clockwise direction, I regret this is all we do, from left to right behind the shrine and out again. I would like to sit here for an hour, letting the place imprint itself on the memory, rather than have it telescoped together with all other halls we shuffled through. Outside a Manjusri has arisen spontaneously from the rocks. All the artisans had to do was paint the face and gown. In a small chapel we file past a smiling young monk who blesses us with a brass-covered baton, stroking down our backs, ending with two taps. To keep us going.

There are many little monks among the 300 residents. We talk to a pair who entered Drepung at five and eight. They desire pens. Pens are forthcoming and they are admonished to use them for their studies. But the elder one has a yellow toy car that rides on smooth blank walls. Spellbinding!

Climbing up steep tunnelled stairs, steps of ancient wood lined with brass strips, we find the wonderful library to see the *Kanjur*. It is in 108 volumes, held with ivory clasps and tiny buddhas carved in lacquer. In the bookroom the black and gold-leaf book still lies in its glass case.

In the kitchen things are unchanged, the brass and copper of tea churns, rice pots and butter pots shining in the gloom. We have seen some large woodheaps for the stoves, but solar cookers are also in use. Old weaponry, dating from medieval times and handed in by people making vows not to kill anymore, rest rusting in corners of cobwebbed halls.

Wandering the alleyways of this mountain city we see much that is in disrepair. Here and there exquisitely painted pillars and beams, or metal fretwork on doors of faded red, remind of the beauty that was. Tsongkhapa images on the rocks have been freshly painted, so are little stupas glowing white and gold on the slate scree. Some walls have seen whitewash recently, window flounces have been replaced. There is life, although 300 monks in a place that housed 10 000 cannot maintain, let alone restore this once-thriving beehive of religious activity. But the monks make the best of their circumstances. Tins of white, pink and red geraniums grace their windowsills and when curtains and flounces billow in the breeze, the place is punctured with beauty.

Standing on the large flagstone terrace, Lhasa lies spread out below, a city swathed in green of trees. Monks gather at the big hall. Each monk entering the terrace stops at a prayer flag pole to prostrate himself. Rising, the robe is swung ceremoniously around the shoulders before he joins the others, sitting down cross-legged. Faces lift to the sun, catching its warmth. Old monks are led by tiny monklets holding ageing hands. The chanting begins.

After a while all monks turn to catch the sun on their backs. An abbot begins to speak and the monks start debating. They ask challenging questions, clapping their hands, letting the right arm sail forward, fingers pointing up like the bow of a ship. Stepping forward and backwards to a pattern, their spines bent, they stretch and recoil as questions and answers escalate. It is a ballet to the music of words, teasing young minds into independent thought. Coming from a country where it is not nice to disagree, it is exhilarating to see students thrown back on their own resources to analyse, challenge or defend what they think they have learnt. The Fourteenth Dalai Lama took his final *geshe* debating exam here, at seventeen, prior to prematurely assuming his high office because the Chinese threatened Tibet's independence. On that occasion he presented each of Drepung's 10 000 monks with a present, then walked away a doctor of Buddhist philosophy.

The monks are becoming self-conscious about onlookers. More tourists arrive like flies to the honeypot, taking videos and photographs from high points. We leave them to it.

Over lunch I bring up the unpopularity of analytic debate in daily life in Australia. One companion argues that since debating is now a popular subject in schools, society will change in the near future as debating youngsters grow up. But I am sceptic enough to reiterate that debating is a mere subject in school, left behind when they enter a society where acquiescence is the desired attitude. Whereupon the conversation switches to the food we are eating. Which proves my point, I guess.

The weather is brilliant for an afternoon visit to Tsangkhug nunnery in a back alley of old Lhasa. I have long wanted to visit a nunnery and am not disappointed. Through a gateway in a row of houses we enter a tiny courtyard. Apartment houses are stacked up tight around a small hall at the rear. Two young nuns in brown skirts and saffron blouses are cutting up meat at a wooden bench. We are invited into a tiny cave of a kitchen.

Here presides the abbess, a round-faced, small woman, grey shaven stubble on her broad skull. With her eyes — intelligent, wise and kind — she gathers us in. She is seventy-five and emanates contained strength. Like a company director she relates the nunnery's circumstances. There are usually between ninety-three and ninety-seven nuns — almost the pre-Cultural Revolution number — ninety of whom go home to sleep, as all accommodation the nunnery once had was confiscated in the sixties. Now the government allows apartments to return to the nunnery as they become available, but these need renovation. Dating from the eighth century, this was the site of a temple and monastery before it became a Gelukpa nunnery in the fifteenth century.

The abbess offers butter tea. The little kitchen is clean and scrupulously tidy, the way women keep kitchens. Hooks and nails hold ladles and bags, pots are scoured. A tomato red jug stands by the centre pole, exquisitely shaped.

In the little *gompa* attention to detail is touchingly evident, the space airy and clean, the atmosphere different from the monasteries, which tend to be cobwebby halls rather than homely dwelling places. Here the shrines gleam from care and attention. Marigolds, peacock feathers and paper flowers sit in well-washed pots. The *kata* are brightly white, as if they get regular washday dunkings. Polished brass butter lamps stand on a spotless tiled counter, above tables with special red *torma*.

Two nuns sit by the window shaping *torma* with skilful fingers. They continuously dip butter in cold water to stop it from melting during handling. An old bent man with wispy beard, wearing a silk-lined *chuba* with Mongolian trimmings, looks on reverently, *mala* around his neck. Two young men with him watch no less respectfully. Even butter in the process of becoming a *torma* is a sacred substance.

One of the nuns takes a break, stretches her back, picks up my day pack from the floor and laces her arms through the straps. Hoisting the pack on her back she pretends to leave. 'Bye-bye', she waves from the door, then turns back gurgling laughter, puts the pack down and returns to her butter sculpture. Her impish face is the colour of ripe peaches, her brown eyes clear as forest pools, filled with laughter, her ears stand wide off her head indicating wisdom. She is very young and I feel great respect for her genuine *joie de vivre*.

In a narrow alley alongside the *gompa* a low doorway leads to Songtsen

Gampo's meditation cave. Bowing, we enter, one pair at a time. Two teenage nuns are scrubbing and mopping the stone floor. The cave is behind yet another gleaming shrine. Fresh paint, polished table, butter lamps reflecting in the glass and behind it the king's small statue.

In this cave the king meditated for floodwaters on the Jokhang site to recede. Songtsen Gampo's era must have experienced particularly wet weather. This is the third place we have seen where he intervened to obtain dry sites for temples. The nuns show us his cave with the reverence of junior intimates. As in so many religious places, you gain the impression that time is not linear and the eighth century is at no distance at all from living memory. All the nuns meditate here. They are a cheerful and happy lot. Yet some of their colleagues are in prison for singing patriotic songs. How do they bear up?

The Nechung oracle, once resident near Drepung, also has a city temple. We find the lane behind the carpet dealers in the Barkhor. A gateway gives access to a courtyard in dappled shade. Seated on the ground under plastic sunshelters, hundreds of elderly women and a few men spin prayer wheels, humming ceaselessly OM MANI PEME HUM and OM AH HUM VAJRA GURU PADME SIDHI HUM. They aim to chant one million repetitions of Avalokiteshvara's and Padmasambhava's mantras. This devotion will take three months. The old ones beam welcome smiles, some stop reciting to ask who we are. Elderly Tibetans don't play bingo; they devote their time to the wellbeing of their society by reciting these prayers with all their energy. Having seen Tibet turned upside down, they believe it will right itself if they remain loyal to the founders of their religion.

Humbled, we take turns to shuffle through the temple where a few chanting monks mind the butter lamps. One is overcome with the seriousness of this business of regulating unseen but real powers by strenuous personal effort, so that constraints are put on suffering. Padmasambhava's statue is the main deity, but buddhas and great teachers are represented. Back in the courtyard we circumambulate the space, big feet treading deftly between folded legs and prayer-filled laps, supported by the old people's goodwill, until we find the lane again.

The sound of a deep drum issues from an upstairs temple room. A dumb woman points, making vigorous noises, gesturing we should climb the stairs. She is exuberant when we do. In the prevailing gloom, images are hardly visible, but we are shown a suit of chain mail and a sword, reputedly left here by Genghis Khan when he decided to give up waging war! This recurring legend is worthy of emulation in our times. Let churches, mosques and temples collect guns, ammunition, hand grenades, land mines, missiles and bombs. Let worshippers melt them down to make wheelchairs and crutches for millions of war-maimed children.

As we leave the lane, a woman pushes a young man in a makeshift wheelchair on bicycle wheels at great speed towards the Nechung temple. Both are laughing and talking. This is a high-spirited place, where the people of a sad city do something about life in the best way they know.

In the Barkhor's side alleys, stalls display chunks of butter the size of cheese wheels and plastic packs of butter for the temple. The travellers buy devotional items for shrines at home. I find a small brass lamp, woven Taras for *thangkas* and a tape of Panchen Lama's speeches. I ask the young trader to play the tape and briefly the Panchen's powerful voice resonates across the Barkhor, as it used to from the Jokhang on memorable occasions. It was in the Jokhang in 1964 that he was arrested for throwing away a censored speech, shouting: 'Long live the Dalai Lama!'.

The boy sits on a piece of snow leopard skin he offers for sale. I frown. He laughs shrewdly. Westerners' sensibilities are well known. He didn't kill the animal, so it's not his karma. Why waste a good skin just because it is from a protected animal? The police turn a blind eye. Animal skins are not their business. They deal with human skins. We meet our Tibetan guide with his family in the Barkhor. On his day off they shop for a *thangka* to present to an elderly relative. His cheeks look very blue. But his limp has disappeared.

An old woman in a skin *chuba* points at my shell earrings. Shells are a novelty here. I want to give them to her. She has one pierced lobe, but the other is torn. I leave her wearing one shell earring, big daughter has the other. My earrings seem destined to split up.

A last lingering at the Jokhang. The entrance is choked with prostrators. I am shy to break in, so we watch a while, incline our heads, and cross the plaza arguing with a desperate throng of Khamba women traders. There is thunder in the air and before long a rainshower settles the city's dust, bringing fresh earth smells. At the hotel we hand our passports to the Tibetan guide who will obtain permits for Shigatse. Gut feelings cry 'stateless', but I trust him implicitly.

On an evening walk, turning the other way to avoid the pavement market, we run into three Khamba women and a big boy, felt hat balancing on hair bound with red sashes. They are decked in silver, turquoise and coral and hang on our arms to make a sale. We would carry our baggage allowance in jewellery, had we the means to oblige every Khamba entrepreneur. But they laugh boisterously at our denials, nothing upsets them. Wanting to rescue the encounter I produce family photographs. Suddenly we all stand in a huddle and one of the women produces a small photo of her little boy. Where are they from? Derge. It is three years since they left home. The little boy is being brought up by grandmother. I take their picture. They pose happily, then walk us home arm in arm like old friends.

The Potala Palace and
Sera Monastery

The golden tombs on the Potala's roof contain the remains of all Dalai Lamas except the Sixth. He was 'removed' because he became an embarrassment, was taken in the direction of Mongolia and never heard of again. He loved wine and women and the people remember his poetry about youth and ageing, about unfulfilled love, maybe worldly but cast in spiritual terms. One telling verse reveals the Sixth Dalai Lama as a prisoner of his high office. In it he laments that although he went to his teacher filled with devotion to learn about the Lord Buddha, he could not take anything in because his mind was full of 'that Compassionate One' who loves him and occupies his mind.

Our little bus crawls up the paved roadway leading to the back door of the Potala, from where once the Dalai Lama was carried in procession to take up residence in his favourite summer palace. Norbulingka is sometimes open for Tibetans, the Potala never is, whereas in the Dalai Lama's time the public attended certain ceremonies there. The Potala's reason for existence now seems to be as a source of tourist dollars.

Here history envelops us like a suffocating quilt. Bastions of walls and towers surround us. Our footfall as we climb the last ramp sounds like the feet of mice scrambling. The entrance, like all entrances in this extraordinary palace, is almost two storeys high, as if in times gone by giants lived here. The effect of a person in a high-peaked cap, standing in such a doorway, must have given that impression seen from below. Of course, given an enlightened ruler in residence — a spiritual giant — this palace in the clouds could be a beacon of hope.

Inside we are shown another cave where Songtsen Gampo meditated before building his palace on Red Hill. The Great Fifth built the Potala as it is now, restoring and extending a fortress palace more than 1000 years old. When he died, a regent nicknamed Flathead kept his death a secret for as many years as it took to complete the building.

Climbing narrow staircases and filing through dark passages, we roam through what once was the ceremonial heart of Tibet. Great shrine rooms fold one into the other, connected by dark wide corridors lashed with murals of dancing deities. The artwork is stupendous. Many Maitreya statues live in the palace. Discussing a gallery of important statues we think ourselves alone when a voice speaks in English from the wall. We jump a little. In a dark niche sits a shaven monk wearing the grey robe of officialdom. He proffers official information and we nod politely. After this encounter we keep seeing monks in many dark corners and surveillance cameras high on the walls.

We come upon a smaller room, the ceiling not so high. It is home to the three-dimensional red copper Kalachakra mandala, hundreds of tiny figures and the wheel of time. We circle in silent wonder. Where else in the world is there such a miracle of metal skills? But what a devastating loss for the Tibetan people, in Tibet and elsewhere, that this Kalachakra mandala and their Dalai Lama are separated. Here stands the mandala in all its burnished beauty. Outside Tibet the Dalai Lama performs Kalachakra ceremonies while his monks painstakingly fashion two-dimensional mandalas in coloured sand. The Kalachakra is the heart of Tibetan Buddhist ritual. It embodies Tibetans' hopes for a peaceful world, coming as it did from legendary Shambhala, where no violence against or between sentient beings existed. Whenever the Dalai Lama performs Kalachakra initiations, be that in India, the United States or Australia, tens of thousands of people attend. In Mongolia in 1995, 2 per cent of the entire population galloped on fast ponies to the capital to sit still for the ten days of the Kalachakra. No public Kalachakra is performed anymore in Tibet. It carries the ideologically unsound message of a better existence achieved without the use of violence.

The great reception hall is having its floor polished by a small army of softly singing Chinese women. The Potala employs no Tibetans except guide monks in dark corners. The mostly Chinese staff numbers 200; they live in. I finger Bhutanese cloth covering columns, raise eyes at the throne. During ceremonies the Dalai Lama would have been visible to all, able to touch anyone. Photo charge is 60 yuan per chapel. No-one bothers.

Surprisingly, photos of the Dalai Lama as a child and young man abound. His private quarters are small and frugal. Descriptions of his rather sombre winter sojourns in this dark city on the rock appear in several accounts. Not a place for children, whereas most monasteries we saw are happy playgrounds for young monklets.

The vast open courtyard on the upper floor is cluttered with starlets in Tibetan costume Chinese-style, made of flowing silks. Cameramen circle and aim. The starlets pose with superior noses in the air. We find a toilet room and make for it. So do two starlets. All noses go up for air here, as we squat communally across slits in the floor, hoisting up flowing silks and trekkers' pants to prevent getting soiled. A 1992 guidebook mentions plans for modern toilets in the Potala. Meanwhile in the courtyard another propaganda piece takes shape before the cameras.

Back in the fresh air we lean over the parapet to see the sorriest sight in all Tibet. The streetworks we negotiated to drive to old Lhasa reveal themselves as a giant Tiananmen square in the making, a parade ground for the PLA to rival

Beijing. this is one of the sixty-two projects to be finished by September. No-one could miss the implications of this grotesque example of dictatorial architecture. To clear that space, a whole neighbourhood was razed to the ground. The little cobblestone street under the Potala walls has gone. Most of Shöl village has been pulled down and a high wall is being built to hide the last ruins from sight. Even the house of my dreamtime in Lhasa, from where I had a full view of the Potala, is no more. That entire area, to the left looking down, is taken up by tall Chinese buildings clad in nailpolish tiles. To the left of Chakpori hill stands the small empty townhouse of the Panchen Lama, waiting for the new incumbent.

To end the Potala tour we are shown the Chinese tearoom on the top floor. Tibetan couches line windowed walls. Chinese propaganda booklets litter low tables. We sit down for a rest. The mood is flat. This is a travesty. Any museum has more life than this 'Chinese national treasure', as it is known officially. The death of a civilisation hangs between these walls.

Walking down surprisingly few internal stairs, then the outer staircase down the front, I keep looking back at towering walls and turrets. To be walking here! The terrible sense of doom disappears outside. Architecturally the place is magic, one of the world's greatest wonders. I pray it will not revert to the dark intrigue of times gone, nor remain a lifeless dollar-extractor for long, but become the headquarters of the Zone of Peace the Dalai Lama proposed Tibet should be for the people of the world.

Below cluster small art galleries, Chinese, Tibetan. I don't intend to buy, but am struck on the inner button by a Green Tara cut in crystal. Green Tara rules my life. I have bought her before I can calculate money or baggage weight, then look no further. Some things are meant to be.

Joking we walk the gauntlet of a fresh posse of Derge women. What a way to make a living, with tourists dwindling. At the Banak Shöl, staff wait to cook our lunch. We are the only guests. Shall I shout: 'Brown rice and vegetables for me'. Hunger drives me to the board laden with *tsampa* cakes, chunky yoghurt, pickles. Afterwards in the street, two Sakya musicians offer to play for a fee. But only I am interested and as the others walk on I must follow. The musicians are also starved for tourists.

Time for another Barkhor round. I stock up on brocade remnants, but a stall selling old scraps is more interesting. Rummaging, I select three small pieces to work into hangings, one with woven dragons. All smell of lives lived as garments on big occasions. Who in days gone by would wear imperial yellow? Could I be holding a scrap of a ceremonial gown that belonged to a high official now out of favour?

I pull a face at the asking price and hastily throw the pieces down. This is no bartering game, I must stop spending. But the Tibetan merchant asks what I am prepared to pay. I offer. He ups. I frown. He moans holding his belly, then his face splits in laughter. He wraps the pieces in paper and puts them in my hand the same way the Dalai Lama shakes hands, putting his other hand over mine, pressing it. The Tibetan way. I pay with small notes of one, two, five and ten yuan, smelling of yak butter. He waves goodbye, gurgling suppressed laughter.

The Derge women wait at the bus, rushing us joyfully, desperately. There are too many of them in a small city. One woman says she has been in Lhasa two years now. There are few young women left in Derge. Entrepreneurs provide the jewellery they sell. In the exile community in Dharamsala stories are told that eastern Tibetans are being coerced to sell first their cattle, then their land, to Muslim Hui Chinese. With their livelihood gone they descend on Lhasa and other towns, resented by locals. Nightly street fights and prostitution are rumoured to be on the increase.

We drive to Sera monastery through streets where Chinese nightclubs and karaoke bars lean closed and sleepy against one another in the midday sun. A Chinese woman in long red velvet dress, split high on her thigh, steps out of a door, closing it behind her and languidly crosses the road to another. Some signboards are in English.

Sera is quieter than last time I was here during a people's holiday. We can walk anywhere. Two little imps, future monklets or workers' kids, tag our progress hoping for small gain. They have their photo taken seven times and never cease laughing at us.

The assembly hall of Je college houses beautiful statues of Maitreya, hope of the future. Strange and not strange how every monastery has an atmosphere all its own. Sera presents a spiritual orderliness in the arresting presentation of the temple's doorway, inner space and artifacts, everything painted, pleated, swept. It is in the stylised Kalachakra mandala on the wall. It is there most touchingly in rows of tins standing equidistant on a plank resting on bricks between pillars, filled alternately with red and pink geraniums. A white pleated pelmet curtain is whipped up by a playful breeze, like a ballerina's tutu in a perfectly timed high jump. Along a row of windows one curtain after another blows up and out, flouncing horizontally. They flutter down like so many stately birds — the second scene of *Swan Lake* in a Tibetan hillside monastery.

High against the ceiling of the assembly hall hang ancient armour, chain mail and many Mongolian hats. Booty from invasions or pledges of peaceful behaviour? The shrine monk bids us to bend down to view an important small statue of Hayagriva, the horse-headed protector. He graciously blesses a new *mala* presented to him by one traveller, touching them lightly on the shrine, mumbling a mantra.

As we walk cobbled streets, cross mossy forecourts, there comes a rush of rapping feet, voices playing ball with Tibetan sounds. We go towards the swelling rush, enter one by one a small gateway to emerge in a large courtyard bathing in dappled sunlight. Under canopies of gnarled knotty trees cluster monks in perpetual motion. We have happened on a debating session just begun. Leaning against old stone walls, we dig in for the duration.

Tibetan Buddhist debating is a superior learning aid. Standing monks launch questions at monks seated against tree trunks, dancing towards them, delivering resounding hand claps with a sliding motion on the last syllable, meaning 'Answer me!' If the seated monk does not know the answer he is rubbed on the head — normally an offence — and must try again. If the questioner swings his *mala* over the seated monk's head it means 'You are confused'. If the seated monk answers well, he may stretch his arms to launch his own opinions. These cannot be from set texts. The monks tax themselves to come up with new questions about texts that have been discussed in this manner for thirteen hundred years! Those who must reply often look genuinely stunned or puzzled. The questioner seems to launch an answer if none is forthcoming, but not always to the enlightenment of the defeated monk, judging from dismayed expressions.

The constant movement of monks questioning and answering begins to flow like a ballet, a choreography testing the litheness of the intellect. Standing on one foot in full flight of speech, the monks give evidence of inner calm by neatly balancing their bodies until they gracefully retract arms, waiting for replies. Wooden prayer beads slung around the left arm are pulled like a string on a bow when the question is fired, then fly upwards in predictable arches, backwards in skating motion. Questions and answers fly to and fro like short sharp arrows. The colours of this ballet of wits are stunning. On light grey gravel, between drystone and yellow ochre walls, maroon robes fly and twist, black heads twist and turn, mahogany faces turn and bow, and in between and over it all the soft bright green of summer leaves on ancient bark, and beams of sunshine.

A monk of great age, benign face, tufts of grey on balding head, has been watching from the other side of the courtyard. He begins circling slowly, watching each group. You see the monks mentally pull up their socks, striving to put even more punch into their performance. The old wise one observes, says nothing, winds his way around the courtyard, then gives a sign. All monks throw their upper wrap across their left shoulder and file out of the courtyard. In the fullness of the stillness they leave behind, we tiptoe to a *thangka* painted on the ochre wall of a raised platform.

Then their footsteps return. Silent, they re-enter wrapped in great pleated capes with red-and-yellow cockscomb hats worn for assemblies. There must be a hundred monks now, mostly young, a few old, and very young ones who did not debate. They sit in a half-circle on the gravel, facing the *thangka*. The old abbot presides. The chanting begins. I listen spellbound, moving in unison with young backs swaying to hold the rhythm of the text. A little boy keeps losing his lines. Distracted by our presence at his back, he continually peeks over his shoulder. But he picks up the text again, bellowing out his little knowledge until his attention is waylaid by something else. His fervour, when it operates, is touching.

Suddenly it is all over. I emerge from my concentration, back stiff, feet cold. The abbot leads the way out and the monks of Je college file through the stone doorway. When at last we follow they have disappeared into their quarters. Only two little monks pose gracefully in the portal to the temple courtyard. When they leave I peek inside. It is empty, but I can hear again the chanting of the *lung*, see the crowd of thousands sitting on the cobblestones in the hot midday sun, as it will be again.

The hermitages above Sera sit stonily between boulders, unused. Goodbye Sera. May better times come.

Changes at Ganden

During the night I wake up to the sound of fireworks. In the middle of the night? It must be gunfire. Restless now, I am awake to hear the muezzin call from the mosque.

Early, the phone rings. I had expressed the wish to return to Ganden and a car from our agency is going there today. The group will be sightseeing in Lhasa. I rush to the lobby to be introduced to an Australian couple. On their way south the woman had shown signs of altitude sickness on the Karo-La. They turned back to Lhasa but she is still feeling awful. Now they do day trips in a Landcruiser with a Tibetan driver and guide, a happy pair. I thank them for taking me on board. The guide speaks English and has information about everything we pass. On the road out of town we pass experimental sweet corn plots, rows of greenhouses with Chinese vegetables grown by prisoners, and a large rubbish tip.

It is exciting to travel a familiar road, recognising Takste Dzong ruin still sitting majestically atop its rock. The couple wants to see a village along the road. We wander off separately through muddy lanes connecting stone houses. A brown calf wearing a halter crosses my path, going home unaccompanied like a pet dog. An ochre door in a stone wall has a freshly painted white crescent moon and saffron sun. The mountains rise slate grey behind the village. On the other side green slopes abut the village wall.

Villagers gather in the gateway of the wall to look at us. A woman spins a fine thread of soft sheep wool on a hand-held spindle. With the guide's help I talk with her. The wool will be dyed and woven for clothing. A man is plying rough wool on a bigger spindle, for bedding or curtains. They spin during daylight because they have no electricity. Why does a village half an hour's drive from Lhasa have no electricity after forty-five years of Chinese modernisation, when military encampments in remote deserts have power?

I produce pictures of my workroom, spinning wheel and big loom. The villagers' watchfulness vanishes. They bend eagerly over the album, pointing, discussing the loom. They scrutinise pictures of me pushing a wheelbarrow, of vegetable beds, pumpkin and squash harvest, apple trees in fruit. The guide says the villagers are impressed that I do these things: spinning, weaving, growing fruit and vegetables. In the absence of a common language the pictures have spoken again, given meaning to a foreigner's life, shown similarities rather than differences.

We leave, waving. The couple is excited for having been invited into a woman's house and offered butter tea. We follow the river, laced with sandbanks compared with the strong flow two years ago. But water is gushing in from eastern rivulets, from the direction of Kham where due to logging water and soil erode away. This is the highway to Chengdu via Derge and Kham. There are no big fish in the river, which has been fished out in a few decades. Tibetans seldom ate fish, because it took too many little lives to equal the life of one yak, which can feed many people.

The first Buddhist precept 'to refrain from taking life' was always problematic in a country frozen half the year. Tibetans used to get around it by allowing a butchers' 'caste', by praying for butchered animals' improved reincarnation, by not feeding on multitudes of small animals. Tibet's birdlife, fishlife and wildlife were the most abundant anywhere this century. Nomads occasionally hunted big mammals. But in forty-five years of occupation the Chinese shot practically all birds out of the sky, fished almost all fish out of the rivers, hunted the wild yak to the point of extinction and decimated mammalian wildlife on the vast plateau. Driving through wilderness landscapes, the stillness of a birdless sky and empty slopes invades the subconscious, causing a sense of doom.

Beyond green fields enclosed by low stone walls, we see a long snake of people following flag bearers. They are singing and chanting. About sixty people circumambulate a barley field to invite the gods to bless the forthcoming harvest in a *bunkhur* ceremony. Five men carry religious banners, playing cymbals, drum and horn. Little sandy apso dogs run ahead, busily pretending to be in charge.

As the procession nears the roadside, the farmers smile and nod that we can take photos, never interrupting their chant. Between the musicians walks a man carrying a basket of the grain to be blessed. Women and men carry on their backs sacred prayer books from Ganden, wrapped in red striped cloths. Especially the women in their dark *chubas* and colourful headscarfs, carrying these striped bundles, form a festive column. The drought is a great worry. Farmers are trying to do something for their crops. If this fails they will probably blame themselves or the karma of their country.

Leaving the singing villagers behind, our vehicle noses up the steep track to the monastery. There is the thrill of returning, the familiar vistas as we negotiate bends on the switchback road. The big mountain in the background is free of snow.

We hear more singing coming from a depression behind a hillock and stop to look. About thirty men sit cross-legged in rows facing each other, beating wool fleece spread in a wide strip between them with only sticks and muscle power. At one end fleece is pulled from a big heap and at the other an old monk wearing hat and apron stuffs the carded wool into bags. Some wear dust masks, but they all sing a repetitive song, beating to the rhythm. Some lose their lines when they see us, folding up laughing. We must look like creatures from outer space looming on the hill above them in big boots, sunglasses and funny-coloured clothes. Although the beaters wear work clothes, they are monks and the wool is to be felted for Ganden's new *gompa's* rugs and curtains.

When Ganden monastery appears above us it takes my breath away as it did the first time. We drive the last hike up to find a new sawmill, operating under a corrugated-iron roof. Stacks of logged forest giants lie nearby.

There are big changes since 1993. Evidence of reconstruction abounds. We hear the government gave money in 1994 for the restoration of Ganden and the new *gompa* is being built. Four enormous wooden pillars support fantastic carvings above the entrance. Presumably the hall will rise to twice this height. Women carry building stones in baskets on their back, pick their way gingerly up steep, uneven steps cut in the rocks.

One debating courtyard has had its wall restored, one tree is growing tall and one seedling in a car tyre promises future shade. The podium is squared off neatly and the small *thangka* wall roofed. Heaps of rubble speak of demolition prior to rebuilding. New buildings are also rising in the central area and on the left shoulder of the mountain which catches the afternoon sun, an important consideration at this chill height.

Since the eighties, foreigners have brought home dramatic photographs of Ganden as ultimate proof of the devastation China has wreaked on Tibet. It seems the Chinese have decided to let the hated monastery be restored to stop adverse propaganda. Looking up at the amphitheatre of ruined walls rising from the mountain, I estimate it will take another fifteen years to erase the damning evidence. Then Ganden will again be fit for 3000 monks or so, but under present restrictions they cannot have more than 300. Is a restored Ganden to become another half-dead museum? It seems inconceivable, as the only reason Ganden was not abandoned forever after its total destruction, was that its monks kept creeping back to look for remnants of sacred treasures, to restore a stupa here, a little temple there, to meditate in the hermitage, to never give up their Ganden. Now their persistence is paying off.

In China, Buddhist and Daoist monasteries, temples and hermitages were also ruthlessly destroyed during the Cultural Revolution. Now the Beijing government doles out inadequate restoration money while monks and nuns who used to exist on family support, trade and donations from the faithful have to raise money from pilgrims and tourists. Tourism destroys the centred atmosphere needed for meditation and the search for truth. In the past, pilgrims would come on religious occasions. Now it is open season all year round. Is this Ganden's prospect?

We walk cobbled streets up the steep hillside, visit temples for Tsongkhapa and Maitreya, then find the library in a small building. Apart from the *Kanjur* in 108 volumes, all the original texts of Tsongkhapa's major work, the *Lam Rim* teachings, are here again, taking up an entire wall, watched over by a fifty-year-old monk. Looking about sixty, he entered the monastic life at ten. During the Cultural Revolution he spent eight years incarcerated, then lived in his village until it was possible to return as a monk and help rebuild Ganden.

You imagine the news travelling the countryside. 'Monks are returning to Ganden' — and dispersed monks getting out their robes, saying goodbye to their families and taking to the road, walking as many days as it took to get home. This monk's bony face is thin and peaceful, his smile shy. To be the keeper of the sacred texts in what in Tibet is old age, and after all that suffering, is a great blessing.

Four monks come carrying scriptures. Two in robes, two in civvies, still waiting to be admitted. Tibet is full of unofficial monks waiting to make the small quotas, or expelled for politically disagreeable behaviour.

We are allowed to see several inner chambers. The room where Tsongkhapa died survived the bombardment. There are rooms for the Dalai Lama and the Panchen Lama. These small dark rooms share the tiny inner courtyard of an old building. The dim interiors remain in a dilapidated condition, sad with unwanted absences. Down the steps to another level where two printers sit under an overhang. They work with minimum equipment — printing blocks, hand-made paper, ink and printing pad — they give a virtuoso performance of text printing with shooting arms and flying sheets. They stop to offer for sale small printing blocks of the wind horse.

At the chapel of Tsongkhapa's tooth the guide and I, being practising Buddhists, receive the blessing of the tooth on bowed heads. The tooth is less well-wrapped than I remember. In another room we purchase small red cloth bags tied with yellow cotton, containing prayers for good health. Small enterprises aimed at pilgrims bring a little cash. This time at Ganden I can breathe, although altitude once more stops my brain acting independently. It is great to be back here, but I would love to experience mountain-top life — to wake here dawn after dawn and see the sun sink behind the mountains would be better than travel itself.

Most big statues at Ganden are new, but the large Sakyamuni was hidden by villagers and later repaired. Perhaps by the villagers from the barley field, who are just driving up in a truck to return the sacred books they carried around the fields. The bond between village and monastery is the warp of Tibetan society. We wave to each other.

We run into another tourist, a rare species this summer in Tibet. An Australian on long service leave, he entered Tibet from the north by bus from Golmud. A truly terribly journey, he assures us. Carrying Chan's massive guidebook, he is determined to see all and on his own. Knowledgeable and well acclimatised, he keenly enjoys what must be a long-planned journey. Robust health, body height and male gender accommodate the spirit of adventure best. My flickering flame relies on willpower.

Wearily the three of us choose a grassy slope to eat lunch, shared with a pack of ravenous dogs, each guarding its own minute territory of the pilgrims' resting place. The canine in charge of us sits at our feet, snapping at every dog who tries a low-bellied advance for a possible scrap, or even so much as raises a nose for a whiff. The slope is littered with rubbish, tins and broken glass. Tibetan pilgrims sit unconcerned amongst the debris where their children play.

Rubbish has become a major problem in Tibet. Formerly it was largely organic and it is now hard to imagine what pre-1950 travellers meant by saying that the streets of Lhasa were full of rubbish. Today not only the towns but the countryside along main roads are littered with plastics and broken glass due to the importation of Chinese beer.

Driver and guide have brought sweet tea for the party and offer me a steaming cup also. When they realise I only have muesli bars, they give me an egg and cake from their lunchbox. I share the spare bars amongst patiently waiting children.

The tranquillity of Ganden is greater than its mechanical noises. Just below us the life of the monastery passes by. The sawmill whines, young monks fill steel cans at the only tap and carry them up the mountain. The small debating courtyard has filled with monks, relishing sunshine while they can. Ganden's unheated stone buildings can't be cosy when the sun sinks behind the range. Three young monks in maroon and one in grey robes bask on a knoll, talking, laughing. When time is up they swing their wraps across their left shoulders. As the maroon cloth flies up against a backdrop of green and slate mountains, they become freedom flags on the march.

As final scraps of food are pounced on by hungry dogs, a fight at last ensues. 'Our' dog chases off the poor bitch that has been salivating on the edge of enemy territory. She flees growling up the rocky slope, licking a nasty nip on the rump. Now as before, the condition of Ganden's dogs indicates the poverty of the people choosing to live here. Two monklets sit in the car. One is 'steering', the other studies the dashboard. A third one close to crying waits outside, too tiny to see, hot and bothered in a maroon plastic jacket. The driver allows him a look too, then we lucky beings climb in and drive off. Life is so unfair. I spin around, scanning mountains and the valley below through the viewfinder, recording last memories of a place that fills me with admiration.

A clutch of girls carrying baskets and boys carrying nothing give us chase. Lithe as mountain goats they skip down one bank after another as the car precariously zigzags on the hairpin track. Around every bend they jump onto the road ahead and reach their village on the plain at the same time as do we. Picnic tents now dot the blessed fields and this morning's singers and musicians are having a good time. We notice the effect of descending. Headaches fade. I did better today at Ganden, a good omen for the passes.

Back in Lhasa, several travellers are not feeling 100 per cent. My room-mate is ill in bed. Our tour leader fears mass food-poisoning. Those who want dinner troop to a small Tibetan restaurant in old Lhasa where a feast is laid out for departing groups. The small room is tightly furnished with couches to accommodate forty guests knee to low table, shoulder to shoulder. Tibetan ladies rush thirty lidded bowls from the kitchen, each a different delicacy. A television crew arrives to record the phenomenon, but we are incapable of doing justice to such largesse. I avoid all meat dishes.

Forty people, television lights and thirty steaming bowls raise the temperature to suffocation point. When a musician and singer cram into the room to perform, several of us rudely make for the door. We sit on the stoop gulping fresh air, observing Lhasa's nightlife with amazement. Beautiful women and young men parade past, only to disappear into a narrow alley. Too dark to see what hides in its recesses. Giggles and salvos of laughter are heard, but no-one returns.

It is nice to think to yourself: 'Here I sit on a stoop in old Lhasa. I dreamed a lifetime of doing this'. But it has been a long day and city life, even in Lhasa, is getting to me.

Lhasa to Gyantse via Khamba-La and Karo-La

A glorious Lhasa morning. Brilliant early sunshine lights up the mountains. Tonight they will be hued altogether differently but we won't be here to marvel. We are leaving Lhasa with two sick travellers on board, oxygen bags, lunch boxes and a case of mineral water. Tonight, Gyantse. I can scarcely contain my excitement, but am also apprehensive about crossing the high passes where previously I ran so dangerously out of air. Yet I can't wait to set eyes on the blue waters of Yamdrok Tso. And a visit to Samding monastery, seat of Lhasa-bound Dorje Phagmo, is on today's itinerary.

The first hitch comes at roadworks outside Lhasa. We just passed a belching factory chimney on the outskirts, wondering what on earth produces such vile black smoke, when there is a detour across a sandy plain. I suggest we get out and walk, but my voice is drowned by the revving of the engine and in seconds we are bogged. Then we get out. There are bogged trucks as far as the eye can see. Ten women travellers push the bus out of the bog as the driver steers it growling across bumps and puddles to where the road is navigable again.

In some places the new road runs barely half a metre from the river, where the water is visibly rising. A car, concrete mixer and bulldozer sit hopelessly stuck in a roadside puddle. Thousands of road workers, Tibetan and Chinese, men and women, are labouring to meet the September deadline. Red revolutionary slogans deface long walls. On opposite rocks, Tibetan mantras voice silent corrections.

The river is still shallow at the bridge to the Shigatse road. The slow climb to Khamba-La begins in clear weather. I feel excited, but look back at Lhasa valley once more. Unfortunate road workers are still camped in the same bend, only tins of geraniums mark a different season. Many reinforcing walls underpin the road to bear heavy traffic. The labourers' work will never be done. The massive pipeline of the Yamdrok Tso hydro-electric scheme snakes down the mountain.

Near a village a woman carrying a milk can rounds a bend. Time to deal out Dalai Lama pictures. They have burned in my pocket and no-one can see us here. When I offer the woman a picture she sucks in her breath and with a movement born from habit presses the image to her forehead, then places it on her head before folding it inside her *chuba*. Climbing back on the bus, I watch

267

her walk away. Joy and sadness. The photo comes from a world where the Dalai Lama is respected, a world that knows why his pictures are now banned in his homeland.

There is no sign of life at the last farm. The crumbling homestead looks deserted. The jumper I keep ready to give to the girl in the thin dress stays in my bag. Some lapses you can never make up for.

When we turn a bend and reach the top of the pass, I am amazed how colourful it looks without snow. The lake is a stunning blue mirror. Tumbling out, shouting 'Lha gyalo', we scatter paper wind horses at 4979 metres. Behind us the green-grey mountains of Lhasa valley capped with fat white clouds against a taut blue sky. Several Tibetan men drive up from the lake, stop to throw wind horses, muttering mantras. Their solemnity makes us careless children in comparison, using big words, not knowing what they mean. Prayer flags rap-rap-rap in the wind. Nursing a minor headache, I stand on Khamba-La, lungs pumping victoriously. Oh for a phone booth to ring home and shout: 'I'm breathing and talking simultaneously at almost 5000 metres!' Childish thought.

Whizzing down the switchback road to the lake, the driver puts his gears in neutral! Past the first village, Chinese settlement, dredging works, and a new mining site to take the lake's minerals. A white bird resembling a gull lands on the lake, fishes something up and flies off. In some places water is clearly receding from the former lake edge. Enclosed, without outlets, evaporation and rainfall kept water levels balanced. The hydro-electric scheme upsets this natural system. Without records, there's no saying until it is too late whether this drop in the water's level is seasonal through evaporation in the hottest month of the year, or due to man's interference.

Driving along the lakeside, another white bird fishing. An orange-breasted robin! Elderberry flowers, bushes hugging the ground. And there goes the boy we shared lunch with two years ago, half a head taller, herding sheep and yak, a timeless occupation. Does he dream of going places? Some men dig at the lakeside, fossicking for gold. May the naga get them. A sand-coloured bird flies by. So clear is the lake that the mountains' reflections mirror upside down images, joined to the real landscape by the perfectly straight line of the water's motionless surface. We could be upside down ourselves, the real world being in the lake where the naga are holding emergency meetings. I recall the concerned eyes of my lama when he spoke of creatures living in this lake, protecting not just their own domain but the weather and land itself. Disturb a closed circuit environment and the powers unleashed are capable of irreversible damage.

The road is as rough as ever and it is heaven to stretch out on a grassy slope at midday, peer through half-closed eyes at floating clouds and snow peaks and contemplate not boarding that bus again. Giant mosquitoes, daddy-long-leg size, attempt to change my mind.

We chew chicken legs and Chinese buns and ceaselessly drink water. Two Tibetans approach, herding four healthy yaklings and a big yak with a raw back, as if it carried packs without padding. One beautiful black yak with long white tail wears on its back a white cloth with three red strips. A deal is struck with the men to take and bury our rubbish in return for untouched food. But what about soft-drink bottles? How soon will the glass litter the valley?

Clouds gather and all the colours of the lake valley change to dramatically deep hues. A large brown bird flies high, etched against the peaks. A vulture? Any bird is a miracle here.

The village of Nangkartse with its imposing *dzong* lies a distance from the lake shore. Here a muddy track turns left for Samding, eight kilometres away. Our vehicle has hardly progressed fifty metres when it bogs. A boy comes running to tell the driver that the road to Samding is impassable due to ten days rain. The bus gets out of the bog with the help of a man walking past with his wife. Both wear traditional clothes and bits of old jewellery. They accept an unopened lunch box and our gratitude.

I am disappointed we can't reach Dorje Phagmo's Samding. But a fine view of Nangkartse is had from this track. Pretty yellow mustard fields skirt the old village, houses climbing up to the *dzong*. On the further side new buildings are going up. Why here? So high, so inhospitable most of the year? A checkpost between Lhasa and Shigatse? But Chinese traffic takes the easier low road. Only tourists and pilgrims cross this way. Are Chinese settlers so strapped for land that even a 14 000 foot elevation becomes attractive? The birthplace of the Fifth Dalai Lama's mother has become a Chinese settlement with flimsy new houses, a truck stop and agricultural expansion.

The weather begins to close in, obscuring the peaks. We stop at the impressive glacier. Its fingers are clearly visible, although the big hand of ice and snow recedes in the mist of low clouds. We drink from a stream so clear you can see every pebble and water plant under the surface. '*Lessay yapushu!*' I hear the driver shout: 'Okay, come in now'. He is impatient to cross Karo-La before the weather gets worse. As we jostle ever higher, a fierce short hailstorm rattles on the roof, but higher still the sky is clear. No headache. I pat Ganden's protective prayers in my pocket.

Just before two o'clock we shout '*Lha gyalo*' on Karo-La, clambering from the bus to inhale air of an unearthly freshness. Wildflowers grow even here. Again that powerful reluctance to leave this place assails me, even though I would not survive one winter's day on the pass.

West of Karo-La another huge glacier hangs like a leaking eiderdown between mountain ridges. At the bottom of the green valley running up to it sits a *drogpa* camp of three black tents. Four nomad women trail a bobbing stream of little children as they run towards us like beads rolling up the slope. They swing strings of yak curd in the air to sell. Peering into the bus they ask for plastic water bottles and get some empties, useful for storing snow and water. Smoked curds are bought.

Unopened lunch boxes also go to the nomads. But again the driver urges us to hurry. Seeing another woman running up, carrying twin children under her arms, he shouts to get going and closes the door on the women. They run to the other side of the bus, shouting through the open window: '*Dzik cho chik theta!*' or words to that effect. I loudly repeat them to Tibetan speakers at the front of the bus and get a burst of laughter from the *drogpa* women. But the message gets across. The sounds I so clumsily repeated mean, 'Plastic bag, give me!' As the bus takes off, plastic bags float from the windows like festive balloons. The women catch them all. I hope they won't let the kids play with them and resent the fact we aren't allowed time to give that warning.

On the descent, tiny terraces of barley and mustard flank the river. A girl washes her long black hair in the river. Her laundered clothes lie draped on the rocks. Sedges, mosses and lichen are still the main natural vegetation. Here and there crumbling mud brick telegraph pillars stand like sentinels not far from new tree trunk poles. A dam under construction. A new road above the dam will pass through a tunnel. Vast construction sites and tent camps near a Tibetan village are bound to become permanent Chinese settlements when dam and road are completed.

Two men labour up the steep road driving donkey carts top-heavy with terracotta pots. They are walking from Gyantse to as many villages as it takes to sell the products of their hands. The landscape is still harsh, but a few stone-walled trees cast shady patches. Below the road a man sows his field, broadcasting the seed from a flat basket with ancient movements.

Gradually the valley broadens, mountains recede and the ranges spread out. Trees line the road. The butte of Gyantse comes in sight and we take photos, walk around, inhale rural tranquillity, but the driver is impatient to reach Gyantse. I scarcely recognise the approach. Via building sites of possible department stores and hotels, we are suddenly on the old Hotel Gyantse's doorstep. The frantic monkey is gone, as is the black yak, a rare white yak has taken its place. The view is blotted by a new high-rise suburb. Gyantse, most Tibetan of towns in 1993, now shows all the signs of rapid sinofication.

We are given Tibetan rooms, two floors up. Pretty painted furniture, Tibetan rugs on the beds. From the corridor window I reclaim the *dzong*. It confirms the impression of ten minutes ago that the *dzong* has been rebuilt. Its contours stand sharp against the early evening sky. Another project to put Gyantse on the tourist map, to be renovated until it resembles every other fast-track Chinese town.

I go for a walk before the light fails. Building activity everywhere. The erstwhile sandy track between hotel and town has become a muddy throughfare lined with Chinese shops and stalls. Chinese settlers walk home with full shopping bags. There are few Tibetans to be seen. At the intersection with the old main street lies a concrete traffic roundabout. A new shopping street to the right, blaring electronic music and television cafes — all the comforts of home for the immigrants. But the main vehicle in Gyantse's streets is still the horse-drawn cart. It shocks to see the new age come so crassly to this most traditional of towns.

I walk halfway up the main street which is busy with traffic, looking for dilapidated houses, wondering how many will be here next year. One house has faded paper strips slapped diagonally across its doors — order for demolition or acquisition of a house belonging to a condemned family? Admirable woodwork under peeling paint, masonry skills evident in walls, but a caving roof. At the back, someone's family life continues in the ruins.

When I can see the monastery at the end of the street I turn back. Keep that for tomorrow. On the opposite side of the street late Chinese market stalls, one selling crude wooden spinning wheels — the first I have seen. A long store is stocked with foodstuffs from China, hardware from China, plastic household articles and shoes from China, clothes from China. Just like shops in Australia!

At the intersection I turn left to the *dzong*. A fascinating climb for future visitors to see how well this restoration compares with old accounts. Along the lane leading to the foot of the mountain is one of those Tibetan neighbourhoods that closes in on itself. I intrude. Thin echoes of hammers on stone puncture the air. When the *dzong* looms again, silhouettes of two men working late high up its ramparts stand out against the night sky. The place gives me goosebumps, I don't know why, yet I am fascinated. However, the light is fading so rapidly that little can be distinguished and I turn back to investigate the long Tibetan street stretching into the distance. It is lined with scungy-looking Tibetan eating houses. Women gesture that food is ready to be served, but nobody is friendly. History has put its stamp on this population. They have been invaded a few times too many and tourists are just another army to be fed. As I turn back, several fierce dogfights break out. I wait in the shadows until they have sorted out their territories. By now it is so dark that I stumble back through potholes and puddles.

Returning to Gyantse is a bit of a shock. The sleepy town, once glad to see a few stray travellers, has been shaken up. Gyantse was far from sleepy when

Tibet was free, but simply was bypassed when the faster road from Lhasa to Shigatse was built. Since tourists stubbornly insist on taking the high road to see the magic lake, Gyantse is back on the special projects list.

The hotel's service directory has been extended to cover more bad habits of the regular clientele, promising dire measures. The management sounds less obliging than in 1993. Only one night in Gyantse.

Gyantse to Shigatse

The great maroon hulk of Palkhor Chöde monastery, built between 1418 and 1425 by Rabtan Kunsang Phag, dominates the perspective of Gyantse's main street like an *arc de triomphe*. Through the imposing gateway we cross the now paved courtyard. No pictures may be taken inside the temple. The sharp scent of juniper incense. A monk points out three large monastic display banners, telling our guide that one such banner was taken by Captain Younghusband in 1904. Where did that banner end up? In the British Museum like so many stolen artefacts, or still in the family? And wouldn't it be nice if the banner was ceremonially restored to Palkhor Chöde, or must it wait until the invasion's centenary in 2004? Having kept the memory of the missing banner for ninety years, the monks will keep it until the banner returns home.

Individually we circumambulate the huge shrine guarded by an elderly monk. As I come upon him in the gloom at the rear of the shrine, he stretches out a parched hand and lisps: 'Dalai Lama photo'. Hairs rise on my neck. Stiffly I shake my head. I fear this monk may be tricking me. Last year it was done to tourists at Shalu. There is a ban now on Dalai Lama photos wherever Chinese control is strict. I have hardly finished shaking my head when two Chinese officers walk around the shrine in the wrong direction, accompanied by a beautifully groomed Chinese woman. High brass. And who would have been in big trouble had I just then pulled a Dalai Lama photo from my pocket? Not this monk, I suspect.

The Chinese party inspects the back of the shrine and finding it uninteresting they leave in the right direction. You wonder what a good communist cadre girl, dressed in synthetics, thinks of this smelly vault of antiquities. What you get used to as a tourist in Tibet is that the Chinese look right through you, as if you aren't there. They do it to most Tibetans. If you see otherwise, you suspect collaboration. That's Tibet's new culture. Sixty seconds to view one of the greatest temples in southern Tibet. They're worse than packaged tourists. You wonder why they came at all.

Monastery corridors hold a special fascination: a giant teapot, washing on a line. At the monks' quarters there are nasturtiums, marigolds, pretty white flowers and carmine geraniums in big clay pots. On a balcony a lovely stand of pink dahlias catches the light.

Our guide leads us to a musty room to see Indian clay statues of old masters, the chapel of a wrathful deity whose dance mask hangs on the wall waiting for a ceremony, and the imposing Maitreya temple. Upstairs, where in 1993 the master painter taught his apprentices, is now the fully painted mandala room. Beautiful but a bit empty, unused perhaps. The sense of sacredness was more palpably there when the painters were still at work.

Palkhor Chöde used to have sixteen colleges for 5000 monks. Now it has three, accommodating sixty-five. Yet its state of maintenance is remarkable. Maybe the people of Gyantse contribute to its upkeep, although no worshippers are to be seen, nor were there any last time. Maybe the tourism department is in charge.

The sun glares on courtyard cobbles when we emerge from cool caverns. I wouldn't mind seeing Gyantse under snow. We climb the Kumbum, released from scaffolding, glowing white and gold and strikingly beautiful. Landings allow surprise views of the monastery's imposing walls, deep maroon with sparkling white near the top under a broad black band. Against beige gravel paving and pale green rocks it makes a great film set.

Knowing I can climb higher than before, I have the camera ready. As far as the eye can see stretch green fields, golden mustard, buff mountains, vivid blue sky and white puff clouds in swan formation with the *dzong* gloriously silhouetted against them. Climbing, I see again the amazingly lively statues and murals in Kumbum's 108 chapels.

The statues, particularly green- and red-faced ones, seem to address whoever enters. Sitting in the semi-dark, century upon century, they receive countless visitors, pilgrims and their close friends the painters. All seem to have just been restored to look brand new. Victor Chan writes that all artwork in the Kumbum was executed by Tibetans, whereas the monastery employed Newari artisans. I do not share his opinion that damaged statues have less artistic merit after restoration. Restoration has always been a key element in keeping Tibet's religion alive. Having a religious artefact repainted is an act of worship. Restorers' talents may vary, but these artefacts have neither been ruined or grotesquely done up. Historians may long for the faded beauty of six centuries of neglect, but this art is for the pilgrims.

On the balconies, doors are flanked by wondrous mythological carvings of elephants, birds, winged horses and fearless riders in gorgeous antique blue and green, apricot and lemon. What stories they tell for those in the know! Another amazing carving is of three serpents embracing golden *Kalachakra* mantras. The fierce but not unattractive face of a feathered monster with bulging eyes and a fine set of sharp teeth sits on top, guarding the mantras. Elegant carved leaves curl down the sides and spotted fishes form the flanks.

On higher floors work still waits to be done. There is a wonderful mandala of simple design on a dark wall, obviously old, but every line visible for the painters to follow when they get this high with their brushes. I make it to the top and lean on the balustrade. The others are already in the courtyard, but I linger just a few moments alone on top of one of the wonders of this world. I wouldn't climb Mount Everest even if I could, but rather admire it from the valley. Standing here, however, where the human spirit has been expressed for centuries in art portraying the processes of the human mind, is exciting. Breathing the soft clear air, I gaze across the valley and the town with its new *dzong*, praying the spirit of those days when the Kumbum was built may return.

I had hoped to walk the main street at midday, but we are running late again and the driver waits with suppressed impatience to take us to the hotel and prepare for departure. At lunch no-one eats meat. We toy with rice, pickled cabbage and chilli noodles while talking about the food we cook at home. Some stomachs are craving for change. I'm lucky. Home fare is brown rice or noodles, vegetables and tofu. As waitresses return untouched dishes, a worried chef emerges from his kitchen. Are we letting down the glorious Chinese Revolution by not consuming pork bred especially for us? Hopefully the staff will write us off as just another bunch of incomprehensible Western vegetarians.

Bags are loaded. A long look at the *dzong*. My fascination with this fortress is not satisfied, but we are already back on the road. I stop thinking, because it is again at Gyantse that departure brings the prickling of tears.

Small farms dot the landscape. Shelter belts of dense green protect the fields. A woman stands in the sun by her gate, spinning grey wool on a spindle, waiting for the crops to ripen. The main crop seems to be mustard for cooking oil, not barley. Cooking oil is used by the Chinese. Tibetans eat barley, peas and lentils ground into *tsampa,* mixed with butter tea. This takeover of crops desired for the Chinese population is worrying. It led to a famine in the sixties.

Twenty minutes out of Gyantse, the ruins of Tsechen. Stone walls partition fields. Yards and houses look picturesque. In a small township some abandoned houses also have old paper strips still stuck diagonally on the door. Houses here are large, two storeys, like northern Italian farmhouses. Yak dung pats are drying on handsome mud-brick walls and there are shady trees.

We cross a bridge over a dry riverbed. After a further twenty-five minutes another ruined monastery, tower still intact. Nearby a new Chinese town. It begins to rain. A family of three Tibetans shelters in a rock cave, their pony and cart wait in the open. Suddenly the rain stops.

Fields endlessly yellow with mustard, the mountains beige, the landscape getting barren, the houses brown. At two points the road is washed out. A

275

woman sews on her doorstep, surrounded by five cows. If there is anything that unites the women of the world wherever they live their lives, it is that they pick up needles to sink their worries into colours and patterns of little stitches. An ancient global link.

On the mountain side a stupa is drawn in white with the mantra OM MANI PEMI HUNG. Our guide says stupa and mantra emerged spontaneously from the rocks. Together with another spontaneously arisen stupa invisible from here, they are known as the three treasures of Shalu. Won't the Chinese Department for Religion love that explanation? We turn off to Shalu monastery. The track is rocky but not flooded. The dry riverbed is a mosaic of red, green and grey pebbles.

Inside the gate the jade-coloured roof dominates the forecourt. Otherwise Shalu has the same gentile shabbiness I remember. Two young monks are putting wicks into 108 brass lamps filled with mustard oil, but are prepared to sell a few. A well-fed tawny dog in white shirtfront and socks lies handsomely curled against a rock wall, watching us through half-closed eyes. All around there are perspectives of elegant rooflines, patina of ancient doors with iron handles, natural rock formations, but only a single tree in light green leaf. The giant pole in the centre has a ceremonial umbrella at its top, tied down until needed.

We are admitted to the main temple full of ancient mandalas and statues. I drink in the colours. We won't be staying long. Shalu's artwork is said to be Newari with Yuan Mongol influence, just as the buildings combine Tibetan structure with Chinese roofs. Only twenty monks reside here.

Soon we must leave again. The bus is surrounded by ragged children from the village. They must have sprinted over the pebbles to offer for sale clay tablets carrying inscriptions, robbed from grave sites. The children look extremely poor, the rags they wear a washed-out grey. They are thin and sinewy and when a little girl grabs my hand, she clutches it like a vice. They fight aggressively over small food items. They even claw at an old greybeard leaning on a staff, when he is given some overripe bananas and a small bag of peanuts. In the midst of the fracas the face of a girl about ten years old stands out. She is so beautiful, in grey rags with hunger in her eyes, that it hurts, bringing home the plight of them all. The kids now attack the bus with their little fists, but fall away when an elderly monk approaches and enters the bus. He is the abbot of Shalu, hitching a ride to attend a meeting in Shigatse. In 1993 the abbot was also at a meeting in Shigatse. But he was the son of a previous abbot. Has there been a change at the top?

We are told Shalu has one hundred monks now, so eighty must live outside. Six are just returning, carrying drums and tall hats, after a ceremony in the village. Shalu village with its depressing poverty gathers up memories of countless

Tibetan children seen begging during this journey. In 1993 the few beggars encountered were professionals.

On the road to Shigatse we pass a large walled compound with an enormous Tibetan gateway. The red doors are closed. Not a monastery, it may be party country headquarters. Here the land is sandy and swampy. A large rubbish tip of tins and broken glass disfigures the landscape. We are nearing a metropolis.

The sight of Tashilhunpo's *thangka* wall towering in the distance is a thrill, but Shigatse is as dusty, dirty and chaotically ugly as before. Above the hotel's entrance a banner declares in faultless spelling: 'YEAR'S CHINA FOLK CUSTOM AMOROUS TOUR'. These Chinese are a proud people, who do not let foreign devils check their English grammar or their intentions, which remain deeply obscure. The abbot says he'll walk from here and struts off, in the direction of Tashilhunpo.

We lug bags up several stairs to the Tibetan wing. More pretty furniture, rugs and a huge shrine cabinet that dominates the room. You can hear tourist bosses telling decorators: 'Beijing directive states that tourists come to Tibet especially to see religious artefacts!' The hotel is being rebuilt, restored, extended. We enjoy views on a yard containing fifty white toilet bowls, forty handbasins, building rubble, rubbish dump, generator shed and a pack of roaming dogs. On the other side a view of the laundry yard where sheets are hung and rubbish is dumped.

At 5 pm a dust storm strikes, the electricity fails and the generator comes into its own. The storm, galloping across the valley like a giant *kyiang*, settles as quickly as it arose, so we ask the driver to drop us at the market. A most amazing new apartment block rises three storeys high between old Tibetan dwellings. Looking like a special-offer pack of film rolls, the facade has four rounded walls connected by three narrow straight ones with tall narrow windows. Whoever lives there has a fine opportunity to spy on what goes on in the marketplace.

The saleswomen are possibly even more aggressive in their approach to prospective buyers than remembered. Our tough travellers resist and few sales are made. I can't find woven *thangkas*, but locate some already made up, costing a heap. I salute the entrepreneurship of the Tibetan merchant. Finally I make a singular move towards a stall offering old textiles, but the asking price is so high that I flee, the merchant calling after me.

The pavements around the market are stacked with Chinese consumer goods. Tin trunks in all shapes and sizes, metal jugs, tubs, boxed electrical goods. Patched sheeting strung between houses and trees makes instant stalls. But under one tree in a side street a man on a chrome chair waits for buyers, staring forlornly at his one by three metre display of wool skeins in shocking pink, lollipop orange, poison green, canary yellow, flat turquoise and sultry purples. Beside the heap leans his bicycle. There seems no limit to what an entrepreneur will carry on two wheels. Try to imagine the hopes that brought him to Tibet with his soft cargo, under the new free-enterprise system.

Many towns women sport Chinese straw hats with coloured ribbons, but the peasant women wear brightly checked woollen headscarfs. *Chubas* are dark, but blouses pretty green or blue with pink cuffs. The colourful crowd is in holiday mood. Peasants have come to town for a three-day religious festival for World Purification Day on 12 July. Tomorrow, as it happens.

At the produce market an older peasant with beautiful chiselled face packs his few lovely clay pots into a nest of ropes, helped by his son. We can only admire, for to carry claypots the rest of our journey cannot be contemplated. But a lady stallkeeper hails the potter and buys his superb big pot for twenty yuan. He seems happy not to have to carry it further.

Five country women in red and green felt boots with lotus embroidery, clutching and carrying toddlers, are mesmerised by a display of vegetable seeds. Twenty-four clay bowls contain seeds with coloured pictures: root and green vegetables, marrows, carrots, tomatoes, capsicums, cauliflower, broccoli and three varieties of Chinese cabbage. Smoothing their boldly striped aprons, they eventually walk on without buying. It takes more than a few generations to change food habits. We walk back through dusty streets, stumbling on broken pavements.

The hotel dining room is run along military lines. We queue at the door for one soft drink per person, are told where to sit and constantly watched for I don't quite know what. But tomorrow the giant *thangka* will be lowered on the great wall and we are fortunate to be here for World Purification Day.

Martial Law on
World Purification Day

We're up and out early for the unrolling at about nine. Tibetans also call this the Incense Festival. Several late-model four-wheel-drive cars are parked at the hotel's entrance. Rumour has it that cadres from Lhasa have arrived for a meeting.

The approach of Tashilhunpo monastery is dominated by the great red Kudhung Lakhang rising above a tight clutch of sparkling white buildings. Thousands of people are about. Peasants show the hand-sewn soles of their felt boots as they prostrate on a low concrete platform facing Tashilhunpo. All along pavements and walls people sit in orderly groups with their baskets and bundles, waiting for the gates to open. A rosy-cheeked monk on the platform looks displeased when I photograph the crowd including himself. The *thangka* wall is still empty.

A young farmer has come to town with horse and cart. His girl wife and little son, decked out in best clothes, rest in the cart between bags of provisions. She examines her boots, her face is blistered. They must have come too long a way for the skinny horse to pull them all.

Our guide leads us to a side entrance to be admitted to the monastery forecourt. Once inside, I realise only our little group has been let in. Between monastic buildings in the distance stands a huddle of men near a blue truck. In the left corner four soldiers in outsized flat caps stand around, hands in pockets. A solitary monk slowly crosses the courtyard to the door through which we entered. There is a slow-motion atmosphere, like stillness before a storm.

From here we have an unimpeded picture view of the great wall. A colourful procession of people is walking up the hill towards the tower for the traditional circumambulation.

We have not been waiting more than seven minutes when an official motions us back towards the door. When we gather, a monk official in grey garb grabs an arm and begins to push people unceremoniously through the narrow door, where a high stone step has to be negotiated. Outside there is a press of people trying to gain admission and a rising murmur of voices. The monk official pushes people out into the seething crowd.

When it is my turn I pull my arm away, feeling threatened. The monk is quick to notice, drops his hand, produces a public relations smile and lets me make my own way across the step. Outside I fight for air and nearly lose my footing as the throng of Tibetans presses to get in, until I reach the open space of the road beyond which the rest of the population stands waiting expectantly, three Westerners amongst them.

We hear that the *thangka* was displayed yesterday, but there are rumours it won't appear today. Through the street leading to the monastery come three trucks carrying teenage soldiers. They stand up like salmon in a spawning wave, wearing riot gear, rifles piercing the air. After a hurried consultation between guides and driver we are ordered into the bus. We will visit the carpet factory and come back later to see if the *thangka* has been unrolled. Something is wrong and we are kept in the dark.

Down the street three fire trucks with big hoses stand ready to pull out of a Chinese yard. Suddenly there are uniforms everywhere. Now we are told a meeting is taking place inside Tashilhunpo, for which the abbot of Shalu was also summoned. The day is taking an ominous turn.

The carpet factory is closed. The workers have the day off for the festival. Those living in the compound stand by the gate in their good clothes, awaiting developments. They must know what is going on, but stand about so quietly that you could be fooled into thinking that armed soldiers in trucks pull up as a matter of course to mingle with festive crowds. On reconsidering, the probability seems all too feasible.

The assistant manager appears on edge, but opens some workrooms. Without chatting weavers and singing spinners there isn't much to see. But the store room is another matter. Several travellers want to buy rugs for their homes. A few hours can be spent here in safety. I content myself turning over piles, pulling out gorgeous patterns to entice prospective buyers. Forms are filled out, bills paid. The spree over, we bundle into the bus. The streets are quiet. In the distance military trucks line up ominously. We are rushed back to the hotel for the obligatory lunch.

Afterwards we go up the street in twos and threes, as our program has been cancelled by events. Closer to Tashilhunpo, streets are cordoned off and the military stand guard. We browse in stalls and little shops. A light-fingered boy zips open the back pockets of our day packs. I turn around before he can put his hand in and tell him off in global language, but he keeps hanging around with that glazed look of a kid programmed to do only one thing, forced by predilection or circumstance.

Then an older trio of young males walks behind and beside us with obvious intent, so we call it a day and hail a rickshaw. Rickshaws are socialist China's gift to the Tibetan battler. They turn tourists into capitalist exploiters and the Tibetan driver into a bargaining serf. Thus rickshaws prove the need for communism.

The young fellow asks ten yuan to cycle from one end of the main street to the other. A stiff fee. We agree on five yuan. Sitting behind his straining back, considering the potholes, dust and heat, considering our combined weight, we feel absolute heels. When he swings into the hotel parking lot he is stopped by an armed guard. He wants to argue his way in to deliver his charges at the door but we assure him we can walk it and hand him ten yuan, waiving the change. To see the look of disbelief on his strained face dripping with perspiration, then his smile breaking through, is enough to rub salt into our guilt.

Room doors are open in the Tibet wing, walkers have returned. The mood is strange. There is something amiss between tour leader, guide and driver. The Tibetans look broody. We have nothing to do and tomorrow is another day of cancellations due to circumstances not yet clear. Tashilhunpo is the seat of the new Panchen Lama, now not approved by the Chinese. I had wanted to see the Tenth Panchen's tomb again.

I lie on my Tibetan couch describing the details of the room in my diary. Room descriptions are rare in travel writing. People have more interesting things to do on tour. But not in Shigatse on World Purification Day under Chinese protection.

The carpets on the beds feel very good to sleep on. When I get home I will promote my Tibetan rugs from floor to bed. There are Chinese quilts and bolsters. The carpet is red, curtains white. The Tibetan furniture is roughly made, but brightly painted with flowers and borders. The shrine takes up most of one wall. The upper half is painted gold and contains eight *thangka*s. On the floor stands a wooden incense burner and a wooden basket containing rice and *tsampa* to make offerings.

There are dragons on the pelmets. The ceiling is stencilled with blue key border patterns, double *dorje* surround the central light and fit in corners. Pale pink wallpaper painted over at wainscot height with the blue, red and yellow bands seen in monasteries, set off with gold. Then sugar pink down to the floor. The upper part of the wallpaper has the eight sacred symbols stencilled all over.

The last solitary walker returns, quietly exhilarated with a tale. Having joined the crowds she completed the circumambulation. Others troop out to try it too. Energy spent, I stay in our colourful prison and turn on the television. My attention is galvanised by an English lesson on the subject 'How to Lodge a Complaint'. Who'd dare to act on this? I'm riveted, but my room-mate is not, so we chase news bulletins. All we get is world golf. Global TV is the pits.

The walkers return, sent back from the town centre without reaching the hill on which stands the *thangka* wall, overseeing the Tashilhunpo complex. Tibetans had to discontinue circumambulations. Streets are cordoned off. Uniforms are everywhere. A bad smell hangs over the town from thousands of people camping out without sanitary facilities. The solitary walker says the military ordered people back to the hotel 'for your own safety in case there is trouble'. I feel moved to write in Dutch in my diary.

Desultorily we descend to the dining room. The doors are still closed and we sit about in the courtyard on broken masonry. A suave young Tibetan in a suit joins us. A Khamba who grew up in Dharamsala, he speaks fluent English. I ask whether he knows Lobsang, the former resistance fighter who became leader of the carpet weavers in exile. In the seventies I imported their rugs. Pondering a little, he says Lobsang is trading between Assam and Dharamsala and is well. This may be another Lobsang, but I remain hopeful I will see him again.

We discuss whether to go for a little walk just down the street. There is a Tibetan village not five minutes away, but we need a permit to go there. Permits will not be extended right now, the guide tells us. A walk in the countryside then? Better not, the guide says firmly but nervously. If only we knew what is going on, but honourable guests must not be bothered with unpleasant news. An ominous atmosphere hangs over what is spoken. An early night, then.

I am just drifting off to sleep when there is a loud knocking on the door. Our leader's voice summons us for a meeting. This is Tibet, where one attends meetings at all hours. We huddle in night gear and listen.

Our tour leader has just returned from a long meeting with the guide and driver. They in turn have been to a meeting with the authorities and the military during the afternoon, where they received instructions handed down by another meeting that has been going on for several days between monks and military, over the choice of the new Panchen Lama. The authorities do not agree with the Dalai Lama's choice, but the monks do. They want the infant to live at Tashilhunpo for his religious education. The military say the Dalai Lama did not ask permission to announce the new reincarnation, who nevertheless was chosen by a Tashilhunpo committee set up by Chinese authorities. The religious festival has been called off and tomorrow all travellers must leave Shigatse for their own safety. Shigatse will be under martial law from midnight.

So the monks of the reddest monastery in Tibet are opposing the Chinese military! But why martial law? Are the Chinese afraid the town will stage an uprising? Is it possible? For ourselves there is a sense of relief. Leaving is better than this enforced inactivity in a city under a cloud. There is nothing we can do in our ignorance to make things better. We return to our rooms to pack, then try to sleep.

Expelled: Shigatse to Tinggri

Just after eight in the morning we leave Shigatse, turning our backs on ominous mysteries. Turning sharp left, the bus leaves the forbidden town in a southerly direction past the 'Welcome to Shigatse' sign. Within minutes we drive through the Tibetan village, streets dug up, houses ringed by rubble. Massive hillside ruins mark another destroyed monastery. Men in green uniforms cycle to work. We catch a last distant view of Tashilhunpo, as seen by travellers coming from India. Then a large Chinese cemetery.

The morning sun just begins lighting up the landscape. And what a landscape! Young, folded mountains reflect all colours seen so far, from fawn and mocca brown to bluish green and greenish grey. Burnt orange and mauve accompany light shifts and changes.

Speaking reverently, our guide begins to relate the life of the Tenth Panchen Lama, whom he once met. Imprisoned in 1964 for having thrown away the speech written for him and shouting in the Jokhang, 'Long Live the Dalai Lama', the Panchen disappeared, spending fourteen years in prisons and labour camps, reputedly being tortured. He surfaced as a 'reformed' man in 1979, was ordered to marry and made Vice-Chairman of the Religious Bureau in Beijing. No prizes for guessing the chairman's nationality. He made his first visit to Lhasa and Tibet in 1982 and began a string of good works. He wanted to restore Tashilhunpo and Ganden and have Tibetan language taught in schools and university. Most Tibetans think he was murdered by the Chinese in 1989.

The guide's voice becomes emotional when he relates what people are speculating about the whereabouts of the child named as the Panchen's eleventh reincarnation. He has either been whisked away to Beijing, put in a Lhasa prison, or escaped to India. The people are upset and rumours abound.

Today's martial law is a first for Shigatse, says our guide. Yesterday, hundreds of monks emerged from Tashilhunpo to demonstrate for the new Panchen Lama, but were pushed back inside. At yesterday's meeting were three Tibetan cadres from Lhasa, whose four-wheel drives stood in front of the hotel. Chadrel Rimpoche, abbot of Tashilhunpo, was removed to Beijing after the Dalai Lama announced the new Panchen Lama on 14 May, because he had passed on the official committee's choice to the exiled leader. That the monks of Tashilhunpo want their abbot returned and the new Panchen Lama to live at Tashilhunpo is, our guide says, a great change of heart amongst Tashilhunpo monks, who have always left opposition to Chinese interference to the monks of Lhasa. So much so, that the Shigatse monks were regarded as uniformly red. Now they have declared themselves loyal to Tibetan religious custom. At what price, no-one knows as yet.

A Westerner on the roadside hails our driver. He stops. The guide speaks Tibetan with the man, an individual traveller needing a lift out of closed Shigatse. The guide explains it is company policy not to take hitchhikers and the traveller stays behind on the dusty road. One of the privileges of package tourism is that you have your privileges all to yourself, even during martial law. A green car lies overturned along the road. A recent accident.

Our guide resumes telling stories from the life of the Panchen Lama from the oral newsbeat. Tibetans never needed newspapers, radio or television to spread news. When in 1989 the Panchen prepared to fly from Beijing to Lhasa to conduct ceremonies at Tashilhunpo for restored tombs of previous Panchen Lamas, his wife and daughter came to the airport. It was goodbye forever. At Shigatse the Panchen had to participate for six days in gruelling meetings on communist policy for monasteries. A communist tactic is to wear out opponents until they agree from fatigue. But on the last day the Panchen Lama spoke out strongly against the Chinese occupation, saying it had wrought more harm than benefit when all was considered. Next morning he was dead. The monks who saw his body said it had turned black.

I keep noting in Dutch. We must travel two days to reach the Nepali border. As if prompted by my anticipations, a red flag pops up near a tiny hamlet. A military man emerges from a hut. The guide collects our passports for inspection. A soldier enters the bus to count our heads while the driver presents his papers at a military tent.

An old man and several children with very black hands look on, hanging around the bus door. We give them sweets and the soldier strokes the old man's hair. It is only the second time I have seen a Chinese touch a Tibetan affectionately. This is a lonely place. The guide returns our passports and we depart.

The landscape becomes increasingly rough. Even a yak might have trouble. Near a large village a bridge is under construction across a river meandering across the wide valley floor. Tibetan work gang members wave. Near the village the ruins of a destroyed *dzong*. A large detour to avoid excavations, then crossing the boulderous gravelbed of what must be a mighty river when there is no drought. I can't keep my eyes off the mountains, wondrously folded and striated.

When we reach paved road again, the going is balm smooth after the bone shaking. Books call this sort of landscape barren. No trees, shrubs, nor even sedges to be seen. Yet the brown hills are covered with a green haze after recent rain. Blue mountains ahead. Colours take on new meaning in this landscape, as if one sees them truly for the first time. We spot a man throwing big stones down a slope, perhaps to build. But there is no sign of houses. I muse about hermits, but empty as it may look, this land is under constant surveillance. Hermits must go high to obtain peace. For hours we drive through the beauties of stone.

At last a river-valley village. Beyond is a valley floor, red streamlets feeding in. Iron-ore country. The hills purple, green, red, ochre. One thin tree with two trunks! I get so excited I take its photo. Then, distantly, a whole grove of dark trees beside a stone building on a low escarpment. More gravel plains follow.

In the middle of more vacant landscape a few huts huddle under the red flag. Three green uniforms rush out. An officer wearing an outsize cap and big sunglasses waves us down and hops on the bus, followed demurely by the others. Pointing at the few empty seats, he tells his men where to sit. They are to be non-paying passengers. We have already paid for this bus but company policy does not apply to the PLA, who are above the law.

One of the officers — young as they appear, they wear stripes — sits down next to me. The seats are narrow. We sit thigh to thigh and I am thrown back to childhood where on occasions I found myself in close proximity to a Nazi soldier and nearly died of fright and revulsion. Something similar assails me now, although I am old enough to be wise, and his grandmother.

After two journeys through Tibet, my original resolve to be open-minded concerning Chinese ambitions here lies in shreds. I no longer believe the Chinese government had any other purpose than to aggrandise its status as leaders of a China vaster than the traditional one of classical culture, to acquire land with untapped resources and farmland for its landless peasants.

This soldier smells like a baby — reeks of diarrhoea and wet clothes dried up. This is an opportunity to come to grips with his reality. He can't be more than twenty-two, if that. He has a mother, somewhere. Maybe a wife and baby. He was born after the Cultural Revolution. What would he know of Tibetan and Chinese history? Having placed him, I think of being neighbourly, a conversation. But I remember his grim boss. The boy may feel compromised. Better to just sit together nurturing neutral feelings. Quite an accomplishment. And then I become aware of his unease. That makes two of us.

We cross four more riverbeds before climbing Tso-La, at 4500 metres. *Lha gyalo!* Two buses are here already, but ours has a slashed tyre. The soldiers rush up the far slope of the pass, which affords splendid views of the next mountain range. They are very fit. The travellers follow more sedately. Thick tresses of prayer flags hang across stacked rocks. I add one for safe passage. Breathing easily enough, I am content to stand and simply take the air.

When the others come down, the soldiers help change the tyre. One traveller manages a brief exchange with one. Ours is the last bus to descend into a seemingly deserted landscape. But in high fields women are harvesting by hand. Stone corrals hold their cattle. Although the road is good for a while, soon it changes to mud, more riverbeds veined with streams, gravel beds and plains covered with huge boulders. A few times we get stuck. Habitation remains sporadic. A tiny monastery tucked in a mountain fold, a huddle of houses near a few acres of crops, solitary people performing mysterious tasks in this wilderness. The air becomes more acrid as vegetation is left behind. Still climbing. The next pass is 5220 metres high.

Sweeping around a mountain, we climb it from the back, away from the road. Halfway along there is a Chinese army camp on a windswept plateau. Between flapping tents and spidery communication towers, soldiers build equipment in the cold wind. At a second strategic post the soldiers leave the bus and the driver manoeuvres back to a main track.

A few villages with a stupa or two and brass prayer drums. Two red thermoses stand side by side near a rock in a long valley. Two men sit at the end of the valley with one bicycle and one pickaxe. Two tourists on bicycles travel towards Shigatse, unaware of the ban. Will they be kept at the three huts? Many outcrops topped by ruins. A lonely horseman trots by. Another Chinese camp with padlocked petrol depot. Purple rocks, mustard fields. Peasants along the road duck our dust. Villages appear and disappear. Houses here have the orange and bluish-white stripes of Sakya. How hard life must be on these vast gravel plains.

We turn off to a distant village for petrol. It has rained heavily and the road is awash. We reach the village mud-bespattered, to gape at a collection of buildings testifying to an imagined civilisation. An incongruous white-tiled Chinese building dominates the unpaved main street, also faced with the Simple Pub, the Star and Moon restaurant, and the inevitable Friendship restaurant. This is Lhatse, home to the biggest prison for dissidents in southern Tibet. The petrol station is out of petrol.

In the muddy street, two boy musicians play to us. One made his instrument from an enamel bowl, a long stick, wooden keys and string. It sounds plaintive, but right. They sing a lovely old Tibetan song I have heard before.

Turning around, the bus meets a four-wheel drive stuck in our path. It's the two American girls from Gyantse, collecting material for a guidebook. One girl seems quite ill. The no-petrol message is the last straw for her. She leans against a wall, while our guys help their car out of the mire. The local kids are banging on the bus windows for pens. We have none left.

Away again. Lhatse's fields are surrounded by white stones the size of men's fists on top of mud walls. Narrow irrigation canals thus formed need frequent repair. But many prisoners make light work.

Hours of bouncing delivers another control post. Begging children surround the bus. An old woman lifts a grimy hand to the windows, saying: 'Kuchi. Kuchi'. The driver gives her fourteen yuan. We pass after brief formalities. The air, crisp this morning, is dust-laden.

Any sense of time has evaporated, but we stop in a beautiful mountain meadow, seemingly deserted, at 2 pm and hot. Stripping off layers, we stretch ourselves on the grass. Instantly ten running children appear on the horizon. Behind them four young women, carrying empty baskets on their backs. The children wear a mix of Chinese, Tibetan and Western clothes, all ragged. They are very hungry, staring the food out of our hands, not content to wait. But a deal is struck. They will have their share if they sit and wait. Mentally I sit with them, not hungry at all. We leave a good supply of food in the boxes. When they receive these, arguing and clawing is quickly followed by frantic eating. The women look on. When we leave, there is just flattened cardboard lying on the grass. Fuel for a village stove.

We now travel through a rocky gorge of vertical strata. It begins to rain as we rise to the last big pass. A single farm with two small corrals. Where do they graze their animals? It is midsummer, and hardly any feed to be seen.

Climbing out on the Gyatso-La we are hit by the coldest wind yet. A solitary boy stands buffeted by the gale. What in heaven's name is the child doing on top of the world without shelter as far as the eye can see, when the eye can see as far as Chomolongma in the clouds? Although this is the main track to Nepal, he regards us as if we just blew down from the moon. The distance is punctured by black nomad tents. Yaks grazing. Then a man with a donkey cart appears from behind a rock. Suddenly the place is densely populated!

The pass is vast and flat. Dust flies. The view is stupendous. From here the Himalayan range kisses the skies of a far horizon, light blue, white, icy. At this distance we appear as high up as Everest. Closer, the starched white aprons of spectacular glaciers hang in a row from slate grey mountains. Could there be grander views? Arms wrapped around myself, mouth shut against the wind, my slit eyes drink in the sights. How glorious it would be to stand here free, without martial law, prisons and military camps at your back. Are the poverty-stricken Tibetans of this region able to ignore these threats and live as they always have? The man with the donkey cart and the little boy begin their descent after paying respects to the mountain gods. If freedom was theirs, it certainly would be the greatest of their meagre possessions.

We stay a little, because our night stop is not far away. It is a long drop to a giant gibber plain. The day's events repeatedly throw me back to the past and my childhood resolve to visit the Dalai Lama child in Lhasa. Tibet was free, my country of birth was not. In central and south-east Asia only Tibet and Japan were free then. Japan was busily annexing neighbouring countries, including China. But Tibet minded its own business, as it had done for a very long time. Traditional traders and artisans came and went. Only diplomats and delegates entered officially via British India or China. But the Chinese already occupied Amdo and parts of Kham.

With the world aflame on two large fronts between 1939 and 1946, Tibet was still partially free and independent, while south and central Asia was colonised by various powers: the British, French, Dutch, Russians, Portuguese, Japanese and Chinese, although they were themselves fighting for survival as a nation.

Tibet, straddling the world's highest mountains, was not dragged into the war, although its airspace was used by American planes flying across 'the hump' from Burma to Kunming to support the Chinese National Army against the Japanese. Tibet preserved independence and neutrality. But only five years after World War II ended, immediately after the conclusion of the civil war in China, Tibet fell prey to full-blown colonialism, aided by the biggest new war machine in Asia, while to its south countries were 'granted' independence by war-damaged Western powers. A war-weary world allowed it to happen. The United Nations put Tibet into the too-hard basket. Hadn't Britain recognised suzerainty of China over Tibet in the 1904 'intervention'?

Today, governments which still recognise China's claims over Tibet do so out of self-interest, be that trade, fear, or both. Much trade is with labour-reform camps and prisons disguised as state-owned enterprises. In 1991 Harry Wu was told by a fellow ex-prisoner in Qinghai — the province that absorbed so much of Tibet — that one-third of its population were so-called resettlement prisoners and their families, engaged in forced labour where the state decreed. They construct roads, build dams, set up mining operations and reclaim wasteland.

The cheapest way to keep on the sweet side of one of the world's biggest military powers is to condone its professed self-image. It costs nothing and returns monetary gain. Tibet has been sacrificed to this policy of complicity by most nations trading in China today. For some, like Australia and the United States, a policy of complicity is doubly desirable because they are nations established in lands illegitimately acquired in recent times. It is fine if countries face up to their past, make reparations and start reconciliation. But it is equally necessary to condemn the past and say:

'No more of these conquests! We want a world where countries develop independently, forging relationships of equality with each other. We want unity in our diversity. We condemn all military invasions of territories and the United Nations must and shall deal with all cases where there is doubt about the legality of the arguments on either side. We shall not condone colonialism out of fear of being blamed for a past in which people now alive had no hand. But we acknowledge being responsible heirs of that past and wish to repair the damage that was done to peoples and countries.'

China's grip on Tibet has already spawned a generation of Tibet-born Chinese who may need to speak words like these one day.

Late afternoon, Tinggri is sighted. The driver steps on it, worried that not all expelled tourists will find a bed tonight. We overtake other buses and are the first of the exodus to reach the Qomolangma truck stop. My room-mate is ill from coughing all day. I have a migraine and crash for two hours sleep. Later, food and acupressure give relief. Another band of tourists carry their own paper plates and preserved food, picking disgustingly through the hotel's offerings, muttering complaints. The food is plain and tasty. Yet some travellers are down with stomach troubles.

It has been a gruelling day, getting shaken like dice for nine hours. These are army transport stages. Fine for teenage soldiers, but they take the glitter off for most tourists. A small truck stop near the green meadow where we lunched would give tourists a chance to enjoy the unique beauty of southern Tibet and the starving people there could earn tourist dollars.

There is no water in our room due to a leak. We make frequent trips up and down the stairs for thermoses and carry buckets for the toilet. After all the chores are done we phase out promptly at 4300 metres.

Tinggri to Zhangmo via Milarepa's Cave

The village of Shelkar, 'sugar crystal', lies a short distance from the truck stop. After breakfasting on porridge and steamed buns, we stop there to photograph 'Crystal Monastery' halfway up the crag, and the ruined *dzong* atop a high peak, walls still striding halfway up the rocky slope.

Main street is Chinatown: ugly official buildings and loudspeakers. The children are just walking to school and the Tibetan speakers amongst us ask to see their schoolbooks. 'Good work!' they praise. The village houses, with Sakya stripes, stand either side of a stone-lined riverbed, two metres deep, a bridge connecting the banks, but no more than a puddle of water. A woman in a pink blouse and brown *chuba* tries to scoop the last bit of water into a bucket. We leave soon, as there is little to see and all adults look the other way. Shelkar looks pretty only from a distance. In the fields high-school students walk spread out at distances of ten metres, books in hand, lips moving, memorising lessons.

Our last day in Tibet. I'd even stay in 'Chinese' Shelkar if I could. But with a blue sky dotted with white clouds and the sun rising over a moon landscape, changing colours in split seconds, there is much else to enjoy. The mountains' shapes and colours remain endlessly fascinating. We meet up with more bulldozers and bridgeworks and more and more Chinese settlements. At the Kosi river checkpost we show our passports.

We see the pass that leads to Everest base camp on the Tibetan side. We must be descending, because crops appear around little Sakya villages in pleasant valleys between impressive rock formations. There are no schools in evidence and what a place to play all summer's day! Many small monasteries in ruins, one of which stands behind a Chinese settlement half in ruins itself. Here and there women walk, back baskets piled high with small shrubberies. Fodder, fuel, medicine or incense. The clouds cast surrealistic shadows dancing on buff-coloured mountains. Walls of granite in ridge formation, like ossified dinosaurs. Rings of blackened stones in this vastness signal that people rested to boil a kettle of tea.

Ahead lies Mount Choyu, pristine snow and 7000 metres high. To the west Mount Everest/Chomolongma is shrouded in clouds. Against the blinding blue-white backdrop, black yaks graze. Herders come running. One grinning youngster holds up his necklace, showing the Dalai Lama's photo under plastic. We repeat after him: 'Dalai Lama! Dala Lama!' That's all he wants to tell us. We wave goodbye and drive to the town where he lives. The usual ruined monastery, some houses and many army barracks. A dismal place in a superb landscape. Tibetan villages merge with the landscape. Chinese settlements despoil it.

Since Shelkar we have seen only ruined monasteries. None has been rebuilt. More villages, people and herds in relatively populated valleys. At yet another Everest lookout we see nothing but clouds. It's nice to know the famous mountain to be there, but I am more thrilled by the ones showing themselves in all their untouched glory.

Suddenly, near a village, there is an enormous square stone tower in the distance to the right. As the road bends it appears to be a half-ruined castle, although the walls stand several storeys high. Our guide says that once, long ago, it was the house of a rich family. Many such medieval-looking towers date from the Nepalese wars in the seventeenth century. Gurkhas repeatedly invaded and the Tibetan government requested the Manchu emperor — then an ally — to send troops to help push them out. Later, Ranjit Singh, maharajah of Kashmir, went conquering east and west. By 1840 he ruled not only Baltistan, but western Tibet as far as Kailash. Further on, a Sakya village appears with a ruined castle atop a giant flat rock, its fields at the rock's foot, a hundred metres below. Although there is life, the overall impression remains that southern Tibet is a land of ruins. Not all can be blamed on the Cultural Revolution.

Again we are ascending. The last pass, Nyelam Tong-La, is 5000 metres high. Here we find brilliant blue-green sedges and clumps of purple flowers that look like lavender but smell nothing like it. The wind is fiercely cold, the views fabulous. You begin to understand why mountain climbers are peakoholics. Here too a man with a loaded cart, a horse and two little boys. They continue north and we, alas, go south. My reluctance to leave this country turns into a pain.

Ten minutes down the pass, agriculture begins again. At a roadside well, guarded by prayer flags, men fill vessels with sacred water. Green shrubs grow around the hole. The first village after the pass is of pebble houses built with river stones, set in green and yellow mustard fields. The houses are low and long, huddling close to the ground. There is no mud here to build high towers. Walls and dykes are also of pebbles, as in the pixie villages I built in the heather fields of childhood. These fields, stone free, are full of barley, potatoes and mustard. Groves of trees grow inside the walls.

It is above just such a village that Tibet's most famous yogi mystic, Milarepa (1052–1135) had his cave. Its houses no higher than an adult, topped with brush and protected by tufts of sacred twigs, the village lies protected between bare hills forming a narrow valley for mustard and barley fields. A small forest shields the village of Nyelam from northern gales.

Small children come running when we stop. A six-year-old boy has severe burn scars about the face and neck. He is unable to blink, the eyelids are gone, and his eyes sit in bare sockets which are infected. His head pulls to one shoulder because of extensive scarring. He is nimble on his feet and runs with the mob carrying our last buns and muesli bars to the village. My thoughts turn to plastic surgery in Australia. The kids wear warm, colourless jackets, but are otherwise poorly clad. Nowhere are signs of modern tools or conveniences. Nyelam sits on the valley bottom as in Milarepa's time.

The travellers walk up to the cave along a narrow winding path between trees and houses, to see if the monk is there to open up. I'm one of two who stay behind. I expect the monk won't be there and feel too tired to climb. It turns out he isn't. The little temple by the cave has the auspicious name, Place of Increase and Expansion, and the view on the Himalayan range at the end of the valley complements the intention. It was rebuilt in the 1980s because even a memorial to a naked recluse was not safe from the Red Guards and their helpers.

In his small cave Milarepa meditated in the nude, scandalising his sister, eating nettles, keeping warm through breathing exercises and meditating on his wicked past and the good teachings given him by Marpa the translator and his equally learned wife. Milarepa's humour made his fame as much as it did his wisdom, and even today his laughter produces a full-throttle echo. Coming to a village where women were celebrating the birth of a son to a rich woman, they challenged his nakedness with typical Tibetan bawdiness. The yogi sang them one of his instantaneous and explicit songs, suggesting their uncontrolled bodies and minds were stirred up by seeing a handsome man.

Like the Buddha, Milarepa gave sound advice shortly before his death. Warning against doing good works unless all self-interest is absent, he said there would be sentient beings needing help as long as there was a sky above, so there were always opportunities to give it. But the main aim should be to achieve enlightenment because that benefited all beings. Milarepa advised his followers to be unpretentious, dress in rags, renounce fame, live alone and give up the idea of the self versus the world in order to become a fit benefactor.

Leaving the quiet valley we travel through the gorge of the Nyelamo river far beneath us. Another checkpoint. Then potato land, all the way down from high up near the pass. Pre-1950 literature never mentions the prolific spud. But we are close to Nepal, where they are grown. We pass three girl hikers. They have chosen the best way to see Tibet. Villages are still built of pebbles in this land of mist-shrouded gorges, waterfalls and summer greenery. A cluster of tents sits on a river flat.

Descending quite rapidly, the vegetation is becoming so green that it hurts unaccustomed eyes. Humidity suffocates dry skin and the nose is assailed by gases of decaying verdure. We enter landslide territory. Last week a car with

Chinese officials was hit by a landslide on this road and three women passengers were killed. A few days ago a truck went over with its driver. We face our first landslide.

Over a bridge spanning a waterfall, the mountainside has fallen on the road. We walk across to wait while many men dig and smooth a path, free a stuck truck and get traffic going. It is hot and steamy. We peel off, slap on hats. There is time to identify plants. I find dock, blackberry, wild carrot, balsam, strawberry, purple stocks, thistle, bamboo, salmon astilbe, dark pink spiraea, and a variety of ferns dripping from the rocks. Just as I start photographing I run out of film. A replacement is in the luggage on the bus across the landslide.

In half an hour our bus comes across to shouts of hoorah. Waterfalls pour down rocks on both sides of the ravines through which we now drive. We stop under one waterfall, windows closed, for a carwash, and arrive clean in the zig zag bordertown of Zhangmo, also known as Dram. At the bottom end of town, we find our hotel built in tiers down a steep mountain slope. All rooms are on downstairs levels, facing a green mountain shrouded in low clouds and a river rushing far beneath our windows. On descending narrow terraces stand iron sheds and hothouse tunnels amidst vegetable gardens on hanging terraces. The views are spectacular wherever you look.

We walk up one zig and one zag, but the town is a bit of a tip, a pit and a bog rolled into one. Shades of Tsetang. The buildings are new Chinese or older Nepalese style. One is entirely built of wood, arching in a quarter circle around a bend in the road, but looking a designer slum already. Although technically we are still in Tibet, we have arrived somewhere else.

Two days of rough riding have left me with an on-off migraine. I apply the traveller's first-aid, acupressure, then bind my neck with a foam-rubber collar and scarf to take off the strain. By evening the pain subsides.

Dinner is vegetarian and delicious. One busload of expelled tourists continued to Kathmandu today. Others roll up and the hotel fills rapidly. Lodgings are sought up and down the street before darkness falls. The Europeans spread plastic plates, serviettes and preserved food, taking only cooked rice from the buffet. They wear clean silk shirts and pressed pants, a new high in tour travel. Our guide talks with their guide. He says his English has deteriorated being with them, they complained continually, did not understand Tibet's situation inside China, and had no feelings whatsoever for the local people. He never wanted such groups again. Our guide sang our praises as being easy people, absolutely obedient! I suppose he thought it was not prudent to disclose our understanding of Tibet's situation.

Our scruffy band eats its last meal on Tibetan soil with gusto. We descended 3000 metres today, from 5000 to 2000. Tomorrow we cross the border.

Zhangmo to Kathmandu

Customs, just down the street, opens at 9.30 am, Beijing time. The Shigatse exodus gathers at the gates. There are several European groups, a scattering of Americans, Germans and Scandinavians. There is talk of gunfire when they left Shigatse. Three times we show passports before being let into no-man's-land, a stretch of seven kilometres as the crow flies, or ten as the road zigzags to the Friendship Bridge.

A Chinese woman boards our bus 'to see the bridge', but is hauled off by customs officers. Then another Chinese woman climbs aboard and takes the guide's front seat. No-one removes her, so she must have connections. She rides away with us, beyond the grasp of Chinese bureaucrats for an hour or so. Maybe her job is to prevent driver or guide deserting their bus and hopping the border.

The landscape continues to be damply spectacular. High mountains blanketed with trees, shrubs, lianas, herbs and ferns, the sound of waterfalls, a heavy fragrance of flowers but very few birds. It rained heavily during the night and I worry about the road ahead. Presently it narrows to a muddy track lined with mugwort, astilbe and buddleia among hundreds of familiar flowering plants. On the edge of a ridge half a kilometre above the Friendship Bridge hangs a village called Khasa, where the road has fallen down into the river, almost onto the bridge. From here on we walk.

Khasa is a row of low sapling and matting huts that look as if they will slip next. Nepalese mountain people inhabit them. These small, hardy ridge-dwellers regard us with eyes of permanent estrangement as we lug past their doorways more belongings per person than they have in their entire settlement. They silently watch from verandahs, dripping rain dividing us like a bead curtain.

So this is goodbye. Our tour leader arranges a deal with a group of local boys to carry the luggage. Standing in the mud on the narrow ridge we say farewell to guide and driver with *kata* and gifts and a wrench of the heart for a cheerful guide who shared our life for a month. He knows the history of his country, the official as well as the prohibited versions. We watch the bus reverse, muddy edges just holding for the wheels to pass before collapsing. Then we wave goodbye. The Chinese woman rides with them, having observed the bridge of friendship.

Taking a pack each we begin a descent down slippery boulders. The luggage boys are already out of sight. Soon I am last. Several boys have offered to take me by the hand and guide me down. I feel safer having two hands grabbing branches and rocks to ease my way, but at a gushing stream I accept help to negotiate wet boulders. A quarter of a century earlier I skipped boulders barefoot across a waterfall river in Papua New Guinea's highlands. Now I clasp young hands.

Trousers dripping I cross the Friendship Bridge, trying to feel historic significance. After all, the bridge is a statement, hasn't been here very long, and may not survive much longer either due to landslides of an environmental or political nature. I look over my shoulder at Tibet, but it doesn't look like Tibet anymore. This is in-between country.

In the middle of the bridge stands a passport control officer. Next to the bridge is a prison for Tibetan escapees. As free people we once more ford the same stream gushing from other rocks, hop boulders, and on arrival at the other bank are handed forms to fill out to enter Nepal. 'Do Not Fold', it warns. This may be a novel border crossing, but procedures must be followed.

Our tour guide gives a cry of joy as a Nepalese friend in flash sportswear walks up. They embrace. He has come from Kathmandu to look for us and brings bad news. There are more landslides to negotiate before we can board a waiting bus.

Three landslides and one mudslide further on, we rest on the stoop of a little cafe in a Nepalese village. I discuss with another traveller, also a writer, whether to file a press report about the situation in Shigatse. She won't be able to for reasons of her own, so I say that in that case I will do it. Someone produces a Kathmandu newspaper and the great news is the release of Aung San Suu Kyi of Burma, after six years of house arrest. No-one believes this came about through a new streak of benevolence in a murderous regime. It happened because people inside Burma and in a freer world did not give up on human rights, no matter how forbidding the odds. Sentences start to form in my head to describe the situation in Shigatse. I repeat, rework, learn by rote, edit, all in my head. It must be concise and no more than what I witnessed and heard.

Four hours later we ride through the wet streets of Kathmandu to a Tibetan hotel in Thamel. On this side of the Himalayas the rains are truly disastrous. As soon as I have a room, I first scribble in the back of my diary the story that has been shaping in my head:

Kathmandu — 15 July 1995, 4 pm.
Martial law was declared in the city of Shigatse in Central Tibet on 13 July during an annual religious festival. Chinese authorities stopped all ceremonies on 12 July and troops with riot gear patrolled around Tashilhunpo monastery. All tourists, mainly Europeans and Australians, were ordered to leave town

for their own safety. Those late to leave heard machine-gunfire. At the heart of the disturbance are several hundreds of monks from Tashilhunpo monastery, the traditional seat of the Panchen Lama, second ranking in the Tibetan religious hierarchy. The Chinese government strongly objected to the exiled Dalai Lama announcing on May 14th the new incarnation of the Tenth Panchen Lama, who died in 1989, as a young boy from a town north of the Tibetan capital Lhasa. The monks of Tashilhunpo, rising for the first time during the forty-five years Chinese occupation of Tibet, want the boy to come to the monastery to begin religious training for his high office. The abbot of Tashilhunpo who advised the Dalai Lama on the choice of the new incarnation has been removed by Chinese authorities. The whereabouts of the child incarnation are unknown.

Good, just under 200 words. After several international calls I dictate the report at 5.30 pm, Kathmandu time. It goes around the globe in hours and just when I'm falling asleep after the longest day of the journey, the phone rings. I'm glad I am only a casual foreign correspondent.

It is the Tibet Information Network in London. Robbie Barnett, TIN's astute director, questions me on every aspect of my report, probes further, makes me repeat facts stated, asks me what I saw and what I heard and from whom, then goes over it all again. He susses out my credentials, assesses motivations. I feel I'm in the witness stand, but realise how important it is that my credibility be tested to make sure I do not blow things out of proportion, do not surmise, assume or take for granted that certain things happened somewhere though I did not witness them.

When the grilling comes to an end, I am told TIN is already aware of what is brewing in Shigatse and Lhasa. My report fits previous knowledge. The new intelligence about the declaration of martial law is just another piece in the puzzling saga of Chinese behaviour in the so-called autonomous region of Tibet. Barnett says he must wait for confirmation from another independent source before he can publish the news. He asks permission to release my name if he does. 'It's really important', he says, 'that news does not always come from anonymous people'. Many carriers of news have good reasons to maintain anonymity. I have not and give permission.

I sleep the sleep of exhaustion until the next phone call. Through the following twenty-four hours I give interviews to the BBC in London and the ABC in Melbourne and talk with representatives of the Tibetan community in exile. Correspondents from the Voice of America arrive and I call in two travellers who witnessed authorities forcibly ending a circumambulation on the hill behind Tashilhunpo. Several times we are asked to say what we think *might* have happened or *will* happen now, or whether there were casualties, but we answer 'I do not know' to all such questions.

Robbie Barnett's grilling has been excellent preparation to meeting the press and its desire for more news than one honestly has to give. Finally he rings again from London. A Japanese report about Shigatse closing down has come through. It confirms my story and it goes on the Internet. The BBC has reported that China denies having arrested the new Panchen Lama. Local Tibetans have unconfirmed news that 200 monks have risen in Tashilhunpo, that twenty were arrested and charged. Now that report is waiting for confirmation.

There has not been a moment to realise that I have lost Tibet. Crossing the border and landslides was hardly a time to reflect. I shall never return to the land that has occupied my thoughts and dreams since childhood. Although Tibet the land has surpassed anything I might have expected, the old dreams of Tibetan life have been replaced by a grim reality that has politicised me far beyond my own wishes.

Although at first I felt relieved getting out of occupied Tibet, I now become aware that Nepal is a communist kingdom, recipient of China's largesse, and hardly charitable to the Tibetan refugee community which has contributed so greatly to the country's most important foreign exchange earners: carpet weaving and tourism. New Tibetan refugees are turned back at the border and often badly treated by Nepalese police. They face imprisonment and torture on the Tibetan side.

Lying on the bed, listening to the rain and the street noises of Thamel, I review the last few days, seeing the mountains of southern Tibet sharper than when I actually travelled between them. The giant shifting shadows travelling faster than a bus as morning light progresses, being drawn away like black velvet curtains from a stage. Dawn painting dark saddles with gold and orange flames before exposing the naked beauty of fawn slopes in daylight. The comfort of them, the strength emanating from their very size. These are mountains a person may walk amongst in solitude, feeling content and protected. If but the land and people had been left in peace.

Later, in the intertwining streets of Thamel, I meet up with two travellers from Lhasa. They flew out, but overheard personnel at the China International Tourist Service in Lhasa advise travellers they could not go to Gyantse or Shigatse because the road was closed. Not letting on there are two roads.

To extend our understanding of the Tibetan exile we visit a Tibetan coeducational boarding school near Kathmandu. We are deeply impressed by the charismatic way it is run, the enthusiasm of the principal and the students' maturity. Nepal has 20 000 Tibetan refugees and about twenty Tibetan schools, mostly tiny and in the mountains. India has sixty-eight Tibetan refugee schools. Whereas in earlier years Tibetan children in Nepal had to move to India for secondary education or forego it, the Dalai Lama financed a land purchase and with donations from an Austrian, benefactor the hillside school we visit started teaching in 1988. It has 500 pupils aged between twelve and twenty. They do the full high-school curriculum with Tibetan language and culture and sit for Nepalese exams. Some parents can pay fees, others rely entirely on overseas donations and student sponsorships. Although education is not compulsory in Nepal, 98 per cent of Tibetan children attend school. Of the teachers one is Nepali, three Indian, the rest Tibetan. There are four female teachers. Two are monks with a BA and MA in Tibetan and Sanskrit studies.

'The teachers have to work very hard', says the principal. 'The pay is more than in some Nepalese schools but less than in private schools.' He clearly works as hard as or harder than his staff, keeping his finger on everything. But the teacher/student ratio is 1:18, very good for any school.

The school day starts at 6.30 am with pre-breakfast prayer and is fully programmed — 'to keep them out of town!' — until bedtime at 9.30 pm. School operates six days per week. The students study geography, history, science and commerce, and the teaching media are English, Nepali and Tibetan. At morning assembly three students speak on current affairs in three languages! They also have games, sports, martial arts and Tibetan music. Sixty per cent of pupils speak English. As soon as one class excels, the students are mixed to even out results. There is no special tuition for very bright kids, but those capable of university studies are diverted to India where scholarships are more readily available. An astounding 60 percent of all Tibetan students in India, Nepal and Bhutan go to universities in India, the United States and other countries.

There are more girls than boys at this school and because they have to stay in the compound they tend to read books and get better results. The boys go hiking and play football in their spare time. We may mumble under our breath about sexist discrimination, but in the light of achievements virtually from scratch and not knowing the circumstances, who can criticise?

The principal, himself a product of Tibetan schooling in India on a sponsorship from an overseas benefactor, worked for thirteen years in Tibetan schools in India before coming to Nepal to set this school on a sound footing, financially and otherwise. There are no profits. A European charity pays for development work but tuition has to come from sponsorships. 'In India I could make five-year plans, but not here', says the principal. 'We have little security here. Long term planning means investments, but the government may say, for instance, that the nearby village must benefit from our beautiful school. If they tell us to give 20 per cent of places to local students, what can we say?'

What indeed? Overseas sponsorships are all directed at Tibetans, to make up for the loss of a homeland and home, often for the loss of parents and family. Some children of ethnic Tibetan groups of Buddhist faith, whose ancestors came to northern Nepal from Tibet generations ago, are accepted. Kids with parents in Kathmandu valley return home once a month, while others go on organised picnics and outings. Mountain children only return home for the six-weeks winter holiday, travelling a whole day by bus, then trekking four or five days to reach their villages.

We are given a tour of the school. Although spartan, it is a cheerful space. To the students it must seem a good life. They keep dormitories and trunk room tidy, do latrine duty, take turns cleaning utensils. Bunk beds stand post to post and all of a student's possessions must fit into a regulation size tin trunk. The kitchen smells good, serving rice, dahl, vegetables and meat, with a separate pot for vegetarians. On Sundays they eat *momos*, beloved Tibetan dumplings.

The buildings were designed by a Tibetan architect who studied in the United States, and comprise a concrete octagonal space surrounded by classrooms, dorms and utility rooms on two levels. Looking rather space-age on the outside, inside the school feels as coherent as a *gompa*. On the ball-court wall a slogan reads: 'Education is Discipline: Do or Die'. This is the refugee's stark reality. It would be an ideal school for Australian high-school groups to visit and undertake a sponsorship.

Colourful drawings and bunting still hang in the staffroom from yesterday's 'Happy Teachers Day', when students did everything the teachers wished. This is complemented at another time with 'Happy Students Day' when teachers do everything the students hope for. Both days include the preparation and serving of food, a major Tibetan tradition.

The music room has wonderful instruments and yak masks, mostly made in the school for traditional dances. But the orderly library is pitifully understocked. Old books and magazines sag on near-empty shelves while twenty students are reading. Two travellers who have access to good books immediately promise to organise a shipment to stock the shelves.

A small dispensary with a Tibetan nurse has recently opened. Proudly she shows her simple equipment. It must be a major benefit to have this caring young woman see to the health of 500 youngsters.

The latest project is the building of a big water tank behind the school to ensure a clean supply of drinking water and so cut down on diseases. It will cost 200 000 rupees. More donations and scholarships are needed. But the principal is gravely aware how desperately poor the villagers in the school's vicinity are and how desirable the school is beginning to look. Yet, he wants to equip his charges to make new lives in as yet unknown circumstances.

Could someone tell these villagers that Nepal is less likely to receive overseas aid if they go the communist road and that they could end up as part of China with all the 'benefits' Beijing bestows on the Tibetans? I myself grew up uneducated, but at age fourteen rejected the beautiful ideologies of European communism because of its repression of religion. Yet here a newly educated class touts communism as the saving grace of a country like Nepal, where refugees have been streaming over the Tibetan border for forty-five years. I suppose the answer, stupid as it is, may be that many Nepalese do not like Tibetans. Some Tibetans did too well in business. A not-so-simple case of neighbourly aversion, added to overt pressure from Beijing, made even the hereditary king of Nepal speak supportive words to Chinese communists and publicly denounce the Dalai Lama.

This is truly sad. Most Nepalese are farmers and it was farmers who starved when Beijing reorganised agriculture, in Tibet as well as in China. Nepali farmers can hardly afford feeding a 'protective' PLA and paying a percentage of their harvest in tax to ever-hungry China. China plies Nepal with massive foreign aid for its own purposes. The Friendship Bridge and Friendship Road are but the beginning of permanent access.

We wave goodbye to the Tibetan students in their good school, enjoying perhaps the only good years of their lives. It starts raining again. Weather reports say it is pouring in Dharamsala, but the road is still passable. In Australia, rain has also come down by cloudloads and the home dam is overflowing.

The next afternoon the group flies to Delhi over green wet lands bathed in sunlight, crisscrossed by silver rivers. By nightfall we are on the train to Pathankot, from where a three-hour drive will bring us to MacLeod Ganj above Dharamsala, on the spurs of the Dhaula Dhar ranges, above the Kangra Valley, elevation 1768 metres.

Dharamsala — Abode of Exiles

Dharamsala sits wrapped on its ridge in perpetually precipitating clouds. The area has the second highest rainfall in India during the monsoon. Slopping through mud and rivulets in the three parallel streets that make up the hub of MacLeod Gunj, I find the carpet weavers' workshop looking slightly more worn than eighteen years ago. I climb the stairs and, a little shy, apologise for my intrusion to one of the Tibetan women in the office.

'I was here eighteen years ago', I say, amazed at the pleasure of returning. But eighteen more years in exile for these women! 'I am Lolo from Australia. I would like to know if Lobsang is still here?'

One of the women turns and looks at me with interest. 'You are Lolo from Australia?' she asks.

I feel fairly stupid. I was a small businesswoman once, importing Tibetan carpets, but now have nothing to offer. Then something in the voice catches my attention.

'Are you … ?' I waver.

'Then you know me?' the woman asks, looking straight into my eyes.

'Kelsang!' I exclaim.

We stand in embrace, hugging each other. She was a slender young thing minding the cooperative shop in 1977. Now she is a beautiful, rounded middle-aged lady. She holds me at arm's length, inspecting my face.

'You look younger!' she shouts gleefully. 'How is it possible? You look younger!'

'I was sick when I was here last', I protest. Perhaps drinking three litres of water a day has a rejuvenating effect. The gods know I do not *feel* any younger!

'I am retired', Kelsang announces happily. 'Last May. Now I have my own shop. And I *never* come here in the office. Only today, just to tell her something …' She points at the other woman who looks on incredulously. 'Just now I think I must go into the office for five minutes and here you walk in. It's a miracle!' And she gives me another hug. It *is* miraculous. Dharamsala is an ant heap of comings and goings and I don't even know Kelsang's second name.

'And Lobsang?' I ask.

'Lobsang is here', says Kelsang, pointing out the door and up. 'He has a room here. But he is not well. Let's visit him.'

In a daze I follow her up elbow-shaped concrete stairs to a balcony with the finest view in Dharamsala, a deep green valley, a rising emerald mountain with tiny houses peeking through layers of mist, clinging to upper ridges.

Bending down we enter, Kelsang announcing our arrival. How lovely to hear Tibetan so soon again. The language pleases my ears. In one of two tiny rooms — the same, I think, as he occupied in the seventies — we find Lobsang seated on cushions and turned grey. There is disbelief when I enter, then a flicker of recognition. My heart sinks. The old fire in his eyes is extinguished. Bitterness is etched in his features. But when Kelsang talks rapid Tibetan I hear his familiar grunts, a sign that he follows every word. Now and then he looks up at me, but there is no smile. I feel I should perhaps not have come. My longing to meet this strong leader of refugees again has led me here. Now I face the fact that time can wreak terrible havoc with exiled people.

Perhaps the last favour he asked me years ago — to chase up a defaulting importer of carpets in Australia — did not turn out positively. I remember explaining to him in a letter the enormous distances in Australia. But one day I was in that city, visited the carpet shop and put considerable pressure on them to pay the Tibetan account. Theirs was a culture-clash story. Instead of buying Tibetan carpets, they provided detailed instructions of patterns and colours that would suit their customers. The result was not harmonious and they had trouble selling the hybrids. However, they did get what they ordered and should have paid up. Maybe they never did. The word 'Australia' may taste bitter to Lobsang.

Lobsang is seventy-four now and retired from running the weavers' workshop. Some years ago, while circumambulating the temple, he fell and broke both legs. Now he walks painfully with a stick. He is being looked after by his son-in-law. The son-in-law's wife, Lobsang's daughter, who miraculously emerged from Tibet in the early eighties when he thought her dead, lives in America. She gained a green card in the yearly lottery, left child, husband and father to spearhead a possible future for the family in the United States, and is now working too hard and having difficulties learning English. Her sad-eyed husband brings tea and biscuits. We sip. Kelsang talks, translates. Lobsang grunts. I ask a few questions, but feel he is not in a talking mood. I tell a little of our travels in Tibet, but that is painful also.

I take photos with his permission, promise to send them, promise to say goodbye before we leave. But it is Kelsang who is most pleased with my reappearance. As we talk, walking the street, I ask Kelsang the name of her village in Tibet.

'Tinggri', she says.

'I was there last week', I reply. It hurts both of us. 'I will send you photos of Tinggri.'

Years ago she told me her family had owned many sheep. Her eyes dim and she nods listlessly. The pain of exile is in all of them. A photo will only rub salt in the wound. Still, I will send it because on other occasions it may revive hope. We get spattered with mud by a passing vehicle.

'Dharamsala is not like it used to be', Kelsang says. Dharamsala is becoming like anywhere else, except on Tibetan festive days. More people, traffic, horrid new buildings. And pressures from new exiles: Indian beggars from the plains, monkeys who have lost habitat lower down, and Kashmiri traders escaping the Kashmir war, diluting tourist income for the Tibetans. There is no escape from suffering in this world.

At the hotel the group meets three Tibetan press people who interview us about the Shigatse situation. They are deeply concerned about the whereabouts of the child Panchen Lama and the fate of Tashilhunpo's abbot. The bad news depresses me.

By the next morning we are gaining impressions of how a refugee town operates. I have long looked forward to visiting the Tibetan Children's Village, having been a sponsor for years. We are led around by Tashi Dolma, who herself grew up here. The children are orphans or have parents working as itinerant labourers and traders. Because it is a school day, we spend time with a happy bunch of babies and toddlers snacking on popcorn. Then we view the inside of a family home where twenty-five children live with a Tibetan foster parent couple. All are out. The house is no bigger than an average Australian suburban house, but scrupulously tidy. The kitchen is small. Bunks fill the bedrooms like so many stacks of drawers. But the sitting room is an oasis of peace with a carpet, low seats around the walls and a small shrine. By the front door grow pretty flowers and there are playing courts and fields nearby and a colourful temple. It's a real home. We visit one classroom where an English lesson is in progress and are impressed with the children's proficiency. It is here that many refugee children find their first home in freedom and begin a new life.

Geden Choeling nunnery is conducting a special *puja* when we arrive. We sit down against a wall of the *gompa* to watch the chanting with drums. When the blessed bread comes around we too receive a piece, with a blessed lolly. No money for a donation. The State Bank of India only opens one hour occasionally and we missed that hour. Only some of these nuns are refugees, most are Indian-born Tibetans.

The heavens pour down immense volumes of water when we emerge, but after a group lunch of chunky Tibetan bread and coffee in our rooms, I run for the bank and gain entrance. I obtain money after an hour's wait, because Indian bank staff successfully obstruct modernisation, preferring yellowing ledgers to computers to preserve jobs.

Passing the Tibet Information Centre window I see a booklet on the Tenth Panchen Lama and enter. Two young women at the counter are busy with correspondence. I wait seven minutes while people come and go and finally reach for the book in the window. Unfortunately there is a glass partition I did not see, so my furtive gesture to help myself sounds like a violent break-in. This finally arouses the women and in a hostile and impolite manner one retrieves the book and takes the money. Born in exile, these two seem different from Tibetan-born young people. There is a steely hardness about them that I subconsciously registered in Kathmandu and some institutions in Dharamsala that reminds me of Chinese staff in Tibet. There is a suggestion that tourists can go to hell — it must be a bore to be a tourist attraction. Yet our Dharamsala Tibetan guide is a friendly, shy young man with an easy smile. Maybe it has nothing to do with being in exile. It could be the freedom to choose with whom one associates.

Reporters from the Tibetan Youth Congress are waiting in the hotel to ask more questions. They too are hard-nosed, pressing for news of casualties and other details I cannot vouch for. I refuse to have my photograph taken. Being spotlighted like this is beginning to sit heavily on me also.

When the rain eases I take a walk to the church of St John in the Wilderness, wandering through the cemetery under the deodars, reading headstones. Apart from early English graves there are recent ones of Indian Christians, tourists, and a South Indian baby who died here not long ago. A solitary white horse grazes near the iron-roofed church. A brook plays forest music nearby. Ferns and mosses dim all sounds from the road. The soughing of wind through fragrant trees sweeps my brain clean of the day's struggles.

After a refreshing hike back, I take to my room with a pot of tea to dry off and read Christine Noble's *Over the High Passes,* found second-hand in the next street. The story of her year trekking on foot through nearby mountains with the Gaddis carries its own sadness. These shepherd people originally lived here seasonally but are being pushed further into the mountains by urbanisation and the growing refugee community.

I listen with one ear to the ceaseless rain and monkeys scavenging across tin roofs. The skies have quite some weeping to do.

✦   ✦   ✦

Sunday, and we sightsee on regardless, despite relentless rain. Down a steep jeep track to Tse Dip Chok Ling monastery to see a new Yamanthaka sand mandala. Tse Dip Chok Ling's monastery's home monastery is in Lhasa and was used as a shooting base by the Chinese. I contributed to the floor of this new monastery's Tara Hall and the abbot kindly wrote some years ago that I was welcome to visit. This is the day, though I do so anonymously. We troop in dripping, wetting the new wooden floor, sitting against one wall while a voluminous and richly decorative ceremony is in progress.

The monks wear yellow brocade gowns in the 'big lotus' pattern and tall black wig-like hats of yak hair, tied at intervals with golden ties to resemble an onion dome grown into a spire. An aura of ancient magic and sacredness surrounds them. They chant sonorously, gracefully hand each other sacred vessels and play drums. I remember the specific earnings I donated to this floor I sit on. May tens of thousands of bums enjoy this floor and gain enlightenment! The abbot waves 'enough, enough' and the public leaves while the ceremony continues. Interest awakened, understanding comes later.

The nearby Dip Tsok temple has superb new murals. A young Buddha Gautama, an unfinished mature Buddha, and a large mandala surrounded by lamas seated on floating clouds are being explained by a knowledgeable tourist we've met somewhere before. The buildings are whitewashed with maroon friezes, yellow or maroon windows set in black frames. Drum-like temple banners stand on the corners of roofs. The only modern details are metalwork grilles on the balconies. The monastery is surpassingly lovely. Later I look down on it, draped in swirling mists, nestled in a hugging cleft of green vegetation. A wonderful place to be, outside the tourist season. I begin to sympathise with the Dharamsala Tibetans.

I share *chai*, Indian spicy tea, with Kelsang in her little shop full of nice clothes and Tibetan rugs. Later the group goes up the hill to visit Namgyal monastery and the temple opposite the Dalai Lama's bungalow. The bungalow gates are guarded by Indian soldiers.

In the Jokhang temple of Dharamsala the guide monk says laughingly: 'Please take many pictures, because you Australians put them in books'. This temple is a treasure cave of stunning murals where Tibetan Buddhism revived itself. Indian visitors ask whether they can meet His Holiness the Dalai Lama. He explains it takes a month after application in writing. 'These Australians here don't expect to just arrive today and see His Holiness tomorrow', he chides them, laughing continuously. We feel reasonable and virtuous as the Indians keep pushing their luck before switching to the topic of the disappeared Panchen Lama. We wouldn't dream of asking to meet the Dalai Lama.

Behind his bungalow, below the hill guarded by armed soldiers on all sides, lies the old people's home. Our tour leader has brought a batch of reading glasses and happy faces discover new sights. We talk with two women from Kham. One is eighty-five, doing her first weaving on a back-strap loom. A gift from a friend, she says. A friend who died, most likely. Sitting on the floor of her tiny room she continues the pattern set up by her friend. The other is a 65-five-year-old nun who lost her entire family. Father killed, mother died, brother committed suicide. She fled Tibet in 1994 to see the Dalai Lama before she dies herself. Now she is happy. A man of seventy-one tells how some years ago he returned to his beloved Lhasa on a refugee pass, but found it so terrible that he hastened back to India. To reach old age is unusual, very few make it to here.

We say goodbye when it is *puja* time when sixty elderly Tibetans gather on cushions in the shrine room for prayers. Delicious smells waft from cauldrons with dahl and stew in the kitchen, stirred by two sturdy elderly cooks wearing 'Free Tibet' T-shirts. This storehouse of human suffering is after all a strangely happy place. Maybe because the inhabitants daily express their gratitude for being here, a few hundred metres from Tibet's greatest living *bodhisattva*, who takes a personal interest in their welfare.

Along the circumambulation path back to MacLeod Ganj lie hundreds of *mani* stones, big and small, chiselled with the sacred mantra OM MANI PADME HUM, painted white, green, yellow, blue and red. Thick tresses of prayer flags connect the deodars. Small temples sit on the rocks with rows of brass prayer drums. An exiled couple, originally from southern Kham, has donated a long-life prayer for the Dalai Lama, cut in granite:

THE SHROUD OF COMPASSION THAT PROTECTS BEINGS OF THE WORLD, THE WISHFULFILLING GEM THAT FEED AMBROSIA, MAY TENZIN GYATSO, THE SOLE SAVIOUR, BE VICTORIOUS WITH PRAYERS THAT H.H. THE DALAI LAMA, THE CRUSADER OF WORLD PEACE IN THE AGE OF THE FIVE DEGENERATIONS AND NUCLEAR WEAPONS, GEM OF REFUGE OF THE TIBETAN PEOPLE IN THIS LIFE AND THE NEXT, LIVE FOR A HUNDRED AEONS AND SUCCEED IN HIS GREAT ACTIVITIES IN THE THREE REALMS.

They also financed the building of 101 hand-turned spurred mani wheels, containing 560 million mani mantras at a cost of 275 553 rupees, proving that religion could relieve unemployment without getting into harmful work or production. And so there are 101 prayer wheels to spin on the road to town to speed heavenwards millions of O HAIL THE JEWEL IN THE LOTUS.

In the evening we see the latest video from Yorkshire's First Television Network, *Escape From Tibet*, in the company of Tibetans. We become aware of the bitter reality that not only Nepal but India too tries to stem the flow of refugees from Tibet, without discussing the cause of the problem. Nepal indeed is hand-in-glove with China to arrest and return them. Refugees must reach the Tibetan community in Boudnath near Kathmandu undetected in order to gain access to the United Nations Refugee Association, which should really be at the border. Here they will be provided with papers to travel to India. There the Dalai Lama decides who may stay and who gets a year's free education before being sent back to Tibet, 'otherwise the culture dies'. Is this his policy statement or is it enforced by his hosts? We sit silent after watching the terrible misadventures of two brothers, one a child, until they finally find a home in a Tibetan monastery in southern India. Australia also prefers complicity with China, afraid to lose out on trade contracts and trusting that the refugees of China's mismanagement in Tibet will be absorbed elsewhere.

I cannot sleep. Although India has absorbed most Tibetan refugees, and private donors from around the globe help to maintain their schools and institutions, Tibetans have no citizenship and the global community is not demanding that China make the Tibetan homeland livable again for its dispersed people. Increasingly, young Tibetans look towards the United States, Canada, Australia and other Western countries where citizenship is attainable if they can make out a case for themselves. Tibetans are one of the largest refugee communities in the world.

✦　　✦　　✦

The morning offers an absence of rain and we drive in pale sunshine to the Dalai Lama's new summer palace in Sidhpur, a tiny Indian village twenty minutes' drive from Dharamsala. The new Norbulingka is an architectural delight. Built on slightly sloping land, laid out like half a mandala in brick and mortar, it combines the revival and continuation of Tibetan culture by being a training institution for all the traditional crafts: *thangka* painting, metalwork, woodcarving, cloth appliqué and temple construction.

The buildings are of square grey stones, walls arching to form the mandala. Architraves are in soft colours, although black door frames and maroon eaves prevail. But decorative paintwork features soft blue with pink lotuses, light red and gold. One- and two-storey offices and workshops are set in delightful gardens where the trickling of water mingles with the sound of a broom sweeping a path, a gardener clipping grass, people talking softly in Tibetan and local Indian dialect, birds singing, the high sound of metalworkers hammering in the distance. There is a guesthouse, a restaurant and a shop. A museum and an institute for higher learning in Tibetan are being set up. Trees and flowering bushes shade every step. Little ponds are sunk in pebble courts under clumps of bamboo. By the staircase to the temple, approached through a pillared portal, lily ponds reflect the sky.

New Norbulingka was built with donations and designed by Japanese architects, who have achieved a happy blend between traditional Tibetan styles and a native genius for blending gardens with structures.

We are shown around by Patricia, an Australian Volunteer Abroad just starting a term as administrator of Norbulingka Institute. Some 250 apprentices live in hostel accommodation behind the temple, receive food and pocket money and learn traditional trades. The refugee community still has an 18 per cent unemployment rate. Some very young boys already produce incredibly detailed *thangkas.*

In the appliqué workshop I watch with fascination the hands of women sitting on the floor. Their only aid is thin wire that comes already wrapped with silk. This surrounds lotus flowers, dragons, deities and sacred symbols cut from silk and laboriously hemmed, glued and stitched onto plain backgrounds of cotton and silk. The women make banners, tents and temple adornments.

Inside the unfinished four-storey temple, a crew of French architects gesticulates with a row of Indian labourers perched on rafters like birds on a telephone wire. Buddha's cross-legged body sits on its dais, but his serene copper head, about my height, stands on the floor between his knees. I am strangely moved by this. Having seen a thousands statues, this Buddha about to be assembled reminds me of those decapitated in Tibet. It will only be a matter of days before this Buddha's head sits where it ought to.

We are allowed to see the Dalai Lama's quarters on the top floor. Three small rooms with unrivalled views of the ranges, a close-up of the Kangra valley, and a perfect snow mountain through the tree branches. From the balcony you see two wings of curved buildings, set amidst hundreds of elegant trees and clumps of slender bamboo. I think I have never seen a lovelier people-made site than this. The entire complex exudes a highly developed sense of beauty, faith in the future to build something so solid, and a pursuit of sacred spaces that have always worked for the Tibetan people.

Before tearing ourselves away, we walk a mossy path behind the temple, through an Indian hamlet of neat huts and healthy-looking cows, past the apprentices' hostel, to Dolma Ling, a nunnery under construction.

Here at last I meet the young nun I sponsor. Her story is atypical. Born in Kham, she became a nun at fifteen, feeling a desire to study. She joined a large group of nuns, monks and lay people going on a Lhasa pilgrimage under the guidance of a lama. This epic journey included five months of progressing by bodily prostration. But they were denied entry to Lhasa and the Jokhang because of the visit of a United Nations delegation. The Chinese authorities feared a confrontation. So the pilgrims' once-in-a-lifetime pilgrimage failed. Travelling on to Tashilhunpo, they were again refused access because of fear of Chinese reactions to the size of their group. So they travelled on to Mount Kailash, where the idea of crossing the border was discussed. One hundred and twenty-three made the hazardous crossing, while fifty turned back. The young nun Delek's desire to study Buddhism, and the treatment of denial by the Chinese, drove her to leave country and family behind. There is no freedom of religion in Tibet.

Dharamsala could hardly cope with the sudden influx of so many refugees.

The nuns, eager to take up proper Buddhist studies, found themselves living in tents and rented housing for several years, until Dolma Ling could be constructed with private overseas sponsorships. Now it is going up at a fast pace. Waiting for Delek, I admire the pleasant two-storey whitewashed buildings of housekeeping and nuns' quarters, classrooms and an office. Linked with stone paths, patches of lawn and garden beds in the making, all it needs is a few good seasons to become as pretty a place as the little *ling* at Samyé.

When Delek emerges from laundry duty she grips my hands, her excitement about the unexpected materialisation of her sponsor strong and obvious. I am surprised how important it seems to her to talk to me. She searches for English words but cannot string them together. I deeply regret my Tibetan is even more inadequate. And so we stand, holding hands, saying simple things that can be translated, looking at each other. She is twenty-two years old now, a strong young woman whose appearance betrays her farming background. She has an English class every day.

The nuns of Dolma Ling are to become teaching nuns when they complete their studies, which apart from Buddhist scholarship include history, geography, science and languages. Delek meets the travellers and, still clasping my hand, looks at them with great curiosity as I tell what little of her story I know. Then we must part. She walks to the gate with me, asks me to come back for a longer period, stay for a while. There is nothing I would rather do. I promise her I will be her sponsor as long as I have life.

All these partings from people and places cause a fatigue of the heart until it whispers: 'Go home'. But the round is not yet done. A quick visit to the Tibetan Medical and Astrological Institute near Dharamsala, where a herbal-medicine display bears English descriptions. The usual herbs, coriander, saffron, also cyprus, many minerals, and to our consternation asbestos. Shocked, we cluster to stare at a substance we have learnt to fear. But the institute keeps alive a medical tradition that served Tibetans in the absence of modern drugs and may serve them again when side effects of chemical medicines prove detrimental.

The Information Office, from where the Tibetan government in exile also maintains its foreign relations, is our next stop. The rabbit warren of an old English two-storey bungalow is a beehive of activity. Both metaphors apply because of the comings and goings and the conditions inside. Here people work under restrictions of space and resources to keep the world informed of what news refugees bring out of occupied Tibet. There is a human rights desk and a computer room. Tibetan newspapers, journals and information booklets are printed on a printing press with lead type. The Tibetan type was made in India, which thirteen centuries ago provided Tibet with a model to script its language. Books in offset are farmed out, but everything else is printed here and collated by hand. The old press does good work, the staff are enthusiastic. And when fatigue forces me to sit on a chair in the hall, a woman finds time to bring me a cup of tea.

Nearby is the Tibetan Library and Archives. We see its exquisite museum of rescued cultural artefacts: *thangkas*, metal mandalas, statues, old books. The library is a resource centre for Tibetan and overseas researchers. Some of each sit on the front steps drinking Coke. The place is not exactly humming, but the afternoon is hot. Across the plaza is Nechung, the state oracle's temple.

In the evening we are off to a performance by the Tibetan Institute for the Performing Arts (TIPA). The group has its own theatre on the edge of a small plateau with a magnificent drop to the Kangra valley floor. On stage, the dancers leap as if to span mountains and valleys. They present a fast program of a dozen traditional dance stories in full costume. The small orchestra's backing and the dancers' vigorous singing express an energy that transcends the requirements of the dance. The beautiful shepherds in sheep-fur hats project their voices as if there were mountains to return the echo. Their singing rushes across the footlights, transporting the small audience of mainly foreigners. Here, as in New Norbulingka, young Tibetans rehearse what is dearest to them, now that the source of this beauty and drama — the mountains, rivers and forests of Tibet — are missing from their birthright.

TIPA performs overseas, but although Europe and the United States see these dancers periodically, Australians saw only the early generation of dancers in 1976. Today's dancers are young and professionally trained. Costumes and sets are made on the premises. Afterwards we are treated to a Tibetan dinner in the TIPA staffroom, but the dancers do not join in.

During these few days in Dharamsala we have seen amazingly energetic expressions of the Tibetan will to maintain their remarkable culture. Tibetans hope to engage the international community in efforts to not only keep the exiled community intact where possible, but to convey an understanding of their deep need to return to a Tibet free of oppression, where all we have seen here can reconnect with its source, the amazing Tibetan landscape.

By the time we are in pyjamas our tour-leader calls a meeting to announce a surprise. We are to meet His Holiness the Dalai Lama at 1 pm tomorrow, even though no application was made one month ago. How amazing. Why? Because of the circumstances of our exit from Shigatse? The guide monk in the temple, he with the twinkle in his eye, must have known!

We fill in small forms with passport details and two of us write down our true profession of writer. After months of pretending, it is a relief.

Lobsang's Story

A bad night. No rain to dampen the multifarious noises of the night. Barking dogs, hammering, monastery drums and piercing flutes, a screaming man living out a tortured existence in the next house — perhaps he was a torture victim? What to say to the Dalai Lama? After midnight an unwilling silence descends, but at 5 am all noises resolutely revive: barking, hammering, drumming, piping, and the running feet of monkeys on tin roofs, looking for breakfast. Only the tortured man is silent now. On flat roofs people face the new day doing obeisance, *puja*, exercises, ablutions, or simply nothing. A woman is picking fleas from the coats of two apso dogs. The little charmers lie on their backs in turn, paws outstretched, having their bellies tickled. The air is fresh and damp.

Early, at 7.30, I visit Kelsang and meet her husband. I tell her I would like to take down Lobsang's life story for the book I will write. Together we call on him. He is unwell. It will be another year before I return to record the brief life story he tells me. Thanking Kelsang Dekyi for her translation, I insert it here because Lobsang's life, and the background to it, is the script of exile itself.

Lobsang's story, recorded in July 1996

Lobsang Rabgyal was born in Markham in Kham in 1917. As a 21-year old he made his first journey to Lhasa where he established himself as a trader. The journey took two months.

When the Dalai Lama fled Lhasa in 1959, Lobsang joined Chusi Gangdruk or 'Four Rivers, Six Ranges', the renowned Khamba resistance movement. He and his party were coming from Kongpo in eastern Tibet and engaged Chinese troops seven times to cover the Dalai Lama's flight to the Indian border. With some companions Lobsang crossed over the Loh pass into Nepal the same year. He went first to Missamari, a refugee transit camp in Assam, then to Gangtok in Sikkim, both south of the eastern Himalayas, surviving for three months by working as a coolie. In 1960 he made his way to Dharamsala in the foothills of the western Himalayas.

Lobsang's son-in-law refills our teacups. Lobsang makes deep throaty noises, indicating he is reviewing what he has just said. I am reminded of how hard the Khambas have had it. Although Buddhists, they are also by nature a fighting people. The Chinese invasion presented a legitimate cause to fight for their own land of Kham, but when they took up the fight for greater Tibet they were continually asked by the Dalai Lama to lay down their arms.

A pacifist, the Dalai Lama advocated a non-violent struggle to Khamba leader Chime in 1959, for fear of Chinese reprisals and because killing is immoral. Yet the Khambas, assisted by the women of Lhasa who carried ammunition and petrol bombs, kept the Chinese engaged in the capital while the Dalai Lama made his getaway in March 1959. Once he was safe in India, the Khambas became guerillas, impeding Chinese efforts to build strategic roads and supply routes for their army. In the mid-1960s they established a guerilla base in Mustang, a Tibetan kingdom in northernmost Nepal.

In 1974 Mao pressured King Birendra of Nepal to rid his country of the Tibetan guerillas. The Dalai Lama, trying to prevent a confrontation, sent a recorded message requesting the Khambas to disarm peacefully. Some committed suicide rather than surrender. Those that surrendered landed in Nepali prisons. The rest fled and were hunted down between the Chinese, Nepali and Indian armies. The Chinese again had their way. Chusi Gangdruk remains a political force in Dharamsala. Younger Tibetans express their desire for an independent Tibet through the Tibetan Youth Congress. Neither the congress nor Chusi Gangdruk agrees with the Dalai Lama's view that Tibet can be truly autonomous within the Chinese People's Republic if the Chinese will negotiate.

Putting down his cup, Lobsang continues his story. The Tibetan government in exile, recognising Lobsang Rabgyal's leadership qualities, sent him to Manali in Kulu where Tibetan refugees were making roads for the Indian government. One of three headmen, he was personally responsible for 3500 men and women refugees doing back-breaking work, living in tents, some dying of tuberculosis. These refugees were organised in groups of one hundred, each with a spokesperson who communicated with Lobsang, so that he dealt with thirty-five representatives on a daily basis under dreadful conditions. To him they brought their needs and problems. He dealt with work schedules, food and accommodation, sickness and death.

Lobsang led road gangs for seven years. In winter they worked around Manali, but as summer came they shifted to higher altitudes, constructing the road through the Lahoul valley to Spiti as far as Kaza, an amazing road through boulder-strewn valleys and through ice walls in mid-summer. When that highway in the clouds was completed, needing annual maintenance from then on, the work gangs constructed roads in the Kangra valley and around Dharamsala.

One feels humbled by the road distances these possessionless Tibetan refugees hacked out of the mountains in a climate that affected their health. Roads that travellers grumble about, but that only existed as caravan tracks and sheep trails before the influx of 100 000 Tibetan refugees in 1959. And during all these years Lobsang must have searched every contingent of new refugees for a familiar face, his wife, his young daughters.

In 1967 the Dalai Lama appointed Lobsang, then fifty, as manager of the new handicraft cooperative in Dharamsala. He remained its moving force and leading spirit for fifteen years. When he came, the weavers and craftspeople lived in tents all year round. Under his guidance they built the cooperative: living quarters, a two-storey workshop, hotel and dining room. Opposite the workshop they set up a creche for the babies of women weavers, so mothers could go down to feed their children when they cried. Within a few years the cooperative received its first export order for carpets. I was the importer and it was then that I came to know of this man who was pulling an entire community up by the bootstraps. From then on they began to export carpets to many countries.

Lobsang does not mention his private life, but I remember some turning points. After living in solitude for eighteen years he found a partner in a lovely woman I only knew as Ani-la in 1977. Was she a former nun? I had dinner with them. He said no-one could make better *momo* than Ani-la. It is the test of excellence among Tibetans and as a foreigner you do not want to be caught in its complexities. I do not know what happened to Ani-la. In the early eighties he wrote me that a miracle had happened. His wife and daughters had travelled out of Tibet on a temporary permit and he had gone to Nepal to meet them. One daughter remained with him, the one now in America.

Although life was difficult, Lobsang says he is happy to have helped thousands of refugees with work and accommodation in Dharamsala. Underneath his remark I sense unspoken regrets. Perhaps he wanted to stay on as manager. His mental abilities are strong as ever. The carpet workshop is no longer the same lively place that greeted me, humming with song and the beating of looms, when I first met Lobsang as director in the front office.

Changing the subject, I ask whether he ever met the Tenth Panchen Lama. Yes, he saw him once in Lhasa, in the distance. Kelsang explains: 'Here we can see our Lama closely, any time. In Tibet that never happened with high lamas'. Exile has broken down many barriers. How the Tenth Panchen Lama, a gregarious exuberant man, would have enjoyed life amongst the people. But his was a life in prison camps or prison palaces, keeping the conquerors honest where he could.

Tomorrow, Lobsang will participate in a presentation of Songtsen Gampo statues by His Holiness the Dalai Lama, at a special *puja* for elderly Tibetans of merit. Every day there are *pujas* for His Holiness's birthday, while he catches up on government affairs, packs his bags to fly to England and Europe, and receives overseas journalists. It is a far cry from his highly circumscribed ceremonial existence in the Potala, with twice-yearly grand processions to and from Norbulingka. From being a nominal figurehead with decisions mostly made by high officials, the Dalai Lama has turned into the vital factor that keeps the Tibetans in exile together and the case for a free homeland before the conscience of the world. Moreover, he has written many books on Buddhism and non-violence for Western readers.

Lobsang and Kelsang talk rapidly in Tibetan. Kelsang says they feel other countries ought to put more pressure on China about Tibet. Although they don't say so, they clearly cannot understand how it is that all the free countries, seemingly so powerful in scientific and economic ways, organised in global bodies like the United Nations, World Bank, Food and Agricultural Organisation and international commerce, cannot simply say to China: 'GET OUT OF TIBET!' No need to fight a war over it, no need to be nasty. Just enough simultaneous communally applied pressure to help China make a decision not to hold on to a resisting Tibet, but to let go and gain a multitude of friends. To the refugees and those who visit refugee settlements, China's claim that Tibetan society is stable and only the Dalai Lama's 'clique' is causing unrest is too preposterous to discuss.

Wanting to leave some hope, I relate how many overseas Tibet supporters make representations to China and their own governments to gain small advances in the understanding of Tibet's case, and express the thought that things will change in Tibet eventually, although no-one can say when.

But what activists do cannot be compared with what governments could do, given political will. I suppose Lobsang and Kelsang know that my government recognises China's rule over Tibet. I cannot hope to explain this and in the light of the facts I fail to understand it. I can only assume that either my government is hopelessly ignorant of the facts, or is hopelessly callous regarding another nation's destruction. How can Lobsang and Kelsang ever hope to go home again?

We leave Lobsang, as he is tired. At Kelsang's home, where her supportive husband is cooking, I am pressed to drink tea with them. My visit has brought to the surface Kelsang's deep longing for her homeland. She tells me how last year, during the troubles over the death of an Indian boy in a fight among Tibetan and Indian youths, all Tibetans feared for their lives. Indians threw stones at Tibetans in the streets and smashed windows. All pent-up discontent of the Indian population about their own poverty was vent at Tibetan survivors who successfully built new lives in a number of locations in India, aided by countless overseas sponsors.

When the attacks would not stop, the Dalai Lama proclaimed officially that perhaps it would be best if the Tibetan refugees and his government in exile left

Dharamsala altogether. He began to look around for a suitable place to resettle. This drew a new reaction. The Indian business community assured him that this was not a desired solution. Things quietened down, the accused boy was acquitted and the Tibetans stayed. There are signs that Indians want to cooperate with Tibetans, but the scars hide deep wounds.

'It would be so much better if we could return to our own place', Kelsang says, 'Not live here anymore'. She waves her hand towards the beautiful scenery outside the window that was shattered by hatred last year. Kelsang came here as a small girl and has lived in Dharamsala for thirty-seven years, nearly as long as I have lived in Australia. But different circumstances allow me to visit Holland and call Australia home, while stateless Kelsang has but one home and that is occupied Tibet.

The Tibetan government in exile continually discusses issues pertaining to the refugee population and the future of the Tibetan homeland. The Dalai Lama has insisted on a democratic course and membership of political parties is growing. The Tibetan Youth Congress is the largest political group. They and the National Democratic Party of Tibet want total independence for Tibet because they do not believe China will keep any promises under so-called autonomy, as recent history has overwhelmingly shown. The Dalai Lama favours the Buddhist 'Middle Way', that is, genuine autonomy with China looking after foreign affairs and defence. His elder brother Takster, living in the United States, is a passionate advocate of total independence, whereas his eldest brother is on speaking terms with the Beijing government and has in the past relayed messages. So even the Dalai Lama's family is divided. The refugees either want total independence or trust the Dalai Lama's wisdom. But inside Tibet there are some Tibetans who, even if they do not trust China, side with the regime to maintain the status they have gained.

That concludes Lobsang's story and Kelsang's comments in 1996. I return now to my last day in Dharamsala in 1995, in Lobsang's tiny room with a view of the mountains.

I take photos, promise to work for Tibet and say goodbye. Now that contact has been re-established, I believe we will meet again. If only we could meet next time in Tibet. In 1977 Lobsang said: 'Come and live with us in Tibet. We'll be back there in two years'. What gave him that confidence then, three years after the destruction in Mustang of the Khamba resistance force to which he once belonged? Now he seems to have lost all hope. Grief is etched on his face, has turned his eyes black with despair. Perhaps he thinks the foreigners with all their promises have done nothing to return Tibet to the Tibetans. It's hard to explain we must grovel before our own governments to get any attention for Tibet. We part.

After a final stroll through the street I start packing, when Kelsang climbs the stairs with Lobsang's son-in-law, carrying presents and *kata*. A soft grey Kashmiri shawl, like those worn by Himalayan shepherds, is laid in my hands. From Lobsang. I am moved. Kelsang gives me a wrapped parcel and container of freshly baked pancakes for the train journey. We sit, have tea and I hear a bit more of Lobsang's story. His daughter in America is his youngest. The older daughter died. Years ago his wife visited on a one-month visa, but returned to Tibet. The daughter came to India in 1981, about the time I stopped hearing from Lobsang. Lobsang's son-in-law learnt English at Namgyal monastery school in Dharamsala.

A last goodbye until we meet again. As always, I feel overwhelmed by Tibetan generosity. In 1977 Lobsang presented me with a Tibetan rug and had it sent to my home address. All I ever seem able to return are small sums of money and photos — and support for Tibet's independence in a form that returns dignity in freedom to the Tibetan people. Perhaps the despair in Lobsang's eyes has to do with the Dalai Lama's insistence on peaceful means and negotiations with Beijing, which to date have not eventuated. Honouring the Dalai Lama with the Nobel Peace Prize in 1989 should have been followed by world action on Tibet's behalf in the eyes of the exiles. Meanwhile families disintegrate in their search for a more secure existence and young Tibetans grow up in stateless despair.

A Conversation with the Dalai Lama

Our moment has come. We approach the gates of His Holiness the Dalai Lama's residence, are frisked and led into a small dark waiting room in the gatehouse. One video and one print camera are allowed to be taken in, all else is deposited. We sit fingering our *kata*. The secretary enters, looks at his papers, calls my name, asks whether I am present. My journalistic exploits have been reported. Embarrassed at being singled out I identify myself. Mentally I withdraw into a shell from where my words will sound like shooting pebbles, even to myself.

'So you didn't have a very good time in Shigatse?' he asks.

'It didn't matter for us', I say, resenting an implication that we would be mainly concerned with having a good time in occupied Tibet. 'But the Tibetans are having a very bad time there.'

He nods. I feel tense. Maybe it is group tension. Having journeyed together for so long, we must be sharing some emotions by now.

A monk sweeps in to fetch us and we proceed to the reception room for a ten-minute audience with the most famous Nobel Peace Prize winner of our times. The same path I remember, the same small garden quite lovely with roses and lawn. But some revamping of the old bungalow has taken place. We cross a porch and enter through wide-open doors into the old waiting room where in 1977 I sat staring at a model of the Potala in a glass case. The genteel faded brocade sofa and chairs have been upholstered in smart feldspar pink. We are directed to sit in a semi-circle, facing a simple upright chair. As soon as we are seated there is a rustle at another door and the Dalai Lama strides in, smiling, followed by his secretary.

I catch my breath at the incongruity of the moment. A bunch of travellers in their cleanest scruffy clothes meet the most celebrated exile in the world, leader of all Tibetans, head of a renowned school of Buddhism and 'just a simple Buddhist monk' as he pleases to call himself. Once more I am struck by what a deep familiarity with this remarkable man I have acquired through a lifetime of following his fate and that of his country, reading his writings, practising Buddhism. He appears larger than any of us in his robes, dominating the circle, drawing all our attention and subdued energies. His face glows as he looks at each of us in turn, a getting-to-know-you gaze that goes deeper than an arrow. Behind that look rises half a century of studies in what drives, assails

317

and moves the human mind. Is this what the Chinese fear to meet at the conference table?

Most solemnly we present *kata*. The secretary lifts them off the Dalai Lama's hands, bowing as he does so. The Dalai Lama begins by asking how things were and our tour leader relates some of our adventures. The subject of handing out Dalai Lama photos in Tibet comes up.

A rollicking giggle. 'A crime! A great crime!' chuckles the Dalai Lama. I remember the village woman pressing his image to her forehead before stowing it inside her *chuba*, and the tearful old nun at the Jokhang. Does he know what he means to them? He refuses to see himself as important, a leader from whom all ego has vanished. I have watched him pick up prostrating people who wanted to touch his feet, kindly dusting them off as if they'd unexpectedly stumbled.

The secretary records the conversation in writing, sometimes offering an English word when the Dalai Lama turns to him. There are more general questions to put us at ease and then he asks about the martial law situation in Shigatse. The travellers who were on the mountain in the afternoon of 12 July tell what they saw. He asks more questions to round out the picture, then launches into the story of how the new Panchen Lama was chosen by divinations.

This child, Gendhun Choekyi Nyima of Nagchuka was one of three final candidates about whom the Dalai Lama received reports from Tashilhunpo's abbot Chadrel Rimpoche, the head of the China–appointed selection committee. Rimpoche's divinations found this child to be the real incarnation of the Panchen Lama. One other child had signs on the tongue indicating he might be a reincarnation, but no other marks. Presumably it is this child the Chinese later installed as Eleventh Panchen Lama. That child's father was connected with the Chinese on a high level. Gendhun's father has no such connections.

The Dalai Lama goes on to tell why he chose 14 May to announce the new reincarnation. It was Wesak, the most important celebration on the Buddhist calender, commemorating Buddha's birth, enlightenment and death. Seemingly, the Dalai Lama was well aware of Chinese plans to announce Ghendun Choekyi Nyima as the new Panchen Lama on 15 or 16 May. The Dalai Lama performed a divination to ascertain the correct date for announcing the news and this told him the 14th was a good day. Divinations usually have the final say in Tibetan decision making, as they did in independent Tibet. Thus upholding all traditions, especially the one that requires the Panchen and Dalai Lamas to approve each other's reincarnation, the exiled Tibetan ruler announced that the Eleventh Panchen Lama had been found and in so doing pipped the Chinese at the post.

The Dalai Lama laughs again when it is related that Lhasa Tibetans were pleased with this very first uprising in Tashilhunpo. Since the Panchen Lama's monastery has long been regarded as a Chinese stronghold, to see even part of its population finally saying 'Enough!' is a recognition for Lhasa, where protest is endemic. The Dalai Lama replies that the Chinese have always played up differences between the two courts and speculated which might be the older, although that it is of no significance. He now fears the child's elimination, unless the Chinese give up interfering in religious affairs.

One traveller asks why the child was not put under protection. Both Dalai Lama and secretary display surprise. The question hangs about. How could it have been done with the child in Tibet? Having approved the candidate chosen by the Chinese-appointed committee, could anyone have expected the Chinese to make the about-turn they did? Not to mention constant Chinese assurances of upholding freedom of religion. It seems a case of rank political spite that they have made an issue of the Panchen Lama's selection. Meanwhile the child and his family are missing. I remark that the Chinese won't be able to pretend a heart attack in a six-year-old child, referring to the death of the Tenth Panchen Lama. The Dalai Lama now begins to tell the story of the Tenth Panchen's demise.

He says that according to a Chinese report a doctor flew from China to Gonggar airport in January 1989, then to Shigatse, managing to land despite high winds. The Panchen Lama lay in a coma the day after he had collapsed with chest pains. The doctor was with him some time before he died. But Tibetans close to the Panchen say the Panchen became sick and the doctor gave him an injection while he lay in a coma and he died that night, not the next day. 'Why two different versions?' asked the Dalai Lama. But it seems then there was heart trouble before foul play or medical interference.

Servants close to the Panchen Lama say his nails went black after he died. When his wife arrived from Beijing she wanted to touch his body but was not allowed to do so. The Dalai Lama thinks the Panchen knew his death was in the offing. 'He said to me: "Both my bodyguard and my physician have been replaced."' When did they talk? Was it during that illicit phone connection between Australia and Germany while both were travelling? And was the Lhasa Holiday Inn doctor, now in a cushiony job, the original Panchen Lama physician or the replacement? Either one may have needed to be mollified.

As the Dalai Lama talks animatedly he laughs a lot, sometimes throwing back his head and rocking gently in his chair. Much has been written about his serenity, but his jollity is harder to comprehend. Yet, we witnessed Tibetans laughing heartily and profusely, no matter how undignified their lives. Culturally this may not suit me, having probably fretted too much about life's vicissitudes, but perhaps this leader of a scattered people would not otherwise be able to sustain his campaign of non-violence, decade after decade, in the face of oppression, global indifference, and Beijing's unrelenting weekly denunciations of himself.

We have been aware of time far exceeding the stipulated ten minutes. Attendants hover on the verandah trying to catch the Dalai Lama's attention; other people are waiting. Surely he is aware of it, but his attention never wavers until he seems satisfied he has heard the more important impressions of our journey and has filled us in on the tragic topic of the Panchen Lama.

Finally His Holiness whispers to his secretary, who briefly leaves, to return with a handful of booklets carrying the Dalai Lama's smiling face on the cover. He signs one for each of us, hands them to us personally. We do not receive our *kata* back as is often the custom, but receive new *kata* from the Dalai Lama himself with a firm handclasp. Then he shouts 'Group photo!' in his deep jolly voice, grabs two travellers by the hand and troops out onto the porch with the group in tow. We arrange ourselves under an arch of roses. The secretary takes the photo with the only allowed camera. Then we say goodbye and walk floatingly, rather transformed, down the garden path and past the sentry boxes. The audience has lasted forty-five minutes. No-one speaks. Each unto her own thoughts.

For three hours we drive the winding road to Pathankot through dusty villages to catch the night train to Delhi. I write in my diary: '3 x met D.L. And never asked for it'. In Buddhism they call it good karma. But good karma carries responsibilities. I went to Tibet because I always wanted to and because the Dalai Lama said: 'Go to Tibet and see for yourself'. Having seen, I have only just begun to tell the world what I saw.

Epilogue: The Tibetan Gulag

THE PEOPLE LEFT BEHIND

After my return from Tibet I would often think of the radiant monk who crossed the Tsangpo river to meditate in a cave for eleven years, until I heard he was brutally evicted. Over one hundred hermit nuns and monks meditating in the Chimpu range near Samyé were first charged a land tax of five yuan a month in September 1996, followed by 'door number' registration in February 1997. Finally, in March 1998, all nuns and monks were evicted from Chimpu by Chinese authorities. Some were beaten for pleading to be allowed to stay. Their simple quarters were completely destroyed. The hermits went to Lhasa to do prostrations along the Lingkor. 'There is too much religion in Tibet' is a frequent Chinese criticism that justifies such acts of vandalism.

Four of the cheerful nuns from Tsangkhug nunnery in Lhasa, aged sixteen to eighteen, were arrested on 13 June 1996 for calling out "Free Tibet" in the Barkhor and imprisoned in Drapchi high-security prison. Pema, Phuntsog and Yangdrol are assumed still to be in detention.

Of more than 500 monks involved in the Shigatse uprising of 12 July 1995, about forty-five were arrested as well as several lay people. Some are still in prison, others escaped to India after release. Chadrel Rimpoche, aged fifty-five, former abbot of Tashilhunpo who informed the Dalai Lama of the choice of the new Panchen Lama, was convicted of 'plotting to split the country' and 'leaking state secrets'. In a closed trial in Shigatse on 21 April 1997 he was sentenced to six years imprisonment. His assistant Jampa Chung, aged fifty, was sentenced to four years.

In May 1996, the monks of Ganden monastery threatened authorities they would walk out if the ban on Dalai Lama pictures was enforced. The ban was enforced, the pictures torn down and walked over, and a fight ensued in which many were injured and two monks killed, one aged fifteen. More than ninety monks were arrested. Over 600 monks fled to their villages. Some escaped to India. Ganden became a ghost town. The seventeen monks known to be in prison were given sentences of from three to fifteen years. The Jokhang, Sera, Drepung and Ramoche monasteries closed their gates that week in support of the Ganden protest.

Since 1995 three Sera monks were imprisoned, fifteen from Drepung including a sixty-year-old monk, and one from Ramoche. Three Palkhor Chöde monks have since been imprisoned, as well as a nineteen-year-old Samyé monk. A hermit nun from Samyé Chimpu was sentenced to three years in prison. And a monk guide from the Potala has completed ten years of a fifteen-year sentence.

Some of the people we met during our travels may now be dead or behind bars. No traveller in Tibet should be fooled by orderly streets and modern developments. These hide ongoing struggles for independence and against Draconian regulations.

Our Tibetan guide did not suffer from high blood pressure. When we met him we did not know he had just been released from prison, after being arrested in Lhasa for giving a taped interview to an American travel agent. His red and purple face gradually assumed a normal colour and maybe he did not really fall off a yak either. Later that year he was arrested near the Nepalese border, kept in a windowless cell in Zhangmo without food or blankets, then transferred to a military prison without bedding, before being released. He eventually made his escape from Tibet and found political asylum in the West. Being a tourist guide is an extremely dangerous occupation in Tibet.

Tibetans keep their distance from the Chinese and are reticent to talk to tourists when Chinese people are about, especially in the cities. They exist in a space warp between their oppressors and visitors who enjoy liberties Tibetans only dream about. Having lived under oppression, I never cease to worry about many Tibetans I met in Tibet, for reasons of their health, safety and future.

Enquiries were made about the possibility to perform plastic surgery on the burnt boy from Nyelam village if he could be brought to Australia, but a specialist doctor connected with a program for cranial reconstruction gave a discouraging reply. He believed that children were often better off staying in their own environment. Our tour leader looked for the boy on a later journey, but he was not with the village children.

CHINA'S TAKEOVER OF TIBET

Apologists murmur periodically that China has brought progress to Tibet, but the reality is that the Chinese have advanced themselves in Tibet at the expense of the Tibetans.

Before 1950 Tibet was an independent country. Its independent status has been established according to international law by the International Committee of Lawyers for Tibet (ICLT) together with the Unrepresented Nations and Peoples Organisation (UNPO). According to their findings, Tibet had a fully functioning government, comprising a civil service, judicial and taxation systems, postal and telegraph services, border control, Tibetan currency and internationally recognised Tibetan passports. Tibet entered into treaties with nations like Great Britain, Nepal and Mongolia. These facts are documented in the pre-1950 literature, as are those instances when Tibet invited imperial troops to assist in evicting invaders, or suffered intrusions by Chinese warlords in its Amdo and Kham borderlands.

Consequently, China's 1950 military invasion of Tibet was an illegal conquest of a sovereign nation. China's continued occupation of Tibet violates international laws including the United Nations Declaration of Human Rights. The United Nations Charter rejects claims to territory based on the illegal use of force as contrary to international law. Tibet's legitimate government is the Tibetan government in exile in Dharamsala, now democratically elected by refugees to represent all provinces.

The Chinese carved Tibet in three. The former Tibetan provinces Kham and Amdo are now governed as Chinese provinces, although they include some so-called Autonomous Tibetan Prefectures. The Tibet Autonomous Region — formerly central, southern and western Tibet with the Chang Tang plateau — has a regional government, not elected but appointed, receiving its directives from Beijing.

Chinese attempts to take control of Tibet by stealth or force go back centuries. The Thirteenth Dalai Lama, predecessor of the present Dalai Lama, was the first to survive into adulthood during the nineteenth century. Four incarnates died prematurely, presumed poisoned by Chinese agents. Chinese rulers have steadfastly tried to influence events in Tibet through the second highest lama in the land, the Panchen Lama, causing a permanent rift between the Ninth Panchen and the Thirteenth Dalai Lama. The choice of Tenth Panchen Lama was forced upon the young Fourteenth Dalai Lama by the communists in 1950. The Tenth Panchen Lama was brought up by Chinese communists, but in adulthood advocated real Tibetan autonomy and paid with his liberty and health. The Eleventh Panchen Lama installed by the Beijing government in 1995 is a candidate chosen by the Chinese regime and lives in Beijing. The whereabouts of Gendhun Choekyi Nyima, the boy chosen by the Dalai Lama, are unknown, but Beijing maintains he is in protective custody. He is the youngest political prisoner in the world.

CHINA'S IMPACT ON TIBET'S SOCIETY SINCE 1950

Since annexation in 1950, Tibet has become to China what Siberia is to Russia: a treasure-house of minerals, fertile fields, rivers and forests to exploit for mainland China's benefit and a place for China's principal nuclear test sites and nuclear waste disposal. Heavy industries pollute air and waterways, while hydro-electric dams and a steel industry are planned for Kham.

But China had no need to send Chinese prisoners to Tibet to do the hard labour. Although PLA soldiers died in vast numbers to make the military access roads connecting China with Tibet, for further developments they organised the Tibetan population into work gangs. The country became one vast prison camp.

China appears to send to Tibet its hard–line cadres who no longer fit the new capitalist China, where state enterprises fold and private businesses flourish. The result is that Tibet, after a decade of hesitant opening up, now suffers an ongoing second Cultural Revolution, while the more than one million dead of the 1959 uprising and the 1960s Cultural Revolution are still being mourned. In some parts of Tibet starvation is apparent again. Despite the existence of collaborators, Tibetans at large have not embraced communism and thereby they may well have prevented China from expanding further south and west.

In the last decade of the twentieth century Beijing's directives for the benefit of the Tibetan people have included the despotic Strike Hard, Spiritual Civilisation and Patriotic Education campaigns. The first clamps down on 'splittism', that is, supporters of independence or splitting off from 'the Motherland'. The second aims at replacing the Dalai Lama's influence and Buddhist religion with communist ideology. The third aims to cleanse monasteries and nunneries of Dalai Lama pictures, expel reactionary monks and nuns and teach the rest communist ideology. Consequently, the cost of administration alone rose to 21.8 per cent of the TAR budget in 1996. The subsidies China spends in Tibet thus largely support China's policy of control. Moreover, these are only a fraction of the value of minerals China hopes to extract from Tibet.

The Chinese assault on the very soil of Tibet has come through the influx of Chinese immigrants, now outnumbering Tibetans in their own land. They own most businesses, occupy the best farmland and mine the minerals, pushing Tibetans to marginal highlands to survive as herders. China has been able to attract foreign investment and overseas aid to finance this genocidal immigration policy.

Lhasa valley has been inhabited by Tibetans since neolithic times. Now Lhasa is one of fifty 'protected' historic cities in the People's Republic of China, but only 180 historic city sites survive out of the 650 recorded before 1950 (*IIAS News* — Summer 1998). Ancient Lhasa is rapidly being demolished. The Dutch Centre on Housing Rights and Evictions estimates that more than 5000 Tibetans have been evicted from their Lhasa homes and 10 000 more face this fate. The Chinese government sees this upheaval of a settled population that has lived here for millennia, as an internal matter not to be criticised by outsiders.

An Australian–aided United Nation's World Food Program in the Lhasa valley, aiming to 'enhance the fertility of the valley', was to settle another 130 000 Chinese peasants, according to the *South China Morning Post* of 30 January 1994. Tibetan farmers in the valley received 'official notification that they will be required to vacate their houses to accommodate Chinese settlers'. Tibetans have been made refugees in their own land as well as a disadvantaged minority. After eviction from their ancestral villages, adults will presumably be pressed into work gangs and made to live in miserable road workers' camps in remote areas.

Travellers cannot fail to see the desecration of cultural artefacts and buildings, the rape of southern Tibet's forests evidenced by trucks transporting gigantic logs northwards, and the desecration of pristine Yamdrok Tso with a hydro-electric scheme that may drain the lake in fifty years. Acquisitions of farmers' land for that scheme were made without compensation.

China's claim that Tibetans were serfs held in bondage and that monasteries gobbled up children, produce and valuables, is still echoed by some observers who apply European medieval patterns to Tibet. For a variety of reasons this does not work. One major reason is the genuine and deep attachment Tibetans have to their religion and those who study or dispense it. Entering monasteries was often a youthful aspiration, supported by the family. It also checked population increase, a necessity in Tibet's fragile landscape, whereas now the Chinese complain that Tibetans are begetting too many children. So-called serfdom in Tibet compares favourably with the lives of industrial workers and coalminers in England during the same period.

Tibet's climate forced frugality on master and servant alike. There was less difference in lifestyle between rich, poor and religious than in most countries. The poor might travel more often on foot than on mule or horseback, but all drank butter tea, took herbal medicines and lived in unheated houses. Buddhism required compassion from all, but more from the wealthy. This nullified many of the negative aspects of Tibetan society. Work in Tibet is determined by weather and seasons. No people work under harsher circumstances than Tibetan nomads. Although apparently free and independent, they live in tents through all seasons to care for their animals, the source of their existence. Yet, there always was time for festivals and pilgrimages.

Massive population transfer was already alluded to in the 1950s, when Mao Zedong planned to raise Tibet's population to ten million. That figure has been overshot by about three million already. This and exports to China and increased grain taxes are depleting the soils of Tibet, which has to feed a population two-and-a-half times larger than ever. The population transfer is accompanied by massive importation of cheap consumer goods, which has caused a rubbish crisis in Tibet detrimental to soils and rivers, as there is no rubbish disposal or landfill policy.

The often touted introduction of modern health services to Tibet amount to Chinese hospitals Tibetans fear to enter, because of the unauthorised taking of blood and sterilisations, and high newborn infant mortality. Thus, finance from the Australian Government has provided for a new wing at the Chinese hospital in Shigatse may contribute to the demise of Tibetan people. Aid to upgrade technology for the hand-woven carpet industry, already producing the best quality carpets in the world in India, Nepal and Tibet, seems something of a symbolic gesture to Tibetan culture.

Education is not free in Tibet and many parents cannot afford to send their children to school. Some are not allowed to attend because they come from black-listed families, formerly wealthy. Education is now delivered only in Chinese, placing Tibetan students at a disadvantage. All schools using Tibetan as a teaching medium were closed down in 1998. Tibetan history is not taught as it proved impossible to separate it from Tibet's religion.

In early 1994 Chinese authorities banned reception and relay of foreign satellite TV in Tibet, ordering ground satellite receiving stations to shut down. In 1993 in Lhasa we watched the BBC, Star TV and CNN, but the authorities were obviously afraid information might reach Tibetans. One of the requirements for President Clinton's renewal of China's Most Favoured Nation status was that China must allow international radio and TV broadcasts in China and Tibet, particularly Chinese and Tibetan broadcasts on Voice of America and the newly established Radio Free Asia. The Chinese jam Voice of America Tibetan-language broadcasts whenever they can and the president turns a blind eye for trade's sake.

Religion, said to be free according to China's laws, suffers inconceivable restrictions. Tibetans may not possess photos of the Dalai Lama even in their closets. Government employees may not practise Buddhism. Chinese authorities determine how many monasteries and nunneries may operate. Tibetans need permission from Chinese authorities to enter religious life and most are refused, sending thousands into exile to get a Tibetan Buddhist education. The Chinese have not restored 1 per cent of the religious buildings and their contents destroyed in the Cultural Revolution. Rather, Chinese authorities continue to pull down small monasteries and nunneries on bureaucratic pretexts and antique religious artefacts stolen during these closures have turned up in overseas art auctions.

Restrictions on the recruitment of nuns and expulsions of politically active nuns have closed virtually all remaining nunneries in the Lhasa valley. Formerly imprisoned nuns who fled to India reported torture by electric cattle prods inserted into the vagina, as well as beatings, food deprivation and solitary confinement. These brave women, often under twenty, are Tibet's counterparts of the Chinese students who demonstrated for democracy at Tiananmen Square in 1989.

No people who 'welcomed the liberators' need a military and police presence like the one Tibet has to put up with. Soldiers, People's Armed Police, Public Security officers, surveillance cameras, military installations and prisons litter the cities and the land. In the Potala, cameras record foreigners and monks exchanging anything more than nods. The monk stands to suffer if he cannot avoid being engaged in 'unpatriotic' conversations. Tibetans live in a police state under a military dictatorship. There have been more than fifty rebellions against the Chinese authorities in Tibet since 1959.

The Chinese fear uprisings on many dates of the Tibetan calendar: Tibetan New Year (February), 1959 Uprising Day (10 March), the Dalai Lama's birthday (6 July), Tibet Autonomous Region day (1 September) and Chinese October Revolution day (1 October). Add to these, visits by Chinese dignitaries, foreign and United Nations delegations, and US foreign policy declarations. When 30 000 extra Chinese troops moved into Tibet in 1994, in case of demonstrations after President Clinton's decision on China's Most Favoured Nation status, it was hardly worth their while to withdraw them.

Tibetans, nuns and monks in the vanguard, also demonstrate at other times, get arrested, tortured and are often never seen again. Monks and nuns arrested for singing prohibited Tibetan songs undergo torture, rape, food deprivation and solitary confinement and are expelled from their communities if released. Nuns have their sentences doubled for singing patriotic songs. One young nun died in prison from maltreatment and her body was cremated to destroy the evidence.

During 1993 when I first travelled in Tibet, the number of prisoners in Lhasa alone was over 400, more than 30 per cent above 1992 figures. Approximately half of them were nuns and monks. Their non-violent demonstrations usually last for only a few minutes before arrests take place. Lhasa alone has six large prisons. One Tibetan is serving fourteen years in Drapchi prison for replying to an Italian tourist who discussed Tibetan independence. The conversation was video-taped and its screening became 'evidence' for the Chinese court. Meant as a plug for Tibet, it destroyed one man's freedom and life.

One 1994 Australian fact-finding mission to China presented Beijing officials with a list of 222 political prisoners, Chinese and Tibetan, including fourteen nuns from Garu nunnery near Lhasa — one of them only fifteen years old at the time — and requested their release. The Garu nuns are still incarcerated and two have died from their treatment.

Asia Watch reported that 80 per cent of the 250 cases of political arrest or trial documented in 1993 alone took place in Tibet. By 1999 it was estimated that Tibet held 1024 political prisoners — 538 are known by name and place of origin — despite two decades of 'quiet diplomacy' and human rights delegations from other governments and the United Nations. China denies it holds political prisoners in Tibet because, under Chinese law, dissenters are guilty of crimes against the nation and thus law-breakers. It denies the existence of torture despite overwhelming evidence to the contrary, because its constitution does not allow it. Words are scrubbed clean of all meaning by totalitarian regimes.

CHINA'S IMPACT ON TIBET'S ENVIRONMENT SINCE 1950

The Yamdrok Tso hydro-electric scheme was so badly built that the official opening by Vice-Premier Wu Bangguo in 1996 was a non-event. The lake's water level is said to have dropped considerably. Tibetans in Lhasa claim the Chinese have taken precious objects from the lake that had been placed there as religious offerings.

The appropriation of the great Tibetan plateau — once the habitat of free nomads — for China's principal nuclear test sites and nuclear waste disposal carries incalculable consequences. Air, soils and waterways are being polluted. Chinese offers to accept other countries' nuclear waste for disposal in Tibet, at a price, increases the danger that major rivers flowing from the plateau will become poisoned and affect half the world's population in ways that cannot yet be determined.

Tibetan animals and birds have been hunted, in many cases to extinction, while rivers have been fished out and polluted. Tibet's abundant wildlife has been brought to the brink of extinction in less than fifty years. The PLA had licence to shoot for food and for sale to China, bringing down wild yak, ass, antelopes, snow leopards, Asian black bear, grey wolf, argali sheep, other high-altitude mammals and all birds. Thirty species of Tibetan wildlife are now listed as endangered.

China has clear-felled so much of Tibet's ancient forests that floods have devastated large areas of China and South-East Asia. Tibet's spruce, cypress and oak forests covered approximately 220 000 square kilometres. Between 1950 and 1990 Chinese loggers clear-felled over 40 per cent, an estimated 130 000 square kilometres worth US$54 billion. Twenty-five per cent of Tibet's flora is unique to Tibet. Apart from habitat destruction for endangered wildlife and destruction of thousands of endemic plant species never recorded let alone researched, the felling of Tibet's forests is causing landslides, soil erosion, destruction of soil fertility and annual floods.

The South-East Asian monsoon cycle has been altered by the massive deforestation of Tibet, bringing heavy rains in Nepal and Bangladesh as well as Tibet, causing annual devastating landslides, erosion and floods. Flash floods along Vietnam's Mekong worsen every year. The rivers now carry unusual amounts of silt and periodically flood their banks, causing widespread destruction to soils, vegetation, human and animal habitat in downstream China, Vietnam, Laos, Cambodia, Nepal, Bangladesh and India. Goldmining along Yangtze tributaries in eastern Tibet adds to silting and destruction of river life.

Weather patterns affecting other parts of the globe are expected to be affected by the changes on the Tibetan plateau, just as the decimation of Amazonian rainforests set tropical and Southern Hemisphere weather patterns into a spin of disastrous droughts and torrential downpours. Tibet's weather patterns have started to do the same. Governments of affected countries will have to address the causes and when they do so, they will realise that environmental destruction and the oppression of the Tibetan people are two profiles of the same monster. Although emphasis on human rights in Tibet must take top billing, Tibet's environmental destruction is so enormous that the effects are bound to be felt globally in the next decade and draw world governments' attention to the Land of Snows. The Chinese do not care for Tibet's environment except to exploit it.

Asia's seven largest river systems originate on the Tibetan plateau: the Yellow River, Yangtze, Mekong, Salween, Sutlej, Indus and Tsangpo-Brahmaputra. Almost half the world population — over two billion people — depend on these rivers for water, irrigation, fish and other river products. In other words, they depend on these rivers for their life.

China is running out of water, soil and trees, three of life's essentials. A fourth, unpolluted air, has been lost already, as anyone who has travelled in China knows. Tibet still has all four. The soil is increasingly being occupied by dispossessed Chinese peasants. It has been said there was no record of oil in Tibet as there was in Kuwait, hence no one came to rescue Tibet. But there probably is oil in Tibet, as there is everything else: uranium, gold, silver, copper and many other minerals. That is why China is in Xizang, the Western Treasure House, as they call Tibet.

WORLD GOVERNMENTS' EFFORTS FOR TIBET

The March 1994 New Delhi Statement on Tibetan Freedom, compiled by a convention of world parliamentarians, recognised Tibet as 'a separate independent and sovereign nation prior to its invasion and subsequent occupation by the People's Republic of China'. On 6 June 1994 a group of Australian senators moved a motion to accept the New Delhi Statement on Tibetan Freedom as a resolution. The House of Representatives declined. Australian governments agree with Beijing that Tibet is an inalienable part of the Chinese Motherland. If asked why, they cannot explain on what grounds.

The present Australian government has conducted formal annual dialogues on human rights with China since 1997, during which period the human rights violations in Tibet have escalated.

In 1993 President Clinton's decision to extend China's Most Favoured Nation trade position — heavily lobbied by the Australian government — gave the green light to China to continue as usual with its own version of human rights in Tibet, in other so-called minorities' areas and in China proper. In the same year a 'fact-finding mission' of six Australian parliamentarians under the leadership of National Party leader, now also deputy prime minister, Tim Fischer visited Tibet. On his return Mr Fischer reported that the streets of Lhasa were quiet! The careless words of a person who knows not what it means to be ruled by fear and the gun. When the Clinton decision was announced, Mr Fischer's comment was that it would directly benefit Australia's wool trade. When I wrote to Mr Fischer asking where he had been in Tibet, he passed on my letter to another member of his party for reply. A reply never came, nor was an official report issued. It is safe to assume he had no clue where he was, apart from having a headache in Lhasa.

Taxpayers everywhere are justified in demanding that politicians visiting Tibet to assess the human rights situation are not on a disguised trade mission but bring their own translators, stay longer, travel more widely, make independent observations, know where they have been, and give full reports on their return. However, China does not allow politicians or journalists to travel privately in Tibet. One American senator who did is now *persona non grata* on the growing list of people who can no longer obtain Chinese visas. Politicians are seldom as well informed on Tibet as interested lay persons. Only Mary Robinson, United Nations Commissioner for Human Rights, was informed, sensitive and critical enough to assess adequately the little she could see.

Australian taxpayers' money flows to Tibet via the Australian government's aid agency. Officially described as poverty alleviation projects, on close inspection they carry little benefit for Tibetans, but much for Chinese settlers in Tibet. An Australian government project in Amdo aims at turning Tibetans whose land has been appropriated into meat producers for Amdo's large Chinese population. It ignores the fact that breeding animals purely for slaughter and intensive animal production in feedlots (as in Shigatse) violates Tibetan religious sensibilities. Australian consultants and Chinese officials were the first beneficiaries from the Australian grant, Chinese middlemen profited next, and Tibetan meat producers had to accept prices as offered. Tibetans were not consulted, since the Australian government recognises Chinese rule over Tibet. The big freeze of 1996 killed off most livestock and scores of nomadic herders in Amdo.

STORIES OF REFUGEES
Although Tibet under the Dalai Lamas was closed to foreigners, borders were open for border people and for Tibetans traders to travel to China, Mongolia,

India, Nepal, Sikkim, Bhutan and other traditional trading partners. For centuries Tibetans travelled, selling Tibetan products and returning with manufactured goods. All that time, desperate 'serfs' could have taken their chances to flee via trade routes or lesser used passes and opt for freedom in Tibetan areas across the border. But flight never seemed to have occurred to them until the Chinese occupied their country and their Dalai Lama fled.

Tibetan traders married into border tribes and settled, but there never was an exodus from oppression until 1959 when the Dalai Lama fled and the Chinese People's Liberation Army swarmed all over Tibet with intent to have total control. Then these world-strange Tibetans, most of whom had never left their villages and towns, packed a bundle and the kids, left homes and monasteries, to trek through snow and ice across the southern borders to the tune of one hundred thousand, hunted by Chinese troops and military planes. Ever since there has been a decisive trickle of hundreds annually, despite armed border guards shooting on sight, prisons where torture and rape take place, and robbery, rape and beatings on the Nepali side. But in the 1990s refugee numbers have risen to 5000 annually. Apologists for China should ask themselves what causes this phenomenon and what prevented Tibetans from fleeing their 'serfdom' before 1950 when the borders were not guarded. Tibet's borders are now more hermetically closed than ever for 'autonomous' Tibetans.

Extraordinary evidence of unbearable living conditions in Tibet comes from the yearly increasing flow of refugees entering Nepal and India. Villagers swamped by a 200 per cent increase of Chinese settlers taking over their lands risk everything to cross the mountains in midwinter when patrols are few. Too many lose hands, feet or legs to frostbite, or freeze to death. In 1994 between 150 and 250 refugees crossed the mountains every month. Some 500 children cross annually. Many escapees are nuns and monks. The consequent strain on Tibetan refugee settlements means that thousands of refugees continue to half-starve in freedom and succumb to tuberculosis and other low-altitude illnesses.

The Tibetan Children's Village in Dharamsala has tripled its population in the last few years, as parents in Tibet send and smuggle their children over the border so they can receive a Tibetan education and grow up free. The Dharamsala Transit School and Tibetan government in exile do not have the resources to deliver even basic living conditions and must rely on outside help to take in the never-ending flow. About 200 Tibetans live permanently in Australia. Refugees who marry Australians cannot bring a child from a previous relationship to Australia if the child has no identification papers, which few refugees can produce. Thus already diminished families are broken up again.

The Independent of 12 February 1994 tells of an amazing Lhasa boy named Tenzin, who at age ten decided with some school friends to cycle to freedom.

But near Shigatse they gave themselves away by asking directions to the Nepalese border. They were caught by police and returned to Lhasa. Tenzin tried several more times, gaining a reputation as a troublemaker. He and a number of his friends were arrested at gunpoint outside the Potala for singing a patriotic song. After his release, Tenzin began to walk south and crossed the border twenty-five days later.

On 20 September 1994, International World Peace Day, I attended the wiping out of a sand painting of the Yamanthaka mandala in the South Australian Museum. For three weeks four refugee Gyuoto monks — who had given two sacred chant concerts earlier that year — painstakingly assembled millions of coloured grains of sand into this amazing work of art. Yamanthaka is an archetypal deity and the ferocious form of the *bodhisattva* Manjusri. Whereas Manjusri's sword cuts ignorance to reveal 'wisdom knowledge', Yamanthaka stands for the wisdom of ultimate reality triumphing over evils causing suffering and death. Hence, the Yamanthaka sand mandala ritual invites Yamanthaka to inhabit the mandala, thus bringing wisdom to the place where the ritual is performed. Additional rituals with chanting and prayers ensure that this wisdom shines out from that place to the region and to the world. A Yamanthaka sand mandala seeks peace for the world.

The museum advertised the event in the normal manner, installed the monks in the only part of the Pacific Hall not taken up by glass artefact cases, and was clearly unprepared for the public response that followed. As the monks started their day at opening time with half an hour's meditation, people began to come in ever larger numbers to join in, until in the third week 300 people squatted down at 10 am. A Celebration of Completion was hastily organised for the Saturday, for which the Whale Hall was appropriately made available. But nothing prepared the museum staff for the turn-out on World Peace Day, when the wiping-out ceremony was to be held.

When I arrived at noon I could just squeeze in the door. The Pacific Hall was packed to the rafters. People had climbed carefully onto the museum's plastic chairs, children sat in rows on the floor. Most of the crowd of a thousand or more could not see the mandala at all, but appeared to want to be there just the same. Hundreds of people left because they simply could not enter. There were white-haired people and students, mothers with babes, businessmen, shoppers. One striped-shirted businessman stood on tiptoes during the entire ceremony, wearing prayer beads around his left wrist.

All this was remarkable enough on an ordinary working day. But when the small procession carrying the urn emerged from the museum's doors and marched towards the River Torrens for the dispersal of the sacred sands, the entire crowd followed the four monks in bright yellow cockscomb hats and maroon robes carrying the urn wrapped in brocade, stopping traffic on two main roads as they crossed.

I realised then that China can try what it will, but it can never undermine the deep interest in Tibetan culture and religion that is growing throughout the world. We have yet to see four Chinese communists attract capacity crowds on World Peace Day and stop the traffic. They may be able to commandeer crowds in China when the regime decrees it, but it is another matter to make people listen in the free world. Jiang Zhemin will never attract the crowds that listen so attentively to the Dalai Lama everywhere. These are facts of life.

CHINA'S CONTINUING EXPANSIONISM

China's claim on Tibet is based on its bizarre view of its own and Asian history, not shared by other peoples of that continent. The China of Beijing and some of the Han people hold to a vision of a great 'Motherland' that gathers all neighbouring peoples to the Han bosom, under Han rule. It is interesting that a country now controlling one-fifth of the world population with an almost totally male-dominated regime speaks of China as 'the Motherland'.

Throughout their history the Chinese have made beguiling use of language to portray and advance the preferred view, as Mao did with his numerous slogans that stirred millions to destroy whatever he dictated as useless, from people to sparrows and temples. Thus the Plum Blossom View of Chinese History often pretends a situation that is the direct opposite of the reality. It portrays PLA soldiers carrying flowers, singing revolutionary songs, helping peasants bring in the harvest, while simultaneously sections of the PLA shoot into crowds of young Chinese or beat up minority populations who request a dialogue with the government. The plum blossom art of old China was itself a deceit, as only the rich enjoyed the aesthetics of plum blossom in their courtyards. The peasants preferred plums for eating, drying and pickling.

Beijing spends an inordinate amount of time trying to impose its own views of history on other governments. When the Dalai Lama travels, host countries are badgered by Chinese communications objecting to his passage or reception. The Chinese government also actively tries to undermine overseas organisations concerned with Tibet. *A Handbook of Tibetan Culture* lists over 600 organisations in fifty-three countries whose main reason for existence is Tibetan culture and religion, not counting all the Tibet support groups and human rights organisations with Tibet on their agenda. China made efforts to impede the release of Martin Scorcese's film *Kundun,* about the life of the Dalai Lama, by intimidating the Disney Corporation and condemns any film about Tibet that does not fit the Chinese view. This Plum Blossom View of History, in which the Han and fifty-six minority peoples are happily united under the Chinese flag, is what Beijing serves up to a world that should by now know better.

Chinese peasants in China itself are still profoundly poor. Many go to the cities to sell craft, produce or labour to earn money. Increasingly they stay on without receiving city registration, thus being deprived of educational and health services for themselves and dependants. Because of this drain to the cities, farm production is declining, putting future food supplies in jeopardy. No wonder the Chinese government encourages peasants to take up farming in Tibet's high altitudes to relieve China's lowland cities and feed the PLA in Tibet, thus saving imports from China.

These migrants know no better than that Tibet is part of China and few would be aware that this is disputed beyond China's borders. The Chinese have always migrated to live among people vastly different from themselves — in Mongolia, Manchuria, Kazakstan, East Turkestan. A great number of young families simply want to transfer from a place where life is very hard to a place where it may be marginally to much better. Most of them will adapt to conditions even harsher than at home in the hope of making good eventually. Unwittingly they contribute to the Tibetan genocide.

Tibet is presently the last fertile area of size and significance to which the Han Chinese can migrate. China's birthrate is still not at zero level and subsequent governments will need to go on looking for territory to settle surplus people. The question is, where will Chinese peasants move after Tibet's valleys are filled up? Demographers forecast that within three decades 50 per cent of Chinese will live in cities. Considering the present size of those cities and problems in food production, who will feed the billions of city dwellers?

China's 'historical claims' go as far south as Sumatra in Indonesia, and parts of Kazakstan appear as part of China in Chinese geography books. Although Australia and New Zealand are about the only countries in the region on which China does not have a 'historical claim', Australia's existence is intertwined with Asia. But our governments have acted as if this continent not only lies *in* Asia, but *in* China. From the way they embrace the Chinese regime they seem to proceed from a European notion that communism has collapsed globally, even though communist China rules more than one-fifth of the world population with an iron fist. Chinese claims to the Spratley Islands, where it has placed a military installation to terrorise surrounding countries, should concern Australia profoundly.

So should China's vote-buying efforts around the Pacific Islands. China now has diplomatic relations with eleven South Pacific nations. The latest is the Kingdom of Tonga, which for twenty-five years accepted largesse from Taiwan. But after the king and his daughter were banqueted in Beijing, Tonga's foreign minister signed a joint communique in October 1998 recognising the government of the People's Republic of China as 'the sole legal government representing the whole of China and that Taiwan is an inalienable part of the Chinese Territory'. The Tongans hope to get better access to the United Nations with China's help and do a satellite deal with Beijing. They have already been presented with a bronze statue of their king, made by the sculptor who made Mao Zedong's statues. Now that the king has had his views corrected, China expects support from Tonga when next it claims Taiwan for the motherland. The way things are going that can be achieved simply through a vote in the United Nations, once China has bought enough small new friends with gifts of bronze statues.

In the twenty-first century Australia is bound to be drawn increasingly into the Chinese sphere of influence, with England, the United States and Europe providing a receding cultural background. This has less to do with preference than with population volume in Australia versus China. Simultaneously, China will be drawn into expanding global connections for its own survival. Hopes of expanding orderly free enterprise in China have been thwarted by the greatest floods this century in 1998, destroying housing, infrastructure and harvests in central China. The magnitude of these floods was due to the rape of eastern Tibet's forests in the Yangtze basin. Tibet's revenge, mounting every year's rainy season, has finally reached the industrial heartland of China.

Nevertheless, unless there is a change to democracy in China, Beijing will increasingly seek to dictate not only commerce in Asia/Pacific countries, but influence the region culturally, socially and religiously, criticise what company we keep and whether we can receive the Dalai Lama or meet the Taiwanese president. To kowtow already at the beginning of this Chinese era in Asia/Pacifica is to leave oneself without room to retreat.

Australian politicians, traders and citizens ought to choose now the principles by which they want to live, trade and associate with China. Fair play, fair go, freedom of speech, human rights and democracy for everybody are principles Australians take for granted and they think they know what they mean by them. If they want to keep them, it would be prudent to explain these principles to China whenever issues arise that violate them, and withdraw even from possibly lucrative projects when China violates them. That means taking notice of Tibet.

In the 1960s I used to dismiss people who feared the Chinese would come south. Why would the Chinese want to leave their new socialist society and thousands of years of heritage? But Tibet shows what is left of socialism and heritage under Chinese communism. For a view of one possible future for the region, Australians needs to look closely at Tibet under Chinese domination. If that does not open eyes and minds, serfdom in one disguise or another is bound to come to 'the lucky country' and its neighbours.

In the words of North Vietnamese political activist Ha Si Phu (the pen name of Nguyen Xuan Tu): 'Marxism–Leninism is just feudalism in disguise. It is dragging down the progress of society and is being used to cover up other negative intentions'. He is a prisoner-of-conscience for his essay 'Farewell to Ideology'.

While China opens up periodically, Tibet's straitjacket is tightened to the point of snuffing out the Tibetan people, their culture and religion. Harsh officials, ruling autonomously in outposts snowbound for half the year, can purposely misconstrue and repackage their actions in approved rhetoric to show they are meticulously following official policy. Beijing meanwhile trots out slogans such as 'the practice of religion is free as long as it is within the law and does not harm the motherland', giving enormous elasticity to local potentates to control, oppress, punish, arrest, torture, maim and kill.

Other governments have this century played blind monkey with Hitler, Lenin, Stalin, Mao, Pol Pot and their successors. Revelations of Hitler's atrocities have been revealed, Lenin's and Stalin's are in the process of being documented. Massacres are uncovered in many countries, but Mao & Co.'s deeds are still largely unrevealed. While the world community remains reluctant to determine pertinent rules for human rights, we are all at risk of genocide and persecution.

If China should democratise and allow more Chinese citizens passports, the international community can expect to meet new travellers who have been kept gagged, misinformed or uninformed, cut off from international discussion and from their own history and culture pre-1949. For half a century people in China were taught strenuously and officially, at school and at work, to destroy anything the communist government does not approve of, to distrust foreigners and spy and report on their own parents and children for breaches of behaviour or uttering criticism.

China is a militarised society where people who criticise the regime are exterminated or imprisoned. There are now so many stories of life inside China that we can no longer think the Chinese are just coming out of a difficult past, waiting to join hands with people of other nations to make a better world together. That mistake has been made before. Chinese regimes have all acted imperially, aspiring to expand, no matter under what label, and have a dreadful record of cruelties and injustices to their own people and their neighbours. Even though communism may have been an improvement for the surviving masses on the period of warlords and foreign exploitation, it has not prepared them for relationships in a fast-changing world. Distrust of foreigners is still endemic and where foreigners make friends in China there is often a desire in the Chinese partners to shake off communist restrictions.

Some tourists only meet friendly people. But curiosity followed by overt friendliness to the odd bicycling tourist is not a good thermometer for testing the atmosphere for living together. It is to be expected that initially only money speaks a useful language in dealings with Chinese people at large. One cannot expect they will take an interest in human rights except their own or have a desire to help the world's underprivileged, or bring a sense of history repeating itself to the international playing field. Only a small number of surviving intellectuals, dissidents and brave political activists, as well as escaped so-called minority peoples, will, when the time comes, be happy to shake off decades of indoctrination with comparative ease. The masses may take a generation to forget their communist reflexes. Refugees from other communist countries have expressed strong racial prejudices. The Chinese have not been exposed to a multicultural world. They have been encouraged to believe that the Han people are superior and their record of treating 'minorities' is atrocious. Governments that cannot be challenged democratically are always right and produce citizens in their own image.

There are comparisons to be made between the present state of welfare of all indigenous peoples who are ruled by governments not of their own making or choosing. The Tibetans have a recognised leader in exile, refugees all over the globe, and a distinctive culture that has adapted itself to absorb foreigners who want to study their culture and religion, thereby re-establishing itself wherever it is allowed to settle.

The confounding position many governments are in today, is that they rule countries conquered 100 to 1000 years ago, resulting in the undermining of the indigenous people, and their language, and culture, through massive immigration. Some encourage the integration of elements of the conquered culture into mainstream society to achieve an impression of continuity, but their own history moves these democratically elected governments to condone the fact that China marched illegally into Tibet and rules it by the power of the gun.

Many people had hoped a worldwide cut-off point for imperialist and colonialist conquest could have been set, if not immediately after World War II, then in the 1960s or 1970s, when global awareness of human rights made some advances. Instead, conquering nations have spread a web of complicity across the lands of indigenous peoples, in order not to have their own conquests challenged. No matter how long ago conquests took place, governments find it difficult to apologise.

China's problems with Tibet, if it holds on to it, will compound as the years pass, just as they compounded in the societies of other conquering nations, who either find themselves increasingly powerless and impoverished (e.g. Spain and Britain), or are seen as dishonest brokers in the modern climate of human rights, fair trade, education for all and similar sound policies. Australia and the United States fall in the second category.

What is needed at the start of the new millennium is a deep and comprehensive study of the patterns of complicity that exist between China, the United States, Canada Australia, New Zealand, the old invader Britain, and all other countries no matter how large or small who have in the last thousand years conquered, 'liberated', incorporated, annexed or otherwise taken it upon themselves to rule and lay down the law for indigenous peoples, while taking their lands and calling these their own. An annual world conference between interest groups and governments needs to sort out the last millennium's mistakes as the next one gets under way. Since an Australian government admitted that Australia was not *terra nullius*, not for their ancestors to take and regard as their own, what stops them recognising that other indigenous peoples have been conquered against their will?

The general belief holds that trade and economic advantage prevent governments from speaking and acting justly. But global trade will continue between all manner of countries, no matter what policies their governments adhere to, because traditionally even enemies have traded with each other. Trade has nothing to do with friendship, although the two do co-exist. The case of China has proven that all countries want to trade with human rights abusers. But all countries also want to trade with the suppressed as soon as they have something to trade. Trade is in people's blood and nothing will stop countries trading. If China can do what it likes and still trade with all countries, than surely all governments can say what they like about China without losing trade. Where would China be if it stopped trading when governments become honest and declare that China rules Tibet by conquest? If China stopped trading, as it sometimes threatens to do, it would soon descend into pre-1970s conditions, when more people died of starvation and violence in China than in any one place on the globe this century. China needs trade to survive as it needs clean air.

Trade has always been a driving force of imperialism, a reason for conquest, an excuse for invasions (as in Britain's 1904 invasion of Tibet). A peaceful world needs trade, but not at that cost. Yet, in a world increasingly hesitant to wage war because of the supremacy of modern destructive weaponry, trade is again used as an excuse for complicity about conquests.

Is there any difference between China's invasion of Tibet to incorporate it into the great Motherland, and Germany's invasion of my country of birth in the name of a greater German *Reich*? I used to believe the Allies liberated Holland from the Nazi yoke to save us from starvation and death, genocide and exploitation. But Tibet has taught me otherwise, because the circumstances are identical and yet no country, no allied forces, not even a concert of official protests came overtly to Tibet's rescue. I realise now that my home country and others were liberated because Germany's occupancy of Europe did not suit the Allies. Had they not found it necessary for their own advantage to come to our rescue, the bones of many more millions would have been added to those claimed by the Holocaust.

Ironically, it was Germany that bit the bullet and incurred China's wrath by issuing a statement on human rights in Tibet in 1996. It has been Germany that first officially recognised that the Tibetan Holocaust was continuing under the eyes of a trade-hungry world. No country can now say they didn't know the facts. The facts have been recorded for decades by reputable global agencies. The facts demand that the world community speaks out. When history is ignored, history will repeat, not necessarily confining itself to the same place.

Politicians inherit the mantle of complicity the moment they take office. Few politicians dare shake off that mantle and speak out about injustices. Instead they acquire the language of justification. Their words weave the pattern of complicity by the conquistadors into an ever tighter web. The public, indigenous and non-indigenous, has to come to grips with and understand complicity's ramifications in order to struggle for reparation for ordinary people, indigenous and non-indigenous. If free citizens adopt the pattern of complicity offered by the conquistadors, they will eventually suffer as suppressed indigenous peoples do. The conquest of Tibet by China occurred with full complicity of the big powers, who stood by and did nothing in their governments or in the United Nations. Only Equador put Tibet on the UN agenda.

The conquest of Tibet will fester in the world's future, as have other conquests, fouling up all the best-laid plans for human welfare and fair trade. The world community has to get to the bottom of the reasons for conquest, for ultimately it is everyone's problem. If this is not done, consequences spawned by conquests will keep on compounding, leaving no space for normal human existence.

HOPES FOR THE FUTURE

The Dalai Lama has always advocated a non-violent approach and tried for decades to meet Chinese leaders at the negotiation table. Nudgings by overseas leaders to the Beijing government have fallen on deaf ears. There has been no progress at all in forty years. Trying to negotiate with Beijing is like throwing margarine at steel, to paraphrase Francis Younghusband.

Hatred can never be overcome by hatred. Hatred can only be overcome by love. So wrote my grandfather in my poesie album during World War II. He was quoting the Buddha. He wrote it after an overwhelming military power had occupied Holland and half a dozen other countries to create a great

'Fatherland', just as by the end of that same decade another overwhelming military power on the eastern end of the great Asian–European landmass, occupied a number of smaller neighbours in pursuit of a greater 'Motherland'. If such patterns are to stop occurring, governments must become strong and decisive about human rights.

One of the countries that stands to benefit most from an independent Tibet is India. Having fought a war with China in 1962, India's military are now stationed, at great expense, along their long northern border. India bore the cost of resettling the influx of refugees in 1959, although some became self-sufficient, overseas non-government aid streamed in and Dharamsala as a Tibetan town is an economic asset. But traditional border trade between Tibetans and Himalayan Indians came to a halt after the Chinese takeover and it would revive these border people's economy if the trade could be resumed.

Other Himalayan countries that stand to gain from a re-opening of the borders are Nepal, Sikkim and Bhutan. Nepal treats Tibetan refugees with contempt, although they have increased tourism and initiated carpet exports, two of Nepal's main hard currency earners. A free Tibet would alleviate Nepal's population problem, as most Tibetans would return home. Yet Nepal supports China in everything it demands, including vilification of the Dalai Lama. The logic is hard to follow, although both Nepal and India have displayed a fear of China that at times seems greater than their sense of self-interest.

Remembering growing up in a country under foreign oppression, with guns in the streets and starvation a natural cause of death, I keep sharing the suffering of Tibetans in Tibet. Through writing these journeys, Tibet resurrects itself in its many aspects outside the Land of Snows, as it does through every person who has come in contact with its down-to-earth magic.

There are many Tibets. There may be as many Tibets as there are people with ties to Tibet. If Tibet were declared a World Heritage Spiritual Sanctuary and Wilderness Area, all these Tibets could be preserved for all humanity. That would preserve Tibet for the Tibetans and for those Chinese who acknowledge its properties as a world heritage. It would do China no end of good. China would reap goodwill from peoples and nations around the world, for there are few who actively support its present rule over Tibet.

It would become possible to restore Tibet's cultural heritage with aid from many willing agencies and develop infrastructure for spiritual tourism. If that term sounds too New Age for some, we ought to ask ourselves what it is we do when visiting medieval churches, Uluru and Kakadu, as well as the temples and monasteries of Tibet. The whole world needs to preserve the few spiritual places still extant, especially such functioning — or recently functioning — places of religious practice as Tibet's monastic institutions. China's troubles in Tibet would dissipate if they went down this road instead of fighting the uphill battle to turn Tibet into a Chinese province, which it will never be.

Whosoever picks up a small part of that task and runs with it, helps to reconstruct the spirit of Tibet. Tens of thousands of non-Tibetans are now engaged in refugee aid, restoration, study, research, translation of ancient Tibetan texts and personal quests such as writing books. The repository of Tibet's spirit now lies in the world at large, amidst more than 100 000 refugees and as many Tibet supporters, who together accommodate Tibet's diaspora until the day dawns when Tibet shall be free again and becomes a world Zone of Peace by international agreement. For it is inconceivable that China's occupation of Tibet can last.

At a Tibetan ceremony in Australia a Tibetan speaker said: 'The Chinese people deserve to be happy and so do we'. A simple plea and an expression of peace from the heart of Tibetan culture. And in Dharamsala a Tibetan trader says: 'We are all sitting on our suitcases here. There will be a new, better Tibet'.

Glossary

ama mother; any elderly woman.

amban representative of the Chinese emperor.

ani nun.

apso Tibetan breed of small dog.

arhat (Sanskrit) one who has attained truth and will not return to this life after death.

artemisia fragrant plant of the wormwood family.

ashram (Sanskrit) a centre for meditation and religious contemplation, usually residential.

bardo intermediate state between death and rebirth.

bodhi (Sanskrit) wisdom.

bodhisattva an enlightened being who refuses to go into Nirvana until the last blade of grass has reached enlightenment. Also, reincarnating life after life for the benefit of all sentient beings.

Bön Tibet's religion before Buddhism arrived in the seventh century AD. *Bön* survives to this day.

bunkhur pre-harvest ceremony to ask the blessings of the gods.

chai (Hindi) Indian spicy tea with milk and sugar.

chang barley beer.

chörten Tibetan for stupa.

chu river.

chuba Tibetan-style woman's dress or man's coat.

chugum cubes of dried yak cheese, carried on a string.

CITS Chinese International Tourist Service.

congee (Chinese) Chinese rice gruel with meat, fish, poultry or other meat, garnished with spring onions and peanuts.

dahl Indian/Nepalese curried lentil dish.

dakini female deity representing highest level of reality.

dekye happiness.

Dhammapada, the The Buddha's collected sayings as used in southern or Theravada Buddhism.

dharma the teachings of the Buddha. Often the teachings of Buddhist teachers are also called *dharma*.

dop dop police monks armed with clubs who keep order at monastic events.

dorje ritual thunderbolt.

dri female yak. See also *nak*.

drogpa nomadic pastoralist.

drumying Tibetan string instrument.

dzo female cross between yak and cow.

dzomo male cross between yak and cow.

dzong fort-like structure, usually on a high outcrop. Formerly home of the *dzongpo* or regional governor, his soldiers and administration. Former homes of ancient rulers.

dzongpo regional governor or administrator.

Gadan namchoi commemoration of Tsongkhapa's death.

Ganden government, as by the Dalai Lamas.

Gelukpa Tsongkhapa's reformed sect of Tibetan Buddhism, also known as the Yellow Hats, dating from the fifteenth century.

geshe highest degree in Tibetan monastic universities, equivalent to a PhD or Doctorate of Divinity or Philosophy.

gompa assembly hall in a monastery where reciting and meditation take place.

guru Indian word used in Tibet for Guru Padmasambhava and for personal teachers.

Kalachakra (Sanskrit) Wheel of Time, a *tantra* introduced into Tibet in 1027, transmitted by the kings of the mythical country of Shambhala.

kalon first minister or president of the government.

kalung an 'authorisation' to teach a religious book after hearing it read by a monastic teacher.

Kanjur literally, 'translation of the Buddha's words', the sacred scriptures of Tibetan Buddhism in 108 volumes.

karma world view of sentient beings weaving their thoughts and actions into a web of consequences that in turn have to be negated, i.e. one reaps as one sows. Karma determines one's rebirths and continues beyond death until, by skilful living, no further karma is created.

kashag the cabinet of Tibet's government.

kata white silk or gauze scarf accompanying greetings, gifts and farewells on all occasions.

khamtshan monastic college within a monastery for monks from a certain district.

khang measure of land, taking 400 pounds of seed grain to plant.

kyang wild Tibetan asses.

kora circumambulation of sacred buildings and structures.

la mountain pass.

lakhang a temple housing image(s) of a deity or deities.

laksh (Hindi) 100 000 rupees.

Lam Rim teaching by Tsongkhapa of the graduated path to enlightenment.

Lha gyalo! a shout uttered when crossing a high pass: May the gods be victorious.

lingka, also *ling* garden or park. Metaphorical meaning: island or continent.

lingkhor the outermost circum-ambulation of a sacred place, usually one of three.

lung reading of the entire *Kanjur* and *Tanjur* by a monastic teacher.

mala string of 108 prayer beads, often with counterbeads for mantras.

mandala symbolic geometric representation of the Buddhist universe with a supreme deity at its centre.

mani jewel, i.e. jewel in the lotus. A stone inscribed with the mantra OM MANI PADME HUM (also OM MANI PEMI HUNG): mani stone. Mantra as prayer: doing 10 000 manis.

mantra sacred prayer formula.

momo Tibetan meat and dough dumpling.

monlam great prayer festival at Tibetan New Year, usually in February.

naga underwater or sky deity.

nak female yak. Also see *dri*.

namtar life stories of sages or revered teachers, biographies of renowned monks, *dakinis*, yogis, *siddhis*, etc.

ngakpa Tibetan wandering yogins and yoginis, often of the Bön religion.

nhamba woollen cloth of the Gyantse valley.

Nyingmapa 'Ancient Ones', oldest and unreformed Buddhist order in Tibet known as the Red Hats.

OM MANI PADME HUM 'Hail the Jewel in the Lotus', Tibet's most universally recited mantra. Also OM MANI PEMI HUNG.

Panchen title for a guru who is a great scholar.

PAP People's Armed Police.

pema twigs used in building construction.

PLA People's Liberation Army.

pö cha Tibetan butter tea with salt. *Pö* = Tibet, *cha* = tea.

puja offering and worship.

radong long brass horns blown from monastery roofs.

rimpoche a high and learned lama.

Sakyapa major southern sect of Tibetan Buddhism dating from the eleventh century.

samgbum auspicious smoke from juniper branches burnt at religious occasions.

sangha the Buddhist monastic community.

shabrack (Eng.) a saddle cloth.

shahtoosh fine wool of Tibetan antelope.

shape government minister.

shikar (Indian) hunting.

sho a game of chance played with dice on a leather pad.

shramanas see *siddhi*.

siddhas an Indian word for ancient Buddhist wandering mendicants who achieved enlightenment through experience. Also known as *sramanas*.

siddhi gaining the goal, or perfection.

stupa Buddhist memorial monument containing remains and/or relics of a great Buddhist teacher.

sutra (Sanskrit) literally thread. Discourses of the Buddha.

swastika (Sanskrit) happiness, wellbeing. See also *wan tze*.

Tanjur commentaries on the *Kanjur*.

tantra, tantric (Sanskrit) weft, context, continuum or system. In Tibetan Buddhism it is the advanced Vajrayana system of meditation.

TAR Tibet Autonomous Region.

Tara the most important female deity of compassion. Also Dolma.

tashi delek a New Year wish, but also a greeting between friends.

thangka religious painting, usually with central deity, on cloth, with red, yellow and blue brocade borders, sloping inwards from bottom to top like Tibetan buildings. Wooden dowels top and bottom.

tofu (Chinese, also *dofu, daufu*) bean curd made from soya beans.

tom street market.

torma votive offering of dough and butter, usually painted red.

tsampa roasted barley flour, Tibet's staple food when mixed with butter tea.

tsamzing (Chinese) self-confession of crimes against the Communist Party or state, after interrogation by the people.

tsangpo river.

tudeche thank you.

ulag system by which villagers provide lodging and transport (fresh animals) for one day's journey to travelling officials, as a form of taxation.

wan tze Chinese swastika, symbol of long life and eternity, meaning 10 000 characters.

Xinhua China's official and only news agency.

yuan Chinese monetary unit.

zi black and white patterned beads found in Tibetan soil, possibly ancient shells.

Bibliography

Ancient Tibet: Research Materials from the Yeshe De Project (Dharma Publishing, Berkeley) 1986.

Andrugtsang, G.T., *Four Rivers, Six Ranges* (Information and Publicity Office of His Holiness the Dalai Lama, Dharamsala) 1973.

Australia Tibet Council News (Sydney), January/February/March — October/November 1994, December 1994/January 1995.

Avedon, John, *In Exile From the Land of Snows* (Vintage Books, New York) 1986.

Barber, Noel, *From the Land of Lost Content: The Dalai Lama's Fight for Tibet* (Collins, London) 1969.

Barnett, Robert and Shirin Akiner, eds., *Resistance and Reform in Tibet* (Indiana University Press, Bloomington/Indianapolis) 1994.

Bass, Catriona, *Education in Tibet: Policy and Practice Since 1950* (Zed Books/Tibet Information Network, London) 1998.

Bass, Catriona, *Inside the Treasure House: A Time in Tibet* (Abacus/Little, Brown & Co., London) 1992. First published 1990.

Batchelor, Stephen, *The Tibet Guide* (Wisdom Publications, London) 1987. Foreword by the Dalai Lama.

Bechert, Heinz, and Richard Gombrich, eds., *The World of Buddhism* (Thames & Hudson, London) 1991. First published 1984.

Beckwith, Christopher I., *The Tibetan Empire in Central Asia* (Princeton University Press, Princeton, New Jersey) 1987.

Bell, Sir Charles, *The People of Tibet* (Oxford University Press, London) 1968. First published 1928.

Bell, Sir Charles, *The Religion of Tibet* (Oxford University Press, London) 1968. First published 1931.

Bell, Sir Charles, *Tibet Past and Present* (Oxford University Press, London) 1968. First published 1924.

Bellezza, John Vincent, 'Quest for the Four Fountains of Tibet' in *HIMAL Himalayan Magazine* (Kathmandu), January/February 1993.

Berry, Scott, *A Stranger in Tibet: The Adventures of a Zen Monk*. (INDUS/HarperCollins Publishers, New Delhi) 1989. See also Kimura.

Beyer, Stephan, *The Cult of Tara: Magic and Ritual in Tibet* (University of California Press, Berkeley and Los Angeles) 1973.

Booz, Elizabeth B., *Tibet: A Fascinating Look at the Roof of the World, its People and Culture* (Passport Books/National Textbook Co., Chicago) 1986.

Broomhall, A.J., *Strong Man's Prey* (China Inland Mission, London) 1953.

Bull, Geoffrey T., *When Iron Gates Yield* (Hodder & Stoughton, London) 1955.

Cable, Mildred, with Francesca French, *China, Her Life and Her People* (University of London Press, London) 1946.

Cahill, Thomas, *How the Irish Saved Civilization: The Untold Story of Ireland's Heroic Role from the Fall of Rome to the Rise of Medieval Europe.* (Anchor/Bantam Doubleday Dell, New York) 1995.

Cameron, Ian, in association with the Royal Geographic Society, *Mountains of the Gods: The Himalaya and the Mountains of Central Asia* (Century Publishing, London) 1984.

Chan, Victor, *Tibet Handbook: A Pilgrimage Guide* (Moon Publications Inc., Chico, California) 1994.

China South West Airlines Inflight Magazine (Chengdu) July 1993.

China Tibet Tour Map (Mapping Bureau of Tibet Autonomous Region) 1993.

Chögyam Trungpa, *Born in Tibet*, as told to Esmé Cramer Roberts (Penguin, Hammondsworth) 1971. First published 1966.

Clewlow, Carol, and Alan Samagalski, *Hong Kong, Macau and Canton: a Travel Survival Kit* (Lonely Planet Publications, Melbourne) 1986.

Coleman, Graham, ed., with the Orient Foundation as compiler, *A Handbook of Tibetan Culture: A Guide to Tibetan Centres and Resources throughout the World.* (Shambhala, Boston) 1993.

Conze, Edward, *Buddhist Scriptures* (Penguin, Harmondsworth) 1959.

Craig, Mary, *Tears of Blood: A Cry for Tibet* (HarperCollins, London) 1992.

Cronin, Vincent, *The Wise Man From the West: Matteo Ricci and his Mission to China* (Collins, London) 1984.

Dakpa, Rinchen, and B.A. Rooke, *In Haste From Tibet* (Robert Hale, London) 1971.

Dalai Lama, His Holiness the, *My Land and my People* (Weidenfeld and Nicholson, London) 1962.

Dankert, Gabriele, 'Mortality and its Sex Differentials of the Tibetan Population of the Tibetan Autonomous Region of China', in *Tibetan Environment and Development News*, Issue 18, 1995.

Das, Sarat Chandra, *Journey to Lhasa and Central Tibet*, edited by W.W. Rockhill. (Manjusri Publishing House, New Delhi) 1970. First published 1902.

David-Neel, Alexandra, *My Journey to Lhasa* (William Heinemann, London) 1927.

David-Neel, Alexandra and Lama Yongden, *The Superhuman Life of Gesar of Ling* (Shambhala, Boston/London) 1987.

David-Neel, Alexandra, *Tibetan Journey* (Book Faith India, Delhi) 1992.

Diemberger, Hildegard *et al, Feast Of Miracles: The Life and the Tradition of Bödong Chole Namgyal (1375/6-1451* AD*)* [includes Dorje Phagmo's history] (Porong Pema Chöding Editions, Vienna) 1997.

Dorje, Gyurme, *Tibet Handbook With Bhutan* (Trade & Travel Publications Ltd., Bath, England/Passport Books, Chicago) 1996.

Dowman, Keith, *The Power-Places of Central Tibet: The Pilgrim's Guide* (Routledge & Kegan Paul, London and New York) 1988.

Ekvall, Robert B., *Religious Observances in Tibet: Patterns and Function* (University of Chicago Press) 1964.

Ekvall, Robert B., *Tibetan Skylines* (Victor Gollancz, London) 1952.

Encyclopedia of Eastern Philosophy and Religion, eds. Stephan Schuhmacher *et al* (Shambhala, Boston) 1989.

Evans-Wentz, W.Y., *The Tibetan Book of the Dead* (Causeway Books, New York) 1973. First published in 1927.

Fang Xiangshu and Trevor Hay, *East Wind, West Wind* (Penguin Books, Melbourne) 1992.

Fernandez-Armesto, Felipe, *Millennium* (Bantam/Transworld, London) 1995.

Fitzgerald, C.P., *The Southern Expansion of the Chinese People* (Praeger Publishers, New York/Washington) 1972.

Fleming, Peter, *Bayonets to Lhasa*, (Rupert Hart-Davies, London) 1961.

Ford, Robert, *Wind Between the Worlds* (Snow Lion Graphics, Berkeley) 1987.

Frederic, Louise, *Buddhism: Flammarion Iconographic Guides* (BUFLIC/Snow Lion, Ithaca, New York) [not sighted].

Geleg, Lopsang, and Nancy E. Levine, 'Ethnic Variation and Cultures of Tibet' in *White Lotus: An Introduction to Tibetan Culture*, ed. Carole Elchert (Snow Lion Publications, Ithaca, New York) 1990.

Goldstein, Melvyn C., *A History of Modern Tibet, 1913–1951: The Demise of the Lamaist State.* (University of California Press, Berkeley and Los Angeles) 1991. First published 1989.

Goldstein, Melvyn C. And Cynthia M. Beall, *Nomads Of Western Tibet: The Survival of a Way of Life* (University of California Press, Berkeley and Los Angeles) 1990.

Goodman, Michael, *The Last Dalai Lama: A Biography* (Shambhala, Boston) 1986.

Goullart, Peter, *Forgotten Kingdom* (Readers Union/John Murray, London) 1957.

Goullart, Peter, *Princes of the Black Bone* (John Murray, London) 1959.

Govinda, Lama Anagarika, *Buddhist Reflections* (Samuel Weiser Inc., Maine) 1991.

Govinda, Lama Anagarika, *The Way of the White Clouds: A Buddhist Pilgrim in Tibet* (Shambhala, Boulder) 1970.

Gyatso, Palden, *Fire Under the Snow* (Harvill Press, London) 1998.

Gyatso, the Dalai Lama Tenzin and Jeffrey Hopkins, *Kalachakra Tantra Rite of Initiation* (Wisdom Publications, London) 1989.

Gyatsho, Thubten Legshay. The Eighteenth Chogay Trichen of New Buddhist Monastery Lumbini, Nepal. *Gateway to the Temple: Manual of Tibetan Monastic Customs, Art, Building and Celebrations* (Ratna Pustak Bhandar, Kathmandu) 1979.

Hadfield, Charles and Jill, *A Winter in Tibet* (Impact Books, London) 1988.

Harrer, Heinrich, *Lost Lhasa: Heinrich Harrer's Tibet* (Harry N. Abrams, New York) 1992.

Harrer, Heinrich, 'My Life in Forbidden Lhasa', in *National Geographic*, July 1955.

Harrer, Heinrich, *Return to Tibet: Tibet after the Chinese Occupation* (Penguin, Harmondsworth) 1985.

Harrer, Heinrich, *Seven Years In Tibet* (Rupert Hart-Davis, London) 1955.

Harvey, Janice, *One Stone For Tibet* (Awareness Publications, Nedlands) 1998.

Hilton, James, *Lost Horizon* (first published by William Morrow & Co., 1933, many paperback editions by Pocket Books/Simon & Schuster, New York).

Himal, Himalayan Magazine (Lalitpur, Nepal), March/April 1994, May/June 1994, May/June, September/October 1995.

Hopkirk, Peter, *Trespassers on the Roof of the World: The Race for Lhasa* (Oxford University Press, Oxford) 1982.

Houbein, Lolo, *The Sixth Sense* (University of Queensland Press, St Lucia) 1992. [Contains a fictionalised story of author's 1977 meeting with HH the Dalai Lama.]

Houbein, Lolo, *Wrong Face in the Mirror* (University of Queensland Press, St Lucia) 1990. [Contains a factual story of author's 1977 meeting with HH the Dalai Lama.]

Huc, Abbé, *Travels in Tartary and Thibet* (Herbert Joseph, London) 1937.

IIAS News, (International Institute for Asian Studies, Leiden, the Netherlands) Summer 1998.

Jackson, David P. And Janice A., *Tibetan Thangka Painting: Methods and Materials* (Shambhala, Boulder, Colorado) 1984.

Jivaka, Lobsang, *The Life of Milarepa: Tibet's Great Yogi* (John Murray, London) 1962. Abridged adaptation from W.Y. Evans-Wentz's original translation.

Jones, Schuyler, *Tibetan Nomads* (The Carlsberg Foundation's Nomad Research Project/ Thames & Hudson/Rhodos International Science and Art Publishers, London/ New York/Copenhagen) 1996.

Jung Chang, *Wild Swans: Three Daughters of China* (HarperCollins, London) 1992.

Kewley, Vanya, *Tibet Behind the Ice Curtain* (Grafton Books/Collins, London) 1990.

Kimura, Hisao, *Japanese Agent in Tibet*, as told by Scott Berry (Serindia Publications, London) 1990.

King, F. H., *Farmers of Forty Centuries: Permanent Agriculture in China, Korea and Japan* (Rodale Press, Emmaus, Pennsylvania). Undated reprint of the original 1911 edition.

Kingdon Ward, F., *Plant Hunter's Paradise* (Jonathan Cape, London) 1937.

Kunga Rimpoche, Lama, and Brian Cutillo, trans., *Drinking the Mountain Stream: Further Stories and Songs of Milarepa, Yogin, Poet, and Teacher of Tibet* (Lotsawa, Novato, California) 1978

Lang-Sims, Lois, *The Presence of Tibet* (The Cresset Press, London) 1963.

Lazar, Edward, Tibet, *The Issue is Independence: Tibetans-in-Exile Address the Key Tibetan Issue the World Avoids.* (Parallax Press, Berkeley) 1994.

Lhalungpa, Lobsang P., *Tibet the Sacred Realm: Photographs 1880–1950* (Aperture/ Time Books International, New Delhi) 1983.

Lhamo [Mrs Louis King], Rinchen, *We Tibetans* (Potala Publications, New York) 1985. First published, London 1926.

Ling, Princess Der, *Imperial Incense* (Stanley Paul & Co., London) no publication date, but presumably mid- to late-1930s.

MacDonald Oxley, J., *L'hasa At Last* (Ward, Lock & Co, New York/Melbourne) 1902.

MacGregor, John, *Tibet: A Chronicle of Exploration* (Routledge & Kegan Paul, London) 1972. First published 1970.

Malik, Inder, *Dalai Lamas of Tibet* (New United Process, New Delhi) 1984.

Marshall, Steven D., *Hostile Elements: A Study of Political Imprisonment in Tibet: 1987– 1998* (Tibet Information Network, London) 1999.

Mascaró, Juan, trans., *The Dhammapada: the Path of Perfection* (Penguin, Hammondsworth) 1973.

McRae, Janet, and Peg White, *The Chinese Way* (Brooks Waterloo, Melbourne) 1984.

Mele, Pietro Francesco, *Tibet* (Snow Lion Publications, Ithaca, New York) n.d. [1988?]. With an introduction, 'Tibet Today', by Michael C. Van Walt van Praag, based on his book *The Status Of Tibet: History, Rights and Prospects in International Law* (Boulder/ London) 1987.

Me-Long, Newsletter of the Department of Religion and Culture, Central Tibetan Administration of His Holiness the Dalai Lama, Dharamsala, 1995.

Miller, Luree, *On Top of the World: Five Women Explorers in Tibet.* (The Mountaineers, Seattle) 1984.

Moraes, Frank, *The Revolt In Tibet* (Sterling Publishers, Delhi) 1960.

Myers, Lucas, *Dolma Ling: A Pilgrim's Progress Across the Himalayas* (Paljor Publications, New Delhi) 1997.

Myrdal, Jan, *Report From a Chinese Village* (Pantheon Books/Random House, New York) 1981.

National Geographic, (Washington D.C.) April 1977.

National Geographic Society, *Map of Asia* (Washington, D.C.) March 1971.

Norbu, Jamyang, *Warriors of Tibet: The Story of Aten and the Khambas' Fight for the Freedom of their Country* (Wisdom Publications London) 1986. First published 1979.

Norbu, Thubten Jigme, and Colin Turnbull, *Tibet: An Account of the History, the Religion and the People of Tibet* (Simon & Schuster, New York) 1968.

Norbu, Thubten Jigme, *Tibet Is My Country: the autobiography of Thubten Jigme Norbu* (Wisdom Publications, London) 1986.

On This Spot: An Unconventional Map and Guide to Lhasa (The International Campaign for Tibet, Washington D.C.) 1994.

Patterson, George N., *Tibetan Journey* (Readers Book Club/Faber & Faber, London) 1956.

Peissel, Michel, *Mustang: A Lost Tibetan Kingdom* (Collins & Harvill Press, London) 1968.

Porter, Bill, *Road to Heaven: Encounters With Chinese Hermits* (Mercury House, San Francisco) 1993.

Potala Palace, compiled by Managing Bureau of Cultural Relics, Tibet Autonomous Region (Cultural Relics Publishing House, Beijing) 1988.

Rhie, Marylin M., and Robert A.F. Thurman, *Wisdom and Compassion: The Sacred Art of Tibet* (Asian Art Museum of San Francisco and Tibet House, New York, in association with Harry N. Abrams, New York) 1991.

Ricca, Franco and Erberto Lo Bue, *The Great Stupa of Gyantse: A Complete Tibetan Pantheon of the Fifteenth Century* (GRSTGY/Snow Lion, Ithaca, New York) [not sighted].

Richardson, Hugh E., *Tibet and its History* (Shambhala Publications, Boston) 1962.

Riencourt, Amaury de, *Lost World Tibet* (Sterling Publishers, New Delhi) 1987. First published 1950.

Sacred Art of Tibet, a catalogue issued on the occasion of the Sacred Art of Tibet Exhibition and Film Festival, at Lone Mountain College, San Francisco, December 1972 (Tibetan Nyingma Meditation Centre).

Saklani, Girija, *The Uprooted Tibetans in India: A Sociological Study of Continuity and Change* (Cosmos Publications, New Delhi) 1984.

Sakya, Jamyang and Julie Emery, *Princess In The Land Of Snows: The Life of Jamyang Sakya in Tibet* (Shambhala, Boston) 1990.

Samagalski, Alan and Michael Buckley, *China: A Travel Survival Kit* (Lonely Planet Publications, Melbourne) 1984.

Schaller, George B., 'Tibet's Remote Chang Tang: In a High and Sacred Realm', *National Geographic*, August 1993.

Schmidt, Jeremy, *Himalayan Passage: Seven Months in the High Country of Tibet, Nepal, China, India and Pakistan* (The Mountaineers, Seattle) 1991.

Schram, Stuart, *Mao Tse-Tung* (Penguin, Harmondsworth) 1974. First published 1966.

Senanayake, Ratne Deshapriya, *Inside Story of Tibet* (Afro-Asian Writers' Bureau, Colombo) 1967.

Shakabpa, Tsepon W.D., *Tibet: A Political History* (Potala Publications, New York) 1984.

Snellgrove, David L., *Buddhist Himalaya* (Bruno Cassirer, Oxford) 1957.

Snellgrove, David L., *Himalayan Pilgrimage* (Shambhala, Boston) 1981.

Snellgrove, David and Hugh Richardson, *A Cultural History Of Tibet* (UBS Publishers Distributors, Delhi/Bangalore)1968.

Snelling, John, *Buddhism In Russia: The Story of Agvan Dorzhiev, Lhasa's Emissary to the Tsar.* (Element, Shaftesbury, Dorset/Rockport, Massachusetts/Brisbane) 1993.

Sogyal Rimpoche, *The Tibetan Book of Living and Dying* (Rider/Random House, London) 1992.

Somerville-Large, Peter, *To The Navel Of The World: Yaks and Unheroic Travels in Nepal and Tibet* (Hamish Hamilton, London) 1987.

Stewart, Whitney, *To The Lion Throne: The Story of the Fourteenth Dalai Lama* (Snow Lion Publications, Ithaca, N.Y.) 1990.

Stewart, Whitney, *The 14th Dalai Lama: Spiritual Leader of Tibet* (Lerner Publications, Minneapolis) 1996.

Strauss, Robert, *Tibet: A Travel Survival Kit* (Lonely Planet Publications, Melbourne) 1992.

Taring, Rinchen Dolma, *Daughter of Tibet* (John Murray, London) 1970.

Temple, Robert, *The Genius Of China: 3000 Years of Science, Discovery and Invention* (Simon & Schuster, New York) 1986.

Thomas Jr., Lowell, *Out of This World: Across the Himalayas to Tibet* (Macdonald, London) 1951.

Thondup Rimpoche, Tulku, *Buddhist Civilization in Tibet* (Routledge & Kegan Paul, New York/London) 1987.

Thubtob, Rev. Ngawang, *Tibet Today: A Statement* (Bureau of His Holiness the Dalai Lama, New Delhi) 1965.

Thurman, Robert A.F., *Inside Tibetan Buddhism: Rituals and Symbols Revealed* (Collins Publishers, San Francisco) 1995.

Tibet Information Network, *News Review* No. 27, Reports From Tibet, 1998: Religion and Culture, Prisons and Protests, Politics and Leaders, Economy. (Tibet Information Network, London) 1999.

Tibet Information Network, *A Poisoned Arrow: The Secret Report of the 10th Panchen Lama* [The full text of the Panchen Lama's 70 000 Character Petition of 1962, together with a selection of historical documents] (Tibet Information Network, London) 1997.

Tibetan Review, November 1995, May 1996, November 1966, March 1997.

Tolstoy, Ilia, 'Across Tibet from India to China', in *National Geographic* (Washington D.C.) August 1946.

Topping, Audrey, *The Splendors of Tibet* (Sino Publishing Company, New York) 1980.

Tucci, Giuseppe, *Travels of Tibetan Pilgrims in the Swat Valley* (The Greater India Society, Calcutta) 1940.

Tucci, Giuseppe, *Tibet: Land Of Snows* (Oxford & IBH Publishing Co., Calcutta and Elek Books, London) 1967.

Tung, Rosemary Jones, *A Portrait of Lost Tibet: Photographs by Ilya Tolstoy and Brooke Dolan* (Thames & Hudson, London) 1980.

Turner, Samuel, *An Account of an Embassy to the Court of the Teshoo Lama in Tibet: Containing A Narrative of a Journey Through Bootan and Part of Tibet* (W. Bulmer & Co., St James's, London, 1800) Facsimile copy by Asian Educational Services, New Delhi–Madras, 1991.

Vietnam Democracy, A Monthly Publication of the Free Vietnam Alliance, Vol. 9, No. 9, September 1996 (Paris/Anaheim Hills, California).

Waddell, L. Austine, *Tibetan Buddhism: with its mystic Cults, Symbolism and Mythology* (Dover Publications, New York) 1972. First published in 1895 under the title *The Buddhism of Tibet, or Lamaism.*

Williamson, Margaret D., in collaboration with John Snelling, *Memoirs of a Political Officer's Wife in Tibet, Sikkim and Bhutan,* (Wisdom Publications, London) 1987.

Willis, Janice D., *Enlightened Beings: Life Stories from the Ganden Oral Tradition* (Wisdom Publications, Boston) 1995.

Woodman, Dorothy, *Himalayan Frontiers: A Political Review of British, Chinese, Indian and Russian rivalries* (Frederick A. Praeger, New York/Washington) 1969.

World Tibet News on the Internet.

Wu, Harry, *Bitter Winds: A Memoir of my Years in China's Gulag* (John Wiley & Sons Inc., New York/Chichester/Brisbane/Toronto/Singapore) 1994.

Younghusband, Sir Francis, *India And Tibet* (London) 1910.

Zhu Li, *Tibet: No Longer Medieval* (Foreign Languages Press, Beijing) 1981.

Acknowledgments

I owe special gratitude to my mother for interpreting newspapers to me before I could read, introducing me to a child Dalai Lama enthroned at almost the same age I was then. And to Oma for sponsoring my reading from the neighbourhood lending library, where I first discovered the fabled land of Tibet.

To name the many people who fed my interest in Tibet since then would be impossible, but collectively I salute them. They crossed my path through the decades to keep my attention fixed, possibly prompted by a *bodhisattva*, an enlightened being, for a purpose I do not yet perceive.

I offer gratitude to His Holiness the Fourteenth Dalai Lama for allowing the use of a quotation from his 1994 letter to Buddhist students and for admitting me to his presence on several occasions. I thank from my heart our Australian Rimpoche whose presence in the country provided inspiration to carry on with this work, despite a million finely honed obstacles and interruptions. I know he hopes this book will make Tibet's predicament known to a readership as yet uncertain about its modern history.

Gratitude to all Tibetan friends in India and Australia for on occasion explaining details of Tibetan culture with grace and patience. Thanks also to all organisations that present news from Tibet, preventing it from sliding into oblivion; to Robbie Barnett and the staff of the Tibet Information Network, and to Phillip Adams for allowing me to talk about the sadly misrepresented Tenth Panchen Lama on ABC Radio's 'Late Night Live'. I thank the Catholic Church office in Adelaide, South Australia, for detailed information on the history of the Vatican, the site most comparable to the Potala complex.

Whitney Stewart, fellow writer on Tibet and Internet friend, exchanged books, references, frustrations and rejoicings about stages completed. Thanks also to John Powers, Kunga Sanggye and Scott Wellenbach for information provided via the Internet. Burwell Dodd endured my states of mind during the writing of this book in particular. Not fond of travel himself, he accompanied me on sidetracks into China, forerunner of the Tibet journeys, listened to ideas I bounced off him before I wrote or discarded them, taught me to use a computer, printed manuscripts, acted as Internet researcher, technician, cook, driver and listener. In the evenings, while I stitched mandalas in wool, he read aloud from books on Tibet, so we did not become estranged while I concerned myself with little else during four years. Most of all, he let me journey in far regions while tending the home garden.

Acknowledgement is made to Impact Books (UK) for permission to use a quotation from Charles and Jill Hadfield's *A Winter in Tibet*; to Dover Publications (USA) for three quotations from John MacGregor's *Tibet: A Chronicle of Exploration* and two from L. Austine Waddell's *Tibetan Buddhism;* to Oxford University Press for three quotations from Peter Fleming's *Bayonets to Lhasa;* and to Snow Lion Publications (USA) for two quotations from Giuseppe Tucci's *To Lhasa and Beyond.*

Finally, a depth of gratitude to all at Simon & Schuster Australia, especially David Rosenberg, Publisher of the Kangaroo Press imprint, who had faith in an overlong manuscript, to my editor Carl Harrison-Ford, for unfailing sound advice, interest and encouragement and to Lachlan McLaine for seeing the project through to completion.

Due to the political climate prevailing in Tibet, all people in whose company I travelled and met with, including tour leaders, guides and drivers, remain anonymous or carry fictitious names. They had nothing to do with my reactions to Tibet's predicament. I alone am responsible for my thoughts and opinions about what I saw and sensed. I am also solely responsible for errors or misapprehensions concerning historical backgrounds and situations perceived. Nevertheless, I thank all companions for sharing the pleasures of the road and for untold kindnesses, especially two travelling genies who crossed my path in 1977 and led me to Dharamsala, India, the Tibetan refugees and an audience with His Holiness the Dalai Lama, where the seed of later events was sown. What started as the one journey of a lifetime to Central Tibet in 1993 became a quest for truth in the politics of conquest.

A book on Tibet will always be inadequate. Information was not only difficult to obtain but frequently incorrect, sometimes purposely so. My best effort must suffice and now the book must speak for itself. May each reader make a difference to Tibet.

Lolo Houbein
South Australia, 1999

Index